THE OREGON BIGFOOT HIGHWAY

By

Joe Beelart
&
Cliff Olson

Willamette City Press, LLC

The Oregon Bigfoot Highway
Copyright © 2015 by Joe Beelart and Cliff Olson

Acknowledgements
 Peter Byrne, F.R.G.S. (Fellow Royal Geographical Society), Field Advisor
 Larry G. Lund, The Sasquatch Sleuth, Historical Advisor
 Cover design by Brainjar Media. **www.brainjarmedia.com**

For information on Willamette City Press, LLC, go to:
 www.willamettecitypress.com or
 www.oregonbigfoothighway.com

Prologue

This book is a collection of Bigfoot sightings, Bigfoot related incidents and non-Bigfoot related *happenings* in the wild area of the upper Clackamas and Breitenbush River drainages. In it we explore a considerable number of seemingly genuine accounts relating to Bigfoot along the main road between Estacada and Detroit, and side roads that venture into secret haunts of the Clackamas Ranger District of the Mount Hood National Forest.

These accounts span over one hundred years and were reported by persons of diverse professions from lawyers to loggers. The quantity and similarity of these reports caused us to conclude that this is, indeed, *The Oregon Bigfoot Highway*. Sighting reports are based only on very select newspaper and book accounts, plus the authors' carefully screened personal interviews. The reader will also find many reports of thrilling real-life adventures of a group collectively referred to as *The Clackamas Sasquatchians* who we will introduce to you later.

Find your imagination, open your mind, sit back and enjoy!

Please visit us at *www.oregonbigfoothighway.com* for color photographs and much more.

USFS Road 46 in Big Bottom. Photo by Joe Beelart.

Road 42 bridge to Bigfooting adventure. Photo by Joe Beelart.

The Power of Nature

Tree struck by lightning in July 2014 three miles south of Ripplebrook Guard Station. Photo by Joe Beelart.

The Oregon Bigfoot Highway

Located in the Upper Clackamas and Breitenbush River Drainages in the Oregon Cascade Mountains.

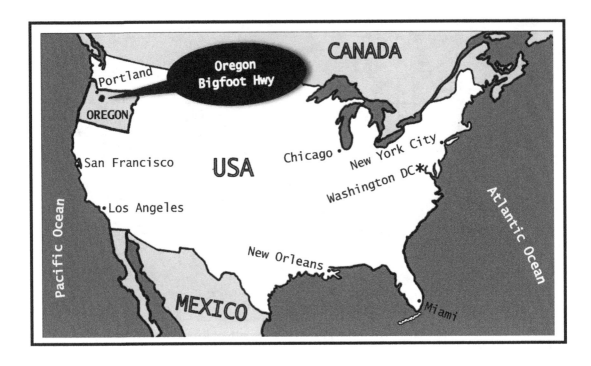

Introduction

For 70 miles, from Estacada to Detroit, *Oregon Scenic Byway No. 5* winds through remote mountains. The Byway hugs the Clackamas River for about 40 miles, and then follows the Breitenbush River into Detroit. It climbs into ancient forests and provides access to serene high lakes and flower filled mountain meadows. From the Byway, travelers find spectacular vistas of majestic Mt. Hood and Mt. Jefferson.

The Clackamas River is so impressive that beginning at the source in the Olallie Lake Scenic Area its first 47 miles are designated a *National Wild & Scenic River*. Not only does *Oregon Scenic Byway No. 5* include the *NWSR* designation, it also contains two other national designations. Adjoining or imbedded within it are five national wilderness areas, collectively titled *The Clackamas Wilderness*; plus the *Collawash National Wild & Scenic River*. So, there is little doubt this stretch of mountain highway is among the most beautiful in the nation.

And by coincidence, *Oregon Scenic Byway 5* also has one of the densest groupings of Bigfoot sightings, track finds, and Bigfoot related incidents in the Pacific Northwest. The first credible track find was reported in 1911. In 1924 a visual sightings of an ape-man was reported on a ridge high above the Indian trail which would become this highway. Reports of sightings and track finds continue to this day.

Nonetheless, to be very clear, this book is not about convincing the reader that Bigfoot exists. Herein "Bigfoot" is consigned to the class of phenomena that includes ghosts and UFOs. In these phenomena the subjects are seen again and again, yet no widely accepted scientific evidence has yet been presented to prove their existence.

It is for the traveler to decide if Bigfoot exists; each to his own opinion. Rather, the purpose of this book is to enhance an explorer's nature experience during a journey along one of the most picturesque roads in the United States, *The Oregon Bigfoot Highway* which we often abbreviate as *OBH*.

The Oregon Bigfoot Highway was originally an ancient Native American trade route, a footpath through regal old growth timber. In 1924 a railroad was built over a portion of the footpath to supply a Portland General Electric power generation project. In 1934 the railroad was replaced by a rock road for hauling logs. Nowadays the highway is still used by the electric utility company and loggers; as well as outdoor recreationalists.

Most high roads along the highway are closed by snow for four or five months of the year. After snow melt, traffic is mainly log trucks and Forest Service vehicles. Seasonally, there are also kayakers, fishermen, campers and hikers with an influx of hunters in the fall.

But, with the only permanent dwellings along *The Oregon Bigfoot Highway* being small work and Job Corps enclaves near Ripplebrook Guard Station, and at Breitenbush Hot Springs Resort, traffic is generally light. During weekdays it is not uncommon for a traveler to drive the entire 70 miles and see less than a handful of vehicles.

Bigfoot along the Highway

In short, if Bigfoot exists, the creatures could live and thrive in relative peace within the vast, remote expanses along *The Oregon Bigfoot Highway*. And according to the stories recounted in this book, they do.

Bigfoot has an advantage in the Clackamas River Ranger District; the District naturally divides into *six geographic areas*. Natural boundaries for the six areas provide clear territorial lines for small bands of Bigfoot. Not surprisingly, reports clustered into these six areas. Thus the book has a chapter for each area with introductory remarks, a description of the terrain and a customized map.

Additionally, within the areas we were able to delineate three *Bigfoot migratory byways*. These byways would make long distance travel easy for the beasts, should they wish to do so. Basically, these natural Bigfoot byways, or Sasquatch express routes, are on the ridgelines above the roads you will travel in the valleys below. So, look up and imagine.

Reports of Bigfoot sightings cover a wide gamut from the mundane, "While I was fishing I saw one on the other side of the river," to the unusual such as, "After it snowed one night, one walked around my bulldozer and then sat on my bulldozer seat," to the truly strange. These especially bizarre reports and happenings are relegated to a special chapter of the book titled *Area 52*.

What is there to make of these many reports? What do we really know about the existence of Our Barefoot Friends? Not much; but in Appendix II titled *Bigfoot Characteristics* we summarize what reports in this book suggest.

To drop any veil of secrecy, GPS coordinates are listed for most locations. So readers, many of our *secret* places are now yours. The exceptions being archaeological sites, and one on-going habitation site. Using our GPS coordinates with Google Earth or another "flying" computer program will visually open the Clackamas River Ranger District, the land of our Sasquatch, to you in a whole new way.

This book chronicles reports from a wide variety of sources including interviews with people who wanted to share experiences, Forest Service and power company employees – most of whom insisted on anonymity; newspaper articles, and especially contributions from the *Clackamas Sasquatchians* who are profiled in Appendix I.

Persons in reports are called *Jakes* per a suggestion by Ray Crowe of the Western Bigfoot Society. Jakes are men and women who come from all walks of life. A few Jake accounts come from print sources, but most were told to a Sasquatchian. Jake accounts were evaluated for credibility before inclusion; so, accounts in this book occurred with a reasonable degree of probability.

We were very fortunate to get permission from Mr. John Green to use his accounts of the four 1967–1968 Glen Thomas sightings and a separate Collawash River sighting. Mr. Green, the historian emeritus of Sasquatch, is profiled at the beginning of his section.

While they are notoriously tight-lipped on the subject, we were also fortunate to get five sighting reports and several other stories from Forest Service Employees (abbreviated "FSE") and Forest Service Law Enforcement Officers (abbreviated "LEO").

Statistical Summary

Based in the six geographic Areas, major events are listed by reference numbers 1 through 100 (Ref. 1 to Ref. 100). References include thirty-one (31) sighting reports going back to 1924 and forty-three (43) quality track finds reaching back to 1911. In addition to the reference numbers assigned to the Bigfoot related events (1-100), each sighting is assigned a number (S1-S31) as is each track find (TF1-TF43). Refer to the maps of sightings and track finds on pages 15 and 16.

We also include sixty-nine (69) probable Bigfoot related Incidents, such as rock throwing and construction of shelters. Thirty-seven (37) unusual happenings are spread through the accounts. There are also seven cougar sighting reports, including one in which a cougar stalks to within five feet of a Sasquatchian.

There are three supernatural Area 52 reports, the first of which makes the supposed Bigfoot – UFO connection popularized by the *Star Wars* movies. Another Area 52 report is about a strange high mountain encounter and the third recounts a bizarre night in the high forest. Area 52 events *are not included* in the above summary totals. All were told by various *Clackamas Sasquatchians*.

Maps of the Region

The Oregon Bigfoot Highway and its side roads run through what we refer to as the "Upper Clackamas Drainage" which includes the Clackamas and Breitenbush rivers. The maps which follow show highways, roads, rivers, mountains and buttes in the region. The area map divides the region into the six geographic areas used to group our reports.

Highways, Roads and Places in the Upper Clackamas Drainage

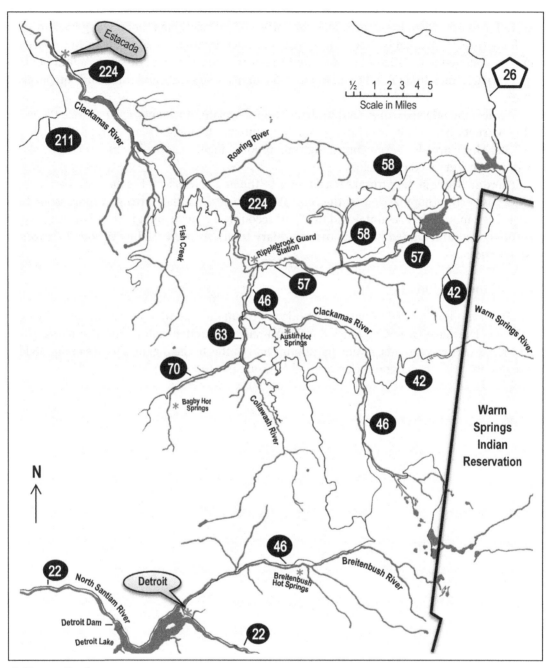

©Sharon Beelart 2015

Rivers and Lakes in the Upper Clackamas Drainage

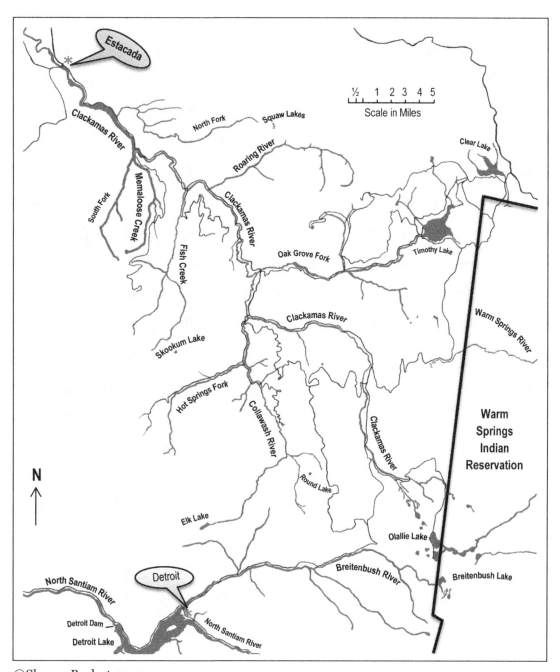

©Sharon Beelart 2015

Mountains and Buttes in the Upper Clackamas Drainage

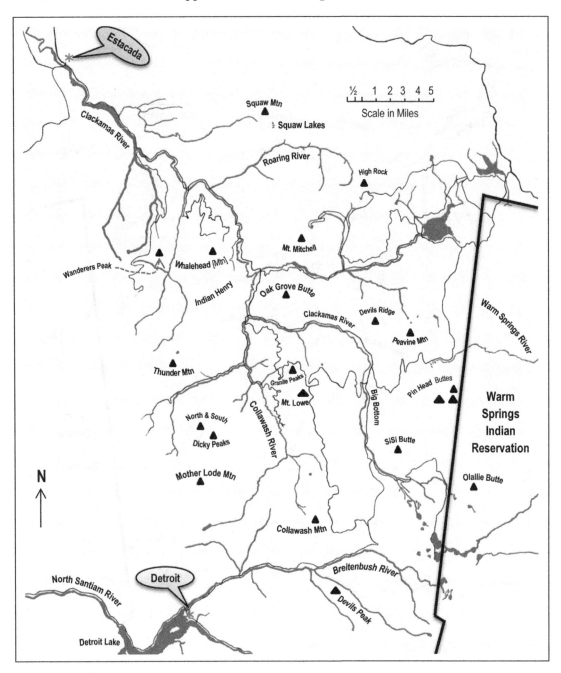

©Sharon Beelart 2015

The Six Geographic Areas in the Upper Clackamas Drainage

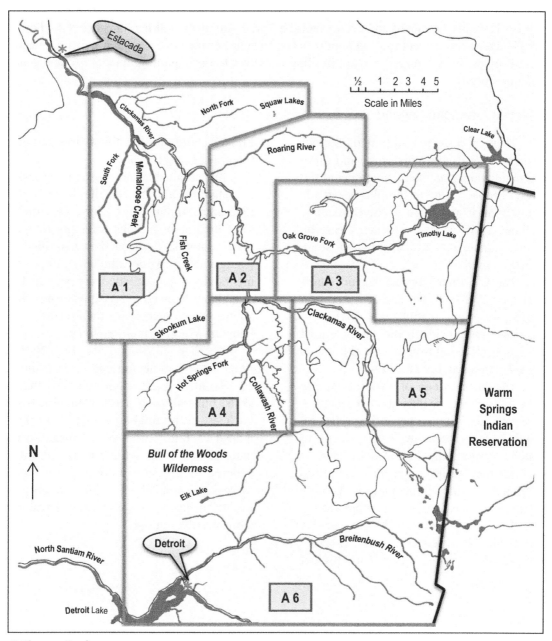

©Sharon Beelart 2015

The Native American Heritage

The authors have no Native American blood and no close ties to Native Americans. So in this book, we are not qualified to represent the Native American culture concerning the Forest People. However, we feel we must address the ancient heritage of Sasquatch living alongside First Peoples. In that regard, we are limiting ourselves to three photographs plus one legend, and one story.

A Native American Legend

There is a deep tradition of Bigfoot Beings in the Pacific Northwest, and there are many names for them, some using the word "People." One of the oldest legends about them is attributed to the Clackamas Indians, a tribe virtually extinct. Please be aware translations are always, to some degree, imperfect.

The Clackamas Indian legend states that for a Bigfoot to become accepted into Bigfoot society as an adult, as a warrior, or, as a mature individual, the Bigfoot must present itself in full frontal view of humans three (3) times and not be seen.

The implications of this legend are enormous. Some are obvious. For instance, to prove the three unseen experiences, other Bigfoots probably were present to watch the events and were also not seen.

Another implication is how do they do it? Can they control human minds? Is there a molecular transformation component?

These are important present-day questions. By selling their cloaking techniques to the military Our Bigfoot

Friends could become billionaires and buy their own gated forests.

But seriously, and most importantly, to establish a basis of the legend, the Clackamas Indians must have repeatedly seen Bigfoot in various attempts to gain mature status. Perhaps they saw Bigfoot young ones, or Bigfoot adults with impaired mental development who were not capable of making themselves invisible; or possibly adults who exposed themselves not knowing a human was watching.

Another likelihood is the Native Americans encountered advanced adolescent Bigfoot attempting invisibility skills, but only saw parts of the creature. Such an event might be very disturbing indeed. But however appearances materialized, the Clackamas Indians believed the creatures were real. And since there is no legend about conflict, we assume the tribe lived in peace and harmony alongside the Bigfoot.

Sleeping with two Bigfoot

Location: Up Fish Creek canyon about 18 miles south of Estacada.

This account comes from a full-blood Yakima Indian, who we cannot name, but will address as Witness 1 (W1). This story was told to me as an example of a Native American experience up the Clackamas River with one condition; it was to end with his exact words, twice.

Witness 1 lives and works in the Portland Metro area. He often travels up the Clackamas River to reconnect with nature. He feels the Clackamas and Wind River drainages are the purest places readily accessible to the metro area, although he prefers the Clackamas because of its open, free feel. He said, "While it may be difficult for a white person to believe, '*this really happened*."

The meaning of *"This really happened."* does not translate well from Native American languages to English. In this story, as well as a later account, the reader will find, *"This really happened."* is not a warranty of truth; *truth is assumed*. Rather, the phrase is a kind of exclamation point.

In this account W1 was far up Fish Creek *"hunting"*. While the witness did not tell me, another part-Native American told me *"hunting"* means more to a Native American than hunting as it is known in white culture. A Native American can *hunt* for mushrooms, herbs, and many other things, but even in these simple examples, the word *"hunting"* in Native American languages does not easily translate into English.

To Native Americans, *"hunting,"* like the phrase *"this really happened"* has complex connotations. In a sense, *hunting* has a spiritual context; and in part it also means reconnecting with nature. It is a reason to go into the forest with a natural purpose. So W1 was *hunting*. For his sleep, he carried a large, thick wool blanket.

When it was time, W1 prepared boughs for his bed and lay down to sleep. After he was asleep for not long, he awoke. On each side of him, lying tight against him was a Bigfoot Being. When he tried to slide out from under his blanket, the Bigfoot Beings pressed tighter against him so he could not rise.

Witness 1 said he was awake for what seemed like several hours. During the time he was awake, the Bigfoot Beings slept. The Bigfoot Beings did not hurt him; they did not even bruise him. They did not move except to press tightly against each side of him.

He said he felt safe, that the Bigfoot Beings were not a threat or a danger. They did not heat his blanket. They were just keeping him between them. W1 said that after hours, he fell asleep from exhaustion. When he awoke the Bigfoot Beings were gone.

He said to close his story with these words, to use "it," and to write them twice:

"I do not know what it meant."

"I do not know what it meant."

Ancient Native American Stone Carving

In January 2003 this stone head was on display at the Washington State Historical Society Bigfoot conference, Olympia, Washington. The stone carving is owned by the Maryhill Museum of Art, Goldendale, Washington. I first saw it on display in the early 1990s; it was labeled as a sheep's head. The photographs were taken through a glass cover and are ©Sharon Beelart 2003.

Maryhill Museum Stone Head – left side

Stone Head
C. 1500 B.C. to 500 A.D.
Courtesy of the Maryhill Museum of Art

Several stone heads have been discovered in the Pacific Northwest with primate-like features. The specimen above, discovered in the Columbia Basin, is of particular interest because it possesses a sagittal crest. These crests appear in great apes, gorillas and some chimpanzees. They tend to be present in the skulls of animals that rely on powerful jaws.

Maryhill Museum Stone Head – right side

Kiley's Principles and Dictums

Steven Kiley has decades of experience in the woods and mountains. The following are simple lessons he teaches people new to the wilderness. The authors believe they apply to everyone who wanders the hills looking for Sasquatch.

Kiley's Principle

Look for the little things,
   Things that are out of place,
      Things that are not quite right.

Kiley's Dictums

Watch the edges.
   Everything loves beaver ponds.
      In the mountains wind and scent follow the sun; up in the day, down at night.

Kiley on the Clackamas Sasquatch

"They are up there, but how do you prove it?"

Finding your way around

Maps

Maps are your friends. Use them, don't refold them as they came. Make notes on them, study them. For most people a suitable map is the Oregon Official State map free from the Department of Transportation. On this map *The Oregon Bigfoot Highway*, purple in color, is easily found east of Salem and southeast of Portland. For field research, or ventures off the main road, detailed maps are a must, except for the foolish.

Two of the four types of maps I use are fifteen (15) USGS 1:24,000 topographical maps with a contour interval of 40′ and, a plastic coated USDA Forest Service Mt. Hood National Forest map with a huge scale of 1:126,720 defined by township lines. The map I use most is the USDA Forest Service Clackamas River Ranger District map with a contour interval of 100′. The fourth map I use is a highly detailed blue-print type forest contractor's map.

USGS topographical maps spread out on the bed of Truck. Photo by Joe Beelart.

Co-author Olson has old maps with precious gems of information printed and noted on them. For a decade, Kiley had many of his collection of Clackamas USGS 1:24,000 maps pinned to a wall in his den. Numerous pins and notes on this large fresco proved very helpful in our planning and field research. Regrettably, this resource was lost when his daughter confiscated the room.

Google Earth

We decided to place great confidence in our readers. We have included GPS, or latitude and longitude coordinates, of most major points of interest with the strict exclusion of archeological sites or when a contributor requested we not use GPS markers.

Following our narratives using *Google Earth*, or a similar program, will greatly enhance the reader's enjoyment and understanding of what is in this book.

If the reader simply types the GPS coordinates as we list them into the "find" box in Google Earth the site will come up. We encourage readers to learn to "fly" with Google Earth to get a feel for the beauty and majesty of the Clackamas and Breitenbush River drainages.

OBH Mile Markers

Oregon Bigfoot Highway mile markers are from Estacada to Detroit followed by the reverse, Detroit to Estacada. For example: Memaloose Bridge 9.1: 58.9 means the Memaloose Bridge is 9.1 miles from Estacada and 58.9 miles from Detroit. There are no *OBH* mile markers along the road. When you are on the road, **do not** confuse mile markers in this book with State of Oregon and Forest Service mile signs.

Woods (wild) Strawberry, *fragaria vesca*, in bloom.
Photo by Sharon Beelart.

Locate the Sightings and Track Finds

The following maps of sighting reports and track finds shows again why we call this *The Oregon Bigfoot Highway*.

Map of Sightings by Sighting Number

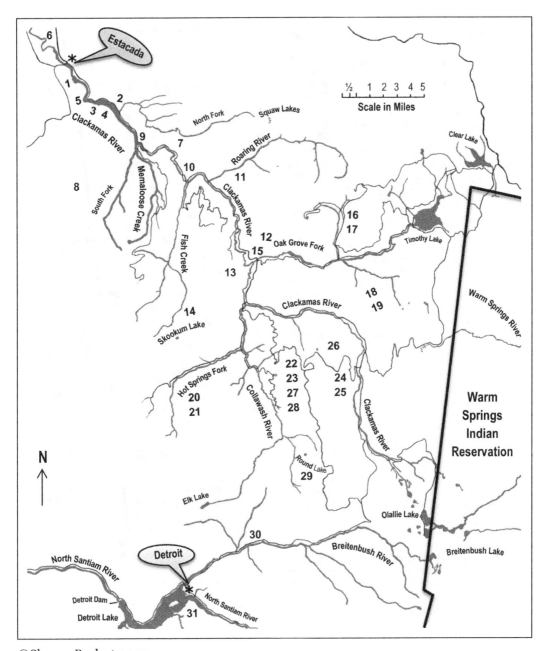

©Sharon Beelart 2015

Map Showing Track Finds

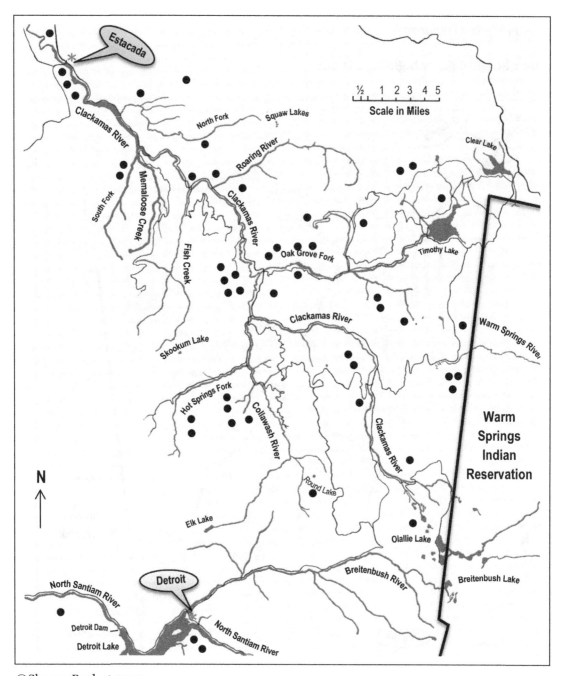

©Sharon Beelart 2015

Area 1: Estacada to Fish Creek

An adventurer will find Area 1 a beautiful, wild introduction to the upper Clackamas River system and home to *Our Barefoot Friends*. The main road through Area 1 is State Highway 224 which makes for an easy winding drive of about 15 miles from Estacada to Fish Creek. The first few miles offer a grand view of the lower Clackamas River gorge.

As explorers drive into Area 1, they will soon find steep canyon walls which in some places are hundreds of feet of perpendicular hexagons of bare basalt rock. Old, tall Douglas fir trees will appear small, giving a sense of the immensity of high country to come. And all along the Oregon Bigfoot Highway, the Clackamas River runs picturesque and supreme, a powerful force in this part of Oregon.

Side areas of Area 1 are large and with little access except on a handful of Forest Service roads which follow the river bottoms. We quickly found reports from Area 1 fell into four (4) districts, two of which are served by Forest Service Roads. The first was the locale around Estacada. The second was the North Fork of the Clackamas. The third includes the South Fork and Memaloose. The fourth district is the Fish Creek drainage.

To truly enjoy Area 1, and all areas in the Clackamas drainage, we strongly recommend bringing along a good set of binoculars or a spotting scope. We also recommend you consider a binocular window mount or a hiking staff with a binocular screw.

If you are buying a set of binoculars for the first time, the general rule is use low power on small diameter barrels; i.e. ~8x22 and no more than 10X on larger; i.e. ~10x50. *Do not* buy 10X small barrel binoculars as they are difficult to stabilize and have limited eye relief.

Oregon Scenic Byway sign near Estacada. Photo by Sharon Beelart

Districts in Area 1

District 1: Near Estacada

The opening set of accounts is from the town of Estacada and places near the town, both on the east and west side of the Clackamas River.

District 2: the North Fork

The east boundary of this rectangle, which is defined by Squaw Mountain, Squaw Lakes, and Squaw Meadows, is pleasant to explore, but be sure to bring mosquito repellant. If your map is new, Squaw Mountain may be named "Tumala Mountain." In the spirit of the times it was renamed in 2005.

The North Fork rectangle is about 4x10 miles east-to-west. Its south boundary is the ridge separating the North Fork from Roaring River. The north boundary is generally pioneer agricultural land. The disagreeable aspect of this district is high frequency of use, often by unlikable characters.

District 2 was heavily logged in the years before required reforestation, so visually it is uninspiring as it is mostly covered with dense, brushy, stunted tree cover. There is little scenery except at the east end. However, after discounting "common" reports, several very high quality and interesting accounts from the North Fork were welcomed into this book.

District 3: the South Fork and Memaloose

The second rectangle in Area 1 is a very large tract of rugged mountains which includes the South Fork of the Clackamas and Memaloose. In the loosest of terms, this district is capped by Wanderers Peak, the highest point in the US Geological topographical map of the area.

District 4: Fish Creek

This part of the rectangle contains Fish Creek, Wash Creek, and Skookum Lake. The southern boundary of District 4 is roughly defined by East Mountain and Thunder Mountain which overlook the Collawash River drainage. Wonderfully eerie Skookum Lake lies in a small basin under the north crest of Thunder Mountain. District 4 covers about 20 square miles and is bordered on the east by Whale Head (a mountain) which is in Area 2.

Map of Area I

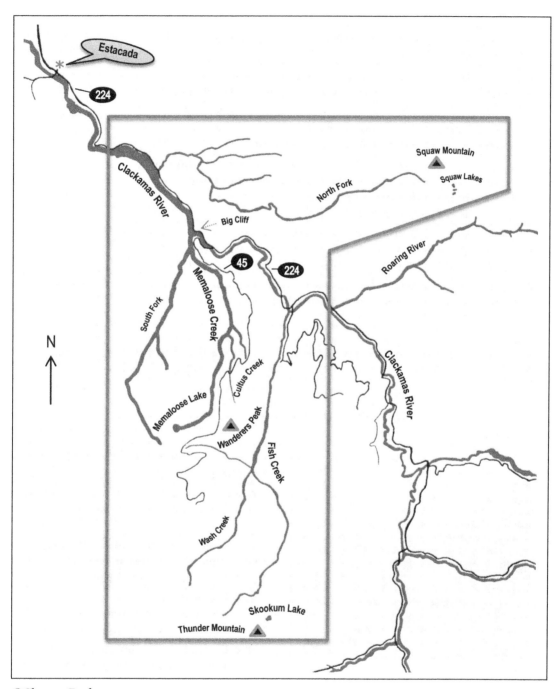

©Sharon Beelart 2015

Area 1 OBH Mile Markers

Miles from Estacada: from Detroit

0.0:	70.0	Intersection of Hwy 224 and 211 in Estacada
1.0:	69.0	Dam Road – PGE West Side Hydro Project
2.9:	67.1	Fall Creek Road; to pioneer homestead land
3.5:	66.5	Clackamas River viewpoint; Whale Head (a mountain)
5.4:	64.6	Confluence of the North Fork; a popular fishing spot.
6.2:	63.8	PGE Promontory Park
6.9:	63.1	Enter Mt. Hood National Forest; sign
7.3:	62.7	End of dam tail water; the Clackamas now flows free
8.2:	61.8	90° turn in road; confluence of South Fork
8.7:	61.3	*Major landmark:* Big Cliff; pullout
9.1:	60.9	Memaloose Road Bridge
11.7:	58.3	Major rock fall zone begins here
11.8:	58.2	Bob's standing wave, a favorite kayaking site
12.6:	57.4	Big Eddy turnout; site of the dynamited outhouse
14.0:	56.0	Carter Bridge: in season, salmon jump the falls
14.4:	55.6	Fish Creek road; ancient Indian fishing site

Zero your odometer to OBH Mile Marker 0.0 at the south end of Estacada near the center of the intersection of Hwy 224 and 211. **Do not** stop in this dangerous intersection.

Approximate GPS coordinates: 45 17 01.73 N 122 19 53.89 W at 474.'

Intersection of Hwy 211 and Hwy 224, Estacada, Oregon. Photo by Sharon Beelart

Just to the right of the intersection is the bridge over the Clackamas River. This was the traditional Native American river crossing from the Clackamas River drainage into the Molalla River drainage. The Molalla River roughly parallels the Clackamas on the west side of the Cascades and also has a rich history of Bigfoot sightings and reports.

Imagine the time when this intersection was covered with tall old growth trees and the only roads were moccasin footpaths through them. Legend and sighting reports from near here lead us to believe Sasquatch has also tread this very intersection.

District 1: Estacada

The beginning (or end) of the Oregon Bigfoot Highway

Area 1 begins in Estacada and is an easy winding drive of about 15 miles to Fish Creek. The first few miles offer a grand view of the lower Clackamas River canyon and dam reservoirs; but, first a few words about Estacada.

Estacada was founded in 1905, not as a lumbering town, but as a base camp for a Portland General Electric power project. Two dams were built nearby and generators were installed to send electricity to a growing Portland. But, those generators were not enough.

To supply Portland with even more power, in 1924 another enormous electrical project was constructed about 30 miles upriver from Estacada at Three Lynx. Water for the project comes from Harriet Lake which was created by a dam made high on the Oak Grove Fork. From Harriet Lake a nine foot diameter eight mile long riveted steel pipeline was built to carry water to spin turbine generators in what is formally known as the Oak Grove Fork Powerhouse.

Workers were housed in Estacada and transported to the construction sites via a narrow gauge railroad built over an ancient Native American footpath. After construction ended the railroad continued as the only transport into the upper Clackamas valley. Then, in 1936 a rock road was built and the railroad dismantled. It is unknown whether the railroad was relocated to another construction site, or was used, as was common in those days, to haul logs down a mountain somewhere else.

About 21 miles upriver from Estacada and just prior to the Indian Henry intersection, on the opposite bank of the Clackamas, is the large white concrete Oak Grove Fork powerhouse. While working on the PGE Oak Grove Fork system, co-author Cliff Olson lived with his family a half mile from the powerhouse in a small company housing and maintenance complex called Three Lynx. It was during those thirteen years that co-author Olson intensely studied the upper Clackamas drainage during his hunting, fishing, and firewood cutting trips.

Ref. 1: Lumber Jack and the Safari Club

For decades *Lumber Jack* (LJ) was Estacada's timber baron and a man who later played a very important role in the future of Bigfoot up the Clackamas. Here, we introduce you to LJ even though the critical part of his story is told in Ref. 88. Ref. 88 is the story of how LJ significantly affected the future of Central Oregon, while simultaneously and undoubtedly inadvertently, conserved critical Bigfoot habitat in the high Clackamas.

After the Portland General Electric Oak Grove Fork project was completed, Estacada became a lumber town. One lumber mill still operates on the north end of the city. This mill was originally owned by *Lumber Jack*. In cooperation with the local United States Forest Service office, *Lumber Jack* did a booming business. One result was LJ had sufficient funds to go trophy hunting around the world.

Lumber Jack also used money to open other businesses. One was the Safari Club in downtown Estacada. Allegedly, his thinking was, "I pay my employees and they spend their extra money somewhere, so it might as well be at my place."

LJ stocked the Safari Club with hundreds of stuffed, trophy animals shot in the Americas and Africa. A huge standing polar bear and Alaskan grizzly bear greeted all who entered. My favorite stuffed animal was the spiral horn bongo antelope from deep in dark African jungles. Some people liked the little arctic hares, or leaping tigers.

The Safari Club was also a zoo by other standards. To paraphrase a beautiful young coed in the movie, *Animal House*, the Safari Club was a study in primitive culture.

As a roadhouse, it rapidly became a spot for folks to linger under the ever-staring, unseeing eyes of the menagerie. For years the Safari Club was *the* underground escape for rich Portlanders; a place to go to dance, to drink, to not be seen.

With three nearby motels, the nicest one allegedly owned by LJ, patrons found the Club a mighty opportune place to perform mating dances to slow rhythmic drum beats, a late-hour house specialty on band nights. But, times change; sadly, the late night drum beats and all they foretold went silent in early 2013 when the venerable Safari Club closed for the last time.

District 1: Reports from near Estacada

Our first seven Bigfoot reports come from near Estacada within three air miles of each other on both the east and west sides of the Clackamas River.

Ref. 2: Millie Kiggins

Estacada #1: This account includes Track Find 1 (TF1) made by Ben Kiggins along the South Fork.

Track Finds 2 and 3 (TF2 & TF3) were reported by the Kiggins family; both were covered by media news.

Millie Kiggins reported roars and screams which we label Bigfoot Related Incident 1. Bigfoot Related Incident 2 is an unusual skull fragment found by the Kiggins.

The Kiggins report comes from interviews with Mildred M. Kiggins (age 87) in November 2012 and January 2013. Millie has lived most of her life on the family farm about three miles from Estacada on the west side of the Clackamas River. Her

grandfather bought the property in 1912 and cleared it to farm. It was replanted to Douglas fir many years ago.

The first encounter with Bigfoot by her family, that Millie remembers, happened in 1911 near "Jacobs Ladder" which is on the South Fork of the Clackamas. Her father, Grover and his brothers were fishing when "Uncle Ben" called out, "Come here!"

What Ben Kiggins found were very large barefoot imprints. Millie says the tracks were found in 1911, a year she remembers because her father bought the property a year later in 1912.

(Authors' note: For Ben Kiggins, a man accustomed to the woods, the footprint, or prints, must have been impressive indeed.)

Please note this is the same area where Kiley and I found a series of 17 inch prints, were roared at, and found crude fishing clubs in 2001. See Ref. 12.

A summer later two of your Clackamas Sasquatchians and a Jake who came along for adventure, again found 17 inch tracks in almost the same spot as our 2001 track find. There is a salmon run up the lower falls of the South Fork which made for great fishing and netting in years past as the spawning area below the falls is shallow water. These days the lower South Fork is closed to fishing.

"We've had him (Bigfoot) here," she said. When Bigfoot was near, they roared several times very near the family farm. The Kiggins, knowledgeable in the ways of wild animals in their woods, knew the tremendous roars were not made by a bear. Millie said, "It sounded like an air horn." She also said that when the beast came around, it stepped over 4 ½-5 foot farm fences like the fences weren't there, leaving big, deep imprints in the soil, and she noted that the imprints were odd, *they were parallel*, not angled like human foot prints.

Note: The authors were permitted to view a copy of the 1968 British Broadcasting Company film on Bigfoot which featured the Kiggins and Glen Thomas, who appears six times later in this book. The BBC film clearly showed parallel foot imprints with no heel drags in the snow. Due to copyright reasons, we were not able to get permission to use frames from the film.

The most important encounter on the Kiggins' farm happened in winter during the late 1960s. There was an unusually deep snow fall of about 2 ½ feet. After several nights of occasional, powerful "high-pitched screams," one morning, she and her father found tracks in the road. The strides in the snow were about 5 ½ feet long. As she recounted the track find, Mille emphasized that the tracks were straight up and down in the deep snow. There were few if any drag marks.

She also said the tracks were also in a straight line, unlike humans who tend to wander off line. She also said the foot imprints were straight and parallel, not pigeon toed. Soon, as in very soon, the word was out. Part of the reason was because Glen Thomas gave the heads up to various people.

Glen Thomas, another local Estacada resident and friend of the family, told the Kiggins of his sightings far up the Clackamas. Millie said that Thomas, who was a Native American from Oklahoma, conducted interviews at the Kiggins' place. She said his sightings "really shook him up." One Thomas interview was with John Green, who Millie described as a very nice man and another with René Dahinden, who she described in less complementary words.

Back to the late 1960s Kiggins track find: a Portland television station (Millie believes it was Channel Two) sent out a reporter and cameraman to record the tracks. Later, John Green came down from British Columbia for his second visit to the Kiggins. She said Roger Patterson of Bluff Creek film fame also visited them for an interview. And even later, a film crew from England came, interviewed Millie and her father, and filmed the site for a TV documentary.

She said, "While I never saw the film, people told us about it. She laughed, "We were internationally famous!"

But there was a dark side to the Kiggins' openness to the media. Some, actually, too many people came to visit just wanting to know "what it was." And then there were small groups of men who wanted to know where to go to find the animal so they could kill it. Millie did not like these men; neither did the local policeman. Chief (Jim) Barden "put a stop to it."

Perhaps too much attention came the Kiggins way for their local barefoot friend. It never returned to the farm that she knows about. Also Millie said that for the decades she operated her barbershop in Estacada, no one ever talked about Bigfoot.

For the record, Mildred (Millie) Kiggins father was Grover Kiggins; his brothers were Benjamin Franklin Kiggins, Everett Kiggins, Armour (spelled correctly) Kiggins, and Gene Kiggins. About 15 years after the incidents at the Kiggins farm, Gene Kiggins son Leslie (Les) saw a Sasquatch on the North Fork.

The Kiggins place remains wild. On January 9, 2013, with great wit, Millie told me before Christmas a sow bear and her cub were coming in every night, ".... leaving their calling cards." They were mainly after fallen apples in the orchard and whatever else they could scavenge from the farmstead.

More on Millie

After telling Vancouver, Washington's *"Sasquatch Sleuth"* Larry Lund about our interview with Millie he said he had an old newspaper article about her which he gave to us. It was *The Clackamas Country News*, Vol. 72 No. 24 of July 25, 1979 and was titled *Encounters with Bigfoot Remembered*. The feature photograph was of Millie and Grover Kiggins. The article contained a long account of the Bigfoot that visited the Kiggins' farm, and an additional track find made by Les Kiggins up the North Fork.

Interestingly, the reporter, Ray Ham, noted that the tracks were parallel. After describing the track finds in snow he quoted Millie saying: "It screeched loudly for a couple of days and then a few days later our dog brought home this portion of a skull." The skull was examined by staff at the Oregon Primate Center and then was sent to the British Columbia Museum of Natural history. 'They couldn't figure out what it was."

Ham also wrote that after the Kiggins became TV personalities the Estacada police chief, Jim Barden told her, "Good God Millie, you've turned a bunch of idiots loose on the town," meaning Bigfoot hunters out for quick fame and lots of dollars.

Ref. 3: The Blank Family

Estacada #2: Sighting 1 (S1) is when Diana Blank sees Bigfoot at her car. Sighting 2 (S2) and Track Find 4 (TF4) is when the Blank women see two Bigfoots in their garden.

Bigfoot related incident 3 is Bigfoot picking vegetables as reported by the Blank women. Bigfoot related incident 4 is when father Blank describes a big "lean-to" he found deep in the forest.

Ray Ham's article also contained a long account about the Blank's, a rural Estacada area family who lived midway down SE Michaels Road southeast of Estacada. Their wooded acreage was about one-half mile east of Promontory Point on the Clackamas, not far from the North Fork, and less than two miles southwest of the upcoming sweetcorn report in Reference 7. Interestingly, the acreage was almost directly east of the Kiggins farmstead on the west side of the river.

One day, Diane Blank (23) was going to her car. From Ham's article:

"When I got to the car *it* was standing – towering – over the other side of the car. It had gigantic bloodshot eyes. I was scared so I tried to joke. I said, 'Hi Mr. Bigfoot, could we be friends?'

After another moment of thinking on the monster staring at her, Ms. Blank decided at that moment her best life choice was retreat, so she backed her way to the house watching the creature by her car. At the house, she turned to open the door; when she turned to look at the Bigfoot again, it had vanished.

A few days later Diane Blank, her sister Debbie, and her mother went to the garden and found, to their surprise, two Bigfoots picking vegetables. When the Bigfoot saw the three women, they ran off. Diane said they had the same "bloodshot" eyes as the one at her car.

Diane's father, Bud Blank, told reporter Ham that he didn't see the house visitors, but in 1976 or 1977 he and two friends were hunting nearby and found a "lean-to" which was constructed from six to eight inch trees pushed over in a circle of about 10 feet. Bud said, "Pine needles covered the floor. Whatever made that up there had an intelligence and a hell of a lot of strength."

End note: The authors find it fascinating that Diane Blank seemed accustomed to the word "Bigfoot," and that she, her mother, or sister were not panicked or terribly surprised to find Bigfoot in their garden.

Were our Barefoot Friends regulars at the house, or in the neighborhood, before her sighting? Was there an informal habituation process in place? Also, see Reference 32 for the description and photograph of a structure found high up the Clackamas very similar to what Bud Blank described.

Ref. 4: Jake the Recluse

Estacada #3: Sighting 3 and Sighting 4 (S3 & S4) by *Jake the Recluse* (J-R) at his forest home.

Like all small mountain towns, Estacada has its share of eccentric people. The most pertinent to this narrative was a crotchety old semi-hermit who lived deep in the forest on the west side of the river well past the Kiggins farm. This solitary man was just the sort of human Sasquatches seem to like.

Through word-of-mouth, this man came to the attention of a major Oregon based Bigfoot research project which was in operation from the late 1980s into the early 1990s. After some difficulties contacting *J-R*, research project personnel arranged an interview.

A Clackamas Sasquatchian associated with the research project, accompanied by a friend, drove to the subject's rustic forest abode. For the purposes of this book, the subject is named *Jake the Recluse*. True to his reputation, he proved somewhat cantankerous, but warmed to our Sasquatchian, perhaps because he had several broken fingers from semi-pro football days which were also the sign of an experienced logger.

Our Sasquatchian reported that J-R was especially memorable because of the number of small flying insects which hovered over his head and seemed to make their home in his hair.

Jake the Recluse made most of his living as a night watchman for a logging crew that worked up the Clackamas. This frequently put him out in the woods alone and able to study nature from a unique perspective. It was on logging shows that J-R developed a habit of setting out offerings, not bait, but offerings, for the creatures around his log landings.

The wood knock telegraph must have tapped favorably on Jake the Recluse since unclassified bipeds seemed to have followed him to his remote trailer location near the river. At home, J-R also routinely set out offerings near his trailer.

Things went along well until there was a timber sale on land next to Jake the Recluse's woodland home.

J-R said that once the logging began, he started seeing Sasquatch regularly; he sensed they were unhappy.

What did that patch of timber being clear cut mean to them? Perhaps it was their wintering grounds. He quickly discovered there were two types of Sasquatch living next to him. The larger variety was tall, black haired, and had a nasty, aggressive disposition.

The other type was about 6 feet tall, a good two feet shorter than their forest cousins. The smaller variety had a very good disposition and was recognizable because of a reddish hue to their hair. One of the "little" Sasquatches was a female who took some solace being near Jake the Recluse while her forest home was being destroyed.

J-R knew when she was around because his dog was afraid of her and went crazy before skedaddling under his trailer. But he said that wasn't unusual, his dog was afraid of all of his barefoot friends, both at logging camps or at his trailer. J-R also knew when Bigfoot visited him while he was sleeping because his dog, which slept with him, snuggled in real close and whimpered.

Anyway, several times he managed to see the "little" female close enough to determine she had blue eyes! He said she smelled "good," that she exuded a pleasing natural scent probably made from a forest plant. J R also mentioned to our Sasquatchian that she seemed to desire human male companionship.

While our man's interview with Jake the Recluse was in 1993, he clearly remembers two of the stories. The first, J-R figured out that his Sasquatches not only liked their offerings served off the ground on a fallen log or stump, they really appreciated it when he set offerings out in folded wax paper with the open end held down by a rock. To some degree, this little trick kept the good eats dry and fresh.

When he put out pastries, often the Bigfoot left a small stone or a limb knot or something similar in return. When he put out sandwiches, sometimes they did not eat the bread, just the fillings. Once, or maybe it was more, when they didn't eat the bread, they filled the bread with forest greens or pebbles and refolded the wax paper over the sandwich.

Jake the Recluse said one night his dog went especially crazy. J-R wanted to know what was going on, so he stepped out and shined his light. Not far from his offering log, one of the big variety had its back turned to him. He remembers well the big fellow holding its arms in a great circle, protecting something in front of it, perhaps a young Sasquatch getting an offering treat. He saw the beast well. He told our Sasquatchian it was probably older because of graying hair he saw in his light. Jake the Recluse decided the polite thing to do was to turn off his light to give the Sasquatch their peace.

Ref. 5: Through a Glass Clearly

Estacada #4: Sighting 5 (S5) and Track Find 5 (TF5) were made by Millie Kiggins' neighbor.

This sighting was a simple affair which the witness told to Millie Kiggins the morning after it happened. Since then, the event has become well-known round Estacada. As retold to the authors, it is often enhanced, but the basic facts do just fine for our report. It concerns a woman approaching 50 years of age who lived alone with her dog about four miles south of Estacada toward Dodge, a rural community on the west side of the Clackamas River.

The subject's house was a single-wide trailer sitting on two sets of concrete blocks which raised it about 18 inches to two feet off the ground. Her acreage was a semi-remote woodlot which was connected to the Clackamas and Mt. Hood National Forest by a creek with a wide riparian tree line. It also lay roughly on the western Bigfoot migration route noted in Appendix IV.

The time was in the late 1960s, a year or two after Millie Kiggins had her visitation. Like at Millie's farm, the witness began finding big, indistinct tracks in dirt, grass and duff around her place. Sometimes at night, the woman's dog, which was a good watchdog, cowered. When her trash was rummaged, she called the sheriff. A deputy concluded a big bear was prowling the property.

Not satisfied with that answer, she contacted Millie, who she knew well. Millie confirmed her own odd nighttime visitor acted in the same ways, but was harmless and only left footprints and ate fallen apples. The woman also mentioned the prowler to other people, but since there was no sighting and there was no attempted forced entry, theft, or the like, the general consensus was it was a bear and to simply let time solve the problem.

One dark winter evening the woman was washing her supper dishes. She told Millie she suddenly began to feel uneasy, very uneasy. Then she looked up to see through her kitchen window the big hairy face of an ape-man staring at her and smiling a beastly smile. Their eyes met, his and hers, but for our lady, there was no magic in the air; only terror.

When she finished screaming and opened her eyes the woman's hairy admirer was gone. The next day, a deputy sheriff reported finding where the ape-man ran into the forest "with huge strides."

That was the end of it. The dog didn't get scared again. After the brief encounter, the woman had no more disturbing feelings. Grass and duff on her place was no longer imprinted by large feet. It was over.

Unfortunately, a description of the face the witness saw is not available. Because of the trailer being on blocks, the Bigfoot was probably about 7 ½ feet tall. The authors find it interesting that the Bigfoot-to-human sighting in this story is roughly equivalent to what happened at *Jake-the-Recluse's* place which is in the same area.

Ref. 6: The Culvert Sighting

Estacada #5: Sighting 6 (S6): Bigfoot travels a streambed in the late 1990s.

Co-author Cliff Olson recounted two instances of brief glimpses of Clackamas Bigfoot. Cliff's first sighting, which occurred earlier than this event, is listed in Area 2 Indian Henry Ref. 37. Cliff recorded both events in his den on a cassette tape which was then carefully transcribed and submitted to him for changes and approval. This Area 1 event was voice recorded on July 30, 2012. After editing, Cliff approved the write-up on August 16, 2012.

"My second sighting, which I think is an authentic sighting, was near the Clackamas River not too far from where I used to live well within the boundaries of civilization. Curiosity about my theory on a Bigfoot "travel way" put me out there. I had checked that area many times before and had never seen anything: this time BINGO!

Anyway, we lived on about a 2 ½ acre place; a woodlot we had cleared off and put a manufactured home on. The neighbor place had similar acreage and beyond that on up to the east was just brushy ground that nobody was using. A creek ran down through the brushy ground, a year around creek that ran through about a 5 ½ foot culvert, a big culvert, but I never measured it.

The culvert was in a narrow place in the road and dropped off into a narrow canyon, narrow like about 20 feet wide that ran between two pieces of property. At the time, the creek did not take up the full bottom of the canyon. The creek was running 5–6–7 inches deep in a 2 to 3 foot channel right in the middle of the canyon. At the culvert there was, in effect, a little waterfall and then the stream went out of sight down over the hill.

Getting back to how I saw it, I was walking out on the road and around my neighbor's place into the vegetation barrier right along the road. I went back in there 30 to 40 feet and was looking around and was moving around in lower brush looking ahead. Now, as you approach the creek, there were two or three gullies that went into the creek. At that point the canyon was six or seven feet deep that the creek ran during spring runoff. There was a house built back from the edge of the, well you can't call it a canyon, the streambed.

The land in front of their house was clear and if they were looking out of their windows, they could see out over the stream toward where I was, but they could not see the stream bottom on their side which was much steeper. I always felt this was a possible highway to sneak out of the hills, if you will, to go to the river. And by using the culvert, you didn't have to go up on the road, you could go through it. But,

there was a problem there. Say you were on the road looking downstream the culvert was pretty high off the short canyon the stream ran in.

So, while I was standing there, I caught movement out of my eye hard to my right, I mean hard to my left, there was movement in the creek bottom. I watched it for just a split second and it appeared to me to be an animal doubled over trying to keep out of sight and it dove right into that culvert. I thought, what in the world was that all about, while knowing full well that at the other end of the culvert there was about an 8 foot drop off the culvert into the creek bottom.

So, I turned around and got out of the damn brush I was in and got on the road, got down the road, got to the culvert just in time to see the last of the muddy water disappear over the edge of the bluff. So whatever I saw which came downstream no doubt and stayed under the line-of-sight from that house and if I hadn't been out there wouldn't have been anyone to see it because it was all in the back of buildings and down in the canyon. And, it was moving pretty fast to get out of sight. I think I caught it out in the open and I didn't see it at first, but it was aware I was there and it was making tracks to get out of sight and doubling over to keep a low profile.

That's how I viewed the back of it; it was stooped and trying to keep out of sight. And it was a dull gray, umm, I didn't notice the back of the head, I just notice the shoulders; heavy shoulders and thick back toward the waist. The head was out of sight. Anyway it dove in the culvert. I think it was, to use Peter's term (Peter Byrne) knuckle walking or running maybe in that creek bottom and then jumped down out of the culvert into the streambed and then ran down what was left of the stream before it broke over the hillside and got out of sight.

But the mud was still riled up. I don't know how long it took me to get untangled from that brush and into the vegetation by the road out on the road and down to the culvert. It took me a few minutes. How long it had been in the creek to muddy the water up before I saw it I have no idea. I think it did travel that way because footprints would not be visible in the moving water. They would silt right back in again.

I think I caught one out in the open; it ran to get out of sight, boosted itself through the culvert, dropped off over the edge and went downstream toward the Clackamas. It took a while for the stream to clear up and that's about when I got there about I think, at the most maybe 10 feet maybe 12 feet of riled up water I watched going over the edge. So I think that was about as close as I've ever been and not known it."

Traveler's note: The Dam Road & West Side Hydro Project on Hwy 224 at OBH mile 1.0 from Estacada (or mile 69.0 from Detroit).

During the period 1905 to 1911 four dams were built across the Clackamas River near Estacada.

These dams blocked the Clackamas River anadromous salmon and steelhead runs ruining one of the most popular sport fisheries in the Northwest. Due to lack of salmon to eat, these dams may have also caused a decline in Bigfoot populations in the upper Clackamas drainage.

After substantive lawsuits, now the norm is to spend many millions of dollars in physical efforts to revive salmon and steelhead runs. For instance, today at Portland General Electric's Estacada Cazadero Dam, wild sea-run salmon and steelhead are penned, sorted, loaded and trucked upriver above North Fork Dam for release and spawning.

Later, fingerlings, and steelhead ready to return to the sea, are penned on the upstream side of the dam, loaded into tank trucks and transported downstream for release. To a degree the trucking program has proved successful. Some seasonal runs of Clackamas wild salmon are roughly equivalent to those prior to the dams and nowadays may contribute to the continuing existence of a remnant population of Bigfoots in the high Clackamas.

Ref. 7: The Sweetcorn Field

Hwy 224 event #1: Jake 1 (J1): Bigfoot Related Incident 5 is when Bigfoot eats sweetcorn and leaves Track Find 6.

Fall Creek road runs east from its intersection with Hwy 224 at OBH mile 2.9 (67.1 miles from Detroit). Events occurring about three miles east on this road produced one of our most amusing Bigfoot stories.

In this account we introduce *Jake* to name people who either do not wish to be named in this book, that are deceased, or who we could not reach to ask permission to use their name. In this case the subject was deceased.

An acquaintance of Cliff Olson lived on a Fall Creek Road farm. We will identify this man as Jake 1 (J1). For many years Jake 1 planted sweetcorn in his big garden. Every year, when the corn was ripe, beasts with human-like feet ranging from great to small came into the field, and like human farmers of old, broke ears from stalks, and ate the corn ears, cobs and all.

However, Jake 1, a stubborn soul of Oregon pioneer stock, was determined to grow his own sweetcorn. So, J1 kept planting and the critters kept eating. He sat out at night with his shotgun, but they always seemed to know when J1 was out and armed, and when he was not. Dogs didn't help. When the beasts came around dogs hid under the house. Strong fences presented no problem to J1's powerful, determined corn field invaders. They simply ripped fences out of the ground.

Worse, every year, the corn robbing bandits generally announced they were on their way with deep, long roars and wails that echoed from nearby hills in the night. Then, on mornings after the calls, and sometimes when there were no calls, J1 went to his corn patch where he again witnessed the devastation made by the corn eaters. He saw huge man-like foot imprints in the loose soil and cursed "The Mountain Devils" as he called them. We designated Bigfoot corn raids as Incident 5 (I5) and the imprints the Mountain Devils left as Track Find 6 (TF6).

Authors' note: Driving on various backcountry byways from Fall Creek road, a motorist can get to Sandy, Oregon. Beyond Sandy, up the Sandy River canyon toward Mt. Hood is a place of many Bigfoot stories. These stories are especially numerous around Portland's highly protected water source, Bull Run Reserve.

Sasquatchian Todd Neiss brought to the authors' attention a pioneer map in Oregon Historical Society archives which notes a place on the Sandy River as *Ape Crossing*. *Ape Crossing* is on the south side of Portland's highly protected Bull Run water reserve and just west of Brightwood (a village). Topographical maps show *Ape Crossing* as the most reasonable route from Bull Run across the Sandy River bottom to Macintyre Ridge and on to the Clackamas. This important information contributed to our migratory routes described in Appendix IV.

Approximate GPS of "Ape Crossing:" 45 22 41.56N 122 01 10.41W.

The Clackamas River Gorge Viewpoint

View of Clackamas gorge from Hwy 224 four miles south of Estacada. Photo by Joe Beelart

Hwy 224: OBH mile 3.7 (66.3.

GPS coordinates: 45 14 46.78 N 120 16 20.23 W at 1,109′.

This pleasing spot is especially beautiful in the early morning when swirls of mist and clouds rise from the river through steep cliffs along the Clackamas gorge. There are three items of interest to note here.

The far mountain lying crosswise (east-to-west) is Whale Head which was named after breaching whales. You will hear much more about Whale Head in Area 2 reports.

Ref. 8: Stoning a '59 Chevy

Hwy 224 event #2: OBH mile 4.5 (65.5 from Detroit): Summer 1962: Jake 2 has his car stoned in Bigfoot Related Incident 6 (I6).

This incident was told to me by a man who I have known for over ten years. He works in the dealership where I have my truck serviced.

This event happened on the old riverside highway which has been obliterated. You will be roughly above the site when you stop at the new clear cut on the west side of the Clackamas River gorge viewpoint.

My friend was driving up the Clackamas with his girlfriend to stoke the embers of affection. About four and a half miles from Estacada they were shocked when a large rock flew out of the air, over the front of the car, and smashed into the trunk lid of his beautifully maintained swept-wing 1959 Chevrolet.

Highly irritated, he turned and patrolled the road, intently watching the woods. He didn't see anybody. The couple drove on up the hill; then on the way back down, another rock flew off the hillside and

From about ½ million to 2 million years ago huge lava flows covered much of Oregon and Washington with 600 to 900 feet of basalt. These gargantuan flows left the relatively flat plateaus seen on the east side of the Clackamas gorge.

The third thing to notice is water erosion has cut through the ancient lava flows to bedrock. Much of this cutting was done by water borne boulders at the end of the last ice age when glaciers high up the Clackamas melted. Later in your tour, you will enter Big Bottom which is an excellent example of these glaciated valleys.

hit the trunk again! This time, my friend simply accelerated out of the area.

The real mystery was the ground wasn't steep; there was no way the flying rocks came from a cliff fall. He said it was a quiet time of the year and there was little traffic that day. From the size of the dents, he seriously doubts the rock was thrown by a human.

Traveler's note: Hwy 224 at mile 5.4 (64.6 from Detroit): This is where the North Fork of the Clackamas enters the main river. This is a popular family fishing spot. Be sure to drive carefully near here.

The North Fork of the Clackamas runs roughly east to west. South of the North Fork is a ridge. On the other (south) side of this ridge is Roaring River. On top of this dividing ridgeline is Forest Service road 4610 which was named Abbott Road after a general who explored the Clackamas trying to find the best route between the Willamette Valley and central Oregon. Your map may show road 4610 as a through route; it is not. The bridge near Squaw Mountain was washed away in the 1996 floods.

Portland General Electric's Promontory Park

Hwy 224: OBH mile 6.2 (63.8): GPS coordinates: 45 13 22.50N 122 14 35.64W at 740'

Portland General Electric's Promontory Park & Marina is river side. In spring, summer and fall, when the Marina is open, it's the last gas until you reach Detroit. At the intersection, the east bound road is Forest Service Road 4610 into the North Fork. We report one sighting and two Bigfoot related incidents along this road.

About 12 miles east on Road 4610, adventurers find Squaw Meadows and Squaw Mountain. This beautiful, little used area has a plethora of anecdotes about *Our Barefoot Friends* and is featured in Sasquatchian Thom Powell's novel *Shady Neighbors*, much of which is based on fact.

District 2: The North Fork, South Fork, & Memaloose

Ref. 9: Sasquatch backs out a fly fisherman

North Fork event #1 is Sighting 7 (S7) made by Jake 3 (J3). Here, we introduce a Forest Service Law Enforcement Officer 1 (LEO 1) who was a friend of this project.

Jake 3 reported this sighting to a Forest Service Law Enforcement Officer (LEO 1) on the afternoon of his sighting. LEO 1 asked detailed questions at that time, and again at a later interview to confirm the facts. The LEO told his report to Cliff Olson. A close friend of Jake 3 at the time, who is mentioned later in this book, also heard the story several times from Jake 3 before telling it to me (Joe Beelart). The details in the LEO and friend accounts matched well.

This sighting, labeled Sighting 7 (S7), was made by a government employee, who we identify as Jake 3. Jake 3 often had days off in the middle of the week. So, one weekday he decided to take his children fishing up North Fork Road 4610. He drove about six miles up to the beginning of La Dee Flats and turned north on Spur Road 4613 for about a quarter of a mile.

In this area Winslow Creek, Whisky Creek, Boyer Creek, and the ever-flowing reach of Dry Creek join the North Fork of the Clackamas. These creeks are prime spawning grounds for steelhead and salmon, plus if you know how to do it, there is fine wild rainbow trout fishing. It is also, "Squatchy" territory as they say on TV.

Jake 3 got his children out of the truck and organized. Then they walked down an eroded old logging road for several hundred yards towards a favorite fishing pool. Jake stopped to rig up his fly rod. While he was doing that, to the absolute amazement of Jake 3 and his surprised children, from out of the sunken grade rose first a head, and then the rest of a big male Sasquatch as it climbed onto the logging road and stopped about 12 feet in front of them.

The gigantic monster stood there simply looking at Jake 3 and his children, who were literally scared speechless in open eyed wonder. To them, this was it! Before them was a Saturday morning cartoon monster come to life!

All was quiet, for a while. Scared into silence by the 7 ½ to 8 foot tall beast covered with short black hair, Jake 3 simply froze. His children followed suit. From the look on its face, freezing in place obviously displeased the Sasquatch. At this point,

Jake 3 became somewhat concerned about his children's future.

While frozen, Jake 3 notices several things. The beast expressed his displeasure by exposing clenched ivory teeth through thin black lips. He said the teeth were larger and squarer than those in humans. J3 was mesmerized by the hominid's large, black eyes.

Jake 3 also said the beast's hands were big enough to crush his head like a grape and while its private parts weren't large, they were plenty big enough.

Ignoring the children, the beast carefully and without threat then approached Jake 3. What to do? Well Reader, there are only two things to do, are there not? Which would you do?

Confronted by a huge, naked man-like creature only twelve feet away on a deserted old logging road, the man simply held out his 9 foot fly rod toward the beast which walked to it, bumped into the tip of the rod; and stood there. Jake 3 took a few steps back.

His kids took a few steps back, staying near their father. Now over their first shock, they start to get animated. Before them was something straight out of the movies! Again, the beast walked forward bumping into the tip of the fly rod. And so it went, all the way back to Jake 3's truck where the beast kindly stood at the edge of the clearing, watched Jake 3 throw his fly rod into his truck, load up his children and drive off.

What to Learn

What is there to learn from this encounter? First, we learn of a few physical characteristics: Jake 3, after several hundred retreating steps, noticed his peaceful aggressor had relatively small ears set close to its head. The head was rather square, with wide set jaws and the top of the head was relatively flat with perhaps a bit of a "butch" haircut look. The Bigfoot was muscular throughout with large shoulder muscles similar to a weight lifter's. It had a short neck, which for some reason it turned with its body when it looked behind itself, which it did often.

The Sasquatch breathed deeply in a natural, non-stressed sort of way through slightly wide nostrils set in a moderately wide nose. Mainly keeping his eye on the upper portion of his hairy new acquaintance, Jake 3 did not register much about the feet and legs.

The second thing to consider is the beast's motivations for the encounter. The fly fisher was going to descend the bank to a pool that generally held quite a number of trout or spawning salmon. The general opinion of members of the Bigfoot community who have read this report think the male's family was fishing in the pool, or was perhaps teaching youngsters to fish. The Sasquatch may have simply wanted privacy for his family.

The third thing is how witness stories evolve. What is known to Bigfoot researchers is often after a Bigfoot encounter, as time goes on and the story is retold, the creatures become more human like and events in the story become more detailed, or elaborate, or both. We might have been able to find and talk to Jake 3 ourselves, but because of the way stories can evolve, we decided to go with the LEO's account. Over the 20 years since the event, perhaps J3's remembrance is not as solid as what LEO 1 remembers from his report.

One very experienced researcher has made a practice of repeatedly asking witnesses to tell their story again and again, often over years. He then compares notes to see how the story has evolved. He says stories from "true" encounters tend to stay the same. In this case, the story Jake 3 tells has remained about the same over roughly 20 years.

Ref. 10: Bigfoot Sits on a Bulldozer Seat

North Fork event #2: Jakes 4, 5, 6: Track Find 7 (TF7): Bigfoot related Incident 7.

Approximate GPS coordinates: 45 10 53.48N 122 08 04.87W at 2765'

La Dee Flats lays along the North Fork in a wide curve roughly following Winslow Creek toward Huxley Lake, which is a small summit lake that drains south down a steep slope into Roaring River. It is a great place to log because expensive spar trees, huge wire ropes, and high-line log carriages are not needed. Loggers simply need to fall trees, limb and length, then drag them to a log loader and the job is done.

In about 1965 a small logging company picked up a Forest Service sale in La Dee Flats. Cliff Olson was a friend of the logging company cat skinner (bulldozer operator) and got this story first-hand almost immediately after the incident. Over the years, the cat skinner retold this story many times to Olson without significant changes.

The timber sale was a great success for the small company, so the men pressed their luck against winter and lost. One night about three feet of snow fell and more was in the forecast. Unfortunately, they still had a large bulldozer fitted with log clamps, a log loader, their fire truck, and other equipment at the log landing. The equipment had to be retrieved before the winter weather damaged it.

Their retrieval plan was simple. Park the truck at a good place below the snow line, walk in about two miles to the landing, use the big bulldozer to clear the road and drive out the log loader and the other rig. Simple plans are always the best, and this one worked perfectly; except when they got

to the landing the men found someone had beat them to it.

To their relief, a quick inspection showed no vandalism or damage, just many large footprints in the snow where their visitor had patrolled all around. We call this set of footprints Track Find 7 (TF7). The men thought it most curious that their snow walker had large bare feet because both toe and foot showed well in the fresh snow.

Further, the footprints were huge! They measured over 17 inches and there were hundreds of them. But the most unusual aspect of the visitation was the creature had stepped up on the bulldozer tracks, sat down on the seat, and handled lever controls and brushed off the instrument panel. The hind end of their visitor was huge. The hair pattern it smashed into the snow made a lasting impression in the men's minds so we list this as Bigfoot Related Incident 7.

Another unusual aspect of this incident was the two lines of tracks in the snow, one coming out of a thicket to the log landing, and the other set going back to the thicket. The cat skinner supposed that, hidden in the trees, the creature watched the men working and when it felt safe, tried to imitate the cat skinner's job.

Probably the most adverse thing about the snow visitor was the psychological impact it had on one of the men. Two of the men belonged to a Christian church that believes Cain still exists alongside man, who descended from Adam and Eve. To him, the huge, barefoot snow walker was proof incarnate of the tenants of his faith. In effect he had seen proof that Cain walks with us. After confirming his brother's account to Olson, this man would not speak of the event again.

Ref. 11: The Scotch Broom Twist-off

North Fork event #3: Kiley and Beelart: Bigfoot Related Incident 8

After learning of the fly rod bumping incident, even though it happened years earlier, Steve Kiley and I decided to take a look around the sighting area in the spring of 2000. Hiking in the vicinity of Roads 4611 and 4612, sharp eyed Steve spied a limb of scotch broom lying by an old, overgrown cat trail (logging road). The stem had a radius of about 1 inch and was cleanly twisted off. The stem was not twisted with tools. Whatever did it had "soft" hands and left bark intact.

This stem was a highlight of the Kiley Principle. Scotch broom grows on strong vine like stems. It is simply impossible for a human to cleanly twist off a stem that size.

Entering Mt. Hood National Forest

Hwy 224: At *OBH* mile 6.9 (63.1) is the *Entering Mt. Hood National Forest* sign.

Notice the grove of red alder trees across the river. This is the end of the North Fork dam reservoir; beyond this point the Clackamas River flows free.

At *OBH* Mile 7 a sharp left turn places the traveler virtually across from the South Fork of the Clackamas. There is ample parking at this turn, but beware of potholes. It is a good place to stop and watch the beautiful deep flow of the river for a few minutes. This bend in the river is a salmon holding pool so perhaps you might see an angler fly fishing for salmon or steelhead.

Since the upper Clackamas is an artificial lure only river, sometimes you will see fly fishermen with long, strong, two-handed muscle-testing salmon rods called

Our supposition was a large Sasquatch twisted off the stem and left it as a boundary or warning marker. The stem was given to Ray Crowe for his Western Bigfoot Society museum, and in 2008 was probably transferred to the archives of the North American Bigfoot Search.

Reader, please know there are millions upon millions, maybe even billions of broken branches in the south Mt. Hood National Forest. Most breaks are the result of wind, ice, and natural aging. Only one in millions is man-made, let alone the possible work of a Bigfoot. In this book there are only three mentions of breaks possibly made by Bigfoot. The North Fork scotch broom twist-off is certainly the most important of the three.

Entering Mt. Hood National Forest sign. Photo by Bailey Olson.

"spey rods." In recent years, a cadre of traditional fishermen cast this pool in likeness to traditional fly fishermen of old in Scotland and the Atlantic provinces of Canada. Look for their beautiful flies, or if a fly fisher is pausing in their labor, quietly ask for a look.

Please notice the confluence of the South Fork of the Clackamas across the river. This was the site of an early major civil engineering project in Oregon. In 1913 polluted Willamette River water caused a severe bout of typhoid in Oregon City. A "Pure Mountain Water League" was established. The "League" built 26 miles of 18 inch wood stave pipeline to the South Fork. Upslope on the South Fork the "League" built a dam at Memaloose Creek to supply the pipeline.

The pipeline carried some of the purest water in the United States to Oregon City, Gladstone, and West Linn. The supply system was improved in the 1930s by the Federal Works Project Administration resulting in hand drilled tunnels and a 24 inch supply line out-of-sight from the highway. The 18 inch wood pipeline and a forester style maintenance cabin were visible just east of the Memaloose Bridge until the 1996 floods wiped them away. Then, a new water intake was installed near Oregon City.

Warning: A professional diver who has participated in several rescues and retrievals along this stretch of river suggested this warning. Currents near the South Fork are very strong and treacherous. He strongly recommends not paddling kayaks, and especially canoes, in that stretch without good river experience, and life preservers.

Ref. 12: The South Fork Tracks, Roaring, & Foul Scent

Kiley and Beelart: Track Find 8 (TF8): Incident #9 is a probable Bigfoot scent emission. Bigfoot Related Incident #10 is a creature roaring. Happening #1 is finding fishing clubs.

The location of this report is on the South Fork of the Clackamas, well off Hwy 224 and south across the main river.

Approx. GPS of the South Fork confluence: 45 11 59.56N 122 13 26.29W at 730.'

Approx. GPS of Lower Clackamas Falls: 45 11 45.62N 122 13 34.46W.

Approx. GPS of Upper Clackamas Falls: 45 11 17.49N 122 13 45.14W.

One Monday morning in late August 2001, Kiley and I decided to cross the Clackamas to see some new country, territory not often visited by humans, especially since the 1996 floods. Using Kiley's canoe, we were amazed by the power of the river through the narrows, even though it was running seasonally low. After furious paddling, we went ashore. With our Duluth canvas packs supplied for a day trip, we began hiking up slope.

After a few hundred yards, maybe a third of a mile, we reached the top of a wide waterfall which was just out of sight from the trail. The smooth flow of the water in the morning sun was spectacular to see and hear.

Behind the top of the waterfall was a pool. As usual, Kiley was in the lead since he walks faster than I do. Just past the waterfall ... for the first time ... I experienced a substantial sulfuric smell which I attributed to Kiley's uncommonly active digestive tract. But, I thought little about it since I was very happy I wasn't trapped in the truck with him grinning "got'ya."

It was an idyllic morning under the timber. Except for the quiet flow of the South Fork, silence reigned. About 100 yards beyond an old, somewhat treacherous bridge built by the water district, Kiley stopped beneath a huge maple tree. As I crossed the bridge, I again suffered a dose of sulfuric gases, but the issue was forgotten as I approached Kiley.

Lower waterfall on South Fork. Photo by Joe Beelart

Steve was standing at the edge of a small grass covered glen full of fresh Bigfoot tracks. How did we know the tracks were fresh? Because there was heavy dew on the ground and the dew was off the tracks. Plus, where the beast shuffled, maybe listening to us walk up the slope, dew was spewed off grass near the shuffles.

One excellent right foot imprint was in a slightly wet, grass free muddy spot. The track measured 17 ½ inches long by about 7 ½ inches wide at the ball of the foot and about 5 inches wide at the heel. The toes were somewhat square by human standards and the two part foot hinge showed clearly.

We marveled at how clearly the two-part Bigfoot foot was shown in this imprint. It was at this point we well-prepared Bigfooters found we'd left the plaster-of-

Paris in the truck on the other side of the Clackamas.

Close examination of the impressions in the grass showed impressions in the earth beneath mirroring the mud track. There were also distinct foot-turning impressions as, we assume, the beast looked over its shoulder as we hiked up the hill.

After photographing the track, and impressions in the grass, Kiley and I continued up the grade through the old construction tunnel. Beckoned by the sound, in not many yards we encountered a beautiful veil waterfall. The dam above still remained out of sight. It was here where the trail was obliterated and our climb stopped.

One of the South Fork tracks. Photo by Joe Beelart

It was also here where I pleasantly inquired of Kiley as to his intestinal problems, of which Kiley said he had none.

"You're joking."

"No, honest, I am not."

"Well, something's making that gas, it happened again only about 100 yards back."

"Well, (laugh), it wasn't me."

With the gas emission mystery unsolved, we hiked back down the slope; pausing at the track find. We paused again at the crest of the waterfall as we hiked downslope. We then circled to the outlet of the South Fork and followed it up to see the face of the waterfall.

Kiley splashed upstream in the shallows to get a better look at the waterfall. I stayed further down exploring the shore line, and since I also wore water-resistant boots I waded into the river to look for potential salmon spawning grounds which I easily found while watching big bright fish splashing and finning around their redds (salmon spawning beds).

After leaving the redds, I waded toward the bank. It was then I found a collection of makeshift wood clubs on a large tree which had fallen into the river.

The wooden clubs were made from limbs. All were about 15 inches long and very sturdy. Two were made from limb knots which generally is the hardest part of the whole tree.

Just as I found the wood clubs, something began calling, actually roaring, from the hillside above Kiley. Whatever the beast on the hillside was, it was obviously greatly disturbed by our presence, but remained out of sight. From the length of the repeated roars, it was certainly not a bear.

Wood clubs on log up South Fork. Photo by Joe Beelart

Steve finally turned downstream from the base of the falls. When we met up, I asked if he'd heard the roars. Steve said no because of the noise from the water fall. He also reported redds below the water fall just beyond the fall pool. I showed him the salmon clubs which were a bit of a marvel to Steve; we were careful not to touch them.

Then we hiked back down to the canoe. Again, with great effort, we paddled back across the Clackamas to the river rock beach and portaged the canoe up to the truck. Due to river conditions, we decided not to paddle back with the plaster-of-Paris. Steve and I were very tired, so that was the end of our day of adventuring.

Note: Track Find 8 was at roughly the same location as Kiggins brothers' 1911 track find TF1 reported in Ref. 2: Millie Kiggins.

Big Cliff

OBH mile 8.7 (61.3)   GPS: 45 12 03.23N 122 13 16.41W

Big Cliff on Hwy 224. Photo by Sharon Beelart

Big Cliff is just past the South Fork confluence after a sharp right turn. This unmistakable majestic cliff marks the north terminus of the Clackamas National Wild and Scenic River which begins about 47 miles up mountain at its source near Olallie Butte. The parking area to view the cliff is at *OBH* Mile 8.7 (61.3 from Detroit).

In the old days, the parking area was a log scaling station. Log scaling stations were used to measure logs for the mills, and thereby reduced truck congestion and time in towns. Now the scaling station is a good place to stop for a break and photography. This reach of the river is very scenic, but be careful crossing the road to see it.

After passing Big Cliff, please notice the basalt overlay throughout the canyon. As noted, several ancient eruptions covered most of the Pacific Northwest with 600 to 900 feet of basalt. The polygonal joint patterns are a characteristic of slow cooling basalt, so at one time the adventurer can know the Clackamas was very hot indeed.

Mines in the Clackamas are mostly located where the hot basalt interacted with existing mineral deposits. Thus mines are generally located high up mountains, or in those rare places where water has worn through the rock to the original substrata. A retired geologist once told me some of the richest mineral deposits in the world may well lie buried under the *OBH*.

The Memaloose Bridge: OBH mile 9.2 (60.8)

The Memaloose Bridge crosses the Clackamas River to the south. Since this is the first turn off since Estacada this is where many people go to shoot and dump trash. As a result, if you go up the hill about a mile, you will find a large flat place paved with broken glass, spent cartridge casings, and a wide variety of blasted targets. These last few years, old flat screen TVs seem to have gained favor as targets ... hey, it saves the cost of taking them to a recycling center.

FJ on Memaloose Bridge 2014. Photo by Sharon Beelart

The Memaloose: A rare westerly mountain pass

Amazingly, Hwy 45, which winds up the hill beyond the Memaloose Bridge, is only one of two places in the south Mt. Hood National Forest where a driver can cross from the Clackamas west into the Willamette Valley. The other is about 10 air miles to the south in the Collawash.

The south crossing, or pass, in the Collawash is the very winding Forest Service Road 7010 which climbs up from near Bagby Hot Springs toward Table Rock Wilderness. The next westerly crossing is Hwy 22 which is the main highway between Salem and Detroit. Hwy 22 is about 18 *air miles* south of Road 7010.

The reason we spend so many words on these crossings is to suggest the ruggedness of the line of mountains dividing the Willamette Valley and the upper Clackamas basin. Truly, the high Clackamas is a territory in itself because of this strong natural boundary.

Almost undoubtedly, in days of old, the Bigfoots of the Clackamas traditionally used this wild boundary as a territorial clan line to separate themselves from Bigfoot clans in the Molalla drainage and the Willamette Valley.

We say this as we speculate before the arrival of white pioneers it is feasible to think there were "flat land" Bigfoot clans living in the expansive, 100 mile plus long valley where salmon and steelhead runs crowded all of the tributaries of the Willamette River. In any event, since the west ridge is relatively flat along its crest, as described in Appendix IV, this ridge line probably also serves as a migratory route.

Ref. 13: High in the Memaloose: Running naked in wild fire smoke

Memaloose event #1: Law Enforcement Officer 1 (LEO 1, again): Sighting 8 (S8)

United States Forest Service employees are notoriously silent on the subject of Bigfoot. Their reasons are open to speculation. But still, sometimes they will share a sighting or event of some kind. In this book, nine sightings and events were told directly to authors Beelart and Olson by two Law Enforcement Officers (LEOs). The Memaloose provides the first three LEO reports.

Early one morning we, meaning authors Olson and Beelart, were topping off our gas tank in Estacada when LEO 1 (United States Forest Service Law Enforcement Officer) drove in. During the years he lived in Estacada, and at Three Lynx, Olson knew LEO 1 socially.

We always treat LEO's with courtesy and respect. Yes, it is the right thing to do to respect their office, and partly it is because of the inherent nature of LEO's to be a bit "crusty" if they don't get treated right. It's probably important to note one reason Leo's get a little "crusty" is, in this area, they generally operate alone. Their backups are normally far away, sometimes hours away, even if they have radio contact. They live dangerous lives. Please respect them.

Anyway, LEO 1 exchanged pleasantries, then, politely inquired as to our business up the hill. He sighed and then told two stories about the Memaloose that he "didn't think would hurt much." The first one was very simple. In the middle 70s, he and another FS employee were driving a 4-wheel drive pickup to check a wild fire high up Road 45 beyond the Memaloose Bridge.

At the big sweeping curve near the transmitting station building, a large hairy body ran from the fire line across the road

41

very close to the front of their pickup. In the smoke, body particulars were difficult to see, but the waist of the running creature was slightly higher than the hood of the pickup. The witness said the body was very

massive, that it looked very strong. The LEO was both glad and surprised there wasn't a collision. We label the naked smoke runner Sighting 8 (S8).

Ref. 14: "Four dark suited fly fishermen"

Memaloose event #2: LEO 1 (again): Sighting 9 (S9)

On another day, maybe a year later, at the same gas station, LEO 1 asked us if we had given up on our quest, yet. We both smiled and both answered "no."

"Well, I'll tell you another little story that shouldn't matter much." He paused. Do you know the little water fall on the main river east of the Memaloose Bridge, just where the river changes direction?" "Yes."

Author's note: the low water fall is sometimes submerged out of sight in high water. It is located just past the bridge at about *OBH* mile 9.4. In a sharp bend, the river changes course from north to west. Just below the fall is a fish holding pool. This is all very easy to see, just be careful walking along the road.

"Well, early one morning in the late 60s when I was just starting out with the Forest Service, I was driving the crummy with a BD (brush disposal) crew up to our assigned area. Just after we passed the bridge, the man riding shotgun and I saw four dark-suited fly fishermen in the water just after the falls where the river turns 90°. Everyone else was asleep in the back."

He paused, remembering: "We wanted to know what was going on, whether they were salmon poachers or what, so I turned the crummy around and drove back. They were gone. We looked for a rig (vehicle), but didn't find one." He paused. "You can make what conclusions you want. Anyway, they were all different sizes."

Note: A "crummy" is a term used mainly by loggers for a no frills drive-to-work, van-type vehicle normally equipped to carry six or more people.

Ref. 15: Circled Map. "Little People." A Mine

Memaloose event #3: Law Enforcement Officer 1 (again): Happening 2 (H2)

Our final report relating to LEO 1 again happened at the Estacada gas station. This was our third substantial conversation with LEO 1. The exchange centered on the forest map open on the hood of my truck, so we label this Happening 2 (H2).

I had the forest map spread out on the hood because Cliff and I wanted to spy our spot of the day before leaving, and because big folding maps are unwieldy inside a

truck cab. As we were looking, talking quietly and pointing, LEO 1 came over with his coffee cup and we started talking about various things Bigfoot, but with serious attempts to avoid using that word.

We were looking at Whale Head (a mountain) on the map when he casually said in words very close to this effect:

"I take a lot of my lunch hours up there to watch an old mine entrance with my spotting scope. It's high up and the ground around it looks smooth like something lives inside the mine." He paused, smiling, "No, I'm not going to tell you where it is."

Then he humorously remarked on how we two fools would go up there and get ourselves in trouble inside the mine. Well, we've looked and looked, but haven't spied that mine entrance. Of course, just one bush might hide it except from a certain angle.

Then he looked at the map for what seemed like a long time. Finally he pulled his pen and circled hard several times around a high basin far up the Memaloose. Then, as an afterthought, he circled Memaloose Lake.

He pointed at the big circles; he paused as he chose his words: "If I was doing what you two are trying to do, I'd go here. That's where little people are."

As we drove, we talked about the remark. Little people! Where did that come from? We heard him right; he said his sentence clearly and carefully. Why did he say it so it meant two things?? Did he mean "few people" or "little people," ... or both! Anyway that was years ago and to date your authors have spent only one day and no nights high above the Memaloose Bridge.

Bob's Standing Wave

Hwy 224: at *OBH* mile 11.8 (58.2) If you are ready for a break, here is a good spot. Be safe finding a pull out and entering traffic. This is also where you can watch kayakers line up for their turn in Bob's Hole. Bob's Hole is one of those rare places where kayakers can remain virtually motionless on a "standing wave;" providing water flow is high enough.

The exploded "outhouse"

Hwy 224: *OBH* mile 12.6 (57.4): The Big Eddy turnout: A major case in point of National Forest vandalism.

The Big Eddy turnout is a good place for a traveler to stop. There's plenty of parking, lots of space for a safe return to the highway, plus there's a nice river view. It is also a historic site for a rather odd reason. In 1998, someone blew up the Forest Service's brand new, top-of-the-line outhouse. (In private conversation, the authors use indelicate generic slang to describe the structure, and it isn't "privy.")

While blowing up a Federal "building" was unusual, vandalism is rampant in National Forests close to a major population center such as Portland. It is undoubtedly disheartening to Forest Service employees to see their hard work destroyed, stolen, littered, sawed down, or shot up. While the authors don't know the pyramid of vandalism in the National Forest, the great outhouse dynamiting episode has to be up there close to the top.

Carter Bridge

Hwy 224: *OBH* mile 14.0 (56.0)

If the explorer wants to stop here there is a large pull out on the southwest side of the bridge but beware of the road lip and potholes. This is a good place to observe a little water fall on the east side of the bridge. When salmon are running and the water is right, you may see the big fish jumping their way up the waterfall, especially on the north side.

Warning: If you walk on Carter Bridge, when you stop always grasp the rail. Air suction from passing log trucks is very strong and may pull small people into the roadway. Do not walk on the roadway. *Never* allow pets on the bridge.

Carter Falls, viewed from Carter Bridge. Photo by Sharon Beelart

The Fish Creek intersection

Hwy 224: *OBH* mile 14.5 (55.5 from Detroit)

Where Fish Creek flows into the Clackamas: GPS 45 09 26.47N 122 09 26.47W ~ 882′

Fish Creek and Whale Head (a mountain) are south of Fish Creek Bridge. Both have a history of Bigfoot encounters and incidents. Consider taking some time to turn off at the intersection, cross the bridge, and park in the area to the right and observe. Fish Creek lies in a narrow canyon running south for about 11 miles. Skookum Lake lies on the high plateau at the head of Fish Creek canyon.

For hundreds of years the large, beautiful pool at the Fish Creek outlet has been a traditional Native American fishing site. You may find pleasure watching the pool as currents swirl and the light changes with movement in the clouds or as local ducks dapple the water. This is also a good place to watch for bald eagles and osprey.

Caution! When you leave the Fish Creek parking area, reenter the road with extreme caution. Summertime brush and leaves often completely block the driver's left view of oncoming traffic, which is frequently moving very fast.

District 3: Fish Creek

Ref: 16: Bigfoot watches a tire change

Fish Creek event #1: Sighting 10 (S10): Forest Service Employee 1 (FSE 1)

The Forest Service employee who had this sighting is retired and seems very comfortable and relaxed telling his story. In fact, he was filmed giving this report by Blake Eckard for Eckard's upcoming Bigfoot documentary.

FSE 1 was changing a tire on his Forest Service pickup just after dark at the north end of Fish Creek Bridge. It was late in 1967, almost Thanksgiving, so night came on early. FSE 1 became uneasy. Then, for some reason, he became nervous. With the pickup still on the jack, he rose up and shined his flashlight about. "There!"

To his left, standing just out of the beam of his pickup headlights, was a huge black man-like creature. When FSE 1's flashlight 'hit' the beast's face, it raised its arm to fend off the light. In politeness FSE

1 then shined the light away from the creature's face toward its chest and legs.

Then, for some seconds, the beast looked at FSE 1; FSE 1 looked at the beast. Simultaneously, both the beast and FSE 1 decided it was time to vamoose.

To FSE 1's amazement, with long graceful strides, the creature walked across the road, and with apparent ease, climbed the steep slope on the northeast side of the road. FSE 1 said it walked, it did not climb or scramble, it just walked up the slope and out of the beam of his flashlight.

At that point, FSE 1, who seems quite a level-headed fellow, decided it was best to jump in his pickup and depart the area. Which, he did by driving off his jack! Unnerved, he drove about a mile before he stopped to tighten his lug nuts. The next morning on his way back up to do his duties, he retrieved the jack and hubcap. He looked for tracks, but didn't see any.

Ref. 17: Bigfoot leans against a tent

Fish Creek event #2: Bigfoot related Incident 11: Jake 7 & Jake 8

Surprisingly, this is one of two "leaning against a tent reports" in this book. (See Ref. 61.) So, take note and beware that not all that walks in the forest night are bears.

In the middle 1980s a Clackamas Sasquatchian and his wife went camping for a weekend about 5 miles up Fish Creek. Before the 1996 floods, a well-maintained logging road went a long way up the creek. Our friends parked and hiked a short distance to a quiet glen surrounded by tree covered bluffs.

Our Sasquatchian has a measure of Native American blood in his family and is proud of his Native American heritage. He also takes every opportunity to study nature. Without witnessing one, he has long accepted the existence of Sasquatch as fact. His wife had recently retired as a state patrol officer, so it's safe to conclude both are very calm and level-headed. Neither qualifies for admittance into an institution for the very, very nervous.

This weekend was for relaxation, professional reading, and to get away from the urban environment. They set up a tent, gathered wood for a fire, talked, laughed, and had a nice time. Then something started walking in the trees around their camp. Their visitor remained unseen and seemed to walk on two legs, but they decided they were wrong, it was a bear.

They remained nonplussed when at one point a limb flew out of the brush onto the edge of their campground. No matter, "probably a natural break." After a while a rock or two landed near their camp. "Probably off the bluffs."

Late in the evening, as the fire died down, something started to whistle from the bluffs. It was a modulated, long, high whistle; not man-made, and was definitely not a night bird. This was not good. However, our hardy souls decided they were not going to be scared from their camp.

Finally it was time for blankets so they got into the tent and went to bed. Shortly after blanket time something making heavy footfalls entered their camp. It marched around, obviously inspecting everything; not caring if the Jakes in the tent knew it was there.

In what may have been a sign of displeasure, it leaned against the tent. His wife certainly wasn't concerned. She had her 44 magnum full of Alaskan bear loads at the ready. Our man wasn't worried because the creature had not tried to harm them, only scare them, which was in accord with Native American legends told in his family.

But, his curiosity was at a very high level. What was there to do? Well, he did it. He reached up to the depression on the side of the tent and pressed against what was on the other side.

Whatever it was on the other side was cold, very firm, and hard. Jake 7 kept pressing; whatever it was leaning on their tent was very heavy, unmovable; and even though it was summertime, it was very cold. Then, the beast outside seemed to lose interest in the camp, rose up, and walked into the forest not to be seen or heard from again.

Incredibly, Jakes 7 and 8 intuitively knew the event was all over and whatever *it* was, was gone. They immediately fell into a deep, good sleep almost as if they were told to sleep. In the morning, upon reflection of the previous day's happenings, they noticed they had camped next to a trail leading from the mountains to a quiet pool on Fish Creek, in short, a trail to a wilderness being's dinner.

Ref. 18: A Watchman's Nightmare

Fish Creek event #3: Bigfoot Related Incident 12: Jake 9 (J9)

One afternoon when Kiley and I were hiking up Fish Creek, we talked for a little while with a forest construction crew night watchman and oiler who we call Jake 9 (J9).

Since Jake 9 worked nights, he was just up and making himself breakfast when we came walking by. He politely stopped us. After we reassured him we were not going into the road construction area and would be out before they closed the barrier, he relaxed.

It seemed that the rest of the crew stayed in Estacada motels. Only he stayed here, alone, at night, filling diesel tanks, greasing, doing routine maintenance, and minor repairs. Then, even though the barrier was closed three miles downstream, he watched for vandals. He asked if we would be out of Fish Creek before 5 when they closed the gate. He said tonight was a busy one for him and the last thing he wanted was to have his routine interrupted to drive three miles on a slow road to let us out.

We assured him we'd be out the gate well before 5, but as it ended up, we barely made the cut. Anyway, since our "business" is Bigfoot investigations of sorts, we engaged him in conversation. He said he'd been with the company a long time as their watchman/oiler. The company did forestry construction jobs all over Washington and Oregon, plus a few in Idaho.

When we gave him a little verbal jostle about strange doings and big barefoot people here in Fish Creek, he got pale and quiet. We sensed that on this job, barefoot people were why he stayed awake almost all night, most nights.

In a shaky voice that gave us pause, he said, "I don't want anything to do with that kind of talk, thank you."

Then he paused. "I will tell you that of all the places we've had a work camp this is the one that I want to leave most." His meaning was obvious, so we exchanged pleasantries and were on our way.

Ref. 19: Rock Marker, Licked Rocks

Fish Creek event #4: Oct. 15, 1999: Bigfoot Related Incident 13: Third Creek Ridge off Fish Creek: Kiley and Beelart.

After an *arduous climb* from Third Creek canyon, Steve and I found ourselves on lower west ridge of Whale Head. On the top we found a boundary monument possibly placed by Bigfoot, and a place where an ambidextrous animal licked the underside of rocks for minerals and nutrients.

On a stump clearly visible from all around, was a flat stone the size of a platter. We looked around for the source of the stone. It certainly wasn't within 50 yards or so. Why was it laying there, just out in the open, on a stump, in plain sight? Maybe it was a Bigfoot boundary marker, a Bigfoot wilderness survey monument?

About 100 yards after the stone on the stump, we passed a little rock outcrop. The outcrop rose up a foot and a half or so and was sedimentary and layered. It was weathered. I asked Steve if he could see what was different about the rock outcropping and he looked only a minute before he said, "not long ago, something pulled rocks off of it and turned them over." What made the outcropping even more special was that the pulled rocks were neatly stacked.

More, there were still lichens and dirt on them from being turned over. They hadn't baked dead under high altitude summer sun. What was even more amazing was that it looked like something had licked the underside of the rocks. In that little rock stack strangeness abounded.

We looked at the rocks carefully. Whatever had done it had a comfortable arm span of about 6 feet. It was very easy to visualize a man-like creature sitting on the soft dirt of the ridge to the left of the outcrop, pulling the rocks with a right hand, licking them for whatever reason, transferring them to the left hand, stacking them, and doing it again.

Licked rocks above Third Creek. Photo by Joe Beelart.

These rocks were not the same as the one on the stump. The one on the stump was dark with weathering. These were tan on the underside and sun bleached gray on the outside. These rocks were very curious indeed because several times Sasquatch have been observed licking rocks, supposedly for nutrients. The best known incident of rock licking was reported by Bob Gimlin at Bluff Creek, California in October 1967.

Cougar #1 Stalks Woman

Fish Creek event #5: Cougar #1 (C1): Jake #10 & Forest Service Employee 2 (FSE2)

This is the first of seven cougar sighting reports in this book. The authors wish to note that while cougar attacks on humans are very rare, they do happen.

But, since cougars are curious cats, they also simply approach and watch humans. So, over the years your Sasquatchians have personally experienced seven cougar events in the Mt. Hood National Forest.

In late August of 2003, Kiley and I decided to go for another Fish Creek hike. At the barrier, we met a twentyish, outdoorsy type woman we shall call Jake 10 (J10) hiking out of the creek. As we mounted our Duluth packs, we exchanged pleasantries. She was from the Chicago area and was in Portland for a convention. This was the "exploring afternoon off" so she decided to hike instead of taking a trip to the wine country.

After waiting to make sure her car started we headed up the creek. Not 50 yards down the trail we saw very fresh tracks where a cougar turned and leapt out of the trail. Mr. Cougar's tracks, and he was a big one, were in the woman hiker's tracks meaning the cougar was stalking the woman we just met. As we walked along,

from the cougar's pug marks, it was clear the cougar followed her for at least half a mile, attracted to her for some reason but held back, just watching.

We thought "short" cougar follows were mainly because of curiosity, but such a long cougar stalk was bad business. We spent the rest of the day finding where the cougar began his prowl and searching the glens and glades along the first mile and a half of creek for more sign. On our way home, we decided we'd better report the incident. What if the cougar was injured, crippled, or old and had begun hunting people?

I managed to get through to a Forest Service biologist who we designate as FSE 2. She said she'd look into it. On Friday she returned my call. She was excited. "I saw your cougar! It jumped off a bench right in front of me!" She said it was a large, young male that appeared in good health. The biologist thought it probably just had a bad case of youthful inquisitiveness toward the woman hiker.

Next, she surprised me. "Hey, did you know some of the people at the office know about you?" Even though I occasionally talked with a contact in the Estacada office, I was shocked anyone else knew my name. Then, she really giggled. "And they know what you and your buddies are doing up there!"

Ref. 20: "Biologist Hits a Wall"

Fish Creek event #6: Bigfoot Related Incident 14: FSE2, again

Continued from the previous report: What an opportunity! A good humored Forest Service biologist was at the other end of the line! So, in words to this effect, I asked, "Have you had any experiences of the Bigfootery kind?" That made her laugh

again; then she paused. "No, I haven't seen one, and I haven't seen indisputable tracks, but once a few years ago one strange thing happened to me."

I waited. I knew she wanted to tell a story. "At the time, I already had over 20 years' experience as a Forest Service biologist. One day I went up to ..." She stopped, paused, thinking; then she changed her tone, "…. to a narrow canyon to check on one of my projects. It was after the '96 floods, so I was on foot. After going up creek for a while, I hit a wall. There was no wall there, but I simply could go no further. Then I got confused, like I was in a cloud." She stopped talking.

After a minute, she resumed. "I don't know why I'm telling you this. I didn't tell anyone then, or anyone since. Anyway I backed away from the 'wall,' left the canyon, drove back to the office, and did paperwork. The next day I went back up again and nothing happened."

I thanked her for sharing and assured her that I would not use her name if I ever told the story. That relieved her. I was also very careful to not comment on, or question her report which I think she appreciated. When I read my notes, I still find it interesting she used the phrase, "… I backed away from the wall."

This ends reports from Area 1.

The Clackamas River in fall color, just above South Fork. Photo by Sharon Beelart.

North-facing slope behind Ripplebrook Guard Station. Photo by Sharon Beelart

Smokey Bear at Ripplebrook Guard Station. Photo by Sharon Beelart.

Area 2: Roaring River, Whale Head, Indian Henry, & Ripplebrook

This stretch of the *Oregon Bigfoot Highway* should impress the traveler with the immense erosive power of the Clackamas River as it wears away rock in the river bottom. It also provides a very real sense of the importance of river and stream bottoms as natural pathways through the mountains.

And, along this part of the highway, the remains of old forest fires show changes in nature as she recovers from unsparing catastrophe into the rebirth of seemingly tranquil, enduring surroundings.

This section of the tour runs from Fish Creek to the Timothy Lake intersection, a distance of about 8 miles. But Bigfoot wise, what a thrilling 8 miles it is! This section of road is so packed with reports that it is broken into three districts:

District 1: Roaring River and the Mt. Mitchell Plateau.

District 2: Whale Head and Indian Henry.

District 3: The Ripplebrook area.

About two miles south of Fish Creek is Roaring River. When you get to the Roaring River Bridge, and if you stop here, park safely, walk onto the bridge and face up the river (northeast). On your right the Mount Mitchell plateau rises out of sight. In front of you, if you are able to hike up Roaring River, you will find yourself in a key Bigfoot territory.

Three more miles up the road you will find Three Lynx Road. A half mile further upriver, the big white Oak Grove electrical power house looms on the east side of the river. Only one half mile beyond the powerhouse, at *OBH* Mile 21 (49 from Detroit), Indian Henry road veers south. Be very sure, there is adventure up that road. Bigfoot wise, Indian Henry is "action-packed."

About two miles upstream from the Indian Henry Bridge is the beginning of the alluvial basin of the Oak Grove Fork of the Clackamas. The base of this triangular basin is easily identified by the Job Corps Center and Ripplebrook Guard Station. Several track finds and a recent significant sighting which occurred east of the Guard Station indicate this part of Area 2 is prime habitat for Our Barefoot Friends.

Easy-to-see landmarks in Area 2: The Roaring River Bridge at *OBH* Mile 16.7 (53.3), The Job Corps Center at *OBH* Mile 23.2 (46.8), The Ripplebrook Guard Station at *OBH* Mile 24.3 (45.7), and the southern boundary marker which is the Timothy Lake Road 57 intersection at *OBH* Mile 24.9 (45.1).

Area 2 OBH Mile Markers

Miles from Estacada: from Detroit

16.0:	54.0	Seasonal waterfall on left
16.2:	53.8	Power line crossing
16.7:	53.3	Roaring River: bridge and campground
18.4:	51.6	Power line crossing
18.8:	51.2	Rock gabions on left: right, low, far: tree across river
19.1:	50.9	Power line crossing
19.5:	50.5	Waterfall on left
19.8:	50.2	Three Lynx turn; power line
20.0:	50.0	Bridge without a name
20.5:	49.5	Portland General Electric Oak Grove Fork Powerhouse
21.0:	49.0	Indian Henry Bridge; Indian Henry Road 4620
21.1:	48.9	Beginning of 1996 landslide
22.2:	47.8	New road; rusty guard rail by design
22.5:	47.5	Gravel pit road; gate is generally open
22.8:	47.2	On left: Five Elk Pond
23.2:	46.8	Job Corps center wastewater treatment pond with cattails
24.4:	45.6	Ripplebrook Guard Station
24.9:	45.1	A large intersection where Timothy Lake Road 57 begins, Hwy 224 ends and Road 46 to Detroit begins

Map of Area 2

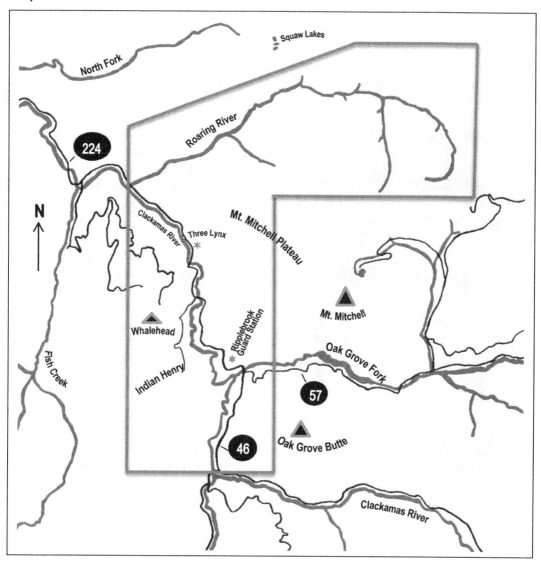

©Sharon Beelart 2015

District 1: Roaring River

Roaring River Bridge: Hwy 224: *OBH* mile 16.7 (53.3)

GPS coordinates: 45 09 32.07N 122 07 02.44W at 964'

It is safe to park at the pull out on the northeast side of the river or at the campground on the southeast side. Do not park on the bridge for even a few minutes since oncoming traffic speeds through this area. Beware of passing traffic if you walk across the bridge.

The steep, zigzag trail to the top of the Mt. Mitchell plateau is accessed through the campground. If parking at the campground, be sure to have a day use permit. A permit is necessary to park at all trailheads, and at Bagby Hot Springs. Permits are available in Estacada Ranger Station and at the Ripplebrook Guard Station, when it is open. Trail heads are patrolled and the no-permit fine is substantial.

Roaring River looking upstream from the Roaring River Bridge on Hwy 224. Photo by Sharon Beelart.

Roaring River enters the Clackamas only yards west of the bridge and warrants a careful hike for a look. Like Fish Creek, this is a good spot to watch a confluence of waters, and perhaps migrating steelhead jumping from the Clackamas into Roaring River.

Roaring River "roars" during spring runoff, especially if you hike into the narrows to listen. The river is shaped like a fish hook with the bridge at roughly the eye of the hook. The hook shank runs almost straight east for about six miles. Then the "hook" part of the river curves south into a high basin on the east side of the Mt. Mitchell high plateau. At the tip of the "hook" is the "bait," which in this case is Signal Buttes.

As mentioned, the plateau on the right (on the southeast side of the bridge) is called the Mt. Mitchell plateau. About nine miles south Mt. Mitchell imposingly caps the plateau's beginning. In 2003 Cliff Olson found an 82 step track line near the crest of Mt. Mitchell which is described in Ref. 44.

Far to the east of Hwy 224 beyond Roaring River is the Salmon-Huckleberry Wilderness, a place rife with Bigfoot reports. What is evident to the serious researcher using United States Geological Survey topographical maps is these territories are connected. Easy-to-see travel routes between each of the areas are illustrated in the Bigfoot Byways & Migration Map in Appendix IV.

Ref. 21: Prospector backed out by "Gorilla"

Roaring River event #1: Sighting 11 (S11): Jake 11 (J11): Reported by Todd Neiss: Follow-up on-site investigation witnessed by film maker Blake Eckard: This is the second report of a human being backed out by a Clackamas Sasquatch. It happened on the south side of Roaring River.

In Ref. 9, one of the beasts backed a fly fisherman and his children out of the North Fork. Speculation is it that was done to keep him away from young Bigfoots fishing in a favorite hole.

A prospector told Todd Neiss a similar story of an incident in the lower Roaring River area. The hiker was shaken by the incident and remembers few body feature details about his assailant; for in this event, the big beast made it clear it was aggressive and determined to have its way.

The time was late summer of 2004. The witness planned a rock hounding trip up Roaring River along the seams of ancient lava flows and underlying rocks. He brought along his Australian shepherd dog. The man and his dog hiked about a mile upriver past the sheer south cliff and over the waterfall rise and then on to a good spot where he commenced chipping with his rock hammer.

After about an hour of chipping, the prospector heard his dog make a low, long growl. He looked up. His dog was standing on a fallen log, back hair up, teeth bared, claws imbedded in the bark, intent on something in the nearby woods. A long scan which in actuality only lasted seconds led to astonishment.

Only about 25 feet away standing on a fallen log, with its right arm braced against a big cedar was a massive "gorilla." And, it was clear to the prospector the "gorilla" did not like the dog, or for that matter him either.

Figuring that maintaining integrity of life and limb was the best option, the prospector pulled his dog from the log; it did not want to leave and was still growling. The waterfall was only about a quarter of a mile away, so tugging his dog he turned and hiked west.

After about a hundred yards, the dog was still trying to break free and attack. The man turned and found the "gorilla" following them, still about 25 feet away and glaring at the dog.

Jake 11 continued on, pulling his dog, who still wanted a fight. They got to the waterfall, descended the "dry side" steep slope, went a few yards and turned to look back. The "gorilla" was standing on the bluff, which is about 20 feet high, looking down at them, still intent on the dog. The prospector turned and went on, stopped after about another hundred yards, or so, and looked back to find the "gorilla" had disappeared.

As happens many times with witnesses not familiar with the Bigfoot phenomena, the prospector sought out someone knowledgeable to talk with about his experience. Eventually he was routed to Neiss who asked for a guided tour of the incident site. Blake Eckard, a young aspiring filmmaker from Missouri was visiting the Beelart's and also went on the field investigation where a sudden accident impressed on him the many dangers of the mountains.

The witness slipped on wet, mossy rocks, fell "like a tree," knocked himself out, gave himself a severe concussion, and ripped off his ear, "… so it hung like a piece of meat." Career soldier Todd Neiss was Army Strong with a combat tour in Iraq. Luckily he had a first aid kit in his pack and he knew how to handle this kind of bloody injury.

Neiss bound the ear with a long head bandage like you see in the movies. After an hour and a half of struggling to get the victim out of the canyon and with fast and furious driving, Neiss got the poor fellow to an emergency room where his ear was saved, if not quite as squared off as before.

End note: In my 1999 journal I made a short entry about a man I met at one of Ray Crowe's meetings. The man told me about an incident earlier in the year when an ape-man backed him and his dog out of the lower reach of Roaring River. Unlike the Neiss witness, he said his dog would barely get from between his legs. At the time I thought his story was too bizarre to believe so I didn't write details in my logbook.

Bottom of Roaring River Canyon, September low water. Photo by Joe Beelart

Ref. 22: The Great Rooster Experiment

Roaring River event #2: Jake 12 (J12): Track Find 9 (TF9): Bigfoot Related Incident 15 (I15).

Warning: Inasmuch as there are strict penalties for baiting with animals; and, regulations about bringing invasive species into our national lands, the authors strongly discourage doing anything similar to this account.

Long ago Jake 12, an eager young Sasquatch researcher joined an organization and through it was led to believe that Sasquatches apparently like chickens for Sunday dinner, although it is unknown exactly which day "Sunday" is to them.

So one February the concocter of this brilliant bit of Sasquatchery set up a chicken baiting experiment above Roaring River, or to be more precise, a rooster baiting experiment as everyone he approached wanted their hens either for eggs or stew.

The "roostel" was a rabbit hutch someone else didn't want. It was solidly constructed, had a waterproof roof, and doors with a screen latch securing them. They placed it upslope under old growth timber in a glen; a very charming place indeed for their "roostel."

For those who care, please don't worry about the mental state of the chickens, they are pretty much oblivious to their surroundings as long as they have feed and water.

So, for nineteen days the research team alternated going up to feed and water the roosters, clean their cages, and check the area. The roosters seemed perfectly happy and content.

One of those involved told me, "It's absolutely one the most unusual things in the world to listen to rousing 'cock-a-doodle-do's' deep in the forest at sunrise. There is no way in hell forest animals didn't know those roosters were there."

One morning a team member drove up early to feed and water and found the roosters gone; as in really gone. He reported to me there were large barefoot imprints in the forest duff all around the hutch, all the doors were carefully opened, *not torn off or ripped off*, and the roosters were so gone he could not find even a feather.

Since there was no indication that the dirty bird work was done by a raccoon, weasel, skunk, bear, coyote, cougar, or hawk, we label this Bigfoot Related Incident 15 (I15).

After his discovery, the researcher went home, returning a day or two later with a cohort to retrieve the "roostel." What did they find? "The hutch was pulled to the bottom of the slope and smashed flat." He went on to say that something mighty powerful did the smashing because it was one well-built hutch.

And, his cohort exclaimed, "No feathers! Not one in the whole area."

All that the authors could imagine was a big hairy mountain guy stuffing the birds under its massive arm pits to take them "home" for Sunday dinner. When it returned for more chickens the beast found the hutch not refilled and smashed it in disgust.

Later when we visited the site, we were surprised to find a few fresh Bigfoot imprints in the duff, so fresh the moss hadn't rebounded and edges were crisp. The imprints were about 16 1/2" long. We label this Track Find 9 (TF9).

Unfortunately, even though I had plaster in the truck, they were all duff prints leaving nothing to cast. By carefully lifting the moss on a number of them we found they were the real deal, not bear double strikes.

When a bear's rear foot steps into a front paw track it makes a double strike print which can look like a Sasquatch track, but are normally easy to recognize upon close examination. Also, there were no claw marks. So, we concluded there was a resident Bigfoot in the area, perhaps still looking for a fresh supply of succulent, tender roosters.

One other thing was sure even though the boards were old. Whatever smashed the rabbit hutch didn't use a sledge or club to do it. It was flattened by a powerful force something like when people stomp egg cartons for the recycling bin.

Three Lynx

Hwy 224 intersection with Road 4630: *OBH* mile 16 (*OBH* mile 54 from Detroit)

Approx. GPS coordinates of Three Lynx: 45 07 34.52N 122 04 18.19W at ~1315′

The Oak Grove PGE powerhouse: 45 07 19.21 N 122 04 11.42 W

Three Lynx is the location of Portland General Electric's Oak Grove Fork electrical generation project. In the forest on the ridge above is the terminal segment of the pipeline. From the ridge, water flows almost straight down to create the force needed to turn big electric turbines which then generate electricity. The water is discharged into its original destination, the Clackamas River. No water is wasted, heated, or contaminated.

About a mile from the power plant are maintenance shops, and a small residential community for on-site workers. This enclave is where Cliff Olson lived for 13 years.

Continuing on Hwy 224, travelers see the power plant about a mile and a half up river after the Three Lynx turn. It is a large white concrete building on the east side of the river.

Portland General Electric Oak Grove Fork Powerhouse in winter. Photo by Bailey Olson.

The importance of beaver ponds & mountain meadows

According to Steve Kiley beaver ponds are the community centers of the forest. Elk and deer are naturally attracted to them, and where they go, so do cougars. Small life abounds around a beaver pond attracting coyotes and bobcats, especially in winter.

Ducks and other birds, especially the colorful wood duck, call them home. In the upper Clackamas, big redhead pileated woodpeckers often feed on insects in rotten trees drowned in beaver ponds.

Beaver dam in winter, Indian Henry. Photo by Joe Beelart

When exploring a beaver pond, be very careful. Often beavers excavate banks for their homes. You can fall through the "roof." Wasps, bees, and hornets also like being near water so they often make nests nearby. Once I barely made it to an emergency room after many stings from ground nesting hornets at a beaver pond in the Coast Range.

And of course, beaver pond banks are often unstable and slippery.

Mountain Meadows

After beaver ponds silt in, they often become "meadows." Meadows are also gathering places for animals, especially ungulates (deer and elk). Along the *OBH* there are plenty of meadows to explore. The best time of year to watch meadows is as early as possible after snow melt. That is when the grass is tender and animals are hungriest after winter.

Black tail buck in velvet. Photo by Bailey Olson

Ref. 23: Steve's first track cast

Under Mt. Mitchell #1: Track Find 10 (TF10): Comparison to the Molalla Cast

GPS coordinates: Approx. center of pond: 45 05 31.91 N 122 01 55.57W at 1,991'

Approx. location of track casting: 45 05 29.39N 122 01 52.47W at 2,000'

The track find story is very simple. Cliff and I set lures in late winter of 1999. Mainly these were hanging, rotating CD mobiles illuminated by LED bicycle lights or orange flying discs with a light sealed in and made to rotate with a fishing swivel. The flashing LED bicycle lights ran on one medical grade battery for as long as three weeks.

On February 28, 1999 I went up alone to check our baits. It was overcast, misty and spitting snow all the way from Estacada to Ripplebrook, but fortunately the road wasn't icy. The river was full, fast and tawny. Hiking in I found it cold and all-in-all, just a nasty day. Not even Forest Service people seemed to be out.

At two of the three sites I found the flashing lights in the CD lures still blinking. In the dark morning light, the CD lures picked up light and tossed rainbows as they twisted in a very light breeze. (I make them with fishing lure swivels and weights to balance them.) The Spam, was, well, in its normal condition...I began to wonder if it appealed to the Forest Folk.

At the last site, I found a barefoot track in the only available spot of soft mud in the area; it was amazing. It was a very clear right foot about 14 inches long. Later, it cast over 15 inches. The big toe was clearly visible. The other toes had dug in and crushed grass, but were also visible.

Throughout the print I saw dermal ridges. At the ball of the foot the force of impact pushed up a little hump of mud. It had been raining the last few days, so the

dermal ridges told me this track was really fresh! It was definitely not from a boot or stocking foot wader. Most important as I puzzled over it, I thought about someone walking barefoot out here and planting this track just for us.

I had a camera along, but no casting stuff. Who would think I'd need it? There really wasn't much more I could do, so I marked the imprint with a distinctive branch and went for a hike further up the Fork.

When I got home, I called Cliff Olson and told him where the print was and that I couldn't go up for the rest of the week. I told him if he went up to look at the print with a critical eye. Cliff called me Monday night. He said he found the stick marker no problem, but because it had snowed several inches the track was covered. He didn't want to disturb it, so that was that for now.

Steve Casts the Track

One of our main early goals was to find and cast a track, and finally, we had one. Weather and time were working against us. But, like many things that take great effort, by the time we reached the goal it became less important than it seemed. Thus my notes are somewhat sparse. In part, this was because details were lost due to rain in the nine days from when the track was found and when Steve cast the track.

March 11, 1999: Steve and I decided to see if the track could be cast after 11 days of winter weather. Steve drove. It was cold and clear with good long range vision. Given the snow lines, we really saw the lay of the land while enjoying the best weather so far that year.

After a week and a half under snow the track was still clear, but sadly, details like the dermal ridges were lost. The big meadow had lots of standing water. Using this water, Steve mixed up plaster-of-Paris in a plastic zip bag, went back and carefully, carefully poured it into the print.

Steve's first track cast. Photo by Joe Beelart.

We waited. Nothing. It was too cold for the plaster to set up quickly so we spent an hour exploring the Mt. Mitchell plateau. When we got back to the beaver pond the plaster was still damp, so Steve dug it out along with a lot of grass and dirt. Luckily, we got our first cast out of the ground with minimal damage. Later on we learned the hard way to not "pull" a cast. The best way to lift casts is to gently dig around it, then a little under, and gently twist them out of the ground.

Thom's Molalla River Cast vs. Steve's Cast

During the winter after Steve took his cast, Thom Powell showed us a big box of casts given to him by a Bigfoot researcher from Colton, Oregon. The bulk of them were taken in the upper Molalla River drainage about 25 air miles west of where Steve cast our track. Remember, the Molalla River and Clackamas River drainages are separated by a high, north-south ridgeline previously described.

Steve holding his first track cast. Photo by Joe Beelart

One of Thom's upper Molalla casts was *remarkably similar* in size and characteristics to the one Steve cast near Ripplebrook. In particular, the foot seemed deformed somewhat between the metatarsal break and the toes, as if a rock fall had broken it. In fact, as years went on, and the casts were compared by other researchers, it was often opined that they came from the same individual, which meant the creature traveled at least 25 miles over a mountain crest into the central Clackamas basin.

Unfortunately, at a Washington gathering, this cast was broken by an irate person inspecting my display. This person had a profound way with words and wasn't bashful sharing his views of Bigfooters and environmentalists.

Trail Cam photo of black bear by Cliff Barackman. Note the position of the feet and the stride that can create a "double strike."

Trail Cam photo by Cliff Barackman.

Ref. 24: A Curious Circle, a Sasquatch artifact?

Under Mt. Mitchell #2: Happening 3 (H3) is finding a circle of small stacked stones: Olson and Beelart.

On February 10, 1999 Cliff and I decided to explore the eastern flank of Mt. Mitchell. It was cloudy down low and clear up high; it was fairly warm, not parka weather; but we put on our Sorels to hike through snow.

We came to an abandoned bridge with rotten timbers. It would be a long deadly fall onto rocks in the creek, but we decided to cross anyway. The hillside was steep, and the creek was really rushing.

Our mile long hike took some time. Lots of big fir trees had fallen across the road from the steep hillside above us. The trees lay at angles forcing us to scramble over or under them. There was no way around as they hung over the side of the road.

Cliff saw a coyote cross the road; all I got to see was his drag marks in the snow

and tracks. When Cliff's knee began hurting him we decided we'd had enough hiking for the day.

It was there, behind a log, Cliff found *a* very curious circle of stones. It was like a child had transported the stones to the road, sat and played in a circle. There was no apparent natural explanation for the circle. The circle was definitely not made from stones rolling off the hillside.

This was not a place for a human family hike, especially this time of year. The shaded areas of the road were covered with an honest foot of snow. Only a fool parent would cross the old bridge with a child.

The circle was in a protected place; behind the tree it was warm in the morning sun. Plus, the site was well screened from any view except standing on the fallen trees surrounding it.

We puzzled over the circle for a long time for it was a *very curious* find; something made it with dexterous hands. Since there was no obvious connection to either humans or Bigfoot, for the purposes of *The Oregon Bigfoot Highway*, we call finding the curious stone circle Happening 3 (H3).

Ref. 25: The Mother of All Turds

Under Mt. Mitchell #3: Bigfoot Related Incident 16 (I16) is when Olson and a friend find a huge scat: Laboratory analysis reported the *Mother of All Turds* contained intestinal parasites from an unidentified hominid. The laboratory immediately changed its findings when told the specimen probably came from a Sasquatch.

On June 9, 1999 Cliff wanted to go up the hill, so we decided to start wandering at the big beaver pond east of Three Lynx. Cliff invited along Bill Harper, a member of the Western Bigfoot Society. Bill is an expert outdoorsman and an authority on edible wild plants, so it was a privilege to have him as a guest.

Exploring the meadow near where Steve took his cast we found lots of elk and deer sign. On the south side of the meadow there was a lot of bear scat indicating early season berries were ripe. Almost all the bear scat was in small piles and squirty, like the bears had the runs. One spot had 4 such piles within 10 feet, all in a line.

Near the southwest tree line Cliff and Bill found *The Mother of all Turds*. The thing was a tad under 3 inches in diameter and in a long roll of coiled chunks. I was some distance away over by the beaver pond when they found it; I heard them laughing loudly. We hiked back to the SUV for a clean plastic bucket. Bill put some grass on the bottom to cushion the thing and eased it in without much damage.

Whatever passed it aside, one thing was certain, *The Mother of All Turds* was a biggin.' And, it was much more cord-like than common bear scat spread all over the

Cliff later found a strangely pleasing pyramid made from non-local stones on Oak Grove Butte. See Ref. 50.

The MofAT. Photo by Joe Beelart.

Elk scat. Photo by Joe Beelart.

place. It was full of vegetable materials, but didn't show evidence of meat grease or bones.

Also, it wasn't like elk droppings. Elk scat comes out like big grapes and the grapes are bunched up on the ground in different sized piles. There was plenty of elk dropping and bear scat all around, so we had something to compare with *The Mother of All Turds*.

To finish out the day, we drove to Devils Ridge to show Bill the big rock quarry and the lay of the land from the ridge. Most of the day we drove with a window or two down and the tail gate window open, since it really, really smelled bad. In fact, Cliff was a bit worried that it might ruin the smell of his neatly maintained SUV.

Disposing of *TMofAT*

That evening, I posted Henner (Dr. W. Henner Fahrenbach) about the big turd. He promptly telephoned me. While he exhibited some repressed excitement about its size, he said a turd is just that, secondary evidence and it could be from something else besides a Bigfoot. Anyway, Henner only wanted just a bit of it, so after contemplation and a scotch in my easy chair, I hit upon a nefarious plan. I called Ray.

Ray (Ray Crowe of the Western Bigfoot Society) said he was interested in seeing *TMofAT* and knew a veterinarian who would probably check it for free. He also said he'd take a piece of it to Henner at the Primate Center.

The next day I drove over to Ray Crowe's house. He wasn't home, so I left the white bucket in the cool, dark of his front walkway. In the evening, Ray's wonderful wife, Theata, called me. She was rather succinct: "Was that YOU who put 'that thing' on our front porch?"

I was going to protest that I actually set it in the shade on the walkway, but decided it was a technical note of no regard, given her rather agitated, yet somewhat amused state of mind.

Ray called later to tell me he took the can out back, opened the lid and saw the "thing." He said (some words redacted) that he was ... well, surprised ... by both the size and odorous strength of the "thing."

Ray called his veterinarian friend and asked if he could arrange to have "the thing" tested. Ray got a note back from the veterinarian's laboratory. The note said the turd contained intestinal eggs of "unknown hominid origin."

When Ray told the vet he thought it was a Squatch turd, the veterinarian promptly telephoned the laboratory that tested the sample. The lab immediately changed their findings and sent the revised analysis report via Federal Express Next Day Air in a signature required envelope. Now, the lab declared the turd was ungulate and probably from an elk; "So sorry, etc."

W. Henner Fahrenbach, Ph. D.

For 30 years, Dr. W. Henner Fahrenbach was a research scientist at the Oregon National Primate Research Center. He wrote one of the few peer reviewed scientific level Sasquatch papers in existence: Fahrenbach, W. H. *Sasquatch: Size, scaling and statistics*. Cryptozoology 13:47-75 (1998). As a member of the Western Bigfoot Society, Henner became interested in our "work" up the Clackamas, so you will meet him again several times in this book.

Bill Harper and Cliff Olson. 1999 photo by Joe Beelart.

Ref. 26: Mighty Roars & Cougar #2

Under Mt. Mitchell event #4: Location: Road 4631 at Silver Tip, a razed sawmill community: Bigfoot Related Incident 17 was a series of mighty night roars heard by Sasquatchian Woody Woodworth. Nearby, cougar #2 kills a deer fawn.

Woody told this account to me and approved the following write-up, noting with a grin, that I used a bit of literary license in a few of my descriptions, but he didn't change them as they made him laugh. But, on the other hand, when he originally told this story, he made me laugh. After all, this Bigfootin' stuff is all just for fun, isn't it? In any event, all substantive events in this account happened as stated.

On a snowy November night in 2000 Woody Woodworth was hunting the late archery season near Ripplebrook Ranger Station. He parked his trailer on one of the concrete pads left when the Silvertip worker housing project was razed in the 60s. Woody habitually sleeps with one of his trailer windows open so he can enjoy pure air and hear what is happening outside.

Woody reported that about 1 AM a beast with huge lungs made four long, extremely loud wailing roars. Each mighty, chilling roar lasted about 20 seconds. The roars originated east along the Oak Grove Power Project pipeline and the sound carried down through the pipeline cut to where he was camped. He said the wailing roars replicated roars he heard on Dixie Mountain about 30 years before as described in Woody's profile in Appendix I.

In a combination of extreme curiosity and concern about his future, Woody, wearing only shorts and a pair of socks, grabbed his bow, left his trailer, nocked an arrow and while keenly listening, went walking silently in the snow. Even though the moonlit sky was thinly overcast, the night was bright from reflections off the snow.

It didn't take Woody long to discover the reality of being out of his trailer in winter without coat or shoes. Since he saw no movement and heard no more roars he hiked zip-quick back to his trailer. Through the remainder of the night his sleep was restive. There were no more wails but an eerie silence settled in and ensued. We designate the Silver Tip wailing roars as Bigfoot Related Incident 17 (I17).

In the morning, Woody asked the fellow on a nearby concrete pad if he heard anything during the night. This man slept in his pickup canopy with closed windows so he couldn't hear as well as Woody. The man said late in the night he heard a screech owl call several times. He said words to this effect, "What else could it be but a screech owl? It wasn't a cougar. I've heard both."

Let's briefly analyze Incident 17. It's a simple report important for several reasons. First, screech owl calls on the Internet indicate the birds are shrill, thin, and their calls are brief; not 20 seconds long. Bears roar, generally for less than 8 seconds and they don't wail. Cougars scream, often modulating their calls, but not for 20 seconds, and they rarely repeat themselves more than twice. Also, *cougars do not roar like big cat lions and tigers;* or at least that is what is written and heard on the Internet.

Let's consider the report source. At the time, Woodworth was a seasoned 57 year old archery hunter. He hunted all over Oregon and parts of north Idaho, with many deer, several elk, and bear to his credit. In southeast Oregon, with his traditional bow, Woody almost accomplished the challenging task of harvesting a pronghorn antelope.

Woody knows the ways of the woods and has heard many animal calls over the years, including cougar yowls, growls, and screams in eastern and western Oregon, and Idaho. He notes cougar screams are more common since cougar hunting with dogs was outlawed and the cats have greatly multiplied in number.

Also, at the time, Woody was attuned to forest calls of menace because during this same hunt he listened to a deer fawn scream while being killed by a cougar. A day later, Woody found the remains of the fawn.

Conclusions about Incident 17 are these: (1) the loud, long wailing roars were not made by an owl or cougar. (2) due to the close proximity of numerous Sasquatch sightings and incidents to Silver Tip and along the pipeline, we concluded it is very possible the deep, penetrating roars were made by an angry Sasquatch.

Why was the Sasquatch angry? Perhaps he was making a territorial announcement to scare off an intruding Sasquatch, or cougar, from his wintering ground. Perhaps he was making a resounding warning to human hunters harvesting deer in his territory. Perhaps it was for something as simple as attracting a mate...after all, Bigfoots probably like to snuggle up in winter just like us, maybe. Unfortunately, without a recording, and with our current knowledge of Sasquatch behavior, we can only speculate on this most unusual event.

Portland General Electric Oak Fork Hydro Electric Project 9' diameter pipeline. 1984 photo by Sharon Beelart.

Ref. 27: Children see a "Tall Dark Man"

Sighting 12 (S12) was reported to me by Jake 13 (J13). It took place east of Three Lynx on Road 4630 near the Forest Service barn in Ref. 40.

This report is an extract taken from a lengthy Area 2 track find report by Jake 13. I interviewed Jake 13 by telephone; mailed her the write up, and she approved her interview notes for publication. During the interview we first talked about Bigfoot in general and some second hand stories she has heard in Estacada over the years. Then she went on with the story of a truly unique sighting.

Jake 13 said when she was young her family lived in Silvertip while her father worked in the Acme mill when it was still operating. She said one day children on her school bus going to Three Lynx School saw a 'tall dark man' watching them from the trees.

The children reported the figure. The incident was investigated and the area was searched with no results. The school bus incident became well known to area residents, Forest Service, and PGE personnel, all of whom kept on the lookout, but nothing more came of the matter.

Cliff Olson was living at Three Lynx at the time. He was on the school board and remembers the bus sighting very well. He also remembers Jake 13 and her family. We list this Silvertip report as Sighting 12 (S12). Silvertip is a locale about one mile east of the Ripplebrook Guard Station. It is now cleared of company houses.

District 2: Whale Head & Indian Henry

Whale Head (a mountain) is included in Area 2 because it has more connection to Indian Henry than Fish Creek. Cliff Olson has long pointed out a clear transit zone between Whale Head and Indian Henry which we designate as *Olson's Saddle*.

Ref. 28: Hundreds of tracks in snow

Whale Head #1: Track Find 11 (TF11) near the top: Olson and Beelart

Approx. GPS where Cliff first saw tracks: 45 06 49.59N 122 07 52.10W at 3860′

Approx. GPS of where we lost the tracks: 45 07 13.13N 122 08 05.39W at 3931′

GPS start of tracks near quarry: 45 06 51.30N 122 07 51.84W at 3864′

Whale Head (a mountain), was named by seamen turned loggers, as it looks like a breaching whale. It is the big, distant mountain directly south of the viewpoint about 3 miles south of Estacada. It also lies immediately east of upper Fish Creek, an important place in our chronicles.

On December 16, 1998 Cliff Olson and I decided to go high to find a Noble fir Christmas tree before snow got too deep. Yes, there was snow, but that was really no problem since it was a nice day; we continued to explore for nothing in particular.

Near the top of Whale Head we saw footprints. After intense study, we discovered several hundred large impressions in 10 to 14 inches of snow. Measured in many places, the longest step (heel to heel) was 56 inches or a startling 100 inch plus stride! A really big boy made those tracks.

My Sorel boots had room left over inside the "track" impressions. Unfortunately it had snowed about ½ inch of light flakes the night before so, we could only see toe imprints by carefully opening up tracks by hand and very lightly blowing away new snow. The toes were big.

Since this was an area with many wild noble firs, Christmas tree hunters had cut a few trees. Some large prints were made over tree cutter boot prints and on old tire ruts in the snow. That, combined with the recent new snow fall, indicated the tracks were probably made during the night or even early in the morning. Anyway, we sensed the tracks were mighty fresh.

We were impressed by the size of the tracks. Impressions were all one size – about 18 inches long by about 9 inches wide. The most important characteristic of the tracks, we think, was that there were no drag marks like humans make on snow between impressions. Whatever made the imprints simply picked up its feet and set them down, in parallel!

The snow condition at the tracks was somewhat firm. It was well below freezing and while there were icy spots on the road there was no ice in the tracks.

We emphasize the imprints were not made by snow falling from trees, rocks absorbing heat, etc. Due to their size, plus with no drag marks and no hoof prints – they were certainly not made by elk, deer or bear. Bears should be hibernating, besides they would have made big drag marks in snow that deep.

Our beast was quite a wanderer. In addition to the road tracks, where it reentered the scrub regrowth on the south side of the road there were hundreds more tracks. Their maker was tall enough to step over fallen tree trunks and snow covered bushes that Cliff and I had to scramble over or around.

The beast came out of trees in the center of the loop, circled to the north and reentered the road where Cliff initially saw tracks. Then it reentered the trees, came back out onto the road again, and finally walked southwest down an old logging road into tall timber where we lost him due to lack of snow.

Cliff said we were at about 3,800 feet; Cliff sure knows the hills, Google Earth elevation was 3,842′. In still, clear morning air, the view was magnificent and must have been spectacular at night! Steam plumes from the Camas paper mill and the St. Helen's paper mill were clearly visible to the north & northwest, as was steam from the Longview paper mills about 80 miles away.

But we spent little time gazing at the view. Cliff and I were both startled by the size, number, and consistency of the imprints. Amazingly, we did not have a camera along, not even a cheap disposable camera. Anyway, with the sun angle, it would take a photographer better than us to take effective photographs.

Driving a truck through snow not knowing what is underneath is the key to having a really bad day in the woods. So, to get a little more exercise Cliff and I walked the hill top loop. At the quarry, we found more tracks coming out of tall timber and paralleling the road on the southeast side of the rock quarry. We laughed, "This big boy was a traveler for sure."

From where the beast reentered old growth on the west crest of Whale Head there was another viewpoint so we stopped there a few minutes. The impressions showed very clearly that the beast turned and stood, looking toward the Willamette Valley, Portland, and SW Washington.

We weren't expecting to see anything like the tracks. They excited us. We planned to return the next day with cameras and tapes, but a new snow storm stopped that. Besides the new snow would have filled the impressions. In winter, it's a treacherous, curvy, icy drive up to the top of Whale Head.

We have gone back up to the site several times since 1998. In fifteen years the trees have grown enough to obstruct all viewpoints.

Connection notes: (1) the bench where we found the licked rocks in Ref. 19 is downslope directly west of where we lost the tracks in the trees. (2) The next report, Ref. 29 happened downslope from the beast's snow tracks at the quarry. (3) Less than a half mile south is Olson's Saddle.

Ref. 29: Two Dozen "Empty" Camera Clicks

Whale Head #2: Bigfoot Related Incident 18 (I18): Jake 14 (J14) and Beelart.

This is certainly one of the oddest reports in *The Oregon Bigfoot Highway*. It involves nothing more than 24 clicks of game camera film with nothing in them but flora, and in one frame, a mouse. We label this strange event as Bigfoot Related Incident 18 (I18). The photographer in this operation is Jake 14 (J14).

The authors strongly emphasize Jake 14 does not believe in Bigfoot, although he humorously tolerates Sasquatchians. J14 is a vigorous athletic man in his early 40's with substantial outdoor experience. Rather than hunt them, he sets camera traps to photograph a wide variety of animals.

Over the years, with knowledge of his "photo want" list, we've cooperated on at least four major camera traps and, as opportunities present themselves, some minor ones. Results are the usual: cougar, deer, coyote, bear, or skunk.

Elk generally allow only one photograph to a trail cam. After hearing camera noise, or seeing a flash go off, they run into the next township. Occasionally birds descend to bait and on very rare occasions, a human walks into a frame.

Anyway, J14 wanted a lower elevation set where few people ventured. I suggested the southeast slope of Whale Head where if you jump brush to the right place, you look down at the Job Corps Center and Ripplebrook Forest Service buildings.

Since the Clackamas River and a steep slope are between the site and Hwy 224, there is no access from the east. And, there aren't trails in the area, so after hunting season very few people drive the lower road. How do I know this? When I find an area with very little litter, I conclude it's not used by many people.

There are serene glades and glens on the southeast side of Whale Head. I guided our friend through a luxurious meadow of clover-like plants under huge virgin timber to a glen I had in mind. Since the prospects of finding undisturbed game were excellent, he decided to set up a deluxe game camera trap using two cameras and an auxiliary flash unit.

A car battery, transformer, and waterproof cables powered cameras and flash units. One camera was pointed at the rim of a big old log and the other toward the middle of the glen.

The actuator, a security light trip beam, was set with great care to avoid accidental clicks. The photographer expected few accidental clicks from falling limbs as our glen was inside tall virgin timber, plus it was early summer, so we expected few if any wind storms.

Our bait for the main camera set was peanut butter on the log. To entice whatever else might be around about 50 yards south we suspended an old freezer burned beef roast high between trees over a seep hoping for tracks from whatever might make them or, we laughed, maybe the back splat of a falling raccoon.

We thought about setting one of my simple camera traps at the beef but we didn't do that because we figured something might come into the beef first and a flash might scare it away from the main camera trap.

The main camera trap used 35mm auto-wind Canons tied into an actuator. The cameras weren't weather proof so they were encased in Styrofoam clam type covers with dark plastic over them. We set up the cameras, tested them without film and then loaded film. From then on, it was just going up the hill once a week to exchange car batteries and see if anything clicked.

A week went by. I had the first turn for the battery change and to refresh the peanut butter; I decided to add some economical jam. Jake 14's turn was the next weekend, and mine was the third. On weekends one and two nothing happened, not even a bird click which was surprising since birds and mice like peanut butter.

On the third weekend, after hiking into the glen with one heavy car battery, I immediately noticed something was wrong. One of the camera stakes was bent over, as was a flash unit stake. Our water-resistant battery box and the cables running out of it were displaced from behind the log. They weren't moved much, more like someone used a foot to nudge them around. I checked the cameras. One camera had clicks. The other one, which aimed toward the center of the glen, had no clicks.

Whatever came into the glen had pulled the plastic off the Styrofoam camera covers. It had also gently pried open the clamshell to see what was inside. Because the cameras were disturbed, and since everything was out of alignment and resetting them was a two man job, there wasn't much to do but gather everything up, pack it back to the truck and go home. Before I left the glen, I checked the hanging roast, which stunk mightily. Nothing happened there.

I hauled all the gear to Jake 14's house. About a week later he called. 24 developed frames showed only a mouse in one frame, and since it was below the trip beam, Mr. Mouse didn't cause the click. J14 was completely perplexed as to what actuated the cameras. Whatever it was seemed to like the flash as all the photos were at night. Limbs in the background showed the wind was quiet.

Jake 14 thought something that liked to see the flash simply passed a "hand" through the actuator beam to see the flashes. He was equally perplexed as to what forest creature could open the protective covers like they were zip bags, something I noticed myself, and was careful to leave intact for him to see.

I asked if I could have the clicks, which were slides. He said "sure." So, that's how those slides came into my Bigfoot collection. Who knows what kind of curious, ambidextrous creature made them?

Indian Henry Intersection & Bridge

Hwy 224: *OBH* mile 21 (49 miles from Detroit)

GPS coordinates: 45 06 58.11 N 122 04 30.66 W at 1,141′

Caution: If you drive up Indian Henry road, safe driving is your paramount concern. The road is narrow, has lots of blind curves, and people descending are often speeding. Heed this warning.

Indian Henry is an exceptional area for Bigfooting. At lower levels, the north side of the road is lined with steep cliffs. At lower elevations, the south side of the road borders Wards Meadow, a mountain meadow that serves as a wintering ground for elk and deer. On the highway side of the Clackamas, across from Wards Meadow is Austin Meadow. If you quietly walk in to them and watch the edges, you might see deer or elk.

High up Indian Henry Road are transit corridors into the Collawash River basin and into the Molalla drainage, as well as to Whale Head and Fish Creek. So, it is no wonder that many track and incident reports come out of Indian Henry, but curiously, no sighting reports are known to the authors.

Perhaps the scarcity of sightings up Indian Henry is because undergrowth is thick and in most places, close to the road which gives creatures time to step out of sight when they hear a vehicle. Indeed, one report you will read in a few minutes is about a place where two Bigfoots waited beside the road for a vehicle to pass, or not pass!

Ref. 30: Olson's Saddle

Whale Head #3: Cliff Olson discovers the saddle in *OBH* Happening 4 (H4).

One of the most interesting pieces of terrain up Indian Henry is at the far northwest end of Road 4622 which is a spur of the road that starts at Indian Henry Bridge on Hwy 224. This is what we refer to as Olson's Saddle which is a roadless, natural transit zone directly connecting Indian Henry to Whale Head and Fish Creek.

While we have not done it, primarily because of cost, Cliff is sure this saddle is the place to mount game cameras which might give us the photographs we desire. He thinks the time to set the cameras is after the last hunting season through winter until roughly the 4th of July. Cliff's logic is solid; Sasquatches, like elk and deer, most probably move low in winter and high in spring. Weatherproof solar powered cameras with transmission devices are technologically feasible. We know this because in the 1990s Thom Powell pioneered live, long-distance, on-site, warm weather movie camera feeds.

It will be expensive to make winter proof setups, but the expense might easily be offset in scientific value if photographs are clicked of the creatures as they make seasonal moves through this mountain corridor. However, there are technological, legal, and physical challenges, not the least of which is how to keep solar panels clear of snow, obtaining wildlife study permits from the USFS, and finding strong people to do packing and snowmobiling, as necessary.

Frog Lake. Ridgeline view from the left: Collawash basin, East Mt., Olson's Saddle, south slope of Whale Head. Below ridge, center, out of sight, Ripplebrook Guard Station. Central right is Indian Henry. Photo by Sharon Beelart.

Ref. 31: Ray Crowe finds a Trackline

Indian Henry #1: Track Find 12 (TF12) near Road 4620.

In the late 1980s Ray Crowe, who is part Native American, began investigating the Bigfoot phenomena in detail. He established the Western Bigfoot Society in 1991 and produced a newsletter, *The Track Record* until 2006. His studies culminated in the publishing of *Bigfoot Behavior I* (Createspace 2012). One personal event accelerated his interest in Bigfoot. In 1998, during his first outing up Indian Henry, Ray found a line of Bigfoot tracks.

Ray knew a Native American who was very familiar with the upper Clackamas, especially Fish Creek and Indian Henry. The man told Ray that if he wanted to experience Bigfoot there was a good chance

he might at Indian Henry. The fellow also told Ray he would guide him the first time. They went up and walked until amazingly, Ray came upon 18 very fresh tracks going down an old dirt logging road toward Wards Meadow.

Searching the area, the men found no more tracks. It was the opinion of the Native American that the creatures had left the track line as a signal to Ray. Crowe took several photographs which show the unusual trait of feet being placed in parallel. After returning to his home in Hillsboro, Oregon, Ray immediately began plans to establish the Western Bigfoot Society.

Ray told the authors the tracks were located about three miles up Indian Henry from Hwy 224. He also said there was an asphalt logging haul road above the dirt road. This, plus the location of Wards Meadow, indicates the probable location of the track line was on the lower section of Spur Road 150, south of Indian Henry's prime road 4620.

Ref. 32: Todd Neiss finds a structure

Indian Henry #2: Bigfoot related Incident 19 (I19).

Approximate GPS of Neiss structure find: 45 04 25.27N 122 04 57.02W at ~1930'

On January 18, 1999 I met Todd Neiss for our first outing together. In summer 1998 I'd met Todd at the Western Bigfoot Society "Bigfoot Daze" in Carson, Washington and occasionally afterward at Western Bigfoot Society meetings. Since Todd was a very experienced field researcher, and a Bigfoot witness, I decided to call him to get an opinion on my baiting sites up Indian Henry and how I set them.

Walking into the sites Neiss scouted around and found a number of crosshatched trees. It's to his credit he saw them as a "made" structure, not just a bunch of blow downs. While I'd seen the cross-hatched trees during earlier wanderings, I hadn't given them any thought. Todd had no explanation for the arrangement.

He showed me where branches were broken off and placed over the center as a wall or camouflage barrier and that it clearly appeared something had used the area beneath the cross-hatched trees, as all the little branches were smashed flat.

Due to the time of year, and because the needles on the limbs were fresh and green, at first we dismissed it as a hunter's blind which we quickly determined was silly since even two or three hunters could not have pulled down those trees without leaving a trace.

Under the teepee, Todd, at close to 6 foot tall, easily stood erect. The structure was right on a game trail. He also determined that the way these trees fell was totally inconsistent with the way other trees had come down under the same old growth canopy.

Since we could not come up with another explanation, we decided the shelter was made by Sasquatch. The authors now list this important find as Bigfoot Related Incident 19 (I19).

When we got to my "baiting" sites up the hill, it didn't appear that Todd was very impressed with the shiny lure I'd set in one spot and the hanging Spam with a feather in another. He did think the camera set was OK, especially the way I used fishing trawler twine and door shims to secure it. Nearby Todd showed me a good set of tracks in the thick moss duff that went past the lures. The imprints were about 17 inches long. The step, at about 50 inches heel-to-heel, was quite long. It was clear the imprints were not made by deer or elk.

We rolled back the moss to get a good look at the "toe" imprints. We discussed them as being bear double strikes, but the distance between the imprints was way too long, unless maybe the bear was running like hell. There were too many tracks for all of them to be double strikes, and even then, there would be the alternate impacts of a four-legged critter. Plus, there were no claw marks in any of the tracks we inspected.

Always a skeptic, Neiss was not quite ready to pronounce them Sasquatch tracks. He thought it a bit lucky to find such a long line of good tracks the first time he visited an area, especially with someone he hardly knew. I couldn't blame him. Maybe it was the Spam that brought the beast in. But, it was near the clacking, shiny lure where it obviously slowed its pace, so, who knows? Bigfooting is for fun, isn't it?

Lean-to structure found by Todd Neiss in 1999. Photo by Joe Beelart, note rain drop line on the lens. See Ref. 3 for Bud Blank's description of a similar find circa 1975.

Ref. 33: Steve Kiley finds tracks & bit skunk cabbage

Indian Henry #3: Track Find 13 (TF13): Bigfoot related Incident 20 (I20)

GPS of first skunk cabbage find: 45 04 20.81N 122 04 40.92W at ~1830'.

February 25, 1999: Steve Kiley found tracks on his first Bigfoot outing. He also found a true rarity, a skunk cabbage stem bitten by human-like teeth. This was very interesting because raw skunk cabbage is not edible by humans.

The day was overcast, gray and cold. Steve wore his heavy wool Filson coat and his beaded hat. I always wear gloves in cold weather or my hands suffer from old frostbite from my younger days on our ranch in Nebraska. Steve seldom wears gloves.

We went up Indian Henry to the game camera site to look around. Many elk and deer were in the area; there were lots of fresh tracks, double strikes and the like.

I dropped Steve off at the washout bridge road; he wanted to walk alone to get a feel for the country. I drove higher to check the snow line and simply look around.

When I drove back down, parked at the washout bridge road intersection and walked down the road. When I rounded a little curve, Steve was waiting for me. He began waving his arm and calling, "come here, come here!"

When I got to him he pointed. "What the?!"

"What the?!" were two clear five toed tracks in the mud going up the little slope toward the game camera site. Clear as a September day … five toed imprints. And they were not bear! They were not double strikes. They were clearly made by a bare, five-toe foot. There were no claw marks. We were both in shock. He took pictures, I took pictures. It was too cold to cast the tracks, plus we would have to make a dam on the slope to hold the plaster. With rain coming, it was just not a good day for casting.

There were clear prints in the watery mud going from across the road and up the ditch to where the imprints were found. The stride was long and the lift to get up over the bank without making another track was also long.

What was even more interesting was a skunk cabbage root stem dropped near the tracks. Raw skunk cabbage is bad on humans, real bad. But this one showed where wide human-like teeth marks had bitten it off. This was most curious so I collected the sample in a zip bag to show Cliff and Ray.

We carefully studied elk tracks in the area. Some of them were within 5 feet of the impressions. None looked like the toe imprints. We didn't talk much about the tracks. Strange that way. Too startling I guess.

Skunk cabbage, *Lyichiton americanus*. Photo by Sharon Beelart.

We then went up to where I'd first placed the camera, the one under the old growth canopy. Even after rain the tracks Todd Neiss found were still visible. Tree canopy protected them and they hadn't weathered much.

Trapper Steve looked at them carefully and at length. He concluded they were not bear and were made by a bare foot with toes. They were about the same size as the ones along the road; probably the same critter.

Again, there were many deer and elk tracks in the area for comparison. Steve's tracking ability found other impressions Todd and I missed last week. Either that or something walked through again. This was near where I hung Spam in cheese cloth about 7 feet above ground by simply tossing a fishing weight tied to a line over the branch and pulling up the Spam. Footprints indicated something had looked the esteemed meat product over, but decided not to eat it. Due to the cold, the Spam was still not "fragrant."

There was plenty of snow on the ground. Steve found numerous cougar tracks along the edge of the old growth. The cougar tended to follow elk and deer tracks; it had wandered all around the place. Kiley thought seeing that many cougar tracks was a rare treat.

On our way back home we stopped by the big beaver pond east of Three Lynx. Steve was really impressed by the size of the pond. He also got a kick out of my "lures." The lights on all the LED's were still blinking strong. Anyway, we didn't find any tracks and the second game cam hadn't clicked. So, we walked again.

Back at the truck, while we were resting, Steve pulled from his Duluth pack a Bigfoot attracting device he had made. Taking all the ideas he had seen at my house, he compacted them into a tight space.

Basically the attractor was a big white vitamin bottle wrapped in water proof highly reflective fishing lure tape for a daytime visual. For a little noise, fish lure spinners hung from the bottom, kind of like forest wind chimes. For night light he'd wired two diodes into the bottom of the bottle. For movement, he suspended the cap from a fishing lure spinner.

What an invention! It needs to be patented! The world's first Bigfoot all-inclusive attractor device! Hear surprise laughter here. Really ingenious.

We drove home. It was almost too much of a day.

Ref. 34: Bigfoot Watches a Sleeping Man

Indian Henry #4: Sighting 13 (S13): Jake 14 again: Shadowing.

By mid-summer 2005 Jake 14 had made new night photography equipment and wanted to go up the hill to test it. He was interested in attempting to photograph two types of animals at night, those being mountain beavers and pond beavers. I told him I knew just the place-Indian Henry.

I didn't know a mountain beaver from a pond beaver until Steve Kiley showed me photos of two big sets of mountain beaver runs. He said the critters looked like the model for *Troubles with Tribbles* in the Star Trek TV series.

Indeed, after I saw a photograph of one, I found them loveable beyond belief, a short, half-round ball of fur with no apparent tail or head. Apparently, they procreate like crazy because forest critters with big teeth like them more as tasty morsels than for their hug-ability index.

So I had that going for me when I said "Indian Henry is just the place." The other thing was the high beaver dam a couple miles up the road from the Clackamas Highway. By high, I don't mean high-up-the-hill; rather, it stands about 8 feet high from the base, which is quite a bit for Mr. Engineer Beaver and Beaver Crew to construct.

We met at Mike's Second Hand Store in Estacada where the Bigfoot carving greatly amused J14. We drove up the hill; I gave him a tour. He decided the place to camp was about a quarter mile below the high beaver dam at the edge of a glen.

Jake 14 parked his Suburban aimed toward the road, I parked my pickup alongside the little access lane. While I set up camp; setting up the tables, canopy, unloading wood, etc. J14 walked back up the beaver dam to plan his layout.

After sunset which was about 9 PM, as darkness descended upon our forest idyll as only dark can under a cloudy sky, it started to drizzle. "Well, photography is out for tonight." We talked and laughed. He drinks very little and as such, retained his wit and humor. We had a very pleasant conversation with considerable silent periods; we let the feel of the glen, evening, and the quiet sound of falling rain envelop us.

Shadowing

After my friend spread his bed roll in his Suburban, I stoked up the fire a little, but not too much, listened to the fall of a light rain, put my thick blanket on the chair for a cushion and pulled my unzipped bag over me. It was time for a night cap of scotch and water.

I still was far from sleep, so I decided to do what I call "shadowing." Here's how I do it. First build your campfire so it is behind some open space, a valley, a meadow, a quarry, or in this case a glen surrounded by trees on three sides. My back wall this evening was the cliff which was just far enough away so it was slightly illuminated by fire light. With its heavy moss ground cover, the glen was very beautiful in the flickering light.

To shadow, I turn with my face to an open area with the fire behind me. That is where our hairy audience is, not in the paying theater seats. I walk just far enough from the fire so the fire projects my shadow into a huge form.

I try to place myself so I can see my shadow either against the black curtain of night; maybe a quarry wall, or, in this case the cliff; or sometimes trees across a meadow, or the vapors above a valley. It doesn't matter really, in my mind I'm in theatre and it's my responsibility to put on a good show.

Then I silently perform; no, I hugely perform with my giant shadow. I do not talk, I do not shout, I make no noise. I do not cavort, although once it was reported to me that I did so and you will read about that very, very strange night later. I raise my arms, I spread my legs. For a time, in my shadow, I am the biggest being in the forest. And hopefully, if one of Our Barefoot Friends is watching, it might investigate this "new" big man.

Mr. Grumpy

The next morning, a Sunday, I was up before my companion, even though I went to sleep hours after he did. I got coffee perking, set out the juice, had a glass, and waited for him to rise which he did at approximately the same instant my Cabela's coffee pot quit perking.

Man was he grumpy! J14 looked like he hadn't slept all night. He poured a big jolt of orange juice, gulped it down, poured a cup of coffee full to the rim, looked at me disgusted like and said,

"Just what were you doing looking at me when I was trying to sleep last night?"

"What?"

"You know, you were looking at me sleep last night. I saw you out the window!" He was now worked up into a just plain mad.

"Whoa, I never looked in your rig last night."

"Yes you did."

I was perplexed. I stopped talking. By then I had known my friend for a couple of years, spent day trips in the woods with him and camped out with him a few times. I had the experience to say, J14 was not given to anger.

Then, I said words to this effect, "Jake 14, I swear I didn't even check on you last night. Let's take a breath. Why do you think I was looking in at you?"

For some reason this calmed him down. "Because you were leaning on the roof of my car looking down at me. Even though it was cloudy, I saw your shadow, and I wasn't dreaming. You looked at me for a long time. It disturbed me."

"Leaned on the roof of your car and looked down at you."

"Yes."

"Did I look big?"

"Yes."

I walked to his Suburban which was only feet away. "Notice anything?"

Jake 14 got real quiet. "Yes."

"Well."

"You aren't even as tall as my car. You couldn't have leaned on the roof."

"And, how big was the looker?" He thought a minute, looking at his side window. He silently held out his hands to about four feet. A strange pallor came onto his face. Then, he was very quiet, even though he wasn't saying anything. He knew of my interest in Sasquatch, but he put little credence to the reality of their being.

"You are tall enough to see. Did something leave any marks on your roof?"

In a minute ... "Yes, something hairy leaned on it. I see hair marks in the dust."

Well that got my attention, so I jumped into the back of my pickup for a look. Sure enough, it was plain in the wet dust; something crossed its arms on the roofline of the Suburban as if it rested its head on them to watch Jake 14 sleep. Well, that was pretty much the end of that outing. Breakfast was perfunctory and very quiet.

Ref. 35: Two Bigfoots Wait to Cross a Road

Indian Henry #5:   Track Find 14 (TF14): Olson and Beelart

Cliff and I both remember this track find well, even though my notes are lost in my files, we decided to include it. It was in the winter after Indian Henry #4, the Night Watcher incident, so it was probably in February 2006. We decided it was time for a winter walk, so we went up the hill to Indian Henry to look around.

I drove slowly along Road 4620 with Cliff looking for tracks in the snow made by any animal. For some reason, deer tracks were few and old. About a mile and a half up, Cliff spied something at the intersection of Spur 130 northbound so we stopped to investigate.

On the west side of that intersection is a flat clearing covered by grass in summer. For some reason, brush hasn't grown in that clearing for as long as we have been

going up there. Each side of the spur road is covered with regrowth timber. On the east side, the trees are about 60 feet high but only about 20 feet on the west.

Intersection the following spring. Photo by Joe Beelart.

Two sets of Bigfoot tracks came out of the shorter trees on the west side of the spur road. One set was big, in the 16 inch range, and the other smaller, only about 12 inches long. It appears the two animals did what happens at a city intersection. They stopped at the road, milled about for several steps, probably listening for traffic.

The Bigfoots would not have been looking for traffic as the straight-away is short there. After milling around they crossed the road side-by-side into virgin timber on the southeast side of the main road.

We lost their tracks under the big timber because snow didn't hold there. We label this Track Find 14 (T14). Unfortunately, due to light reflecting off the snow, my photos of T14 made at the find are not usable, but they do bring back fond memories.

It was really quite startling, to realize we had seen a very advanced adaptation of Bigfoots to man's environment. And, obviously the big one was probably a parent teaching off-spring what to do in that situation.

Ref. 36: Indian Henry tracks & a second bit Skunk Cabbage

GPS of the tracks and skunk cabbage: found near the intersection of Road 4620 and 4621:

45 04 25.27N 122 04 57.02W at ~1936'

Indian Henry #6: Track Find 15 (TF15) and Bigfoot Related Incident 21 (I21): Possible territorial markers: Steve finds a second set of tracks up Indian Henry with another bitten skunk cabbage lying next to them.

Spring 2000: We went up Indian Henry again for another hike. This time the plan was to check for activity near the structure Todd Neiss found. But mainly we wanted fresh mountain air and exercise by hiking the lower road. But! On spur road 4621 not 20 paces from the steel forestry gate alongside the road Steve found fresh tracks in water and mud and, another fresh, partially eaten skunk cabbage.

Since a picture is worth 1,000 words, or more, here is the find. Note the tracks' sharp edges and deep imprints. We may have surprised the Sasquatch; note the tiny grains of mud on the top edges of the tracks are in place. The tracks were made minutes, at most an hour before we walked into the site! Since the track maker dropped a fresh; and freshly bitten piece of skunk cabbage, perhaps we even scared the creature away.

If looking at the site on Google Earth notice the marshy area immediately north of the intersection and downslope maybe 20 feet. This marsh always has a fine crop of skunk cabbage. The little swamp is a good place to study. It is a popular gathering place for forest animals, with tracks and slide marks around it mostly made by bear. We strongly suspect this small swamp was probably where the skunk cabbage was harvested by Bigfoot even though the watery mud around it only held indistinct tracks.

Tracks so fresh dirt grains were falling from the edges. Also see Ref. 33. Photo by Joe Beelart.

Ref. 37: Sighting below High Lake

Indian Henry #7: Sighting 14 (S14): Cliff catches a glimpse below High Lake

GPS of High Lake: 45 04 43.09N 122 07 17.31W 4523′

Cliff Olson tells two stories about brief glimpses of Bigfoot. We suspect "glimpses" are what most people see of the beings, but since most people are not attuned to the subject, they either pass off what they see as a shadow, or don't report solid "glimpses."

In any event, Cliff recorded both of his brief events on a cassette recorder while relaxed in his den. Then, I carefully transcribed and submitted to him for changes and approval. You read the first account in Ref. 6. This account was recorded on July 30, 2012 and approved by Cliff for this book on August 16, 2012.

Olson Sighting #2

"I have two incidences where I thought I had a glimpse of the creature. The first one was up the Clackamas above Indian Henry on the High Lake road on one of the forks to the left. It was a real steep road up to a very small landing. I pulled up there a little after noon in the summer, stepped out of my Jeep and looked around.

Right off the bat I got a feeling I was being watched so I did a quick look around and couldn't see anything out of the ordinary so I did a much slower look around the perimeters of the unit and when I cased the far corner I saw movement, so I

83

watched it closely. I guess it was out there a few hundred yards, a pretty good distance, a large black creature, a dark creature walking out of the unit into the heavier timber.

It wasn't moving real fast, it wasn't running, I'll put it like that. I believe I saw the right forearm reach up and catch hold of some vegetation, I think probably a vine maple because of the altitude and pull on it for assistance to go up the grade. I think I saw the flash of soles of the feet, shouldn't say a flash, but they were lighter than the legs they were attached to.

Looked to be a shaggy creature; I don't think it was a bear. Bears by that time of the year have shed their heavy coat from winter. Must have been a much shorter coat that did appear dull, but it was out of the sunshine or direct sun and, by the way, on a very steep hill too, and was quickly out of sight.

I wish I had done my quick scouting around a different way. I might have caught it out in the open and had a better look at it. That's the first one. Oh by the way, my binoculars and camera were still in my day bag. Not where they should have been, they should have been right where I could have grabbed them, but I had walked around the Jeep and was on the passenger side looking back across the top of it and I would have had to sprint around to the driver's side to get either one of those things out of my day bag. Poor planning, poor planning.

This happened in the later part of June 1994. I was in the area to check the snow chute below High Lake; this is where we got snow for snow cones for my children and later grandchildren late in the snow year. As I recall that year the snow was already gone, as in every year since."

District 3: Environs near Ripplebrook Guard Station

The Ripplebrook Guard Station and maintenance facility is about 25 miles south of Estacada. As noted earlier, it sits at the base of a geographic triangle made by the alluvial fan of the Oak Grove Fork. The moderately sloped alluvial fan is an acute triangle of roughly 1½ x 3½ x 3½ miles, or about 9 square miles.

The Guard Station is used as a landmark because it is obvious and quite a number of sightings, track finds, and Bigfoot related incidents have been reported near it. One probable reason for the high level of activity in the triangle is simply because a number of people work in, or pass through this area.

Snow at Ripplebrook Guard Station. Photo by Bailey Olson

Ref. 38: Three year slide repair; three years of rest

Ripplebrook #1: Hwy 224: *OBH* mile 22.25 (47.5): Road 224 slides out and takes three years to rebuild resulting in Happening 5 (H5).

Explorers, please note that for about a mile, a new stretch of road runs uphill in a sweeping curve. It is easily identifiable by the rusty guard rail designed to rust, and smoothly sloping banks. The State of Oregon built this grade when the old road, which was down next to the river, washed out during the spring 1996 floods. The slide effectively closed the upper Clackamas watershed from casual traffic from March 1996 until late April 1999.

What does this mean to the few Bigfooters researching the upper Clackamas? Some, as noted, stopped working the Clackamas and moved their research elsewhere, mostly to the Coast Range and Gifford Pinchot National Forest. But, we stayed keyed on the Clackamas, occasionally entering from the east on Road 42, and were among the first up the new road when it opened.

One day when I was excitedly describing the numerous Sasquatch signs we found in May, June, and July 1999 to Dr. Henner Fahrenbach, he cordially laughed in his Alps accent. I shall never forget his words:

"Well Joe, what did you expect? They've had three years of rest from humans."

Then he continued on to gently chide me, in his professorial fashion, that I had not talked to him before spending so much unguided energy at this most opportune time. We regard Henner's remarks and the implications of them, as important; so we designate them as Happening 5.

Five Elk Pond

Ripplebrook #2: *OBH* Mile 22.8 (47.2): Happening 6 (H6)

When you see elk you are in wild country. On my many trips up the Clackamas I first saw them at the first big pond on the east side of the road after the new road. I don't know the official name of this pond, but I call it Five Elk Pond because on the far banks of it was Happening 6.

Note: It is not the cattail filled Job Corps wastewater treatment pond a little further on.

Elk are herd animals with social structure within the herd in any given territory. A key element of the social structure is a prime bull that has a herd of cows through which he passes on his genes.

Then, there are, if you will, the bulls-in-waiting who spend their time practicing fighting each other in anticipation of the glorious moment when they knock off the prime bull and get their own herd of cows with which they anticipate making much elk whoopee.

The other primary function of sub-prime bulls is to avoid making themselves targets for hunters who prowl the forest every fall. The herd bull has a less difficult time of it during hunting season because he has a herd of cows looking out for him. Happening 6 wasn't during hunting season. It was in winter just before bulls shed their antlers, so the immature bulls were less wary.

The event was very simple. Cliff and I were driving up for an outing when we spotted a herd of five lesser bulls gathered on the far side of the pond. We pulled completely clear of the highway and for quite a few minutes watched the bulls shove each other around until they noticed us and casually wandered into the trees.

It was a rare sight. The range of antlers went from a two year old spike to a three point western count which doesn't count the eye guard tine. They were in fine condition; ready for winter which Cliff figured was coming early as it was before Thanksgiving and Mt. Mitchell already had a thick blanket of snow.

The Timber Lake Job Corps Center

Ripplebrook #3: Hwy 224: *OBH* mile 23.2 (46.8): Job Corps sign & intersection: The Job Corps is a division of the US Forest Service, so employees are technically Forest Service personnel.

The site of the Job Corps Center has historical significance in itself as it was the site of Acme Sawmill, the only known long-term sawmill situated within a national forest. Acme sawmill was originally built to supply wood for the 1924 pipeline project, and later for Forest Service buildings up the Clackamas.

Until 1936, excess lumber production was shipped to Estacada via the railroad, and after the rock road was built, by truck. Shipping dimensional lumber, instead of whole logs from the forest, was economically efficient, so due to intense demand for lumber during and after WWII, Acme sawmill remained in operation until about 1960.

However, allowing a sawmill in the middle of a national forest set a dangerous precedent. As noted, since logs were hauled only a short distance to the mill, the owner had an extreme profit advantage over competing sawmills in Estacada and other downriver locations that had to pay for hauling whole logs over long distances. Remember Lumber Jack in Estacada?

Well, ole' Lumber Jack sure didn't like having a competitor up the hill and neither did any other sawmill owner who knew of Acme, no matter their location. "If he can have a mill inside a national forest, why can't I?!" Then environmentalists got into the fray. Circa 1960, Acme sawmill was dismantled and all buildings were razed.

Three final notes on Acme: the pond in the middle of the Job Corps Center was the mill pond where logs were floated until selected for sawing. The residence area for many mill workers was called Silvertip and was located about 2 ½ road miles east of Ripplebrook Ranger Station. The Area 2 Ref. 27 report of the school bus sighting happened between the Silvertip residence area and the Three Lynx primary school.

A Sasquatch enthusiast can only speculate about what the workers, loggers, and family members knew about Sasquatch during the decades when the mill operated. During that time, many of the roads in the upper Clackamas were built. What did those people see?

Did children attract the beasts at the Silvertip residence area? Were habituations and perhaps friendships developed by housewives while their husbands were at work? Are there old notes and records of Bigfoot from those people? This last question leads into our next report, the alleged Bigfoot log book.

Indian Henry: Den made under root overhang. This den was used for several years, but no tracks of any kind were found near the den. Photo by Joe Beelart.

Ref. 39: The alleged Bigfoot log book

Ripplebrook #4: *OBH* mile 24.3 (45.7): Ripplebrook Ranger Station: Forest Service Employee 3 (FSE 3): Happening 7 (H7)

GPS coordinates: 45 04 45.76 N 122 03 1065W at 1519′

Ripplebrook Ranger Station was manned until the 1996 floods destroyed the road below the "new grade." While the Ranger Station was operational, allegedly one of the staff, reportedly a woman, kept a logbook of Bigfoot reports made by USFS personnel and loggers who knew of her interest. We label this alleged logbook Happening 7.

While he never saw it, Cliff Olson heard about the logbook when he lived at Three Lynx. This logbook was also mentioned to me by a friendly USFS employee who we address as FSE 3.

FSE 3 was very concerned about our keeping his identity secret. While he never told us anything earthshaking, from time-to-time, he candidly answered questions, or offered juicy tidbits of information like mentioning the logbook.

We have not made a sincere attempt to find the alleged logbook. Why? First, USFS people are not open to inquiries about such things. I made one half-hearted attempt to get staff names from a USFS person but was politely rebuffed. He said words to this effect, "you should know that we can't give out employee information."

Even so, at one time we were given a woman's name. She was not well and it was inappropriate to contact her. Perhaps we will try to contact her next year, or maybe the opportunity will never happen.

We suspect the alleged logbook is a collection of notes, once again supplying no scientific proof; but it sure would be interesting to study. Could it tell us something about Bigfoot seasonal concentrations or possible family groups?

Even better, it might also lead us to the people making the reports. Then if we were very lucky, one of those people might have photographs to share.

So for now finding the alleged Ripplebrook Bigfoot logbook is a task for one of our readers. Best of Luck! Be mentally prepared for this question: "You are looking for what?!"

Hwy 224: mile 24.4 (45.6): Road 4631

The intersection of Hwy 224 and Forest Service Road 4631 is on the left, or east side of 224 just past the Ranger Station. It is recognizable by a wide two lane turnout. The next four accounts are identified as Road 4631-1 through Road 4631-4 as they all happened on or near Road 4631.

Note: If you have passed the Ripplebrook Campground and are at a large, dangerous intersection with paved road #57 to Timothy Lake on your left, you have passed Road 4631.

Ref. 40: The 2001 Ripplebrook Sasquatch Sighting

Ripplebrook event #5: Internationally Newsworthy Sighting 15 (S15): Track Find 16 (T16): Forest Service Employee 4 (FSE 4) plus Job Corps students.

In the authors' opinion, this is an important sighting with perhaps an even more meaningful long-term follow-up.

Wednesday, February 21, 2001

Time: About 10:30 AM
Weather: Mild temperature, few clouds, bright, illuminating sun from the southeast directly onto sighting site.
Place: Mile 1.7 on FS Road 4631 east of the Ripplebrook Ranger Station.
Approximate GPS coordinates of the sighting: 45 05 13.63N 122 01 25.12W at 1884'
Location: The road is paved. In this area it has sweeping curves. On the north side of the road, is a steep bank about 20 feet high backed by a patch of old growth timber. The south side of the road slopes down to a creek area about 100 yards away. It was logged long ago so large rotting stumps still remain. Second growth forest has left the area under the canopy mostly open with good visibility.

Behind the old growth on the north side of the road is the old Forest Service horse pasture from the days when the Forest Service used horses to supply fire lookout towers and get around the back country on trails.

The pasture is 10 to 15 acres. On the west end is a large old barn and the remnants of three houses used by people who worked at the barn. The majority of the pasture is surrounded by a sturdy fence, at one time to keep horses in, now to keep people out.

Witness

We designate the witness Forest Service Employee 4 (FSE 4). He was an unassuming, quiet man about 5′ 10″ tall. The witness is single, about 40 years old, is fit with weight in proportion to height. He wears neat clothes and states he does not use drugs and drinks only minimal amounts of alcohol.

The witness is articulate, not given to excessive talk, and seems quite intelligent. He lives in the Forest Service detached housing enclave near the Ripplebrook Ranger Station. He teaches technical classes at the Job Corps Center. His students told us he is proficient in his trade. Later we were told FSE 4 was promoted and transferred within the Job Corps system.

What the witness was doing

He and three Job Corps students were taking a lunch break so they drove up the road intending to eat sack lunches and go for a walk. He was backing his white king cab, long box Job Corps truck into the turnout per Forest Service procedure when to his left, and about 60 feet away, FSE 4 saw a Bigfoot run across the road.

What happened?

The Bigfoot jumped south from the high bank on the north side of the road and ran downhill into the flat wetland area. According to the witness, the length of the sighting was about "one second," although we estimate more. The witness termed it "like frames from a movie." He said the creature was excellently illuminated by background sun and the rising asphalt road.

Immediately after the sighting, the three Job Corps students said FSE 4 leaped from the truck and ran up the road shouting "Come back, come back." Both the witness; and the students, who were not in a position to see the beast, became overwhelmed with a "feeling or a warning" to get out of the area, which they did.

All three Job Corps students also reported they felt "spooky", as if they were being "watched" before they decided to leave. FSE 4 said that although the students had not seen the creature, when he returned to the truck, they all told him, "Let's get out of here!"

What he saw

He said the creature was over a foot taller than Steve Kiley who is 6 feet tall. He said it had a very stocky build and was in a classic running pose with its arms swinging forward and backward when out on the road. He said hair hung down under the extended arms by 4 to 6 inches, that the hair color was red-brown and that the creature was "very hairy;" it was covered all over with long hair, including the head. He said it was hair, not curly fur.

He made a point to say that the raised foot pointing toward him as the beast ran was "padded like a dog's." He described the pad as "dark colored." He said the head appeared to have a crest or peak, but due to the direction of travel, could not see the face. He said the creature was very muscular and fast. We list this event as Sighting 15 (S15).

Ref. 41: The Sighting is Investigated and Reported

Ripplebrook event #6: The 36 hours after the sighting: Sasquatchians make two trips to visit the witness: A new Track Find (TF17) is made: After FSE 5 (not FSE 4) reports the sighting to the Western Bigfoot Society; then, to his later chagrin, the witness, FSE 4, is put on television

First, the witness (FSE 4) told Forest Service people at the Job Corps Center and Ripplebrook about his sighting. Likewise, the students told other students. Soon, the sighting was blazing wildfire gossip.

One Ripplebrook employee, who we list as Forest Service Employee 5 (FSE5), and who was a member of the Western Bigfoot Society heard about the sighting. FSE 5 called Ray Crowe the next day (Thursday Feb. 22) with the news. Crowe, Director of the Western Bigfoot Society, reported the event to all major television stations in Portland. By Friday, February 23rd, a vortex of mayhem was descending upon Bigfoot witness FSE 4, and the Forest Service at Ripplebrook.

Ray Crowe also called me on the evening of the 22nd. Ray had the witness' telephone number, so I called FSE 4. He agreed to meet me the next day at 10:30 AM, the approximate time of the sighting, at a road intersection near the site, along with the three students who were with him. I called Steve Kiley and asked him to change his workweek. We drove up together.

Friday, February 23, 2001: Kiley and I visit the site: Leaving early, Steve Kiley and I found the crossing point on our own. It was identifiable by smooth, large pad marks going down a game trail. The tracks on the game trail, up by the barn, and down by the creek we label Track Find 17 (TF17). Only 20 feet away two deer and elk trails paralleled the one used by the beast.

On the north, or uphill side were large indistinct prints, but one was identifiable as a left foot. Due to slope angles and forest duff, we made no casts. On the slope, toe marks, the ball, and the curve of the foot were clearly visible. Lying on the forest duff, in the old growth, was an old bottle of ant killer. This bottle yielded fingerprints which we describe shortly.

On the southern downhill side of the crossing, Steve found a short, rotted stump where something tall had curled up to hide. A close examination of the "bedding site" by both Steve and me revealed no hairs, but fortunately, due to the complete lack of rain since the preceding day, the "lay" was undisturbed, as were footprints on the trail.

A *Devils Trail*: On the slightly swampy southern side of the crossing, Kiley also found a worn path with no deer or elk tracks in it, except to cross the trail. There were large indistinct imprints in the forest duff in this area which were possible Sasquatch tracks; so, we decided to call this type of path a "*Devils Trail*." Devils Trails are also reported in Areas 3, 4, and 5.

Continued: February 23, 2001: **On site, emotions heat up:** FSE 4 arrived on time with the three students. We had a very nice talk. Then, about 15 minutes later both USFS and Portland General Electric vehicles begin driving by us; vehicles filled with occupants obviously interested in our meeting. FSE 4 and the students became uncomfortable. It was time for them to leave.

We made rapid, fond goodbyes. Before Steve and I left, we both individually told FSE 4 that no matter what else he did, that he should absolutely, under no circumstance, talk to the media, period! Don't talk to the media! Unfortunately, FSE 4 did not heed our warnings.

A TV crew arrives

As noted, Ray Crowe had alerted the local TV stations to the sighting, and gave them FSE 4's contact information. After we left, a TV crew arrived at Ripplebrook and requested an on-site interview with FSE 4.

Unfortunately he went on camera. The sighting report was on Portland's 6 o'clock news. The TV report went national, and by early Saturday morning, I saw it on one of the international cable TV channels. (BBC I think). This was not good.

This part of the story ends, sadly. Later on Friday, after the TV interview, Cliff and

Woody drove up to Ripplebrook to meet the witness. Now, a Forest Service supervisor was watching FSE 4's every move. In Cliff's words, FSE 4 was, "Like a cat on a hot tin roof."

During this era, the Forest Service was dealing with controversial rulings that limited logging including severe restrictions on logging Federal forest land in efforts to protect the endangered spotted owl and marbled murrelet (a bird)

It is easy to speculate on a number of political situations, but we will never know all that was involved.

Ref. 42: Two More FSE 4 Sightings

Ripplebrook #7: We revisit the Ripplebrook site: Forest Service Employee 4 (again) mounts a research project resulting in new Sightings 16 and 17 (S16 & S17): Bigfoot related Incidents 22, 23, 24 and 25 (I22, I23, I24, I25) happen: Forest Service Employee 6 (FSE 6) chastises Beelart for doubting his word.

Our discussion of the aftermath of the Ripplebrook sighting is in seven parts. The first three relate directly to the sighting. The first is about elk feed stored in the barn and tire tracks squirrelled in the barn yard. The second is the witness reports "seeing things in his sleep." Part three is when possible Bigfoot fingerprints are dusted.

Parts four through seven relate to FSE 4's ongoing quest to see Bigfoot again, which he does. Part four is about one approaching him in camp. Five is when he gets Sightings 16 and 17. Parts six and seven are about his attempts at habituation and recording the creatures. Finally, stress causes FSE 4 to request a job transfer out of the Pacific NW.

Part 1: Elk feed and "squirrelled" tire marks near the barn: Incident 22 (I22).

On Friday, February 23, 2001 Cliff and Woody arrived on site and briefly met FSE 4 as arranged. As noted, a Forest supervisor was also at the remote intersection, watching; listening. After the two Forest Service vehicles left, Cliff and Woody walked the area.

In the horse fence line they noticed one gate was "ripped" off its hinges, a truck had driven into the meadow and had "squirrelled" around in several places as if to obliterate Bigfoot tracks. Developing a bit of conspiracy theory, Cliff and Woody supposed the reason for having the gate "ripped" off was so the Forest Service could say vandals did the damage, but that is pure speculation. In any event, we label the "squirreled out tracks" Incident 22.

About a week later when I was able to go up the hill again I encountered FSE 6, a Forest Service employee of casual acquaintance. We engaged in conversation. He'd heard about FSE 4's sighting. He said, in a matter of fact way, that the beast just went into the barn again to eat sacked food the Forest Service stores for elk in winter.

I immediately thought why did he use the word *again*? I asked him about "going into the barn *again*." He looked at me like why question me. "It's what they do in winter. They (the Bigfoots) eat our elk feed. That's no news up here; just don't mention my name."

Then, FSE 6 coldly repeated, "Don't mention my name." Once again, I sensed Forest Service people know a lot about Bigfoot, and to some degree, study and protect them in their own way.

(Sacked elk food resembles large dog kibbles. It is made from minced hay, molasses, and nutrients.)

Part 2: FSE 4 gets the hint, plus he sees "things."

Two days after the sighting I drove up in the evening to meet the witness at the site. The following is from a letter I wrote to Dr. LeRoy Fish about this meeting:

"The witness seems stable, but upset. He mentions Forest Service reactions to the TV reports. Then he said he sees "things" in his sleep. He doesn't exactly know what he sees. Not nightmares, but something.

FSE 4 repeated two or three times he sees 'things' in his sleep. He kept using various phrases as if he was attempting to get a handle on his night thoughts. He got a little more agitated each time he mentioned 'things,' but he can't describe them. He seems like a pretty down-to-earth guy who doesn't need this kind of stuff happening to him.

Without official permission to use his Job Corps vehicle, or using his own car, he said he went back to the place of the sighting, day and night, at least 10 times during the 48 hours after his sighting."

This means since Friday the 23rd, getting very little sleep, he returned to the site every 4 to 6 hours. I also wrote LeRoy, "He looks it."

After meeting with FSE 4, Cliff and I remained in contact with him. FSE 4 was very interested in my experiences as a witness and questioned details at length, both about my sighting and what happened afterward.

Also, he again repeatedly mentioned "seeing things in his sleep," "visions of things," and the like. At times he again became very agitated. One day I told him I could drive up to see him where he worked. That was OK with him so I went up the next morning to meet him during his morning teaching break.

The man at the Job Corps entrance desk was very pointed and asked penetrating questions as to why I wanted to see FSE 4. Since I worked in the trades business I told him I wanted to talk to him about new, improved equipment. The gate keeper saw through this lie but let me in. In his office, FSE 4 told me to only stay a few minutes and to meet him later off-site. The gate keeper apparently gave him a stern warning about further media contact.

So, FSE 4 and I, sometimes in the company of Cliff Olson, talked off and on for months, both in the woods and on the telephone. FSE 4 steadfastly refused to use email. What he told us he did during the months between winter and spring when snow melted from the mountain tops, and when snow again fell in winter was, to say the least, fascinating. FSE 4's continuing search for the scientifically unclassified beasts seemed to test the limits of ingenuity.

Part 3: Incident 23: possible Sasquatch fingerprints are dusted.

During the afternoon of the sighting Kiley pointed out an empty small, green glass ant poison bottle sitting upright on forest duff about half way between the

Forest Service horse barn and the sighting site. About the only thing I did right at that time was to pick the bottle up by its top. I was wearing clean yellow cotton winter gloves, and was very careful not to touch the sides of the bottle.

On May 3, 2001 I mailed the bottle to a fingerprint expert interested in the Bigfoot phenomena. On May 25th he responded by sending me a copy of the "latent print card" with these comments:

"Just a note to say the bottle was printed .... I found two human prints and one unidentified print. The texture of the unidentified print is similar to a cast I have examined but it could be a glove print also. Sorry I can't be more positive but it's just not that clear."

I reminded him I wore cotton gloves and fortunately noted such in my submittal letter of May 3rd. On May 28th, he sent me an email with a little more detail:

The glove print I was referring to was a cotton glove. Cotton gloves have ridges on them but no characteristics like human prints. These ridges are twice as wide as human ridges. That's why I said they could be Sasquatch prints."

Part 4: Incident 24 (I24): At night, a Sasquatch approaches FSE 4 from behind while he is camping on the Mount Mitchell Plateau.

The following quotation is from another letter I wrote to LeRoy Fish who lived near Eugene, Oregon. Dr. Fish, Ph.D., (1943–2002) was a respected ecologist with an interest in Bigfoot. He was very interested in FSE 4's sighting and FSE 4's continuing investigation, as well as my other experiences in the Clackamas River system. From my letter to Dr. Fish of July 12, 2001:

"FSE 4 continues to teach at the Job Corps Center. He has been in regular contact with me. After the hoopla with the TV people up there, he wants limited contact, but welcomes it from people who are responsible and will not bring him into the spotlight. The best way to contact him is through a voice mail. Mention me and he will call back.

He continues to spend a considerable

Probable Sasquatch finger prints. Dusting and photo by Jimmy Chilcutt.

number of nights alone in the area trying to establish contact with the creature. He bought an 80cc scooter to use instead of a noisy motorcycle.

His most recent incident occurred during the late evening of June 20th. He had no fire. He was cooking a freeze-dried camp stew on his little pressure stove which makes a hissing noise. When his dog snuggled close to him and acted scared the subject turned off the stove to listen.

FSE 4 then heard very heavy, deep breathing close to his camp. He said he forced himself to stay for at least one minute listening to the breathing. He thought it was well within 20 feet, but due to the dark and shadows, he couldn't see anything. Finally, he and the dog took off for the scooter. He said he could hear the breathing animal coming after them as they skedaddled to the scooter. It was bipedal."

My detailed notes reveal more about Incident 24. Dr. Fish and I already had plans for a book on Sasquatch when the Ripplebrook sighting occurred. Dr. Fish encouraged me to just write him the basics and to keep good notes on what happened with FSE 4.

Unfortunately, soon after he retired, LeRoy died from a heart attack thus ending our book plans. As we used to say in the USMC, LeRoy was good people.

Here are additional details I didn't send LeRoy. The incident happened on the Mt. Mitchell Plateau at about the same place where we talked to the Subaru owner—which is toward the end of Spur 140 of Road 4635 (See Ref. 45.) The Mt. Mitchell Plateau is also where Cliff fell and fortunately only gouged off a big chunk of skin.

The following are more notes on my conversations with FSE 4. FSE 4 told me to write 20 feet because he first became aware of his night visitor when it was about 20 feet away from him. He said he heard it carefully step closer and closer, which filled him with a mixture of apprehension and near terror.

Just before FSE 4 and his dog bolted for the scooter, he said it was either standing within an arm's length behind him, looking over his shoulder at the stew; or, his hearing had remarkably improved as he was hearing every detail of the creature's deep breathing.

He said his dog forced itself between his legs and began a plaintive almost silent whine. That's when FSE 4 grabbed his pot and threw his dinner over his shoulder at the "breather." He said when he came back the next evening to pick up his gear, the pot was licked clean and he found no left-overs lying in the area.

Part 5: FSE 4's further Bigfooting adventures: Sighting 16 and Sighting 17 (S16, S17).

After FSE 4 had his sighting, he did three things attempting to relive the event, or to be more accurate, see the creatures again. This is a common thread in the lives of witnesses, which make his sighting even more credible.

When he told me what he'd done, I honestly thought it was a stroke of genius. It surprised Cliff and Steve so much they both laughed, and they weren't together when I told them. From another letter to Dr. Fish:

"FSE 4 has bought an 80cc motor scooter, mounted a battery box on the back, a spotlight on the front and he uses it to coast down logging roads at night."

FSE 4 didn't buy a motorcycle because they made too much noise under load going uphill. Motorcycles also don't have a place to mount a battery box or a spotlight. He especially liked the battery box because his dog liked to ride on it. He said when they got close to a Sasquatch, the dog would snuggle up real tight. FSE 4 said then he "knew adventure was near."

His technique was simple; motor to the top of an asphalt logging road, wait a while to let wildlife think he was gone, and then coast down the road. He avoided gravel roads because they made too much noise and were unstable traction in the dark. "Sure, I have to replace the brakes, but that's not hard. I keep a stock on hand."

Generally he went coasting when the moon was a quarter and above, the nights when wildlife move. When he heard a noise, he stopped and clicked on the spotlight. Most of the time he saw deer, sometimes an elk, and occasionally a bear. Twice he saw Bigfoot.

These are listed as Sighting 16 and Sighting 17. In each instance the Bigfoot was standing on the right side of the road. In both instances, the creature raised its forearm to cover its eyes and turned its head, just as FSE 1 reported in Ref. 16 at Fish Creek bridge, and as any human would do if hit with a spotlight. After recovering from the shock of sudden light, the Bigfoot of Sighting 16 retreated into the forest. The Bigfoot in FSE 4's Bigfoot Sighting 17 walked across the road into the forest on the other side.

The one that retreated back into the forest was large with long black hair. The one that walked across the road was a smaller female, he could see breasts, but still very muscular. While the big one was about 7 feet tall (he returned to check branches, etc.) the smaller one was probably just over 6 feet. He speculated the female was following another Bigfoot which crossed before her.

When I asked him about giving me a recorded interview (suggested by LeRoy) FSE 4 said words roughly to the effect, "No way, not after what happened at Ripplebrook. Tell your friends, but no one else." That was OK by me. He also declined to tell me the roads, but said, "You should be able to figure them out."

Part 6: FSE 4 makes a video and audio recording device.

Virtually everyone I know who has gotten into serious Sasquatch field research tries camera traps, and some of us try audio recordings. FSE 4 was no different; but unlike investing in his scooter, which had some residual value, his self-designed and built video and audio recording apparatus probably had little residual value even though he told me he spent $10,000 on it.

While I think the apparatus eventually went to another Bigfooter, I doubt he got a lot of dollars for it. He offered it to me but at first I couldn't afford it and later, I couldn't think of a good way to put it to use.

Basically it was a water resistant, condensation resistant black box full of relays, sensors, and recorders with the ability to connect to a variety of cameras and microphones. A separate battery box provided the power. Unfortunately, he built it just at the advent of wireless www communications, so it did not have that capability.

When FSE 4 wasn't using his "black box" at his house, once or twice he set it up in the woods and used his scooter battery box to transport recharged batteries. His electronic gear gave him no results that I know about, but by then FSE 4 had started to quietly immerse himself into the Bigfoot community. He may have shared some recorded information with them.

Part 7: FSE 4 tries habituation: Incident 25 (I25).

The results of habituation efforts lead to episodes which proved unsettling to FSE 4. The authors' collectively label these episodes of FSE 4 as Bigfoot related Incident 25.

Approximate GPS coordinates: 45 04 56.49 N 122 02 32.97 W at ~ 1600'

Unfortunately, for FSE 4 enticing the critters to his Ripplebrook forest backyard worked too well. One day he told me he was about to go crazy, that he had to leave Ripplebrook and was looking for a position in the Forest Service far away from there. It should be noted that FSE 4 had retained a stable personality throughout the times after his sighting so, when he told me he was about to go "crazy," I listened.

As mentioned, FSE 4 lived in the Ripplebrook housing compound separate from the Job Corps Center. The creek below his sighting site ran near it. One day I showed him the Devils Trail along the creek with no elk or deer tracks on it. His backyard, while some distance downstream was open to the forest, creek side. FSE 4, being a thinking man, instantly put a Bigfoot critical path flowchart together and it led to his backyard.

He said, "All I have to do to see them is to get them to come to me."

And after he began putting out offerings on his picnic table they came. Next they left him little rewards, generally shiny things like old aluminum cans and clear plastic bottles. Then they invaded his sleep with thoughts and dreams. Never was he threatened, rather they silently, but clearly said things like, "We like this better than that. Where are you? Why didn't you put anything out for us?"

In short, FSE 4 had completely connected with Sasquatch. He was a human accepted by them. However, from my observations the Sasquatches telepathic intrusions into his mind were slowly destabilizing the once solid man we first met more than a year earlier.

Finally, I decided to pointedly ask FSE 4, "Have you started using drugs or alcohol?" He said no, the Job Corps gives random drug tests, so none of that for me. He also said he'd never used any of that stuff anyway. And, he said he still only drank beer once in a while.

He tried to record visitations with a video recorder and his black box but only had unsatisfactory results. FSE 4 said his dog was still the best indicator when Sasquatch was around; the dog either desperately wanted into the house, or if he was inside, the dog snuggled tight to him.

One day FSE 4 told me over the telephone he was transferring to a position in the east. "Are you interested in my scooter or black box?" Again, I explained I just didn't have the money at the time. He thanked me for all I'd done for him, which perplexed me since I hadn't done much but talk to him. That was the last I heard from FSE 4.

Game cam photo by Joe Beelart. Note cougar claw scar on doe deer's left shoulder. Cougar home ranges vary with deer population. In the upper Clackamas, territories are probably about 10 x 10 (100) square miles.

Ref. 43: Sasquatch Territories

Next is a case report about a possible Sasquatch territorial marker, or warning sign. So, this is a good place to talk a little about Sasquatch territories. Perhaps the authors haven't done enough research, but it seems few words are written about this important subject. Probably the lack of words has to do with the sparsity of repetitive, satisfactory sighting reports in any given area, plus the seemingly ingrained habit of Sasquatch researchers to write a sighting report and end their inquiry with it.

Based on the authors' research, we present a hypothesis on Sasquatch territories: *There are areas where continuous breeding populations exist. In general, these territories are defined by geographic places, such as plateaus, ridgelines, valleys, gorges, and riverbeds.*

Specifically, the authors believe, from information in this book, there are twelve Sasquatch territories in the Clackamas and Breitenbush drainages. The twelve territories are illustrated in the area maps for each chapter, but "boundaries" will have to be dashed or dotted in the reader's mind.

Territories imply population. Appendix III is our Sasquatch population estimate by territory, in the upper Clackamas and Breitenbush drainages. Assuming a female and youngster as the basic territorial group, we estimate up to 31 individuals, including roving males, as the summer population between Estacada and Detroit, with spillover into the Warm Springs Indian Reservation.

Territories also imply movement, or migration; which has been passingly mentioned in Sasquatch literature. Appendix IV describes probable migration routes in the upper Clackamas and Breitenbush drainages. These routes might be important to field researchers since migration may recur certain times of the year, and also cause Sasquatch to be less wary than when confined to a home range.

With over 30 Sasquatch wandering the hills south of Estacada a realistic skeptic will say, "So what's the problem with getting proof?" Well, there are sightings every year, and have been for many decades, so we know they are "up there." It seems there are six barriers to getting scientific proof.

(1) Night ... night is the cloak of Sasquatch and sleeping time for man.

(2) They are alert to human intrusion into their surroundings and stealthily avoid people.

(3) Lack of skeletal remains indicates Sasquatch bury their dead.

(4) Winter ... even if Bigfoot descends to low altitudes and remains in a territory, after rifle elk hunting season, few people wander in winter.

(5) People waste most of their time afield looking down. Look up, look into the trees.

(6) Money and the right crew. We think our approach, calm exploration and approach is the best way, but it takes a lot of money and time.

Next, we look at three cases in the upper Clackamas which probably indicate territorial signals. These are followed by a few words concerning the Sasquatch territorial protection issue.

Ripplebrook #7: Track Find 18 (TF18): is when film makers Blake Eckard, Alec Jennings; and an adult skeptic, Jake 15 find a good track near FSE 4's sighting. The track as a possible territorial marker is Bigfoot Related Incident 26 (I26).

During the winter of 2003 Blake Eckard from NW Missouri enrolled in an advanced film class at the Portland Art Museum Film Sciences Center. With his interest in a Bigfoot documentary unabated, he spent most of his spare time in the mountains. Through the Film Science Center, Eckard met skeptic Jake 15 who was interested in his documentary.

Under the tutelage of Cliff and me, in February Eckard set up a baiting or offering site, depending one's point of view, about 200 yards south of FSE 4's sighting. The offerings were placed slightly up hill from a little creek near the Devils Trail found after FSE 4's sighting on USFS Road 4631.

The Devils Trail we found near the sighting remained well-compacted, open for walking, and had no deer tracks so we decided to set up near it.

The site was formed by two big fallen trees about four feet in diameter lying at right angles to each other. A good canopy was above the site, offering some shelter from rain. In addition, while the view from the site was not expansive, it was open allowing a visiting hominid the security of seeing what was going on around him or her.

Importantly, one of the commonly accepted standards in setting up baiting sites, or making offerings to Bigfoots, is to place them as high as practical off the ground. It is said Bigfoots do not like to bend to offerings on the ground. So, to our minds, the fallen trees were ideal, veritable wilderness buffet tables for our Forest Pals.

We set the spread well with varieties of tinned cat and dog food plus raw carrots on each tree trunk, with the intent to find if one flavor or another was preferable. The tins were the little expensive kind you see on TV.

Why carrots? They are easy-to-see orange, they last a long time in the wild, are healthy and cheap. Why the little tins? In those days we were searching for DNA ... blood, skin, etc. The little tins leave a sharp rim when the lid is pulled which might make a little cut and leave residual blood.

Also, in our wonderfully inventive minds, we decided to not pull the lids clean off, to leave them only cracked. This served two purposes, we thought. First to tell us if critters with no fingers got at the goods, and second, we figured we might get better fingerprints if the cans were handled. Neither supposition paid off, but one thing did. Something ate the carrots, pulled the lids and cleaned out the cans.

It was very interesting that all the cans were emptied and left upright on top of the logs, not strewn about. The pull-off lids were laid next to the finger emptied cans.

Whatever ate the goods, left big imprints in the duff. Just image a Bigfoot wandering up to the log smorgasbord wondering, "What tasty morsel next?"

In any event, we know our epicurean was certainly not raccoon, bear, weasel, or another usual forest denizen. (Yes I knew that word; I didn't have to look it up.). They make a mess of offerings if they get to them before Sasquatch, which they usually do.

Bears probably make the worst mess, because they are strong and tear at things with their claws. While a raccoon is a possible, it would have strewn cans and lids, or at least several of them.

Anyway, we didn't mail the cans for fingerprinting because we were pretty sure the smell of spoiling residual cat food would get us negative vibrations from the Post Office. And, in retrospect, we felt good there was no blood trail.

On the first maintenance visit, after picking up all the empties using latex gloves, I set out another eight servings. Later I arranged for Eckard and Jennings to come up and see the results.

When the day came, Eckard brought along interested skeptic Jake 15, and Jennings; who, as usual, lugged along one or another huge black box covered with knobs and dragging wires to connect them to whoever knows what.

Blake toted his movie camera and did whatever movie makers do for scenes, commanding directions in clipped lingo while holding his hands in little rectangles in front of his face.

A Marker

The day of our little expedition I pointed the filmsters toward the offering site while I stayed up in the trees near where FSE 4 had his sighting. After a while I heard loud exclamations down by the creek reminiscent of when Cliff and Harper found The Mother of All Turds. This time what Eckard and crew found was a footprint: A good, recent, distinctive footprint in wet stable soil beside the creek about 50 yards below the baiting site.

This important event was Track Find 18 (TF18). And while 18 may seem like a lot of tracks to find, keep in mind years before we set stringent standards on what we label a Bigfoot track and both Blake and Alec were well aware of them.

This imprint met our track find standards with (1) clearly defined toes, (2) no claws, (3) evidence of a two part foot, and (4) heel proportional to the ball of the foot (not narrow like a bear paw). We also like to find some evidence of dermal ridges, and other things. So, this was a big deal.

For yards in all directions, this was the only ground cover that would capture a track. In it was an excellent impression! Was this Sasquatch giving a signal; was it "signing" its territory? The filmmakers, and I, felt the footprint was not a warning; rather it seemed a small gesture of forest friendship. We term this possible territorial sign Bigfoot Related Incident 26 (I26).

Skeptic Jake 15 didn't know what to think, other than, "That's really big!" And, "Why aren't there more tracks?"

So to explain why to him, I fell back on the very same thing Cliff and I tell people we take up the Clackamas. It's very seldom to see four or more tracks made by the same deer or elk except in large muddy areas. For most people, even tracking a deer in the duff is an impossible task. The forest simply does not leave sign, and that is good, because lack of spoor means safety for the animals. And, our Sasquatch friends in their mountain world are expert at leaving little or no spoor.

So, what happened? After a lot of "oohing, aahing," taking of still photographs, and a few feet of film run through the Bolex before it seized up, someone, thank goodness it wasn't me, slipped into the track and ruined most of it! And this time, I had plaster along. Just what does it take to get a good track cast?

With no casting to do, the excitement was over. We went up to the buffet site where the condition was the same as the first time; no carrots, an orderly arrangement of empty cans, and stomped down duff next to the logs. We put out more tins and carrots, which, when I went back a week later, were not eaten. So, I cleaned up the site and that was the end of it there. Like the great chicken baiting escapade, this "experiment" was over.

Territorial Signals: Cases #2 & #3

Cliff's 1957 Track Find

In this book Track Find 18 is not the only single Bigfoot track which seems to stake out a territorial claim, or leave the signal "I am here."

In upcoming Ref. 48 Cliff Olson reports his 1957 find of a single track on Oak Grove Butte. Soon after finding Track 21, Cliff independently formed the opinion his 1957 track was a territorial marker.

Steve's Broken Trees

During our 15 years in the Clackamas Ranger District, Sasquatchians reported two possible examples of territory boundaries signed with wood breaks. Both were found by Steve Kiley who is not given to seeing things. His first find was the scotch broom twist-off found up the North Fork and reported in Ref. 11. This unusual break, requiring an enormous amount of hand strength, was placed at a fork on a trail.

The second Kiley find, as reported in upcoming Ref. 50, was high on the east side of Thunder Mountain between Indian Henry and the Collawash. Along a highly visible road, a series of three inch, evenly spaced trees, were freshly broken in a consistent manner, seemingly to define a territorial line.

Territory Protection Issues

Two stories I recall fondly, but are not included in the book, make a point on animals' sense of territory. In what I refer to as the *Attack of the Killer Grouse*, a hen grouse defending her chicks caused me to spring laterally about 4 feet, sending Kiley into a fit of laughter.

In Charge of the Mouse Warrior, while I was lifting duff, a mouse, ears up and little teeth barred, charged me from his den. These allegories on animals and their territories remind us that all animals in one way or another protect their "homes."

The territorial concept truly calls out two questions needful of campfire talk and contemplation. The first is, if Sasquatch exists as a typical Earth animal, what has Sasquatch done, or will he do, to protect his territory? A derivative question is, "Does Sasquatch need to protect his territory from human encroachment?"

Showing signs of aggression when surprised by a human is personal protection, a far cry from territorial defense. Arm raising incidents – like action in a monster movie – are listed in *Appendix II*. These acts, from reports in this book, were clearly done to scare away intruding humans, after which Sasquatch also left the scene.

Perhaps the best examples of territorial defense are found in the rock throwing incidents in Ref. 8, Ref. 51, and Ref. 83. These are interesting reports because in each, there is possible territorial intrusion by humans. In each, the rock thrower was not seen yet the rocks were of substantial size. There were no nearby cliffs for a rock fall. Something powerful, and upset, threw them.

To close this brief discussion of Sasquatch territorial protection issues, the authors offer an additional thought. W*hat if* Sasquatch's prime resting territory is above us, in the trees? Up there, with humans mainly watching their footing down there, what benefit would they derive from attracting the attention of passing humans?

This ends reports from Area 2.

Summit Lake in the southeast sector of Area 3, near the northeast border of Area 5.
Photo by Sharon Beelart.

Loggers call these Widow Makers! Photo by Sharon Beelart.

Area 3: Oak Grove Fork, High Rock, Devils Ridge, & Peavine Mountain

Area 3 is a large rectangle with its centerline based on Forest Service Road 57. The rectangle is about 20 miles long west-to-east and about 15 miles wide north-to-south. The west-central area of Area 3, the alluvial basin of the Oak Grove Fork, is winter holding ground for elk, deer, and the Big Hairy Folk.

Along Road 57 researchers will find themselves immersed in dense tree and vegetation growth which is common in lower elevations of the Clackamas system, thus giving a clue as to how animals remain unseen. However, even along the river bottom there are occasional vistas.

In the first few miles on Road 57 massive Mt. Mitchell raises high in the north. The long, barren, dripping gray stone icicles on Mt. Mitchell's face are talus slopes. Talus slopes are large rock covered areas bare of vegetation.

During the 15 miles from Ripplebrook to Timothy Lake, (the road sign saying 7 miles is wrong, it is 7 miles to the intersection of Road 57 and 58), explorers will not see much except dense greenery as the road winds through the narrow canyon of the Oak Grove Fork of the Clackamas River.

Since Timothy Lake recreationists are notorious drivers, getting sprayed with gravel by passing vehicles is not unusual. Persons driving rental cars who plan to travel Road 57 should consider purchasing the loss and damage waivers.

However, once you arrive, the Timothy Lake area provides a traveler with hiking trails and camping areas as well as a sizeable clear-water reservoir that covers about two square miles. The lake has a 10 mph speed limit for all boats so kayakers and canoers can enjoy the peaceful waters and beautiful vistas. On a cloudless day you will see a picture-book view of Mt. Hood looming over the lake.

Also, in recent years PGE and the Clackamas County Sheriff's department reestablished control over Timothy Lake campgrounds so they are no longer the legendary, outrageous party spots of old. Now, the four lakeshore campgrounds are among the best in the west. (You knew I had to work "... the best in the west" in somewhere didn't you?)

Map of Area 3

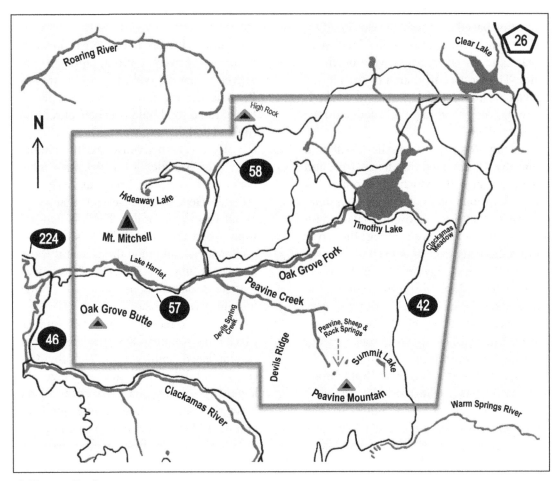

©Sharon Beelart 2015

Are we lost yet?

Spur roads branching off Road 57 sometimes yield awesome vistas, but are often full of pot holes, slumps, and washboards, plus many dead-ends leaving intrepid explorers wondering, "Where am I?" A good Forest Service road map is essential to traveling side roads, unless a traveler goes straight up and straight back with few diversions. Beware; getting lost in the eastern section of Area 3 is very easy. The authors have led lost drivers out of this maze several times.

Area 3 OBH Mile Markers

Miles from Estacada: from Detroit

24.9:   45.1   Timothy Lake intersection Hwy 224, FS Road 46 & Road 57
50.0:   35.0   Intersection of Road 42 with FS Road 46 (in Area 5)

Area 3 mile markers for the traveler going to the Timothy Lake area start at the large Timothy Lake road intersection and run east past Timothy Lake to where the road intersects with Road 42 Road 42 turns south, runs through Area 5 and intersects with the Oregon Bigfoot Highway going to or coming from Detroit

0.0   Timothy Lake intersection of Hwy 224, FS Road 46, and Road 57
0.5   Road 5710 to top of Oak Grove Butte
4.3   New bridge; landslide zone
4.5   Road 5720 to plateau east of Oak Grove Butte summit
5.0   Road 5730 to Devils Ridge
7.0   Intersection with Road 58 north to Hideaway Lake, High Rocks
13.0   Timothy Lake dam
13.2   Road 5740 to Summit Lake plateau not many views
14.0   Hood View Campground
15.75 Road 5750; views require hikes
16.25 Oak Fork Campground (Sharon's favorite)
17.8   Intersection with Road 42 at Clackamas Meadows

Just off Road 57 on Spur 5730 is Gee Zee quarry. This is a fine example of some of the odd quarry names along the *Oregon Bigfoot Highway*. The USFS drops huge tree stumps and root masses from landslides at Gee Zee quarry

The Timothy Lake Road Intersection

Mile 24.9 (45.1): The Timothy Lake intersection marks the end of Oregon Hwy 224, the beginning of Forest Service Road 46 to Detroit and the beginning of Forest Service Road 57 to Timothy Lake. Road 46 ends in Detroit at the intersection with Oregon Highway 22 thus ending, or beginning the *OBH*.

GPS coordinates: 45 04 45.01N 122 02 33.80W at 1430′

Caution: this is a dangerous intersection, so drive defensively. If you park here, clear the roadway and be extremely vigilant when you reenter.

The bridge immediately north of the intersection crosses the Oak Grove Fork.

Near here, the Oak Grove Fork makes two hard 90° turns before joining the main Clackamas River about a half mile to the west. When salmon and steelhead (read Bigfoot vittles) are running (or really any old time), it is worth taking Trail 723 for a fun, easy walk along the river.

General

Timothy Lake is a large dam reservoir 15 miles east of the 224/46/57 intersection. The dam was built in 1956 to provide a stable source of water to power the Portland General Electric Oak Grove / Three Lynx powerhouse. This dam would never be built today as it drowned a great high mountain ecosystem and the lush environment it provided for flora and fauna.

The only remaining large high mountain marshland ecosystem in northern Oregon is about a mile east of Timothy Lake at Clackamas Lake Meadows. Clackamas Lake Meadows extends into the Warm Springs Indian Reservation where it is called Big Meadows. Carefully observing edges of this area with binoculars, or better, a spotting scope reveals an abundance of wildlife. Be sure you have insect repellant.

Approx. GPS for Clackamas Meadows: 45 05 53.25N 121 44 45.29 W at about 3345'; approx. GPS for Big Meadows: 45 05 57.53N 121 42 03.41N at about 3480'

Warning: An officer of the Warm Springs Tribal Police suggested the authors insert this warning since the Warm Springs Indian Reservation boundary line is only a few miles east of Timothy Lake.

In effect, the Reservation is another country with its own laws, regulations, and judicial system.

Do not enter the Warm Springs Indian Reservation without a tribal permit. In this area, unpermitted reservation entry and transit is only allowed on Forest Service Road 42.

Trespass violations are strictly enforced often resulting in substantial fines and other penalties. The Warm Springs boundary is clearly marked along its length, so "I didn't see ...." is not a valid excuse.

Timothy Lake Road 57 ends where it intersects with Road 42 about a mile east of the lake. Forest Road 42 is also called the *Oregon Skyline Road* which originates at Hwy 26 southeast of Mt. Hood, and for practical purposes, ends at Olallie Lake north of Mt. Jefferson. If you decide to drive the Oregon Skyline Road, beware! A southern segment of the Oregon Skyline Road, as drawn on some maps, is not passable with a passenger car.

Traveling from Timothy Lake to Government Camp or Timberline Lodge on Mt. Hood is an easy trip using Hwy.26. The GPS of the intersection of Hwy 26 and Road 42 is 45 10 35.33N 121 40 33.93W at 3645'

Once at Timothy Lake or Clackamas Meadows, the authors suggest adding a five mile side trip north to Little Crater Lake. A short, flat, easy walk from the parking area rewards visitors with an on-the-banks view of one of the clearest small lakes in the world.

Little Crater Lake GPS: 45 09 06.18N 121 45 24.38W at 3284'.

Bigfoot Activity bordering Forest Service Road 57

Except for the alluvial delta behind Ripplebrook which was discussed in Area 2, the Oak Grove Fork is generally a narrow, V-shaped valley with a moderate river gradient. Here is another of the places in the Cascades where water erosion has worn away volcanic overlay to bedrock laid millions of years ago.

Because of the narrow valley, there are not many Sasquatch reports from the canyon, aside from an occasional "I saw one cross Road 57." However, the story is quite different on the mountains north and south of the valley where significant Bigfoot activity is reported in four areas.

According to reports, on the north side of Road 57 two active areas are (1) above upper Roaring River and (2) east of High Rock. Active areas on the south side of Road 57 are (1) the high forested plateau east of Oak Grove Butte and (2) Devils Ridge. Little is reported from immense Peavine Mountain, probably because it lacks ready access.

Timothy Lake with Mt. Hood in the background just before sunrise. Photo by Sharon Beelart.

District 1: North of the Timothy Lake Road

First, we report events above the upper Roaring River drainage, and points east to the Reservation boundary.

Ref. 44: Cliff Finds 82 Tracks

Near the top of Mt. Mitchell: September 27 & 28, 2003: Track Find 19 (TF19): Jake 14 again, plus Olson, Mann, Beelart, and Sharon Beelart: Near the high end of Road 5830.

Our early fall, high mountain, last-of-the-season campout under the crest of Mt. Mitchell took a surprising turn when author Cliff found a Bigfoot track way of 82 exceptional, fresh foot prints.

GPS of the intersection of Road 58 at Road 57: 45 04 42.52 N 121 55 18.11W at 2210′

GPS of Cliff's Lake is 45 06 19.72N 121 57 40.73W at 4034′ (A bit north of Cottonwood Meadows Lake.)

GPS of Mt. Mitchell summit: 45 06 31.31N 121 58 47.94W at 5039′

September 2003 was very mild, so on the weekend before rifle deer hunting season started, five of us, including my wife Sharon, decided to have a last fling at almost wilderness fun. Cliff knew of a pothole lake high on Mt. Mitchell that might be a good place for a campout.

So we all packed up our gear and followed Cliff over hill and dale to the lake of his fancy, which proved to be a very nice spot. The lake's size in fall was about 100 yards long by about 30 yards wide. The shallow pothole lake receded during summer leaving a rather large, moist beach along its south side

A good time was had by all. There was easy walking for a mile or two in most directions. Somehow I managed to hike to a viewpoint giving me a grand vista of upper Roaring River, High Rock, Signal Buttes, and Mt. Hood! The weather was spectacular.

From my logbook: "I stayed up until 3AM! Watching stars. Listening. An absolutely beautiful night. No moon, but so much Zodiac glow I walked on roads without a light!"

In the morning after breakfast, Cliff decided to stretch his legs by walking around the lake to look for deer tracks. I happened to be watching him at the east end of the lake when he stopped short and began furiously looking right and left.

Cliff looked over at me and waved me to the backside of the lake. Normally unflappable, Cliff's wave was more than gestures, he was meaning, no, commanding: "Come here now." What he found was absolutely amazing.

During the night, on the southeast side of the lake, a bipedal creature walked up a seasonal outlet stream and stepped over a limbless fallen tree. It then walked to about the center of the lake and stood watching the fire, and perhaps our going's on. It then turned and made a parallel set of foot prints from whence it came to disappear into the forest.

Cliff's Track Way

We counted 82 distinct tracks, including tracks made by turning, scuffing, etc. In short the whole gamut of walking. They certainly were not made by a deer, elk, or cougar. The logical answer was a bear, but these were not bear tracks for three big reasons.

First, the prints lacked a pad and were elongated, not oval. None of the imprints showed claw marks and the rear of the tracks were not tapered. None were double strikes. If there were only a few tracks, the obvious answer was bear double strikes, but not with a raceway of 82 distinct steps.

Second, the toes were not in a partial circle, they were slightly angled, well defined, and paralleled each other. Also, the imprints were very clear and fresh. Grains of wet soil were still falling from toe imprints and edges of the tracks.

Finally, and probably the most important thing regarding the tracks, was the fact that the imprints penetrated the damp "beach" soil to a depth of 2 inches with a maximum depth of 3 inches. In contrast, none of us penetrated the soil much more than 1/8 inch. We knew a small four pawed bear weighing maybe 200 pounds would not make tracks deeper than ours. Obviously whatever made the tracks was very heavy, or dense, in relation to foot size.

The track size was most interesting. They were 9 to 9 ½ inches long. The width of the heel on both feet was about 3 inches. The ball of the foot was a bit over 3 ½ inches and they seemed to show a two part foot, as the mud in many of the steps had an angle of raised soil behind the ball of the foot.

Heel to heel step was about 24 inches with a two-step stride of about 48 inches in the straight-away. We label this important discovery Track Find 19 (TF19).On site we decided the track way was made by a curious juvenile Bigfoot. So we hiked around the woods and the seasonal outflow stream looking for adult Bigfoot tracks. We found none.

Later we decided the night walker was maybe 4-5 years old, or about 10-11 years old in human terms. How we decided that was from a lot of conjecture; but, almost ten years later, it still seems like a reasonable supposition.

Note depth of track and no claw marks. Buck 110 hunting knife - 4-7/8" closed. Also see photo page 136. Photo by Sharon Beelart.

Amazingly, none of us brought any casting material along, clearly indicating our level of expectations while doing Sasquatch field research. Worse, one roll of film was lost in processing, so there are few images of the track way. The next day was Monday, the start of the work week. None of us could return during the week.

I tried to get several other people to go up and inspect the track way and hopefully make castings, but after they found out it was a three hour drive, no one wanted the job. The next weekend was the first day of deer season. The first weekend of deer season is a foolish time to drive mountain roads unless absolutely necessary.

(The suction of mud possibly indicating a two part foot is also mentioned in References 12, 43, 44 and 99.)

View from our camp looking across the lake. Tracks found on the far side of the lake. Photo by Sharon Beelart.

Ref. 45: Night Walker at Hideaway Lake

Jake 16 (J16) describes Bigfoot Related Incident 27.

Hideaway Lake GPS is 45 07 17.40N 121 58 02.60W at 4095′. Virtually everyone drives to the lake via Road 5830 even though we know Jake 16, and years earlier, Thom Powell, made the challenging northern hike. We met Jake 16 at GPS 45 07 11.22N 122 01 04.65W at 4100′.

In June 2009 Jake 16 told us his story at the 702 trail head on the north end of the Mt. Mitchell plateau. At first he got a worried look when I parked my truck near

his almost new Subaru, but we calmed him down and got him laughing a little.

After we straightforwardly told him about our interest in Bigfoot, and asked if he'd ever seen one, or the tracks of one, he looked upon us with a quizzical look amounting to "What kind of nut cases are you?"

Then he got quiet, thought a while and said, "Well, there was something that happened just before last winter."

It turned out Jake 16 was an avid hiker from Beaverton, Oregon with hundreds of nights in the woods. He had neither seen footprints nor made contact with one of the beasts, until his Hideaway Lake episode which we label Bigfoot Related Incident 27.

"I went for my last outing at the Hideaway Lake campground before the first snows. It was cold so I had extra blankets in my hammock to wrap around my sleeping bag. I was pretty cozy, but couldn't move around much. So, about midnight when this really big man started walking around the campground I couldn't see much of him.' He paused, 'I knew he was big because his footsteps were so heavy."

J16 paused again, thinking, then without encouragement, continued on in partial sentences as his mind recreated the scene. He was obviously a thinker as he answered our questions, unasked.

"No I was alone; there was no one else around' ... pause ... he repeated, 'I know he was big because his footsteps were so heavy' ... pause ...Just about the time I was going to roll out and turn on my light, he walked into the forest ... (pause) ...the next morning I looked around pretty carefully, there were a few imprints in the duff, but nothing really definite."

Hideaway Lake is about 4 miles from where we were parked and is roughly in the center of the upper Roaring River basin. The day we met him, he was going camping at Serene Lake. J16 said he'd keep a watch for us and let us know if he ever saw anything. Although we've kept in touch, five years later, he still hasn't seen tracks or beast.

Ref. 46: Hiker photographs Bigfoot tracks

Track Find 20 (TF20) with an indication of a two-part foot: Jake 13 again, and Jake 17: Half way up High Rock Road 58.

In April 2001 a photograph of a Bigfoot track (Track Find 20) made the front page *of Estacada's Clackamas County News*, (Vol. 97 No. 13: April 11, 2001). Surprisingly the photographer was Jake 13 who I previously interviewed about the Three Lynx school bus sighting. (See Area 2 Ref. 27).

J13 called sighting witness FSE 4 (Ripplebrook sightings Ref. 40 & 42) because she was acquainted with him, and knew he had a sighting. FSE 4 in turn told her what to do, which was not go on camera. Next FSE 4 called me with Jake 13's telephone number as he felt I should talk to her in a knowledgeable way.

When I talked to Jake 13, she said a friend of hers also saw the tracks so we call that person Jake 17. The following is from a letter I sent to Dr. LeRoy Fish:

"She (J13) was quite excited about the find. The location was about a half mile, or slightly more, past Road 5830 on Road 58 going to High Rock. Jakes 13 and Jake 17 were walking a new dog up the road and found the tracks in a shady area in the snow. She repeatedly described them as 'very fresh' and not melted out. She knew that would be one of my first questions, followed by, was there any possibility they were made by a bear.

She was ready for both questions as she lived 15 years in Alaska and worked at a remote lodge her parents owned. Anyway, the dog, a Cocker Spaniel, went a bit wild and ran through most of the tracks which went up a steep snow covered bank. So, she has only one really good photo. She said she'd never seen anything like them before, but almost instantly knew the beast which probably made them.

J13 said the big toe was larger than a big walnut and the foot seemed to make a 'considerable arching' effect in the snow. The tracks were 14 ½ inches long and the step was about 4 feet. Six of the tracks were very clear as the creature left the snow covered road and walked up a slope into brush.

On an interesting side note, J13 repeated the story of when she was young and her family lived at Silvertip when the mill was still operating. She said one day the children on her school bus going to Three Lynx School saw a 'tall dark man' watching them from the trees. The children reported the figure."

Jake 13 and I went on with a long chat about Bigfoot in general. She asked if it would be wise to let the local newspaper know. I told her I was no authority on the subject of Bigfoot public relations, but thought doing a local news article would be OK since it shouldn't draw wide media attention.

When I received my copy of the newspaper story I was very surprised to see the footprint photograph strongly resembled Yeti snow track photographs. Track authorities who I sent copies of the photograph agreed that the tracks looked Yeti, but without knowing, and seeing more, could not confirm them.

One, a retired Ph.D. biologist, said in wildly amusing speculation, "There may be two species of unidentified primate living in the Cascades." He also said the "considerable arching" she mentioned was apparent in her photograph and was possible evidence of a two part foot.

Ref. 47: A FSE points to a "good place"

Bigfoot Related Incident 28 (I28): FS employee 7 (FSE 7) points to a good area for field research.

The following encounter took place in early March 2004 on Road 58 at the intersection of Hideaway Lake Road 5830 near the location of Track Find 20.

Three years after J13 and J17's Yeti-like track find on High Rock Road 58, I had a day off during the week so I decided to drive up to the same area to look for tracks. I parked my truck near the intersection of Roads 57 and 58 at Shellrock Campground.

It was March and cold so I wore my down parka, insulated gloves, and Sorel wool lined boots. Carrying a light pack with water, a snack, my walking stick, and with my 357 magnum strapped to my side, I walked up High Rock Road.

It was chilly climbing the road, but not insufferable. The only tracks I saw the first half mile were deer. Snow was still fairly deep on each side of the road, getting thicker as I walked higher. The roadway was plowed and clear. I was simply enjoying pure air, sun, and exercise when about an hour later I magically found myself miles up the hill at the Hideaway Lake intersection.

From below a Forest Service 4x4 pickup came up the road at moderate speed. When it got near, I saw it had a light bar and several antennas. I was expecting a Law Enforcement Officer (LEO), but instead, when the truck stopped beside me, I got a fit, middle-aged man with no badge I could see. We will call him Forest Service Employee 7 (FSE 7).

Inside his truck was an early laptop arrangement similar to those seen in police cars, and several radios; but I didn't see a mounted shotgun or rifle. Because the FS employee gave me directions, so to speak, this little episode is termed Incident 28.

I opened my parka so he saw my 357 revolver. He stared at it.

"What's that for?"

"In case an early season bear comes after me."

"Sounds reasonable." Then he got quiet for what seemed like a long time. One of his radios 'talked' but it was a monitor channel so he ignored it

Finally, "Is that your truck down below?"

"The white one, yes Sir."

He seemed to like the word "Sir."

"Well, you shouldn't leave your bucket, shovel, and axe in the back, someone will steal them." "Right."

Then he got quiet again.

"You walked all the way up here?"

"Yes Sir."

"Why?"

Now, I was not offended by his questions. This was his forest to protect, and to know what was going on in it. Plus, he was polite and reasonably pleasant.

"Well, I thought by going for a walk up here I'd get lots of fresh air and good exercise."

Then, I realized he knew I wasn't up here just for a hike; he didn't want to hear it. But, on the other hand, FSE 7 didn't really have a clue as to what I was doing; it was way too early in the season for me to be a pot grower and no mushrooms were up. So, I decided to get right to the point.

I said words to this effect: "While I'm getting a little exercise I also look for big man-like tracks."

A small grin appeared on his weather beaten face. "Bigfoot."

I smiled. "Yes."

Then he said words to this effect: "You're probably one of the people they told me about."

"I really don't know."

"Well, you do spend quite a bit of time up here, don't you?"

"Probably more than most people."

He got quiet again. I was getting fidgety, enough is enough.

"You want a lift back to your truck?"

"No thanks, I'm good. It's all downhill from here."

I pointed to the snow where the plow quit plowing. This was the end for me. He smiled. Then he said something important. These are almost his exact words:

"If I was doing what you do, I'd do it right up there." He pointed to the northeast. "Do you know Anvil Lake?"

"Yes."

He didn't elaborate. He'd passed on enough information: "Well, I have to go." He pulled the lever for 4 wheel drive, gave me a little wave, rolled up his window saying "good luck" through the glass and drove up the snow covered road kicking snow from his tires.

For once I planned right. From where I talked to FSE 7, it was a pleasant three mile downhill walk, making it six for the day; not bad for me.

GPS at Hideaway Lake intersection: 45 07 08.06N at 3151' and at the Rd. 57-58 intersection: 45 04 42.77N 121 55 18.40W at 2210'.

When I got down to the truck I was a little relieved that my "stuff" was still there even though an old pickup was parked nearby, indicating the general honesty of most people up the hill. While I sipped hot coffee I made notes of my conversation with FSE 7 which I feel is among the most important in this book.

Notes: Anvil Lake is about 3 air miles northwest of Timothy Lake at 4024' at coordinates 45 08 14.03W 121 51 25.78W.

Anvil Lake has proved out as a good place for stimulating field research. While you can access Anvil Lake from the west via the signed spur road, plus a moderate hike about a mile from the top of Road 58, I think the best access to Anvil Lake is from the east on Spur Road 5820 and a mild dead reckoning hike through second growth timber.

Cougar #3: The Snow Sweeper

North of Timothy Lake: At night Cougar #3 (C3) watches Beelart.

From the time it happened, I thought of this encounter as "the snow sweeper." Cougar Encounter 3 happened the Saturday night before rifle deer season opening in October 2007. Since bambi-blasting is the end of Bigfooting until winter sets in at low altitudes, I took the opportunity to camp and look for tracks in spectacular mountain fall weather.

Functionally, I was alone; I had endless square miles to myself. Quite honestly, I almost wore myself out walking and walking in the fresh mountain air. Back at camp I only heated up a turkey sausage for dinner because I didn't want to attract a bear. Hungry bears are a damn nuisance when they come around in the dark.

Sleeping in the bed of my truck, about 1 in the morning I began to hear the supremely soft sound of snow falling on my dew shield. Some slipped on air currents to melt on my face. I simply eased my thick cocoon of blankets up and thought nothing of it. I was out in nature, not a four-star hotel surrounded by asphalt and automobiles.

Later, I awoke to an acrid, rotten meat smell, a very strong smell. I listened; probably a damn bear. I touched my 357 to make sure where it was if said bear started ripping up my ice chest, but heard nothing. I went back to sleep.

In the twilight time of predawn I woke up. There was, without exaggeration, one and a half to two inches of powder snow covering everything, including my dew shield. Well, I had to get up, so that was it for the night. Then, in the light of early morning, tracks in the fresh snow showed I'd had a nocturnal visitor.

A cougar had walked out of the woods, pausing directly alongside the left side of my truck bed, probably listening to me snore, walked over to the picnic table, looked that area over, and then the big cat, from the paw prints it was big, returned to the rear of the truck.

No more than six feet behind the open tailgate of my truck was a large somewhat flat rock. The cougar sat on that rock watching me sleep in the bed of my truck. His tail had swished off the snow on the back side of the rock kind of like a kid makes a snow angel.

From there, the cougar silently jumped away and walked down to the river, stopping to inspect my offerings, none of which appealed to him or her. Then, the cougar walked south on the river bench for maybe 100 feet before it slipped back into the forest.

A tip for field researchers: One method to "patrol" is to make ever larger circles, or something along those lines. After losing the cougar's tracks, I circled and about 150 yards south of camp found the cougar's tracks again where it ambled down a trail.

This ends our stories from the north side of Timothy Lake Road 57. Next are stories from the south side of Road 57.

District 2: Oak Grove Butte

Stories from Oak Grove Butte, Devils Ridge, and a single account from Peavine Mountain.

Ref. 48: Cliff finds a big track in 1957

Oak Grove Butte #1: Cliff Olson's first track find is designated Track Find 21 (TF21).

Please note this event occurred one year earlier than the 1958 Jerry Crew well-publicized track finds at Bluff Creek, California. Cliff had not yet heard or read the word "Bigfoot."

In September 1957 Cliff Olson joined Portland General Electric, working out of the Three Lynx maintenance shop. One of his first jobs was clearing brush around the microwave repeating towers on top of Oak Grove Butte. While Cliff was working up there he saw several deer, all does but knew that where there are does and rutting season is near, horny bucks also bound. That's "not abound, horny bucks, bound."

In October, Oregon rifle deer season opened. Cliff was stalking near the top of the Butte at the upper west end of a big clear cut because big buck deer love sloping clear cuts where they can watch over big patches of their territory. He said,

"I was finding lots of tracks with nothing in them."

Then he looked down at a spring seep in the duff and saw a huge man-like footprint. Unfortunately he was descending too fast to stop himself on the muddy soil. Olson's boot heel slid through the middle of the track destroying the arch of the print, but leaving the toes and heel intact.

The track was at least 16 inches long. The toes were well defined and another thing Cliff noticed straight-away was that the little toe was splayed out, not curled under like most shoe wearing humans.

Cliff said he marveled at the size of the track and the definition of the toes, which were large and somewhat square. Then it hit him. The place where the track was made was the only bare ground for hundreds of yards around. He said,

"It suddenly came to me that the track was a signal, a sign, saying 'This area is mine!'"

Later, Cliff speculated the beast was unhappy with loggers clear cutting its patch of trees and was doing about all it could to express its displeasure. Cliff also thinks the track might have been left as a territorial sign.

Ref. 49: Log Landing Night Stalker

Bigfoot Related Incident 29 (I29) is when a beast messes with logging gear at night near Road 5710.

For decades Millie Kiggins (Ref. 2) operated a barbershop in downtown Estacada, and in Estacada there actually is an "uptown" and a "downtown." Uptown is on the bench above the river valley; downtown is the ancient riverbed bordered by Highway 224.

There were two barbershops in town. Loggers tended to favor Millie's; that's the one Cliff patronized. "Big tracks" were sometimes discussed in Millie's barber shop so Cliff immediately recognized what he saw up on Oak Grove Butte. However, Cliff said when a stranger entered the shop, the subject was immediately dropped.

With new and improved roads up Oak Grove Butte, Forest Service timber sales made big clear cuts on the Butte. In those years loggers despised thinning operations, so the USFS complied with lumber boss wishes.

As more clear cuts were made, loggers began noticing more large "Wildman" tracks around landings and in "cat" (bulldozer) tracks. Soon, the "Wildman" tracks were subjects of discussion at the barber shop.

Then at night the local "Wildman" began moving things around on log landings, tipping over oil drums and the like. One of "his" favorite targets (it was assumed "it" was a he) was rummaging hinged top wood crates containing large handled tools, like firefighting rakes. "He" then carried the tools around, dropping, or tossing them helter-skelter like forest Frisbee's. There was never any evidence the night stalker stole or vandalized anything; or started a fire. This relatively benign activity we label Bigfoot Related Incident 29.

Ref. 50: On Rock Stacks and Broken Branches

Virtually all rock stacks in the mountains are man-made; to think otherwise is wishful. For example, Happening 8 (H8) is Cliff finding a really fun rock pyramid high on Oak Grove Butte. We also depreciate billions of broken branches as evidence of Sasquatch. However, Happening 9 (H9) is an exception when Steve finds of a series of very unusual tree breaks which might have indicated a territorial boundary.

Cliff's Rock Pyramid

In the forest, virtually all rock stacks are signal routes to campsites, hunting grounds, huckleberry fields; or primitive art. There are a few exceptions. In Ref. 70, a witness watched Sasquatch stack rocks while hunting ground squirrels. So, some stacked rocks are a result of Sasquatch hunter-gathering. Ref. 77 and Ref. 78 describe rock arrangements very similar to those in Ref. 70.

For some strange reason, fun examples of rock art seem to abound on Oak Grove Butte. In Sept. 1999 Cliff spied a very pleasing pyramid of small tightly stacked stones. Strangely, there was absolutely no evidence of recent human activity nearby such as cigarette butts, trash or shoe scuffs.

We circled quite a ways to finally determine the rocks were not local; they were transported from somewhere. After taking several photos I disassembled the pile, numbered each rock, and stored it in my garage.

Steve's Broken Trees

The only broken trees which may have been made by Bigfoot were found by Steve Kiley early one spring high on Indian Henry. That day, I walked high, and Steve walked across the east face of Thunder Mountain.

I didn't find anything, but did collect several nice specimens at the rock crystal vein which had fallen as the result of winter freezing and thawing. Back at the truck, when Steve walked out of stumble, tumble vine alders he told me he'd found something out of place and would tell me about it on the way home.

Generally, Steve pays little attention to broken branches; nevertheless, during his hike he found a series of strange tree breaks running along about half a mile of an old logging road, inaccessible to vehicles. They were made in regrowth trees about 3 inches in diameter and were evenly spaced about 50 yards apart. The breaks were all made on the topside of the road.

The breaks were consistent at about eight feet up the trunks; the tree tops were angled into the road like the hypotenuse of triangles. He said they were definitely not like other snow breaks along the road. Steve said since the needles were green and sap was in the wood the breaks were fresh.

Since the slope below was mostly open and the high-line of tree breaks easily seen, Steve thought the breaks might be Sasquatch territorial markers made by a powerful, tall adult male. That made a certain amount of sense because of where the road lies in relation to the Clackamas River valley, the Collawash, and East Mountain. Due to the oddity of Steve's find, we assign it Happening 9 (H9).

In general, the authors think these are more than enough words about signs and "forest art" in relation to Our Forest Pals. When you see stacked rocks and broken branches, think man-made or nature-made. One in a billion may be made by Sasquatch.

District 3: Accounts from Devils Ridge

Approx. GPS of the center of Devils Ridge: 45 02 34.59N 121 53 00.05W at 3905'

GPS coordinates of the Big Rock Quarry: 45 01 43.66N 121 52 33.23W at 3685'

Approx. GPS of Devils Spring: 45 03 13.81N 121 53 34.17W at 3135'

Google Earth Notes

1. Devils Spring is a long seep in the forest along the ridge's north base. Water is not visible on Google Earth. The spring flows NE under the road as Devils Creek, thence steeply down mountain to the Oak Grove Fork.

2. In 2013 a forest fire, probably caused by a cigarette, burnt a stand of tall, magnificent virgin silver fir at the south end of Devils Ridge. The approximate center of this supremely wasteful burn is clearly seen on Google Earth at GPS 45 01 42.73N 121 52 56.52W at 3727'.

Devils Ridge is one of our *secret* places. With several reportable events happening on it, a few words describing the terrain seem appropriate. Devils Ridge is a rectangular landmass that runs perpendicular on an almost exact north-to-south axis.

The top of the ridge is about 2 miles long and a half-mile wide. The western side of the ridge has a steep to moderate grade, but the whole east side has a very moderate grade. The top of Devils Ridge is basically flat, almost as if a prehistoric airport once operated there.

Devils Ridge seems to be an ancient granite monolith. In far distant times, the great northwest lava flows abutted the monolith. The steep grade along the southwest side of Devils Ridge was caused by water erosion wearing away volcanic basalt toward granite bedrock. However, in general, the geography of the ridge indicates little reason to warrant its name.

The top of the ridge is dry, but holds enough soil to root large old growth white fir trees, a tree which succeeds at high, dry altitudes. And, except for the top, animals have ready access to water around the ridge.

Devils Spring and Devils Spring Creek are at the north end. It also seems like animal tracks are always found along Cabin Creek which flows south between the ridge and Peavine Mountain. Pot Creek falls down the ridge's southwest slope. And, a bulldozed animal watering pond, similar to the one behind Oak Grove Butte, is located at the seep below the Big Rock Quarry.

Devils Ridge is one of our secret places for two reasons. **Reason 1** is that for a logged, and now partially burnt area, it is still a beautiful place to camp and hike. Hiking is easy and offers magnificent views from several points, points being a key word. The ridge abounds in rich mountain flora and fauna depending on altitude and exposure to the sun.

For some reason there seem to be few deer and no resident elk on the ridge itself. In the case of elk this is possibly because creeks for drinking water are down slope. However, under the Bonneville Administration Power Lines, there is seasonal evidence of heavy elk and deer browsing.

Reason no. 2 is the Big Rock Quarry makes for an exceptional place to dry camp, providing a stupendous view of Mt. Hood, both by day and moon-lit night. Plus, the glacial valley below provides an exceptional opportunity to listen to booming night hawks during their transonic dives while hunting large local insects, which will bite you with great vigor.

From 1998 until 2004 an uncomfortable feeling about Devils Ridge bothered me to the point I didn't camp there. From 2005 thru 2012 I camped on Devils Ridge a minimum of four nights each year, at first by myself, and then with others.

As I suspected, after only a few nights on the ridge, by use of long-tested attraction techniques, unusual things began to happen. Oddities in the "normal" sense are reported now; but, the events of one highly abnormal night are reported in *Area 52*.

Happenings include events like a urine circle left just outside our campfire light halo. Another time a large rock was thrown. There have been vocalizations not attributable to normal forest animals to telekinesis. So, in short, reports from Devils Ridge range from the usual to the bizarre and unexplainable.

Thom Powell clearing the road to Devil's Ridge. Photo by Joe Beelart.

A Beautiful Happening

Devils Ridge #1: Happening 8 (H8).

The first memorable event suitable to report in Area 3 South happened on a fine September day in 2009 before school began. Steve Kiley, his son Jamey, and I went camping at the Big Rock Quarry. Late in the afternoon, we drove downslope on Road 4661 to the upper reaches of Cabin Creek between the west slope of Peavine Mountain and east slope of Devils Ridge.

Steve and Jamey went exploring in the woods along the creek because what grows and happens along waterways is always interesting to youngsters, and naturalists. I stayed at the truck near where Cabin Creek crosses the road, making notes, watching sun shadows and trees, and then taking a good walk.

After my walk, for a rest I settled into my well-used director's chair. While I was taking in simple wonder all around me I heard a light sloshing noise coming from up the creek. Slowly, the noise came closer and closer; it was as if something was walking in the creek ... a deer?

Finally, about 30 feet from the road, the sloshing changed to splashing and got real. "What is going on?" Was a deer or coyote, or a bear rolling in the little creek?

Finally, in perfect view from where I was sitting on my much valued director's chair a grouse flew to the top of a stump. My view was partially obscured by leaves and branches, but was still clear, with the late afternoon sun providing superb backlighting.

The grouse spread its wings and beat. Droplets of water from its bath sprayed everywhere creating visions of prisms and rainbows in the sunlight. The deep rust and brighter burgundy colors of the magnificent bird's feathers shone through backlit sun.

It was a sight never to be seen again, by me or anyone; flying silver water droplets, late summer green, a miraculously big wing span full of earth tone colors, always changing, and the proud feather crowned head of a male ruffled grouse in the prime of his life.

It was in these moments I froze in my chair watching in wonder at the spectacular dance performed before me, a dance not to be excelled by graces in the coffee houses of Morocco.

And, it was at this very instant I remembered one of the sage bits of advice said to me by the great Bigfoot researcher René Dahinden during our only meeting: **"Always carry a camera."**

Of course on that day, in those circumstances, I had my camera at the ready; only it was on the console of my truck, far from my hands. When Steve and Jamey hiked out of the forest near the truck, Steve asked,

"See anything?"

"Just a grouse spreading its wings."

How else was I to describe an event of such wonder in words? While I had no photograph to share, I have the image of that wilderness cinema stored where it will never leave me. Therefore, I term the grouse dancing as Happening 8 (H8).

Devils Ridge #2: Happening 9 (H9)

The night of the Devils wind was so impressive I assign it Happening 11. I was camping on Devils Ridge when close to dark the wind began to pick up. So the truck would not get sand blasted, I moved it from the quarry and backed it facing east very close to trees on the west bench, hoping blowing branches would pass over me.

I took a walk to the west. I had to lean into the wind to walk. Grains of granite dust impacted me like tiny bullets, so fearing for my eyes, where I could, I walked backwards, leaning into the wind. That was not difficult. Returning with the wind at my back I felt almost like I was flying.

In the dark of night the wind rose. The windows in my truck pulsed. When I opened them, the truck sighed.

Outside, leaning against the wind with my kerchief taking the brunt of pellets of blowing granite sand, I again "walked" to the part of the road open to the far Pacific. My Brunton wind meter registered gusts over 100 kilometers per hour (60 mph).

In the virgin forest; great white fir trees fell, smashing into the earth. It was magic. Branches cracked and flew; huge feathery spears piercing the night sky.

At the height of the storm I could not hold my Brunton steady enough to gage the wind. Then, I experienced feelings ranging from wonder of nature to concern (not fear) for my well-being.

About 3 AM the wind began to abate, then, quite suddenly it died. Exhausted, elated at the experience, I fell into sleep. When the rising sun woke me the forest was quiet, but seemingly pulsing with new found energy.

I sucked down a little Mandarin orange fruit bowl. Then slowly, enjoyed granola and cold milk from one of the blue plastic bowls I favor. Tepid coffee from my old, dented Thermos completed a splendid breakfast.

With downed trees barricading the routes to Road 57, it took me an hour to find a way to Road 46. Finally, I was on my way home, filled with wonder about the Devils Wind, a force I had not felt since a typhoon in my Marine Corps days.

Ref. 51: The Night Watcher

Devils Ridge #3: Two film makers, a special guest, and Beelart make Track Find 22 (TF 22) and Bigfoot Related Incident 30 (I30). A warning rock is thrown at the filmmakers.

GPS of the seasonal creek bed: 45 01 48.47N 121 52 37.61W

On August 19, 2009 I led Missouri filmmaker Blake Eckard, his friend and production assistant Alec Jennings, and Blake's sister, Natasha Eckard, up to the Big Rock Quarry on Devils Ridge. Before this trip, Blake and Alec had camped with me up

the Clackamas and in northwest California. Although still novices, they had enough experience to qualify them as Honorary Sasquatchians.

Natasha proved a sport and a good campmate, so she also gained the status of *Honorary Sasquatchian*. In any event, since all three were in Portland, Blake and Alec wanted to show the mountains to Natasha and thought a night out with Mt. Hood as the central scenic feature might impress her. I think it did.

It was a pleasant afternoon. They went for a long walk down toward Cabin Creek while I set up camp and made ready a fire.

As the guest of honor, Natasha got to sleep under the stars in the bed of my truck. I made myself a gravel mattress which was just fine for a couple of reasons. First gravel moves when you turn in the night and, I also had my sleeping pad to soften things up. Second, gravel stays cool.

I brought along a couple of wiener sticks, so for supper we roasted big kosher franks. Later we watched shadows grow over the mountains; a sight that is always impressively happy, and quietly talked and laughed around a small fire.

At 11 PM I suggested we start on my usual night walk which we planned earlier. It was a very simple plan; leave the quarry and walk about a third of a mile on Road 5731 to Spur Road 017 which runs north–south along the spine of Devils Ridge.

At that point, the plan was they would walk north on the spur road, which is covered with bright rock dust, to allow the three, and especially Natasha, to absorb the vistas of a mountain night in their own manner.

I planned my walk to follow the main road around the 90° curve, explore toward the power lines and check out the night view to the west. If it was a good view, I planned to lead my guests to it.

Just in case, I gave Alec a "I'm lost, come find me whistle;" plus I gave each of them a small "just in case" flashlight, but as usual, the procedure was to walk under Zodiac glow and the faint light of a moon far from rising.

Things went well getting to the intersection, there was plenty of light, heck, I could even see down the spine of the west road where it was covered by tree shadow. When we got to the intersection, I pointed for them to follow the spur road and said words to this effect:

"OK, I'm going this way. If you really, really need to get me back use the whistle. If you want, feel free to hike back to camp.

I'll be gone for at least half an hour, maybe more."

I wasn't too worried about them because none of the three were of the nervous persuasion. Then, into the gloom, I happily hiked. During my walk back I rounded the 90° curve and abruptly stopped. At the intersection, on the road, back lit by a crescent moon, I saw a clump of dark figures.

Hmm, I thought, Bigfoots, hardly. As I walked closer I saw against the light gravel of the road that the clump of figures was my Honorary Sasquatchians.

Don't make IT MAD!

As I got closer, my first clue something was going on was when I heard one of them loudly whispering words to this effect: "Don't say anything, don't flash your light. Joe's right there! I see him. Don't make *IT MAD!*"

IT ... Mad? What's going on? Then, I thought of Blake's movie making in which forest monsters are *IT* ... creatures somewhere between the real and imagined. At that thought, I had to smile. Fortunately, there was not a black lagoon between Estacada and Detroit, at least not that I knew about, an inter-dimensional portal maybe, but not a black lagoon.

When I got to the adventurers, one of them, and then all of them excitedly began whispering words to this effect: *"It's in there!"* Like out of a 30s movie comedy scene, they simultaneously pointed toward the 30' trees on the south side of the road.

Now, I have spent a lot of time wandering the south side of that road, it covers quite a big area at the end of Devils Ridge, so I knew there were lots of old dozer trails and remains of logging roads. It is easy traveling and occasionally quite pretty when stumbling on to a view of Big Bottom or Mt. Jefferson or places south. But never have I seen a Bigfoot track there.

As I was walking back to my friends I heard a little movement in the trees, I thought something was in the trees on the south side of the road, probably a curious deer or two. I whispered, "Is it a deer?"

"No, no! It's on two legs and it's been watching us since you left."

"You didn't walk down the north road?"

Again, "No!" No!" I was astonished. They had stood at the intersection for about 45 minutes. Then came whispered words which greatly amused me .... We've been waiting for you to come back so we could warn you!"

Well, at least now I felt safer with the Bigfoot Protective Corps covering my back. And, the thought crossed my mind that the Protective Corps had plenty of time, about 40 minutes; to let their imaginations cook up a story of a wild monster lurking in the trees only feet from them, ready to pounce!

So I whispered something to the effect we should probably hike on back to camp, build up the fire, and figure out what was happening. I got no arguments whatsoever from my companions. Then I suggested they go ahead of me by at least 100 yards.

"Can you 'see' your way by yourselves?"

"Yes, yes, yes."

So I walked a few yards with them to make sure they were on track and I stopped, silently leaning on my hiking stick "hiding" in dark shadows; listening.

To my astonishment, behind me, a bipedal creature crossed the intersection and entered the trees on the north side of the road. Then, it proceeded to quietly follow the Bigfoot Protective Corps. Whatever it was, I could not see it, but I could hear it moving, and it was stepping carefully so as not to be heard.

I let the creature get ahead of me. Then, using every bit of concentration I could muster, I began to take silent steps, mainly by carefully placing my footsteps on the road shoulder which was primarily dirt. Continuously I watched for sticks in the ditch because I didn't want to break one.

Finally, after about a hundred yards, the creature turned north into a dry seasonal creek bed and left us. I stopped some minutes to listen for its return which never came. Then I speedily hiked down to camp where the others had already built up the fire to the point it lit half the quarry. Quietly, they were excitedly talking.

They were not astounded to hear the news about their night follower; after all, they'd been listening to it in the trees for over 30 minutes before I returned to the intersection. By then, they were convinced one of Our Barefoot Friends was watching them.

One of them said while they waited for me that a rock impacted the ground in the trees like a hard thrown baseball. This they took as some sort of warning signal. To myself, I silently agreed. The rock probably meant, "Get the hell out of my forest."

Sleeping Well

Surprisingly, after going to the blankets sometime after 1 AM we all slept well. Everyone was up early and cheerful as I made coffee and a hot breakfast. After breakfast, we explored the area of the previous night's events. Where the creature walked past me in the forest paralleling the road was another of the well-used trails where a man can walk with little impediment, but that has no elk or deer tracks on it. It was a true Devils Trail.

We found impressions but no clear foot prints in the forest duff where the creature shuffled while watching Blake, Natasha, and Alec. We didn't find the rock that was supposedly thrown, but the next weekend I went back and found the fresh impact of the clean, ball shaped rock, and the rock about 100 feet away from where we had searched. It weighs about eight pounds and is in my garage. The angle of impact indicated it was thrown from the area near the intersection.

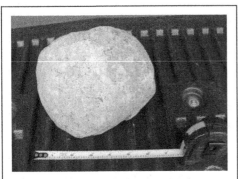

Rock thrown. Photo by Joe Beelart.

On a last note, I must say I thoroughly enjoyed the company of my friends from Missouri, although Natasha now resides and works in Washington, D.C. She said she'd have some real stories to tell when she got back. What will Washington D.C folks think of her stories from "out West?"

Natasha has a degree in mathematics from the University of Missouri and, she's an excellent estimator of distance in the mountains. When I pointed out Government Camp lights on the shoulder of Mt. Hood I said they were about 30 miles away, Natasha gently corrected me. "That's only about 15."

I let it slide, how could a city girl be right and me, the great Bigfoot researcher wrong? When I checked it on Google Earth the distance from where we were camped to Government Camp was 16 air miles. Oh well...

I suspect Natasha's cool demeanor contributed to her calm, simple reporting of the night's events. Of course, Blake and Alec's renditions had the wonderfully refreshing perspective of brave young men confronting a fierce wilderness challenge and overcoming it, albeit a challenge they couldn't see.

Ref. 52: A Devil on the Rim

Devils Ridge #4: In August 2010 Jake 18 (J18) has Sighting 18 (S18).

Sighting 18 happened to a long-term associate, and a Sasquatchian, who does not want to be named, so here he is identified here as Jake 18. Jake 18 went up to Devils Ridge to spend a night alone. His story of that night was very simple. It reflects in many ways the events of some nights I spent in the Big Rock Quarry.

J18 had a pleasant evening and did not drink alcohol or smoke any weed. He planned on sleeping in his vehicle. Not wanting the rising sun in his face, he turned his SUV so it pointed west toward the drilling bench or, the shelf where rock was not yet dynamited to begin the process of crushing rock to gravel. At the Big Rock Quarry, the bench is about 40 feet high.

About dawn J18 reported he got restless and was rolling and turning in his sleeping bag. About 8 AM he woke up. He reported that for some reason he became keenly awake as soon as he opened his eyes.

On the bench, looking down at his SUV was a tall, wide dark figure which we identify as Sighting 18.

Even though it faced the sun, the figure was far enough away so he could not make out facial characteristics, but it was definitely man-like and was looking *at* him. As soon as he rose in his seat, the figure turned and disappeared. Due to the angle of observation, J18 did not see it walk, he said it just disappeared.

When J18 climbed to the bench to investigate, he did not see any clear imprints as the area is covered with gravel. There were random depressions in the gravel going from the bench to the forest. The forest duff also showed imprints of a biped walking west, but no clear tracks.

When I interviewed Jake 18, he was emphatic the figure was not an elk or deer. Later when I went up to the quarry with him and walked the route, I found the sighting was only about 150 yards from where the "IT" creature watched Blake, Alec, and Natasha in Ref. 51.

Ref. 53: The Devils Ridge Offering Incident

Devils Ridge #5: Bigfoot related Incident 31 (I31) and Track Find 23 (TF23) happen to Beelart.

Notes on several different offerings at the Devils Ridge Big Rock Quarry are combined in this report as Incident 31 and Track Find 23 (TF23). From 2008 to 2011 I have camped out at the Big Rock Quarry at least four nights a summer with my high being seven nights in 2009. Almost every night I've set out offerings ranging from salted in-shell peanuts suspended in large paper grocery bags, to apples and other vegetables, to pie slices and tarts.

Some offerings are made on thick plastic dinner plates, others in aluminum

pans, or in the case of most apples, simply set on elevated stumps or in limb crotches.

All offerings are set off the ground, either on a pile of rocks, on a log, on a boulder or a stump. Offerings are always placed at least 100 yards from the campsite, and generally much further.

The locations I've used most are on the bench near the forest on the west side of the quarry and in a gravel storage area just northeast of the quarry. Other locations I've repeatedly used are in the area near the intersection of Road 5731 and Spur 017 just northwest of the quarry, behind the big pile of gravel on the southwest side of the quarry; and, on old logs below and east of the quarry on Spur Road 130. Occasionally I've left offerings in crevices on big rocks up-slope on the south center of the quarry.

In total, during four summers, I set out about 60 offerings in the area surrounding the Big Rock Quarry. Amazingly enough, at least 20 offerings were rewarded with either tracks, small gifts, or careful treatment of the containers.

David Mann inspecting the prior night's offering plate. Photo by Joe Beelart.

During the summer of 2008, one of our Forest Friends was especially considerate when we put out pie in pie plates. It would generally place the empty plate on top of the paper towel originally covering the offering. In 2009 we tried the "experiment" again, intending to take finger prints. During several offerings, nothing even touched the pies. Very odd indeed.

In one case, my wife camped with me overnight at the high rock quarry. We camped up on the bench next to the tree line. We slept in the back of the truck open to the sky. In the morning there were Bigfoot tracks around the truck. The beast watched us sleep in the night.

Glass pie plate with only a few crumbs left. Paper towel covering the offering tucked under the plate. Photo by Joe Beelart.

I'm sure it thought my wife smelled a lot better than I did, plus I had her laughing at the fire, and I imagine Our Barefoot Friends liked that too.

The tracks around the truck bothered my wife a good deal for two reasons. First, here was physical proof that the creatures existed, something she seriously doubted. Second, it made her uncomfortable to think about one of the Forest People watching her sleep. However, she was pleased that they took her carefully prepared offerings, so she wanted to go back again, and we have.

A Small Lesson from 18 Tracks

Perhaps the most important aspect of the tracks around our truck came from the thin layer of soft dirt in the quarry where the creature left the forest to walk up to the truck. This point was a little to the southwest and below us, behind the big pile of crushed rock. Our Forest Pal left a series of 18 reasonably distinct tracks in the

One of 18 tracks. Notice the heel impact, the flex of the two-part foot and the toe push off. Photo by Sharon Beelart.

shallow dirt from where it left the forest and approached the truck.

Unknown to me, my wife secretly set out special offerings behind the pile of crushed rock. (I can imagine her smile and look of anticipation while she was doing it.) The Sasquatch took her "secret" offerings, again leaving the plates as they were! But getting back to the tracks; the foot prints were parallel, not slightly crow footed as humans make.

This is why I think that track line is an important example of how Bigfoot walks. Stand up. Place your feet parallel. Notice how your knees come together? Notice the

change of pressure in your lower back? Now imagine walking that way.

Take a few steps keeping your feet parallel. Now do one other thing. Make a few parallel steps raising your feet up and putting them down. Do not "drag" them or drop your toes. This is how I think our

Track line in bright morning sun glare. Photo by Sharon Beelart.

barefoot friends walk in the forest without tripping and without having to continually watch where they are stepping. My conclusion is they have different bone geometry than humans; but it will take a person with more education in anatomy than me to explain such things.

I am disappointed to report, that to date, no fingerprints have been obtained from offering vessels. Your authors cannot figure out the reason. For instance, I bought six economical, relatively heavy, hard plastic white dinner plates at a discount retailer.

The plates are smooth and a finger print expert said they should pick up prints well. We often use these plates for offerings. Before placing them in the wild we handle them with latex gloves, wash them in soapy water, wipe them dry, and store them one-each in clean plastic bags.

In the field, they are again handled with latex gloves and returned home dirty in clean plastic bags (not the ones we take them up in). In the forest, when these plates are set out after dark, they are turned upside down and empty, within one to two feet, if not exactly where they were originally placed.

Upon first seeing this, Cliff offered the opinion that the creatures were not used to eating off of plates, so they simply turned them over to put the content of the plate onto their other hand. I think Cliff's idea is the most reasonable explanation, but why no fingerprints on the plates?

When bears get to an offering plate they knock them around half way back to Portland and chew on them to get the last of the good stuff. Coyotes chase plates a long way, licking them as they go. Raccoons are gentler on the plates, but still lick the plates clean and move them several feet away. There are no raccoons at the Big Rock Quarry; no nearby water. Chipmunks are somewhat rare in the area, but when they come in, they can't turn a plate upside down.

Ref. 54: Commentary: The Economy of Bigfooting

Since my wife is much attuned to the money I spend on my hobbies, Bigfooting being one of them, this is a good place to address the issue in brief. It costs money to drive the Oregon Bigfoot Highway, so make good plans. Like any hobby or profession, you should understand both the short term and long term costs, to minimize "surprises" and frustration.

First, let's look at the basic issues involved. People are generally surprised, even after being told, to find the drive from Oregon City to the Big Rock Quarry takes over two hours, meaning in 2014 dollars, it takes about $60 worth of gas to make the round trip in a truck or SUV.

A single night out in a good area such as this one generally costs a minimum of an additional $40 in food and supplies. The cost of gas makes spending multiple nights advisable whenever possible. Also, since I'm way over 30, my younger days when a pillow, a half case of beer, and a fishing rod were ample supplies for a night out are long gone.

In short, dollars and days available are the factors in our "research," time. And that is before we start talking about technological devices to aid in our research.

Once I was earnestly approached to conduct a Bigfoot research fund raising effort. The project planned to raise ten million dollars. In the preliminary budget I quickly found a hole in the numbers which was explained as compensation for executive leadership.

Sadly, I concluded this was a plan to make money for an individual, not a research project. I declined. Unfortunately, there are spoilers in every walk of life, even in the crazy pursuit of Bigfoot. It is no wonder that some people, including potential financial backers, think Bigfooters are "nuts."

I can go on ... and on. Well, that's enough on money matters for now. I've spent money on my outdoor activities including Bigfooting for decades and do not regret one penny, but I have always been mindful of my resources. It's time to move on to a report of a really fun outing with three "out-of-towners," which with the

A Saga of Intrepid Explorers & Bears

Devils Ridge #6: Above Devils Springs: Jakes 19, 20, and 21: Happening 10 (H10).

The following is a tale of intrepid explorers and bears. It took place on the far northeast crest of Devils Ridge above Devils Creek.

One of the most wonderful moments I've had in the mountains was near the center of the Devils Springs while standing in a glade of yellow flowers in full bloom. Hundreds of small lightly buzzing bees darted about harvesting nectar. It was truly a moment from the poet's "bee loud glade."

This is also one of those places in the forest that has plentiful water and browse, but few signs of deer. However, there is the occasional bear in the vicinity spending part of its beary life searching for bee honey, which leads to our story.

Once, during one of Ray Crowe's Western Bigfoot Society Portland conferences, I took three out-of-town Bigfooters up the hill. We walked in to the ridge above Devils Creek. Two of the conference attendees were from Washington, D.C. or thereabouts. One was from the southern California megalopolis. As I remember, none had experienced northwest forests. All were 40 years or older.

One thing I do when I take new people to the mountains is make them sit still and say nothing for 15 minutes. I position them some distance apart for privacy and where they cannot make eye contact. For many people it is really quite a test, even though I allow them to rise if they must.

It was a wonderful summer day; the air was warm, clean and fresh; the sun was shining, but not directly on us. My new

lunch I supplied, cost me $100 for the day trip.

friends sat in the woods; I found a spot to watch and make sure no one wandered off.

At the end of our contemplation time, we gathered to drink water and compare notes. One fellow was simply awed by the experience. It turned out that his time in the woods was only camping a few times in the Boy Scouts. Another man, one from Washington, D.C. surprised me.

"You said we were alone out here, but I can hear traffic on a road down there." Well, there was a logging road below us, but I hadn't heard a thing. The first fellow agreed with the second. "There's traffic down there, I heard it too."

What a predicament! I knew full well a truck hadn't traveled the gravel road, I would have heard it. What was this about? I was sincerely puzzled.

So I thought, and thought. My standing as a woodsman in the last great hunt was on the line - in my imagination at least. I listened, I walked a few steps and listened some more. I had an audience; every eye was intently watching my every move. The pressure was on, well just a little, as I looked around and up. Finally, I pointed to the tops of the trees.

"By any chance, is that is what you heard?"

Sure enough, a light breeze through the tree tops misguided their thoughts. We all smiled. It was a tiny thing. I was very pleased they had paid close attention to their surroundings.

The third fellow said that from where he sat he heard an animal moving around down slope from him. So after cautioning everyone to stay quiet, we all hiked a little way around the bluff to where he sat.

Sure enough, downslope a sow bear was tearing up a tree trunk and grunting up a storm in the pleasure of her success finding grubs or honey. I say "her" because the plaintive calls of a cub rose too. I motioned everyone to stand still and remain quiet.

We listened. It was fun. Finally one of the fellows motioned we should gather round him. He excitedly whispered words to this effect: "Let's go down there for a look!"

Well reader, let me tell you, my head rose at that suggestion. The others were figuratively stomping, ready for a downhill charge. The suggestion was wonderful! See a real bear in the wild! What a story that would make! What an adventure!

Well, this was one of the few times in my life when I could actually grasp a situation and convey my judgment in few words. I said, "I'm not going down there, and I suggest you don't either."

Well, these were smart men and the message came out clear; all three, almost in military unison, stepped back from the precipice, a wise choice. Anyway, I wouldn't have let them go down. Disturbing a bear sow with a cub is calling for a mauling and I didn't want to have to contend with that.

The combination of a "road in the tree tops'" and hearing the sow bear and her cub, we label as Happening 10 (H10) for truly, they were two memorable events during a fine day up the hill. For a couple of years, as the story circulated around the Bigfoot community, I heard differing versions of this adventure. In one, I was a bit surprised to learn huge grizzly bears inhabit the Oregon Cascades and I was afraid of them, which I would be, if grizzlies lived here.

District 4: Peavine Mountain

Peavine Mountain is south of Road 57 at about mile 10. Like the lake plateau north of Road 57, Peavine Mountain has not been the focus of your Sasquatchians; the area is ripe for research. Thus I only have brief notes about this large area.

Crest of Peavine Mountain: 45 00 50.03N 121 50 06.88W at 4817′

Approx. GPS of Sheep Spring, Rock Spring and Peavine Springs: 45 01 46.66N 121 49 33.05W at ~4150′

Road 4661 climbs along the west side of Peavine Mountain. Spur Road 140 crosses the north end of Peavine west to east, but beware: Spur 140 is impassable with cars and small SUVs. Peavine Mountain's crest road, Spur Road 350 is also impassable with small vehicles. So, if you don't have a big 4x4, bring water and a trekking staff.

In the South Mt. Hood National Forest, Peavine Mountain is as wonderful a place as Devils Ridge, only much larger and more difficult to wander. At its peak of 4,817 feet, Peavine is about 500 feet higher than Devils Ridge, its neighbor to the west. Like Devils Ridge, Peavine Mountain is a loaf type mountain with a generally flat top sloping gently south to north.

A good portion of the relatively flat top of Peavine Mountain was clear cut in the late 1980s and due to elevation and weather conditions as of 2014 regrowth has been slow. So, there remains an expansive view of the area from the top.

Ref. 55: Bigfoot watches a Sasquatchian sleep

Peavine Mountain: Sighting 19 (S19): Bigfoot Related Incident 32 (I32): Track Find 24 (TF 24): Mann and Beelart have a night encounter at Cabin Creek.

This incident and sighting happened at a place we call Cabin Creek camp. This classic, picturesque, tree covered camp site is immediately north of the intersection of Forest Service Roads 4660 and 4661, which in turn is about six miles above Road 46 at the north end of Big Bottom. GPS coordinates are: 45 00 32.99N 121 52 06.42W at 3018'.

At the time of Incident 32 and Sighting 19, David Mann was about 65 years old and one of our most technically educated Sasquatchians. As noted in the profiles, David is a highly skilled outdoorsman with years of Bigfooting experience throughout the United States.

I had already toured and camped with David several times in the Clackamas system. When I showed him Devils Ridge, David took a special liking to the whole area and wanted to camp several nights up there. He said he felt "their" presence, and what was more, "they" were not unfriendly, which when the word applies to Sasquatches, means something much different from friendly.

In early August 2009, David and I drove to the Cabin Creek campsite. When we arrived, David immediately declared the site one of the best he had ever seen in all his wanderings, and he is a true wanderer. Tall virgin fir trees provide a wonderful natural canopy. Cabin Creek babbles quietly along the east side of the site.

Across the road to the west is a cleared area under trees used by horse campers. By fall, this area is covered with straw and dried horse apples. David immediately, and with subdued excitement, pointed out the horse camp. David said that Bigfoot is attracted to horses and having the horse camp across the road was a very good sign.

David, who is fluent in Russian, courtesy the U.S. Army, reads Russian books in that language. He said he was especially impressed with Russian researchers' descriptions of horse and Russian Bigfoot (Almasty) connections. Since David has visited Russia, later in the evening he talked with some authority about the Almasty and its similarities to our Sasquatch.

We made up a nice camp. I set up my highly experienced camp table, director's chairs, and piled wood around the substantial rock fire ring. I parked my truck so the bed looked toward the road and pitched my sleeping bag, pillow, and blankets. In a glade of trees, near the whispering creek, David carefully prepared an open bed on fresh cut boughs.

After about an hour at the camp, David said he was having a premonition, a feeling to prepare for some event. He did not know what, but he was sure something was going to happen during the night. But night was still a ways off. We had hiking to do. When we got back, it was time for supper.

After supper while we were sitting around the fire, the oddest thing happened. About 8:30 David began to get restless and groggy. His speech became hesitant, not slurred, but hesitant, as if he couldn't put together full sentences or thoughts. There was no reason for it. David was in excellent health, had imbibed little alcohol and, he doesn't smoke, if you can figure what I mean.

I finally asked David, "Are you OK?" He took a minute to answer. He looked at me with slightly glazed eyes. He acted as if he didn't want to say words, but finally, he did.

"When they are near, they sometimes do this to me. I get ... very tired and a little confused."

Shortly, David silently rose from his chair, walked directly from the fire to his bed roll and crawled in. I checked my watch: 9 PM. From my experiences camping with David, it was most unusual for him to go to sleep that early in the woods. He enjoys the night.

This was also the only time where he didn't say "goodnight" to me, or something like "Be sure to have the coffee perked when I get up." For our purposes, since there was more of it to come, we call David's unusual behavior Bigfoot Related Incident 32.

So, I hung out until midnight. Nothing happened; it was a very silent night except for the low gurgling of the creek which, since it is spring fed, runs about the same most of the year. I went for a pleasant night walk. The moon was rising low in the southeast, casting long shadows.

A Face in Moonlight

I turned in and slipped into a sound sleep. At about 2:15 AM, I awoke to the sound of light steps near the fire ring. Why I woke up I don't know. Maybe something left over from my Marine Corps days, who knows?

The steps were carefully, slowly being made on forest duff which thickly covers the whole campground. I soon realized they were coming from a heavy biped since the duff was crushing under its weight. Also, from the one-two pace, I knew our intruder was not a big bear with four paws.

It walked over to where David was sleeping and stood there a very long time. I was now wide awake. I checked my watch which I habitually lay beside my bed roll along with a water bottle and a flashlight.

For some reason I did not feel threatened, and I did not feel David was in danger. Yet, I felt my 357, loaded with Alaska brown bear cartridges, but did not unsnap the holster tab. That would make noise.

The moon was now high, but in the south, so light filtered through the trees over my head. I made every effort to not move, other than to lightly adjust myself in my bed roll. I was especially careful to not make the truck creak with my movements. 2:30 became 2:45 on my digital watch. For some reason I thought, "Don't turn on the light."

I decided the creature had either evaporated into the ethers, or was very patient in its observations of Mann, when I heard a step, or to be more precise, a turning step. Slowly, the steps came toward my truck which was about 50 feet from where David was sleeping on the ground. The steps stopped on the lower left side of my pickup just past the end of the bed. The creature was close.

I tried to adjust my eyes to the light, but not hold them in one place too long for two reasons. The reason is at night, eyes don't focus well if fixed on one spot. That's why if you stare at one point in the stars, they begin moving around; the stars are not moving at all, but your brain is making them move trying to fix on an invisible point in infinity with no background references.

Well, on the ground something similar happens if you fix your eyes. Try it some night in your backyard. I'm sure that's why novices see things moving, especially shrubs and small trees which morph in their brains into lurking Sasquatches.

As I let my eyes focus for a moment here and there, I saw the upper body of a big human like form standing near my pickup bed, as in probably 3 to 5 feet near. With a 7 foot pickup bed, which is the length in my 2000 Tundra, it meant the form was about 12, maybe 15 feet at most, away from where my head lay in the bed. Since the moon was in the southeast and I was looking southwest, in the moonlight, I saw my watcher very clearly.

For the purposes of this book, let's label this Sighting 19 (S19). All is black and white and gray at night. This face was dark, leathery looking, long and rectangular. The top of the head was not pointed. I couldn't see ears, although there was a hint of one on the moon side. In any event, the ear didn't seem large.

Reflecting moonlight, the man-beast had large eyes which were intently watching me. Its nose seemed long, but not wide. The lips were thin, but the mouth seemed, in proportion, about human width, but straighter.

To my surprise, the face seemed clear of whiskers or stubble. The face had a weathered, leathery look, like that of an old man after a long outdoor life. While I couldn't see it clearly, the hair on its head was short. The creature was dry, so its body hair was dull. I was also surprised ... our night visitor did not smell.

I was not afraid, so I do not exaggerate when I say the creature stood still for many minutes, only slightly turning its head when it noticed my eyes resting on its face too long. Then, it was gone, striding – without any pretense of being quiet – southeast down Road 4660 toward Peavine Mountain, down the same road I used for my night walk.

Did it follow me back on my night walk? Had it watched us from the slope on the west, or from the little ridgeline that bordered the east side of our camp?

It's over!

At no time did I feel endangered. There was no reason to make a sudden move, or to pull my 357 magnum revolver from the holster, a holster I left snapped even as the beast walked away. What I did feel was something like what happens when a dog looks hard at you wanting to tell you something, only at a much higher level.

And I felt there was a try to peacefully intrude into my thoughts, nothing malicious at all, just an entry to maybe "talk." I didn't know what that was all about then, and after much reflection on the issue, still don't know.

After the creature left, I was unnerved; I got up and relieved myself. Then I walked near David who was still soundly sleeping. I watched him a short while. He didn't move and he didn't talk in his sleep.

On my digital watch it was almost 3:10 AM. I walked over to the fire ring and sat in my chair. As it should be the dead fire made no heat so I soon chilled in the mountain air. I went back to bed and slept until about 6:30 when morning was well lit.

I walked the road a ways, saw scuff marks, but decided not to track the hominid's path, to look for where it stepped into the forest. Let it have its privacy. So, I drank steaming cups of coffee and ate a croissant or two spread with berry jam Sharon made from hand-picked berries, many picked by me.

Amazingly, David didn't roll out until almost 8 AM. He stayed in his roll for 11 hours. Even though he appeared to sleep soundly, unlike me, David reported a horrible night's sleep. He said he had long surrealist dreams which he had no way to describe. Over coffee David said he didn't hear anything in the night. He also said he didn't remember waking up all night long.

Where the creature stood to study David was clear; it was about five feet from his bed. The duff there was heavily compacted. Under the duff were imprints of toes and the ball of the foot. We label this and other tracks it left in the duff around camp as Track Find 24.

David looked terrible. I told him to rest by the fire and I'd cook us up a nice breakfast. After peaches, a lot more coffee, and a big bacon sandwich, he seemed to perk up. Later I told David what I had heard and saw during the night. He silently listened. Sometime during our mostly silent drive home David summarily announced he would never camp at Cabin Creek again.

Places of the Ancients

West of Peavine Mountain: the *Green Cathedral* and Summer Solstice Spear of Light: Happening 11 (H11): Powell & Beelart: Forest Service Employee 8 (FSE 8).

This is one of the places where we decided not to list GPS coordinates.

However, the location of this segment lies somewhat near the northwest slope of Peavine Mountain. Persons using USGS 1:24,000−40′ topographical maps of that area, in collaboration with solstice tables adjusted for about 10,000 years to graph a declination line in the northwest, may find the locations after a good deal of physical effort.

Thom Powell found the *green cathedral*. After several hikes in to the location, he began to see the trappings of an ancient place of gathering. He said after times there, the vine-hung site began to leave him with a feeling of spirituality, of perhaps ancient worship.

Visiting the site with Thom, I found the *green cathedral* has what seems to be a flat prepared rectangular floor of about 100 x 150 feet if not larger. The floor appears to be built in three small increments of elevation, possibly to give people a line of sight to what now is an elevated, barren stage at the south end.

There is much more to the *green cathedral* than the words we allow here. Suffice it to say, this prehistoric site, in our opinion, needs professional archaeological investigation and has been reported to the USFS archeologist.

The Solstice Spear of Light

It was serendipitous; on June 20th, 2008, I decided to go up and watch the setting sun at Solstice. First I decided to hike in to Thom's *green cathedral*. At the *cathedral* I perceived an ancient faint trail going up the hill. Following it, I found myself on the hillcrest.

Not wanting to leave my gear and truck in the open below, I hiked back down and drove up and around the plateau to where my map indicated a place where I could park and then hike to the northwest crest. My driving and hiking took almost three hours; the distances involved are not short.

When I got to the crest and followed it out to the point, the sun was already low. Below me shadows vanished on the northwest face of the hill. Again, in that light, the trail I originally hiked up now seemed to be an ancient roadway leading downslope toward the cathedral.

As the sun fell lower, a point to my left became the obvious vantage place. The point was stone, flat, and large enough for one, or maybe two, men to comfortably stand. It also appeared to bear the signs of creation by ancient hands.

One of several ancient stone works. Photo by Joe Beelart

From this place, as the sun set, two truly amazing events happened. It was difficult to believe what I saw. First, the sun dropped into a "V" in a far mountain ridge. After the sun set in the "V" came the spectacle. For seconds a grand slash of red and yellow light burst from the "V" rocketing into the heavens!

I hiked out. I slept, but dreams of the marvel were with me in the night. The next morning, I hiked back in. My investigation of the nearby area showed what may be an ancient burial ground and very ancient rock works, hidden for the most part by forest duff and growth, but still discernible after careful scrutiny. I list these finds and the follow up with a Forest Service archeologist as Happening 11.

I notified the Forest Service archeologist at Mt. Hood headquarters about the possible ancient stonework. We list her as Forest Service Employee 8 (FSE 8). Some months later she called me and asked me to not show the place to anyone but those I deemed most necessary to see it. She said the site might be 10,000 or more years old.

This ends reports from Area 3.

Black bear yearling near Timothy Lake. Photo by Richard W. Johnson. Courtesy of Judy Johnson.

Notice the size of the paws with protruding claws. Compare these to the track photograph in Ref. 44 (Cliff finds 82 tracks), and to the bear paws in Cliff Barackman's photographs in Ref.22.

Timothy Lake dam bunger valve at full open. The valve controls water level in the Oak Fork. Photo by Sharon Beelart.

Collawash River, low water in September. Photo by Sharon Beelart.

Area 4: The Collawash River Basin

Cliff Olson ... "One word describes the Collawash...'*Rugged.*"

Another word often used by first time visitors to the Collawash River drainage is "primitive." Indeed, as researchers first explore, or are introduced to this area, they report a feeling of going back in time, to a time when man had not yet intruded on this quarter of Nature's grandeur, time when trees were new to the rocks below, a time when perhaps, just perhaps, there were beings on earth we do not now know.

Bigfoot in the Collawash

The Collawash drainage offers a great deal to our forest friends. In addition to being remote, rugged, and protected over much of the system, the river provides a substantial food source from significant salmon and steelhead runs throughout the year. A number of large meadows and swampy areas offer browse for deer and elk which to some degree are probable Bigfoot food. These wet, open spaces also offer good places for growing another favored Bigfoot food, root plants.

Geographic Territories within the Collawash Drainage

The Collawash drainage is roughly a 12 mile square lying west of the Clackamas River. It is one of the four major tributaries of the Clackamas River with the others being the North Fork, South Fork, and Oak Grove Fork, each of which has been previously discussed.

The East, or Main Fork, of the Collawash runs south to north along high steep cliffs and is designated a *Wild and Scenic Waterway*. The Hot Springs Fork originates high above Bagby Hot Springs and flows west to east along the north side of the square.

A mountain ridge, or "spine," separates the west side of the Collawash drainage from the east. This "spine" is anchored by Dickey Peaks. South of Dickey Peaks, Bull of the Woods Wilderness (refer to map of Area 6) contains the upper reaches and basins of the Collawash drainage and holds one of the few major stands of unlogged, big virgin timber remaining in Oregon.

The name "Bull of the Woods" is a reference to a big, tough, logging crew foreman. Big and tough were key words when many logging operations operated out of remote logging camps where productivity and peace among the crew had to be maintained.

Natural territorial barriers abound and protect the Collawash. On the east side of the main fork, steep cliffs run for several miles. These cliffs are about 1,500 feet high in only ½ mile of slope, thereby establishing a natural fortress wall, a boundary for family groups. For an example, on Google Earth, check the Collawash cliff line just west of Mt. Lowe (enter Mt. Lowe, Clackamas, Oregon and it will come up).

On the north side of the Collawash, high mountains, specifically Thunder Mountain and East Mountain make a natural boundary line with Area 1. These mountains will also come up on Google Earth. Look for Skookum Lake just north of the crest of Thunder Mountain. In 1987

Sasquatchian Steve Lindsey took a series of footprint casts near Skookum Lake. The west boundary of the Collawash is a high ridge line of mountains which separate the Collawash from the Molalla River and Willamette Valley beyond.

The Collawash Palisades

One of Oregon's first environmental battlegrounds

The first miles of Road 63 are buttressed by impressive granite cliffs we call *the Palisades of the Collawash*. Millennia ago, these hard granite cliffs blocked the flow of the Clackamas River from running east-to-west, diverting it north. At the end of the last ice age, huge floods rich with rock from melt-off in the Collawash basin scoured the cliffs to create their present spectacular appearance.

These magnificent cliffs were also the prime reason for one of the first major, long-lasting environmental battles in Oregon. Economy minded planners saw the Collawash Palisades as perfect bedrock for a dam to flood the Collawash basin.

The plan was for a dam to make a flood control and tourist lake for the Portland metroplex, somewhat like Detroit Lake is for the mid-Willamette Valley. Plans included a major access highway from the Willamette Valley up the Molalla River, affecting part of what is now the Table Rock Wilderness.

The plans for the dam and road caused uproar. A brutal, emotional fight lasted into the early 1970s before environmentalists won the vicious, mean-spirited political battle to defeat the dam. But in practical terms, the Collawash dam controversy still left terrible consequences for this bountiful drainage.

Since the basin was presumably going to be flooded, clear cutting proceeded at a breakneck pace in the 1960's. No care was taken to replant clear cuts. As a result, sections of the basin are full of some of the grungiest regrowth in the northwest.

This reforestation was later used by environmentalists as a prime example of poor logging practices and led in part to setting the southern part of the Collawash aside as Bull of the Woods and Opal Creek wilderness areas. The Bull of the Woods and Opal Creek wilderness areas are in Area 6, but they include the headwaters of the Collawash River which flows through Area 4.

To their credit, the Forest Service is now thinning randomly in attempts to reset the Collawash eco system.

Map of Area 4

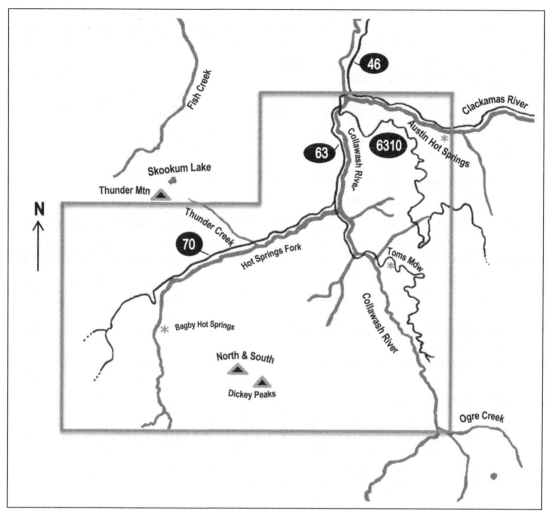

©Sharon Beelart 2015

Area 4 OBH Mile Markers

Miles from Estacada: from Detroit

28.5: 41.5 Intersection of main Road 46 and Road 63 into the Collawash

The boundary landmarks begin at Bigfoot Mile Marker 28.5 which is the Road 46 and Road 63 intersection. This is the northeast, and for touring purposes, the only entry and exit point into the Collawash River watershed. It is also Area 4's only intersection with the Oregon Bigfoot Highway.

Mileage Markers within Area 4

Collawash River Road 63 to the Bagby Hot Springs intersection

0.1 Bridge #1: look north to see the confluence of the Collawash and Clackamas. The big pool is a holding area for salmon. When they are in, and when the water is clear, it is worth the hike to watch salmon. Do not park on the bridge.
- 1.5 Beginning of the Collawash Palisades!
- 2.1 Across the river; the beginning of a huge landslide from Granite Peaks
- 3.2 Right turn on Road 6320. It rises southwest toward Thunder Mountain.
- 3.4 Road 70 intersection. Rd 70 goes to Bagby Hot Springs.

Bagby Hot Springs Road 70 to the Hot Springs parking area

- 5.1 Peg Leg Falls
- 5.8 Bagby Hot Springs parking.

The hike into Bagby Hot Springs is about 1.6 miles. Visitors must have a paid parking pass or soaking permit. Passes are available from the Ranger Station in Estacada or the Ripplebrook Ranger Station when it is open. Soaking permits at $5 per body soaked are available at the trailhead. Do not leave valuables in your vehicle.

Collawash Road 63 from the Bagby Hot Springs Intersection to Graham Pass Road 6350

- 3.4 Intersection of Road 63 and Road 70
- 3.7 Bridge #2; Little Fan Creek Campground
- 4.6 Beginning of rebuilt washed out road
- 4.7 Look east for a view of the giant landslide
- 5.3 Bridge #3
- 5.5 Road 6340 to Dickey Peaks (Bull of Woods trail head 10 miles)
- 5.9 Bridge #4, entry to adventure land
- 6.0 Slope and cave, now washed out, where Cliff found his 1999 track-way
- 6.6 Toms Meadow just south of road
- 7.5 Barrow road where Steve found tracks and root
- 8.4 Road passes through creek: Beware of high water
- 8.7 Intersection with Graham Pass Road 6350
- 14.0 End of road and Elk Lake trailhead (mileage approx.)

Collawash GPS coordinates

GPS of the Road 46 and Road 63 intersection: 45 01 59.90N 122 03 32.90W at 1495'

GPS of the Road 63 and Road 70 intersection: 44 59 20.47N 122 03 59.00W at 1649'

GPS of Bagby Hot Springs: 44 56 09.08N 122 10 25.62 W at 2277'

GPS of Bagby Hot Springs parking area: 44 57 27.38 N 122 09 36.21W at 2079'

Bigfoot reports from the Collawash basin are arranged roughly north to south rather than by date.

One last note on roads in the basin: In a couple of places Collawash roads are covered by seasonal streams. If you encounter a submerged roadway with more than brook flow DO NOT CROSS IT.

Ref. 56: A French Visitor's Luck

Location: Granite Peaks, high on the Collawash side: Road 6310: Our guest was French researcher Jean Roche who is familiar with Neanderthals and European wild man history.

Track Find 25 (TF25) and Bigfoot Related Incident 33 (I33) resulted from a chance track find near the crest of Granite Peaks.

The most important particulars garnered from the Roche site were (1) the escaping creature jumped into tree tops below the road and (2) its hair pattern matches hair patterns in the Washington Skookum cast. Note: There are numerous references to the Skookum cast on the Internet.

Location: Road 6310 near the top west end of Granite Peaks *on the* Collawash River side.

Approx. GPS of the incident: 44 59 10.26W 121 59 23.84W at ~ 4845'

In late summer 2001, Jean Roche, a French hominid researcher, visited the United States. One of Monsieur Roche's goals was to explore the upper Clackamas River and see the Thomas site. So in late August he became a guest at the Beelart home to plan an expedition which, because of time constraints, became a very long day trip.

On August 30, 2001, Roche, Ray Crowe of the Western Bigfoot Society, and Beelart and Olson, went up the hill in Olson's "new" Jeep. It was to prove a day with substantially more action than we expected.

At the Thomas site Jean caused some concern as he excitedly walked the site with little regard for the unstable footing. But, since he was fit and athletic, in the end things were OK.

We then decided to return via the Collawash River to show Jean the majestic granite palisades at the mouth of the river. At about 5:15 PM, within 150 yards after making the hairpin turn at the west crest of Road 6310, Cliff saw a remarkable set of fresh skids on the steep slope above the road.

Later, we decided that what happened was, as our vehicle approached the hairpin turn from the east, a Bigfoot picking late season huckleberries on the little plateau above the road panicked, jumped to the Collawash side of the hair-pin turn, landed on its rear end in soft ground, slid down the slope, stopped itself, stood upright, turned to its left, ran down the rest of the slope, crossed the road, and dove into big fir trees on the other side. The reason to use the word "dove" is the slope on the west side of the road is very steep.

Following are notes Roche and I made the evening of the find. The set of tracks is labeled Track Find 25 (TF25). The angle of the skid slope was very steep. Casting the skids would have been very difficult even if we had brought plaster.

Due to the mass required to generate the skid trail only bear, elk, deer, or a large hominid could have made it. We ruled out elk and deer because no fresh hoof prints were found. A hard running large bear is the obvious and easy explanation as to what made the tracks and skids. However, the bear theory must be questioned for the following reasons:

- No oblong paw marks; or claw marks were found anywhere.

- The first two tracks found at the top of the slope. Where it was almost flat, were hominid foot imprints, not double strike bear tracks.

- The undergrowth should have had some hair on it from a low-slung animal. After careful examination no hair was found indicating that the animal making the tracks and skids was tall enough to partially clear the low brush at the top of the slope, or step around it.

- The first photo shows what looked like a large buttock sitting down very hard on the slope with the legs extended and the feet throwing up dirt stopping the animal's initial skid. Inspection of this spot and later examination of enlarged photographs also discount the possibility an elk made the "butt" print.

- The exit below the water seep line on the slope was about a 30 degree angle to the left (south). The foot imprints in the very soft soil were staggered at about 50 inch intervals and were man-like

imprints with no pad or claw marks.

Two experienced Ph.D. wildlife biologists have informally studied enlarged photographs of the site and offered the opinion that a bear did not make the skids. They indicated the skids looked like a big person sliding downslope trying to catch itself with hands and heels.

The Jump-Off Issue

There are two curious issues about the Granite Peaks incident. First the creature jumped off a very steep, tree covered slope into what is locally known as *Whiskey Bottle Gulch*, so called because that's where loggers tossed their bottles, either going to work, or on the way back to Estacada.

Whiskey Bottle Gulch, from road to bottom, is about 500 feet deep. Depending on whether the reader uses Google Earth or a topographical map to obtain the measurements, run of the slope is about 2 to 1, which is very steep indeed.

Our supposition is that the creature that leaped was skilled at landing in big trees and descending from them. This implication has many ramifications when studying Bigfoot; so we identify it as Bigfoot Related Incident 33 (I33).

The second curiosity is the hair patterns in the "butt" print at the top of the slope are precisely the same hair patterns in the Skookum Cast.

Top of skid marks, photograph does not show steepness of the slope. Photo by Joe Beelart.

Comparisons to the Skookum Cast

In 2000 the Skookum Cast was taken near Skookum Meadows in Washington's Gifford Pinchot National Forest. When I went to Bellingham, Washington for a Bigfoot conference, I found the Skookum Cast on display in the hallway outside the auditorium. Noticing my interest in the cast, two members of a major Bigfooting organization engaged me in conversation about it.

Then a presentation started and the organization members went into the auditorium. I stayed behind to further inspect the cast. Noticing I was much more interested in the cast than the presentation, a man remained in the hallway. He turned out to be tall dignified ecologist Dr. LeRoy Fish (1943-2002).

Fortunately I brought along photographic enlargements of the Granite Peaks skids, two of which clearly showed hair imprints. I showed LeRoy the photographs and he wanted to hear more. So, we spent the next hour and a half going over the Skookum cast, and among other things, comparing hair patterns in it with my Collawash photographs.

His opinion was *if* the Skookum Cast was not made by an elk, and he suspected not, then an animal with similar hair patterns made the butt prints at Granite Peaks. I also told LeRoy that elk hair samples from several sources such as fly tying houses and taxidermy shops did not have the same hair patterns as in the

Granite Peaks butt print and now, as I saw them, in the Skookum Cast.

This was my introduction to Dr. Fish. He thought the hair comparison an interesting challenge and pursued the idea. A few months later LeRoy told me by telephone his opinion was the hair patterns were not elk or bear. But, he wanted to do even more research before offering an opinion on what animal made them.

By then, LeRoy had also decided we should write a book on the upper Clackamas. Unfortunately Dr. Fish, a brilliant, perceptive man, died much too soon from a heart attack, so our collaborative effort never came about. I feel the loss of Dr. Fish's friendship; the loss of his editorial guidance comes in a distant second.

A final note on the Roche site; due to erosion, the slope where the incident occurred has lost most of its loose dirt and is now rocky. Virtually every August since 2001, I have made it a point to explore the Track Find 24 area with no reportable results. Of course, every year the huckleberry field above the road, which I leave to the forest animals, is neatly harvested.

Ref. 57: From John Green: A Collawash Night Sighting

Collawash Hot Springs Fork: Road 70: Sighting 20 (S20): John Green Report of June 1973.

The following quote is reprinted with the written permission of John Green from: Green, John, *Sasquatch, the Apes Among Us*, second paper edition, 2006, Hancock House Publishers, Surrey, B.C. pages 419-420. Begin Green quote:

"The encounter took place in the following locality – along the Collawash River, a small tributary of the Clackamas River, about 40 miles above the town of Estacada. This region is extremely rugged, heavily timbered, and very seldom visited by man.

The sighting took place about six weeks ago. I and my nephew decided to go on a weekend fishing trip to this locale. I have fished the Collawash for 12 years, and it is one of the most beautiful, totally unspoiled places I have ever seen.

We had fished all day Saturday, and were very happy to build a fire circle on a large gravel bank close to the stream. We built a fire, prepared our meal, and settled back for a much needed rest and conversation about the day's activities.

My nephew proceeded to fall asleep rather early, but I remained awake until fairly late, perhaps 11:00 p.m. feeding the fire, and feeling quite content and at peace with the world.

This peaceful attitude was rather quickly shattered. First of all, I heard a sound exactly as if someone was walking along the gravel bank close to the river. I could distinctly hear the crunch and grinding of each step.

I strained to see who or what could be making such a noise, and at that time a very large form came within view of the fire light. It was walking erect, with a very determined gait, almost fluid in motion. The creature swung its arms as it walked, almost as a man would, but slightly more pronounced. As it passed directly in front of the fire, about 20 yards away from me, it paused slightly, and gave almost an *indifferent* glance towards me and towards the fire.

Needless to say I was virtually thunderstruck. I rose slowly, turned my flashlight on the creature, drew my .22 pistol and fired three shots. Upon my execution of this action, the creature emitted a high-pitched scream, and moved with really astounding speed over a huge log, and into the heavy timber.

I was so upset that I could not sleep the rest of the night. Early the next morning my nephew and I searched the bank for signs or tracks but found only a few depressions in the coarse gravel which could have been foot prints. We also examined the point at which the creature moved into the timber. There we also found no trace of its movement. The log which the creature literally stepped over was waist high, and I had some difficulty climbing over it.

In a later letter he noted that the creature had a 'truly nauseating, acrid odor,' and that it was breathing very heavily, almost wheezing, like someone with asthma or emphysema, although it was not exerting itself at all." End quote.

The *indifferent* italics are by Mr. Green. This sighting is designated Sighting 20 (S20). The authors strongly recommend enthusiasts and researchers acquire the Hancock House edition of Green, **Sasquatch, the Apes Among Us**, 2006 for study as it is a foundation stone of the literature.

Authors' opinions on this report: One, there are many more gravel bars on the Hot Springs Fork than on the steeper grade of the main Collawash River, plus access to the Hot Springs Fork is much easier. Thus, the encounter was probably on the Hot Springs Fork, which generally has much better fishing than the Main Fork where trout are often blown out by spring runoff.

Second, in regards to the wheezing, there are quite a number of alders and other leafed trees and bushes in the lower Collawash. Due to the time of year, perhaps as many humans do in late spring, the Sasquatch was suffering from allergies.

Ref. 58: Another Collawash Night Sighting

Bagby Hot Springs: Road 70: Sighting 21 (S21) is when Jake 22 (J22) sees a Bigfoot in moonlight.

Approx. GPS of S14 location: 44 54 51.81N 122 10 23.89W at ~ 2405'

Jake 22 told me his sighting story three times with very little variance in each rendition. The first time was at a coffee house in West Linn's historic Willamette area when Ray Crowe interviewed the witness for a *Track Record* article.

Since J22 lived only two miles from me, we met several more times to compare notes and discuss Bigfoot history. Before his Collawash sighting, J22 thought of Bigfoot as only a legend. J22 was a calm, mature man. It turned out he was a successful stockbroker for a large national firm.

Jake 22 reported seeing a Bigfoot about one mile south of Bagby Hot Springs near the confluence of Hot Springs Creek and Alice Creek. Using Trail 544 Jake 22 said he hiked past the hot springs and scouted the northwest section of Bull of the Woods Wilderness, an area he liked to explore because of its solitude.

The evening of the sighting, before dark J22 backtracked and set up camp next to Hot Springs creek, pitched his tent, and gathered a sizable pile of firewood for a long night fire. He lit his fire and shortly after dark decided to slowly heat a pan of freeze dried stew for supper. He said the night was very bright because of an early rising moon;

it was warm, and there were few insects. J22 said his surroundings were very pleasurable.

Just as his stew was ready to eat, he heard rocks rolling in the creek. This most unusual event attracted his attention, so he began watching the creek, scanning to not generate false night images in his mind. After some minutes, only about 10 feet away a huge black man-like beast emerged from the gloom into moonlight.

J22, of an analytical rather than emotional mind, at first felt he was just an annoyance to the creature. So, he instantly decided to study it. J22 said it was very muscular, about 8 feet tall and had arms longer than a man. He saw it was covered in hair, but due to lack of color in moonlight, could not see hue. He was particularly careful about describing the head and shoulders since the beast stopped walking in the creek and began to intently watch him.

He said he saw some facial features which resembled those of man. He said the ears were small and the neck was short. The top of the large head was rounded, not pointed. Muscles tapered from neck to shoulders like those of a weight lifter. While he could not see genitals, he thought the creature was a male because it lacked breasts.

Jake 22 said the creature continued to look at him, and he looked back, for what seemed like a very long time, "An eternity." Then the witness realized he might be in tremendous danger as the beast kept looking at his fire and stew. What to do?

"Basically, at that point I panicked."

Jake 22 grabbed his camp pan and threw the stew at his intruder! At that point, the Bigfoot also had enough of this intruder into its forest. It turned, and with no apparent effort, walked up the steep slope on the other side of the creek into darkness. J22 was especially impressed with the beast's exit. In several different ways he described its walk up the slope and out-of-sight as effortless.

Well, the night was young, a real-life monster was near and moonlight was wastin' so J22 did what any reasonable person might do when confronted by an 8 foot tall naked, hairy beast in the wilderness. He quickly stuffed his 'stuff' into his pack and hiked all the way back to the Bagby Springs parking area, a distance of over two miles. He said he almost broke his ankle a couple of times stepping wrong in the dark, but it was no matter. He wanted out of there.

Unfortunately, J22's sighting played havoc on his life. He couldn't get it off his mind. He began spending every available day and night up the Collawash trying to see the creature again. I suggested to him many times to let his mind take a break from the event. He tried, but always renewed his efforts.

A smart man, he began studying Sasquatch sightings in Oregon and Washington. He determined that southwest Oregon held promise for his search. So, he left his Portland position to start a branch office down state. It is my belief that effort failed. J22 then dropped from sight, possibly to a big city, as he told me at least twice he was thinking of moving far away from Sasquatch land.

Cougar #4: Stalked

Southwest of Granite Peaks: At Graham Pass Cougar #4 (C4) follows me. I fire a warning shot.

GPS: 44 57 44.44N 122 00 14.81W at ~ 2975' at the road intersection

In early spring 2005 I decided to patrol the area of the Collawash in the vicinity of Toms Meadow and Kiley's barrow pit where he found a cleaned root dropped by a Sasquatch. I also wanted to take a quick look at the two Devils Trails which were only about one half air miles apart.

I should mention that the shady side of brush is often clear of obstructions, offering natural trails, along which deer saunter. Where there are deer, there are cougar, especially since the cougar population in Oregon exploded after the 1994 dog hunting ban.

After scouting lower Buckeye Creek and Toms Meadow, I crossed the road to explore upper Buckeye Creek. There is also an old logging road which runs in that general direction and since the upper creek was still surrounded by snow, I walked the logging road.

The logging road had a foot or more of rotten snow on it, but that was no matter as I was wearing my Sorels which are leather, wool lined boots with rubber footpads. It was a very pleasant, refreshing day. I came to some winter tree falls after which, I returned to the truck parked at the intersection of Road 63 and 6350, the Graham Pass road.

Graham Pass Road, named for Joe Graham, the first superintendent of the Mt. Hood National Forest, is a very important part of the geography of the Collawash. Due to the cliffs, it's the only route to haul logs out of the east side of the Collawash.

After taking a break, drinking plenty of water, and eating a light lunch, I decided to hike up 6350 to look around from higher ground. After about 30 minutes, or a half mile of climbing, I began to feel uneasy. Then, letting my mind go wild, I became very nervous but not quite nervous enough to make me ready for the Mel Brooks institution for the very, very nervous. But rest assured I was awfully nervous.

I purposely walked about 30 yards up a straight stretch of the road and spun around. Below me I saw a flash of tan as a cougar leapt into the brush and made a noisy get-away.

Whew, damn!

When the mountain lion felt safe, crashing stopped and the forest descended into deep silence. I walked down to where the cougar made his bound off the road. From there, I saw the cat's tracks in mine as it followed me up the hill. I drew my 357 and fired a shot. The roar of the powerful revolver echoed through the canyon. Message sent, and undoubtedly received.

After that, I decided to go back to the truck. As I walked down the road I discovered the cougar had followed me all the way up from the intersection. I hiked over to the old logging road. Earlier in the day the damn beast followed me out of the logging road. I saw where it bedded in snowy, shadowy duff, watching me while I took my break.

I will let readers make conclusions about this incident as they may. It was not yet late spring. The cougar tracks still showed winter hair pads. A big cougar's tracks can approach 5 inches. I measured this one at a little over 3½ inches so it was either young, or maybe a female.

Since I was wearing my light parka, I probably appeared larger than normal.

Why the mountain lion trailed me for over three quarters of a mile on two different roads is unknown; probably it was just curious and had nothing else to do.

Ref. 59: What's in a name? Ogre Creek

Southeast Collawash: Road 6355: Bigfoot Related Incident 34 (I34): Unknown surveyor Jake 23: How did Ogre Creek get its name?

GPS of Ogre Creek culvert: 44 53 49.83N 121 58 44.44W at 3260'

Ogre Creek enters East Fork of Collawash: 44 53 32.72N 121 59 52.60W at 2395'

Round Lake: 44 52 31.65N 121 58 13.76W at 3597'

Ogre Creek feeds into the East Fork of the Collawash River near its far south end. Road wise, it lies just south of Spur Road 6370. Road 6355 crosses the upper reach of Ogre Creek, but at that point the creek requires no more than a small culvert crossing.

What an odd name: **Ogre**: from Webster's Desk Dictionary, "A monster in fairy tales and fable that feeds on human flesh," or "a monstrously cruel person". Whatever ogre gave the creek its name, the implication is clear.

To compel a surveyor, who we label Jake 23 (J23) to give a geographic name like Ogre to a site, he must have experienced or known of a monstrous happening. So, we decided to label the unknown event Bigfoot Related Incident 34 (I34).

Notes: Please do not confuse Ogre Creek with Ochre Creek which is about two miles north of Ogre Creek. In Ref. 95 three youths encounter a Bigfoot at Round Lake in 1953. Round Lake is less than two miles south of Ogre Creek.

Ref. 60: Summoned to the Collawash

Tracks at Bagby Hotsprings & Camp Broken Arrow

When Sasquatchian Jeff Rone is "summoned" to the Collawash we have Happening 12 (H12). Rone makes Track Find 26 & Track Find 27 (TF26 & TF27) at, and near Bagby Hot Springs.

This report comes from Jeff Rone, a man with over twenty five years of service in his career with the Federal government. In his spare time, Jeff is an active outdoorsman who lives about 15 miles south of Portland, Oregon. This begins his story.

"This particular Monday in fall 2012 was a holiday and I was going to be able to sleep in. I woke up around 4:00 a.m. and found myself wide awake! Not being able to fall back to sleep, I made a pot of coffee and began surfing the Internet. I did some reading and some research on Sasquatch and checked out my top websites as usual. About an hour into my morning, a "voice" in my head says very clearly, "Go to Bagby Hot Springs."

Now, I love to go on drives and look at nature and wonder if I'll ever get a glimpse of a Sasquatch. Over the last 30 years or so, I have been down the Clackamas River and the Collawash River corridors many times in a car or motorcycle. I have driven to Bagby Hot Springs several times but never took the time to hike the mile and a half up to the springs.

I looked around after I heard this *command* in my head to see who or what else might be in the room to make such a suggestion. After about 30 minutes, a nagging feeling told me that this was NOT a suggestion. I had better obey this voice. I had heard this voice before and disregarded it. I put myself through a lot of unnecessary turmoil because of that rebellion.

So it was; the "voice" and I decided that I would get my stuff and hike on up to the hot springs. I got to the trail head, paid the day use fee of $5, crossed over the bridge and down the path I go. The rains weren't quite here yet, so the ground was still hard but a little moist from overnight dew.

As I took every step, I searched for any signs of larger-than-human foot prints. I scoured the trail, looked over my shoulder, stared into the woods, and made my hike into a mission to find Bigfoot evidence of any kind. I saw plenty of human boot and shoe prints but no signs of my big forest friends. I made my way to the tubs and surrendered my mission to check out the structures and community tub.

After looking around, I walked away from the main area toward a building near the edge of the woods. Turning my eyes to the ground ahead I stopped dead in my tracks. There before me were three (3) very distinct foot prints! The third was just in front of me and I dropped to my knees for a closer look. I was no expert on tracks but these were without a doubt those of a Sasquatch! The moist bare feet of a person walking on the hard dirt ground would easily lift the layer of pine needles.

These tracks were put there for me to find. *They* told me to come here. Once I gave

up the search, there they were, *as if THEY found ME!"*

End quote and postscript; the subject told me that about two weeks later in late October, for some inexplicable reason he went to the Bagby Hot Springs area again to camp. He said that this time he was not "summoned," but something made him want to revisit the area. Trekking, he was surprised to find a series of 22 inch and 15 inch tracks crossing a glen and going into the forest. The tracks paralleled each other, so he supposed the Forest People were traveling together.

Jeff named the place "Camp Broken Arrow" because of a broken arrow in a nearby tree. He spent a comfortable, uneventful night camping at the site. Note: Jeff does not want us to list the GPS of "Camp Broken Arrow" as it is a place of continuing interest to him.

Bagby Hot Springs track, photo taken with cell phone camera. Note arch of foot leaves no impression behind little toe. Photo by Jeff Rone.

Ref. 61: The Camp Broken Arrow Expedition

The expedition happened June 7, 8 & 9, 2013 (Friday thru Sunday). Participants were from Oregon, Washington, and Idaho. Given the maturity of all participants, and their experience in Sasquatch field research, they reported an amazing eight separate and unusual Bigfoot Related Incidents.

Daytime Bigfoot Related Incident 35 was loud-roaring calls. Daytime Incident 36 was Sasquatch making greeting grunts at camp. Daytime Incident 37 was Sasquatch leaving a "glyph" symbol in camp.

Nighttime Bigfoot Related Incident 38 was when two Sasquatch walked into camp and inspected lots of things. Nighttime Incident 39 was when the two Sasquatch simulated individual human speech during their night time intrusion.

Nighttime Incident 40 was Sasquatch mimicking raven calls at night. Nighttime Incident 41 was Sasquatch's interest in the fire ring and cooking area. Nighttime Incident 42 is Sasquatch pressing a hand against tent and an expedition member finds Sasquatch hand is warm to human touch.

Track Find 28 (TF28) happened in camp during the morning of the last day of the expedition.

Originally, this story was told to me by Thom Cantrall and polished by Jeff Rone the expedition leader. On April 12, 2014, I went to the FootStock NW symposium where I met Jim (Elk) DeMain and Sue Funkhouser who also participated in the Camp Broken Arrow expedition.

At the symposium, or soon after, DeMain and Funkhouser privately and individually told me their versions of the expedition. Surprisingly, given the usual variety of human observation of startling or accidental events, all four versions coincided to a great degree.

Let's first meet Thom Cantrall. Now retired in southeast Washington, Thom Cantrall's career was in forestry as a logging road bridge contractor and owner of a logging company. Long interested in Sasquatch, Thom spent 40 years of spare time in the woods of British Columbia and the Northwest researching the creatures. In recent years he has expanded his research territory into the American southeast.

Thom is the author of three well-received Sasquatch books including his newest release, *Sasquatch, the Search for a New Man*. Through his books, Thom became acquainted with Jeff Rone. Thom learned Jeff found two sets of fresh tracks in the Collawash River basin so they planned a follow-up expedition.

Thom easily recruited eight experienced researchers for the long trip to the Collawash partly because of the distinct possibility of new track finds and Sasquatch contact, plus the attraction of "nearby" Bagby Hot Springs. The expedition base was at Camp Broken Arrow, elevation 3,200'.

After Jeff led a lengthy orientation tour of the western Collawash, and the dividing range between the Collawash and the Molalla River basin, the area was divided into sectors. These sectors were searched by expedition members.

First contact was vocalizations late in the day on Friday. Initially there were long, modulated, guttural "roaring calls" up mountain far away from base camp. "Whatever made them had mighty powerful lungs." In the evening Sasquatch reconnoitered close to the camp and made Sasquatch "greeting grunts" which Thom said he has heard many times before.

Thom was careful to explain the grunts were not bear, and the vocalizations they heard were not 5 to 8 second bear calls. He also said there were no elk in the area to give the many sounds elk make. Even though it was good habitat, since there was no elk scat, Thom was sure there were no elk around. Confirmation happened at the Sunday debriefing when expedition members reported finding zero elk tracks in any research sector.

Later Friday night the basin was visited by night hawks making their thundering dives after large insects. While the night hawks hunted, Thom, and the others talked while sitting around the fire. But, they, as one, became silent when expedition members noticed movements near camp. The expedition was being watched and from crunching sounds, the watchers were not curious doe deer.

Nine of the expedition members reported no daytime Sasquatch activity on Saturday. However, at about 3 in the afternoon on Saturday, Thom returned to camp from up mountain. To his great surprise he found a "glyph" placed in front of his tent, a photograph which is on Thom's Facebook page.

Thom says that over the years he has seen the same design left in other camps and thinks it might be a greeting sign or message from the Sasquatch People. However, after circling camp, no tracks were found near Camp Broken Arrow before dark on Saturday.

Enter the Sasquatch

What followed very early Sunday requires a description of the camp layout which looks like a very large comma. The head of the comma is the turn-around ring of an old logging road. The cooking, fire, and social area was in the turn-around. On the comma's outside curve were three tents and a pop-up trailer. Toward the tail of the comma, on the other side of the road, a little down slope from the other tents were Thom's tent and another tent.

It was very cloudy, so despite being close to Solstice, the night was long. About 4 AM weird, powerful, long vocalizations began close to camp. Several people, including Thom, and his tent mate Sue, reported the volume, or frequency, or both, of the vocalizations caused their whole bodies to vibrate. Then the vocalizations went silent, but by now, with the exception of one expedition member, the entire camp was awake and alert.

Next came a series of raven calls, odd raven calls, not quite right raven calls; and, they were out of place. Ravens do not call at night. Then, heavy footsteps came out of the forest and crunched up the gravel road to the fire pit. The Sasquatch circled tents on both sides of the road. Amazingly, and surprisingly, each participant I talked to said they never thought of unzipping their tent to look at the Sasquatch.

At one point, Thom saw the side of his tent indent. He reached up and for fleeting seconds, his fingers met the palm and fingers of a Sasquatch. Thom said it felt warm, and big, and strong.

Footsteps continued; from the cooking area, expedition members said they heard pots rattling and other minor inquisitive rustlings, but in morning light, nothing was missing or terribly out-of-place. Participants agreed the night visitors were in no hurry, they stayed in camp for at least 10 and probably closer to 15 minutes. After inspecting the tents, their night visitors spent much of the rest of their time close to the fire ring.

In the morning, Jeff, and other expedition members who were tented near the turn-around, asked Thom why he and Sue were out walking and talking after the great vocalizations. "Don't you think you might have scared them away?"

Thom was startled. He and Sue never left their tent and they had not talked, except in whispers. Thom asked about the voices. Several campers told Thom they were sure the voices were his and Sue's, but they could not make out words even though the voices were distinct and reasonably loud.

Something Odd about Field Researchers

Camp Broken Arrow was an unmitigated success. First, a good time was had by all ... always a major goal in field research.

To the point, good track finds and an almost astonishing set of eight different Bigfoot Related Incidents were noted by several, or all, expedition members. So, the logical question is, "What did they do to follow-up." The answer is, little.

Jeff and a companion or two have camped several more nights at or near Broken Arrow. A large follow-up expedition has not been planned. While there are exceptions, in the authors' estimation, this is the usual, although somewhat odd, behavior common to experienced field researchers.

This book is full of good results at many locations, yet with the exceptions of the High Rock Quarry and the Big Rock Quarry, sites are seldom revisited or camped in again. A good example is the High Rock Quarry; we have not camped in it since 2008.

Why?

In fact, of the eight other people on the expedition, seven reported hearing Thom and Sue talk in near dawn darkness as they walked around camp. Examination of the grounds revealed two sets of tracks, many of them very clear, but not impressed enough into the earth to cast. One set was made by about a 16″ foot and the other set slightly smaller. No contact was made during Sunday daylight hours before camp breakup.

There are several theories as to why "adequate" follow-up to "results" is generally not made. The first is that Sasquatch happenings are so rare, experienced researchers think them not replicable. The second is Sasquatch may send subliminal messages to the effect, "We contacted you, now stay away."

Third, experienced researchers realize there are few of Our Barefoot Friends. Once one of their places is found, let them alone. Another idea is that it's too expensive and time consuming to replicate some expeditions. Letting someone else have their turn at a site is one reason many GPS coordinates are in this book.

The last idea we offer is more basic. Man is an explorer. Like prospectors, Sasquatch field researchers like to cover a lot of ground. After a gold find and the pay dirt runs out, prospectors move on. Field researchers are a little like prospectors. They have many canyons, ridges, and basins subconsciously tugging at their exploratory minds.

Around Toms Meadow

GPS of Toms Meadow: 44 57 48.15N 122 02 16.96W at 2005'

It is common practice to omit the apostrophe on some topographical names, so Toms is spelled correctly per a variety of official USFS, MHNF & CRRD maps. When you read Appendix V on Meadows along the OBH, you will also notice that the "s" is also sometimes omitted, as in Bob Meadow and Jim Meadow.

Toms Meadow is about a half mile past the fourth bridge on Road 63, or about three and a half road miles from the Bagby intersection. As noted earlier, it appears to be a silted in beaver dam with brush along the north (road) side and scraggly regrowth on the south side. It is important to us and we use it as a landmark because eight reportable track finds and incidents happened within a two mile radius of Toms Meadow.

Toms Meadow. Photo by Joe Beelart.

Ref. 62: Cliff finds tracks on the East Fork

Toms Meadow #1: Cliff's Track Find 29 (TF 29) were tracks going up a long dirt slope next to Road 63: Track Find GPS: 44 57 56.33N 122 02 38.17W at ~1830'

GPS of bridge #4: 44 57 59.56N 122 02 42.25W at 1785'

Notes from 1999 put into sentences: 'I can't believe our usual Bigfooting day is on April 1st! If we had a mind to, Steve, Cliff and I could pull some really good hoaxing! There are plenty of people out there who want to see things, real or not. Anyway, faking just isn't our style and besides, we don't need the attention.

We went south, several miles past bridge four. On the way, we tried out the new five gallon bucket call. The sound threw itself across the valley, and then came back a couple of times with an excellent echo. It was a quiet, cold day. Something replied from quite a ways off, probably a coyote.

Tracks up a steep slope

Driving back just south of Bridge 4 Cliff saw a series of imprints going up a steep dirt slide. It was a very steep and soft land slide slope about 40 feet wide and about 60 feet high with no vegetation. On one side was a rocky ledge and the other side was steep and covered with low thick brush as is usual along the edges of tall timber.

The imprints definitely were from down to up where they stopped. We couldn't figure how the maker got into the forest. Later it came to us, not as a group, but individually after looking at photographs; the creature reached up, seized a branch, and vaulted into the forest!

It took amazing upper arm and shoulder strength to do that.

While the series of tracks was very easy to view, nothing was perfectly clear due to the soil condition. It appeared that the imprints were fresh, dirt crumbles were still in place; and, they hadn't been damaged by rain. They certainly did not look like climbing elk or deer since the penetrations were clear, large, deep, and there *was no throw back.*

Besides, toe impressions were present and they did not show hoof or bear claw marks. There were lots of dermal ridges showing and many barely balanced grains of soil on the edges of the tracks. The tracks were very fresh.

I scrambled up one side of the track line. I took two "steps" for every imprint step; whatever made the prints was strong and agile. The ground was very loose. The first three imprints had about 51 inches between heel strikes – on an uphill slope.

Toward the top, the stride decreased to 43 and 40 inches.

This was our first major track find. We were perplexed. Were they real? Was it this easy to find Bigfoot tracks? Anyway, there wasn't much to accomplish with the tracks. We didn't bring casting material along.

Steve went exploring along the river. Since the slope above the tracks was steep and Cliff's knee was bothering him, he and I walked up the road to Toms Meadow. Later, Steve reported finding a big cave below the road alongside the river but there was no sign in it.

While we were optimists about our search, we simply didn't plan, or were inherently pessimistic, and left simple small things like casting plaster in a bucket at home. Plus today, we could hardly believe what we saw. But the tracks were clear, so for this book they become Track Find 29 (TF29).

Ref. 63: Giant blow downs. Tracks in duff. Spooky Times

Toms Meadow #2: Track Find 30 (TF30) was tracks in forest duff in an area of big blown down trees: Getting "Spooked" is Happening 13 (H13): Road 63.

Approx. GPS of the center point of blow downs: 44 58 04.49N 122 02 29.97W at ~ 2040'

Note about the Google Earth view: The blow downs are out-of-sight under the tree canopy.

In mid-April 1999 Steve Kiley and I drove up the Collawash River to see what remained of Cliff's Track Find 29. It was cold and rainy. We worried about ice on the road. We saw no other vehicles, not even one from the Forest Service. If we slipped into the ditch or worse, slid into the river, we had instant major problems.

To our amazement, the tracked slope was still much like we left it a week ago because the overhanging tree canopy had protected it from direct rain. The main rain damage we noted was the smoothing of the toe lines, but they were still distinguishable. Of course dermal ridges and hanging grains of earth on edges were gone. Unfortunately, track edges were also beginning to show weathering.

About 50 feet away was a dim uphill route, so we climbed the steep slope to the ridge above the track find. It was slippery, but there was plenty of vine maple to grab when we needed it.

There was a big ravine up there. I hiked up the north side of the ravine and Steve hiked up the south. My side dropped off a 100 foot cliff down to the river, but I did find one game trail angling down from the ridge to the river bottom. Later, we would put up a bucket baiting site near the bottom of that trail.

It was all old growth timber up there, the good stuff, nice and big and tall. Viney brush was under the canopy, but there was a lot of open space too. Visibility was good since leaves weren't open and spring growth hadn't started.

There were many big blow downs on my side which told me a big wind of some kind passed through there like a tornado. It didn't clear a swath; it just knocked down a lot of trees. That old wind must have come out of the east-by-northeast as almost all the trees laid west-by-southwest.

The blow downs were virgin Douglas fir with shallow, round root masses. When on their side, many root masses approached 10 feet tall. At the base of each fallen tree where the roots had been, there was a hole filled with soft dirt. With no luck, I looked at many of these holes expecting to find where something slept in them.

A giant Collawash blow-down. Photo by Joe Beelart.

"Spooked"

It was eerie under the canopy. Due to wind, branches in the canopy were moving a little, but on the ground it was very quiet. I couldn't see Steve. I felt like something had become aware of me and was behind me. Almost automatically, I began to approach each fallen tree very cautiously. My search took time; there were many of them.

After almost an hour, toward the upper road, I heard Steve calling me from the other side of the ravine. It took some time to cross fallen logs, drop down into the ravine and climb up the other side. It wasn't a great effort, but it took time. Falling off of one of the blow downs meant a big hurt, so I went slow and easy.

When I got over there, Steve asked me to look around and see if I noticed anything strange. I didn't see anything out of the ordinary. Then he pointed out that while there was a well-used game trail, there were no deer or elk tracks in it, none ... later we began calling this type of path a *Devils Trail*. I told him I searched plenty, and carefully on my side of the ridge and there were no elk and few deer tracks over there as well.

Then, in the duff, he showed me a clear five toe footprint about 15 inches long. The heel didn't show too well, but there it was partly in the mud (toe area) and the rest smashed into the forest duff (soft stuff on forest floor). A little further up the trail was a complete print smashed into the moss. The moss, or forest duff, was really smashed down, something heavy made the prints.

While it was a duff track, this track was complete and about 16 inches long. Gently lifting the mat showed five toe imprints, large toes. It also showed a sort of break between the front and back part of the foot in the soft ground, but due to the duff, that part wasn't as distinct as the toes.

We wished we had better sun; we couldn't get a good grasp of a pattern and we knew my basic camera, even though it had a flash, wouldn't capture the detail we needed. As we went along we found another good print with the toes clearly showing in the mud.

Where this foot struck, a stone about 2 inches in diameter was pounded into the ground near the heel. These were definitely not bear or elk double strikes. The toe imprints were rounded. We note these imprints as Track Find 30 (TF30).

17" duff track in big blow downs. Note rock smashed into ground at heel. 1999 photo by Joe Beelart.

We measured the prints. They were all about 15 to 16 inches long and a bit over 7 inches wide at the ball of the foot. I took a few more photographs. Due to the ground and duff, there wasn't much to cast and for some reason, we both wanted to move right along, to get up to the logging road above us.

We separated again, heading upslope. At first I felt nothing, but then something really disturbed me. It was intense. Steve decided to stay near me, but had wandered off on another game trail, looking for more prints. When he came back I told him we'd better get out of there until we had a plan. Steve agreed, he said this place spooked him; that we should have a plan to study it.

Ref. 64: Spooked Again

Toms Meadow #3: Bigfoot Related Incident 43 (I43) was another spooky and unsettling feeling.

Late April 1999: In Ref. 63 we felt 'spooked.' While this is a report of minor substance and hardly worth noting, another 'unsettling, spooky feeling' happened in the same place later in the month. But, we include it because a year later, in the same place a third episode, a much more disturbing incident of being 'spooked' happened.

The purpose of this adventure was simple. I was going up alone to check cameras and replenish baits at the two game cam sites. At the first site none of the baits were bitten or eaten. Something had been at the site, packed down the duff and kicked a few of the apples around with distain as this was before we learned they like their offerings elevated off the ground. I wondered why deer hadn't gotten them, and then remembered there are few deer tracks in the big blow downs.

I decided to dump the bucket since the vegetables were getting soft and mushy—plus it stunk. Amazingly, after three weeks the bicycle blinkers were still blinking, maybe because I put medical grade batteries in them. There was only one click on the camera, probably just me. The camera looked dry and stable, so I didn't change the film.

I took my time climbing up to Steve's other trail cam. It was warm under the trees, finally. Only one pic fired on that camera. The bait was OK, so I decided to explore the big blow downs. To make it easier, I started by walking up the overgrown logging road at the head of the ravine. Suddenly I felt like someone was watching me.

I was amazed by the intensity of the feeling as it swept over me, for it did sweep over me like an invisible wind; and it clearly wasn't just my psyche. Before the feeling I was in fact having just a great day in a beautiful neck of the woods.

Then I got a little worried. The feeling didn't pass. It wasn't threatening, it was just like something detected me and was tossing me some kind of thought. I should note three weeks ago, unprompted, Steve remarked on manipulated thought.

As I moved along, north of me an occasional branch snapped. I decided to come to a fast halt a couple of times. Both times I heard more snaps. They were about 50 yards away in green leaf brush. Something was following me, something much heavier than a cougar. It wasn't a bear—bears run from people.

I then decided I must not see or hear things that were not real. There was no wind movement under the tree canopy. I decided to hike to the upper road, traverse to Peat Creek and return to the truck on the road via the south side of the ridge. I checked my .357 for a little reassurance and, left the holster buttoned.

During my hike paralleling Peat Creek I didn't hear any more snaps. I watched the ravine between me and where I hiked uphill. Was it some sort of natural territory line? Or was cover on the north side of the ravine better? Or did my woodland follower simply lose interest in me?

Steve called shortly after I got home. Inexplicably, for some reason Steve had decided we should shift our area of interest from the Collawash basin to above Big Bottom. After talking it over, Cliff wholeheartedly agreed with Steve's idea.

The first step toward our new area was for me to go to Captain's Nautical Supply and buy topographical maps to study. For now, we decided to leave the cameras up the Collawash. When we went up to retrieve them, something pretty interesting happened.

Ref. 65: "Leave here now!"

Toms Meadow #4: Bigfoot Related Incident 44 (I44) Steve Kiley and Joe receive a *telepathic command*.

This happened in late July 1999 in the jumbled, blow down trees mentioned in Ref. 63 and 64. Please keep in mind Steve and I both have substantial outdoor experience. I was raised on a ranch, spent five years in the USMC, and have hunted and fished my entire life. Kiley is also a lifelong hunter and fisherman, plus he is an accomplished woodsman and trapper.

Earlier I retrieved the cameras and reset them in Big Bottom. But in late July Steve and I decided to return to the blow downs to see what they were like in the heart of summer. The plan was very good and simple.

First, park above the big cave on the bank of the Collawash ... a cave we still thought might make a good place for the creatures to rest, sleep, or hide, if it had a less rocky floor, which it very well could have before the river's spring blow out.

Then, we'd separate, with me hiking up the north side of the big ravine along the breaks of the Collawash. Kiley's route was up Peat Creek south of the ravine. We were going to walk the north ridgeline upslope to meet at Road 63, and then walk the road down past Toms Meadow to the truck.

We figured on about an hour and a half of hiking and exploring time to get to our meeting place.

We left the truck with our Duluth packs. He wore his .44 magnum; I wore my .357 as we thought we might run into a sow bear with a cub. We parted at the road.

Leaves were out thick and green on shrubs, bushes and low trees. Vines were full and elegant in their draping. Indeed, under the canopy, the forest was at its prime and growing, a living emerald gem of nature. Anyway, within minutes of walking into the green we could not see or hear each other as we climbed and explored.

15 to 20 minutes later, I stepped out of the forest near my truck, crossed the road, and simply stood alongside it, dazed. Within one minute, Steve appeared from Peat Creek and without speaking, walked over to the truck. We took off our side arms, put our Duluth packs behind the seat, and got in the truck. I turned the truck around and drove slightly over 6 miles back to Road 46.

I then drove over 4 miles down to Ripplebrook Ranger Station. I continued on to near the end of the big slide repair, which is another 2½ miles. So, after walking out of the forest, loading the truck, and driving over 12 miles on curvy forest roads, all in silence, one or the other of us (neither remembers) asked this question:

"Did you hear anything back there?"

"Yes."

We both remember there was quite a pause before we resumed talking.

"Something told me, *Leave here now!*"

"That's exactly what I heard."

We were near Roaring River Bridge before we spoke again, and that was in clipped short sentences. Again, neither of us knows who said what first.

"Was what you heard in English?"

"Yes, it was like someone was talking to me in perfect English."

"Same here."

We spent the next hour and a half driving home, talking little and saying *nothing* about what happened up the hill. It was a day or two later before we compared our thoughts. Both of us were surprised that we walked out of the forest within about one minute of each other. We were both perplexed that at least one of us had not continued to the upper road.

We do not list this event as a bizarre happening, even considering it was highly unusual, especially given our level of outdoor experience. We list it as Incident 44 (I4), just another of the out-of-place things that occasionally happen in the woods.

Note to explorers: In 2009 a landslide collapsed the road just past bridge No. 4 on Road 63, the road nearest to Incident 44. Unfortunately the landslide swept away most of the lower slope where we found Track Find 29 and obliterated the cave alongside the Collawash.

Ref. 66: Turning Tracks & Wild Parsley

Toms Meadow #5: Bigfoot related Incident 45 (I45): Track Find 31 (TF31): Kiley finds cleaned roots and a turning track; Steve finds *another Devils Trail*.

Road 63: Barrow pit GPS: 44 57 40.42N 122 01 41.63W at 2395′

One day during the week after Incident 38 when Steve and I were told, *Leave here now!* Steve didn't have to work. So he decided to go up to look around on his own. With all his outdoor experience he was uncomfortable with what happened and thought he may be able to find, or think, of a rational explanation for the incident.

First Steve walked Peat Creek all the way to the upper road and back down past Toms Meadow to his truck. Nothing materialized. Next, he drove up to a small, old barrow pit at Collawash Road 63 mile 7.5.

The barrow pit road is a short, hook shaped, high bank affair with no view of the hook until making the turn into it. Steve made the turn and parked his truck for a look around. Intending to go into the forest behind the berm on the east side of the pit, he took a few steps and was surprised by what he saw lying on the ground: Two freshly cleaned roots. The roots were an off-white color with fronds which were respectively about 6 and 8 inches long.

Thinking he didn't see cleaned roots lying on the ground in the forest every day, Steve thought he'd better take a photo or two of the roots as they lay. So, he took three photographs. Then he hiked into the big timber.

Cow parsnip, *Heracleum maximum*, a member of the parsley family, grows 3′ to 10′. The plants in this photo are 4′ to 5′. Photo by Sharon Beelart.

In the big timber, he found *another* of the trails that are heavily used but have no deer or elk tracks; a trail a man can walk on upright with little brushing. Steve had found yet another *Devils Trail*. He spent a lot of time exploring it and the area around it, but found no Bigfoot tracks.

When Steve returned to his truck, he picked up the roots and brought them home. The next day I went over to Kiley's rod shop where we talked about the incident. The roots were a secondary matter at the time. The new found trail was important.

We looked at Steve's big wall map and talked about it and the area around it. Then we spent a few minutes talking about the roots. Both of us remembered Green's report of Thomas watching female Bigfoots cleaning roots (see Area 5 Ref. 72). We vaguely remembered other mention of roots in the literature. We talked about the two skunk cabbage roots Steve found with bites taken out of them.

I asked Steve if I could take the roots to my place. By the time I got home I decided to call the Oregon State University Extension Service in Oregon City. They in turn referred me to a person in the Oregon State University Botany Department.

A man in the Botany Department said they needed a flower to positively identify the roots. He suggested trying to grow pieces of the root to maturity and made a couple of suggestions on how to cut them to get best results. So I propagated the roots and they grew into plants.

Very Near a Sighting

Just two days after the find, Steve called me and told me to come to his rod shop as soon as possible. When I came by late the next afternoon, Steve showed me his photographs of the root find. We were both shocked by what we saw in the photographs.

About 9 inches from where the roots lay, there was the clear impression of a turning bare foot. The partial footprint

Cleaned wild parsley root and turning toe print with 45-70 casing. Photo by Steve Kiley.

clearly showed the ball of the foot, a right big, big toe, and the two toes next to the big toe, both somewhat dragging in the damp soil. What had surely happened was a creature carrying cleaned roots from the marsh lands below was enroute to the *Devils Trail.*

We speculate that as Steve drove onto the barrow pit road, the Bigfoot braced itself and quickly turned to look over its right shoulder toward the noise of his truck rounding the short turn into the barrow pit. Anxious to make a get-away, the creature probably dropped the two roots as it stepped into the trees. Conclusion: Steve Kiley was literally seconds from seeing a Sasquatch carrying roots!

So, in great anticipation, Steve took me up to the pit to cast the partial print. Unfortunately, 4-wheelers destroyed the shallow impression. We rationalized it away, like most imprints we'd seen. "It probably wouldn't have cast well anyway."

Ref. 67: Aggressive Baiting

Toms Meadow #6: Road 63: Happening 14 (H14) is our first and last aggressive baiting. We change from "baiting" to presenting "offerings." Track Find 32 (TF 32) happens on the "pulpit."

This account marks the beginning of our transformation from "baiting," to "offerings." By mid-1999, we decided we didn't want to kill one of the beasts, even if presented the chance. Even at this early stage in our research we knew we were dealing with a much higher intellect than found in game animals.

One night at a Western Bigfoot Society meeting, Dr. Henner Fahrenbach, a loosely connected associate of Cliff and mine, but still unknown to Steve, said collecting blood, hair, and tissue samples in a somewhat controlled, amateur experiment might prove enormously helpful to science.

We explored the forest and the *Devils Trail* behind the barrow pit. But fortunately, this account didn't end then.

After several weeks, the root starts I planted matured to their flowering stage. Three were sent to Oregon State University for identification. They were a variety of wild parsley that is poisonous, but not normally fatal to humans. Humans can eat the plant if it is well cooked and the liquid drained.

Back to the barrow pit. After the lay of the land was clear to us from studying topographical maps, it became obvious the pit road was a transit zone between the Graham Pass area and the expansive landslide under Granite Peaks.

On another day we followed the trail east toward an interesting area which is mentioned in the next episode of Collawash exploration. It was not far off the Devils Trail, and between the two areas, where Thom Powell cast a track two years later.

Later we assured Henner we were the right crew and one of us told Henner (he forgets who, but thinks it was Cliff) said, "You better get your lab ready."

Since Henner had been a quiet Bigfooter for quite a few years, he certainly appreciated our enthusiasm, but probably had more realistic expectations for results than us. So, things went about like they usually do with the Oregon City Bunch which was us back then.

Steve conceptualized, I made, and Cliff cheered us on. Actually, Steve's plan was simple, so simple it was pure. We'd make a bucket containing a scratching device, hang it up in the air since we now figured they didn't like things on the ground, and fill it full of good eats.

We also decided not to use a camera trap since camera traps hadn't produced results. Steve thought they might emit some frequency that scared off the critters. We knew the Collawash from our time up there, so we decided that was the best place to hang our bucket. What could go wrong? In little more than a week, we'd find out; and it didn't have anything to do with the advancement of science. First, we did a really good setup.

Our attractant was something from Steve's trapping days. He called this scent "Big Stinky" because it was so strong that he stored it in not one, but two glass jars to try and hold in the scent. He used substantial rubber gloves to handle it. On his own, Cliff, unbeknown to us because with his knee, he knew we wouldn't have let him go alone; went on his own to scout for likely sites. We only wanted to start with one, and Cliff, the old frontiersman, found a great one.

This site was basically along the river just past Bridge 4 below the ridge with the big blow downs. Even though it was only about a quarter mile, it was a hard walk through river bottom brush to get to Cliff's site.

There, Cliff found a slight rise above the river banks which had a small flat next to the cliff face. It was also "near" the game trail down the bluff that I'd noticed in Ref. 63. There were a few deer tracks along the river bank, but no elk tracks, not enough space there for elk.

The Tissue Sampling Device

Hey, the title here is not ours; it was what Henner called the contraption. On the advice of my comrades, I made the bait bucket out of a clean, white 5 gallon plastic pail. Using ½ inch hardware screen wire, I cut and bent it at an angle at virtually every weave. These barbs would hopefully catch skin and hair.

Using a piece of 2 by 4 to catch the stapler's impact, Steve and I stapled the hardware screen to the inside of the bucket with an industrial duty staple gun. The prongs that the cut wire left seemed severe, but to us, they were no worse than blackberry vine thorns, and certainly no worse than Devil's Club thorns. At least, that's what we told ourselves. If a human got an arm ripped by one of the sets of cut wire, it would take a hospital visit and lots of stitches to make basic repairs.

Next I drilled a few drain holes around the bottom rim of the bucket and crammed in a layer of first aid cotton cloth near the bottom to help catch blood. Finally I attached a tripod line hanging apparatus with a hardware swivel at the apex since one of our salmon fishing swivels would have allowed the bucket to move too easily.

Now, our masterpiece was ready to hang about 8 feet off the ground and a long ways from surrounding trees and overhead branches (squirrels). Cliff also selected the place because it had an open glen completely shielded from view by brush and trees.

Using my PVC line lift, in short order we had the bucket up and hanging. It was just as we envisioned; it suspended at a slight upward angle so the bait stayed in and rain could drain out the drain holes. Just before the lift into place, we loaded it with 2 cans of Spam, lettuce, apples, cabbage and some other stuff that was on sale at the produce department.

Remember this, on a branch we were able to reach from the cliff, Steve hung the neat little visual attractor he developed. At bucket level, on the far side of the glen, I hung a lighted CD revolving lure. Scrambling up the cliff, we set a LED bicycle warning flasher with medical grade batteries. We also put a flasher down closer to the river in the brush. All in all, we figured we'd put out enough advertising stuff so a Bigfoot would know to "eat here."

So What Happened?

A lot more than fits in this story, but basically since Cliff's knee was bothering him again, Steve and I went back in a week to check our blood and skin collection device. Our bucket was still hanging there, undisturbed. The Spam was getting really stinky since the temperature went up. And, it was clear our bucket had been inspected by the Forest People.

Underneath the bucket the duff was smashed down from a lot of stomping. Whatever did the stomping was heavy and looked our bucket over up close and personal. But, whatever it was sure wasn't a bear for there was not a bear track or claw mark anywhere near.

I couldn't see the blinker high up the slope. Thinking the battery was dead, I climbed up to change it, but when I got there, the blinker was gone. Something had grabbed it and pulled it off the string which also broke the branch. Nearby there was a "pulpit" sort of place on the hillside that was heavily stomped down. Something had stood there looking down, watching our sampling device.

Several toe prints and partial footprints were visible, but we decided nothing was worth casting. Now, for the record, we designate the bucket stomps and the tracks on the pulpit overlooking the site as Track Find 32 (TF 32). From the pulpit, our consciences began to kick in.

We fought our way through the brush tangle to the truck and as we drove along, talked the situation over. These were Our Barefoot Friends and we were trying to harm them.

What had they ever done to us? Why were we now calling them "our friends?" Where had our cold blooded callous advancement of science attitude gone? This was all very perplexing to simple people like us.

Probably an adult had inspected our offerings and visual aids and rejected them. But what happened if a young one wandered into the site and hurt itself, maybe crippling fingers for life? How would it get medical assistance? Honestly, we thought and talked about those things.

So, three days later when I had a day off, I went up the hill and cut down the bucket. Now, the degenerating Spam stunk terrible nasty, plus grease from it dripped out along with rotting vegetable fluids through the drain holes to the ground. The drippings had attracted a bear which from the signs of it, seemed to try everything in bear ingenuity to get to the goods, but failed.

It was a hassle getting that damn bucket out of the brush, even after I dumped the goods, because I didn't want that stinking gooey thing rubbing on my jeans. I put it in one of my contractor trash bags, duct taped it shut and brought it home. Fortunately the next day was garbage day. So, that was the end of our aggressive baiting tactics, no matter the benefit it might give science. Those are Our Barefoot Pals up there.

Large beaver pond below Granite Peaks found after a three mile hike. Photo by Joe Beelart.

Ref. 68: Joe's Private Bigfoot Reserve

Toms Meadow #7: Forest Service Employee 9 (FSE 9) offers a suggestion: Happening 15 (H15) is the creation of Joe's Private Bigfoot Reserve.

Approx. GPS of TF33: 44 58 23.61N 122 03 0013W at ~ 2135'

GPS of upper beaver pond: 44 59 46.66N 122 02 09.32W at ~ 2305'

Sometime after the turn of the century I saw a Forest Service advertisement saying they were seeking input on road closures. Combining the information we'd gathered in 2001 on the area near Toms Meadow, plus with the Forest Service request for input, I decided to write a letter suggesting closing a Spur Road.

At the time I had a mildly cooperative contact in the Estacada Forest Service office we call FSE 9. So, one afternoon I got brave enough to call FSE 9. Since he knew me, FSE 9 had no illusions as to what I was conniving.

My contact, now retired, and not a Bigfoot believer, has over 30 years of experience in the woods. He laughed when I asked about sending a letter suggesting closing a Spur Road to protect Bigfoot. In fact, for a fleeting moment, I was under the impression he was sure I was mildly ... batty?

He paused, then his words were to this effect: "Send me the letter and I'll pass it on. I know that area. Don't mention your interest or your letter will drop in the trash faster than a brick. Say what is real, that's an area where elk and deer drop their young so it is best 4-wheelers and the like not disturb them."

So, through my letter, the hoped for winners were *my* Bigfoots in the Collawash; although, I sincerely think *my* Bigfoots do not think of me as their human, their *Jake*.

Happiness: Three months later about 100 yards from Road 63, a big berm with a deep excavated ditch behind it was thrown up on my Spur road. It was now closed to vehicle traffic. My suggestion worked and I was very happy.

Few people walk more than a quarter mile off a road and the good part of the area was about a mile in. The distance in became an unintended consequence on my part because now I had to leave my truck on the main road where it was vulnerable to vandals and theft, especially gas siphoning. Oh well, that was the price, so I paid it.

Later, someone I guided into the area called the place Joe's Private Bigfoot Reserve. Was I proud when I heard that? Sure was! Now I had my very own reserve, but it really didn't matter because by now, Cliff, Steve, and I decided to move our research yet again, from Big Bottom to Devils Ridge and the Pinhead Buttes.

Ref. 69: Bigfoot Watch Towers

Thom casts Track Find 33 (TF33) and finds Bigfoot Watch Towers which is Happening 16 (H16).

Late the next summer Thom Powell and I were talking. We decided it might be a good idea to walk into Joe's Private Bigfoot Reserve to check things out. So, we went up the hill and walked over a mile on the closed road. The hike was very easy as there's little elevation gain and the day was not hot.

About half a mile in we passed a salmonberry bush lush with berries, so we stopped and ate our fill. The succulent salmonberries also told us people hadn't been on the road for a while...Yes, salmonberries talk, if you take the time to listen.

About three quarters of a mile in, there is an old overgrown logging road running toward the base of Burnt Granite, and, toward the beaver ponds. Reader, does that give you ideas? The area is very pristine. Where it's been logged, new grown has become a park-like setting with a verdant carpet of duff, moss, ferns, and grasses.

Walking the abandoned road, it was only about 100 yards into this green mansion, when Thom saw a line of tracks in the duff. Let us label this Track Find 33 (TF 33). We were both startled, but I shouldn't have been. The tracks were about the same size as those we'd found a few years earlier on the bluff above the breaks of the Collawash.

These tracks were fresh, and whatever made them was heavy enough to leave indentations in the ground beneath the duff (For tracks in duff, gently lift it to look for impressions). But, now was not the time to cast. As a general rule, when a field researcher finds tracks, in the authors' opinion, they should do two things:

- First, follow the tracks to see where they begin and end. Normally, this is not a time consuming process. But, it can be baffling; sometimes track lines begin and end for no apparent reason.

- Second, the best tracks may not be the first ones found. Walk a big circle or two around a track line to look for more.

At about 150 yards, this track line was unusually long. The step between tracks was about 48 inches and the stride was about 90 inches which indicated a sizeable critter made the impressions. Tracks were

about 17 inches long, but the problem was, as with all tracks found in duff, we could only make approximations. This was where step two panned out the real gold that day.

Track line that yielded Thom's track cast. Photo by Joe Beelart.

As we began independent circling, we found other imprints in the duff. This clearly showed the creature habituated the area. While I worked the north, or river side, of the area, Thom circled to the south along the "rim-of-the-bowl." It was here were Thom made a really astounding find.

Thom found three places where the ground was cleared of duff and small limbs. Two were on large flat stones and one was a clearing beside a fir at the crest of the slope; below the clearing was the road we just walked. It was immediately obvious these cleared areas were watch stations. Standing on each of them gave us different views of the Spur Road and one provided a view of main road 63.

Thom had found Sasquatch watch towers! We designate this very important find as Happening 16. While it is not unusual for animals to have vantage points to watch territories, we think Thom's find is the first mention of it in Sasquatch literature.

While we marveled at the find, it was only later during the drive home we discussed a logical extension of Thom's find. If Sasquatch uses high ground for watch towers, why not trees?

Again, the problem was what to do. Well, the general rule of thumb with animals is to let sleeping dogs lie. We figured that was probably the best thing to do now.

On site, I took photographs and circled some more while Thom cast one especially deep duff track. Obviously the track couldn't provide much useable information, but it was a nice memento of the day.

So ends this account. Neither Thom nor I went back to the site until I returned alone late in the fall of 2010, and not since. Why? Honestly we have never talked about it much that I can remember. I think it was because we wanted to respect the home of the Sasquatch.

Postscript & Warning

The 2013 Jazz thinning sale raised havoc with part of the area, but as of July 2014, not all the good places were gone. Also, there is now a deep and dangerous rut early on Spur 170.

This ends reports from Area 4.

Bonneville power lines. See Appendix IV, Bigfoot Byways and Migration Routes for photograph of the trimmed area under the power lines. Photo by Sharon Beelart.

Area 5: Big Bottom and Surrounding Mountains

We feel Area 5 is the most beautiful part of the Oregon Bigfoot Highway, especially if carefully planned side trips allow the traveler to see the mountains, ridges, and buttes which form the east and west boundaries of this large habitat. While it is easy to quickly drive through this area, please do not. Take some time to walk the bottom lands, use binoculars to scout the highlands, and contemplate the life of Bigfoot in this great Area.

Area 5 is rife with Bigfoot reports and Bigfoot adventuring. Because of the large number of accounts in Area 5, it is broken into *three districts* generally delineated by major mountains, ridges, valleys, or landmarks within them.

District 1: Big Bottom, or the upper Clackamas River basin proper

District 2: is the mountain ridge dividing the west side of Big Bottom from the Collawash River drainage. The north end of District 2 is Burnt Granite (a mountain). The south end of the ridge terminates south of Mt. Lowe near Collawash Mountain.

District 2 is very special as it is the place where Glen Thomas had four sightings in 1967 and 1968. Soon after, Thomas was interviewed by John Green for inclusion in Green's seminal book, *Sasquatch, the Apes Among Us*. We are pleased that Mr. Green has graciously allowed us to quote his accounts of Thomas' sightings.

District 3: is a large almost square area east of Road 46 and south of Road 42 to the low plateau near SiSi Butte. District 3's east border is the Warm Springs Indian Reservation.

The highest elevations along *The Oregon Bigfoot Highway* are on the three Pinhead Buttes in District 3. West Pinhead Butte at 5577' is higher than Mt. Lowe at 5334' on the west side of Big Bottom. After sometimes demanding hiking, viewpoints high on the Pinhead Buttes reveal vast vistas to all points on the compass.

Map of Area 5

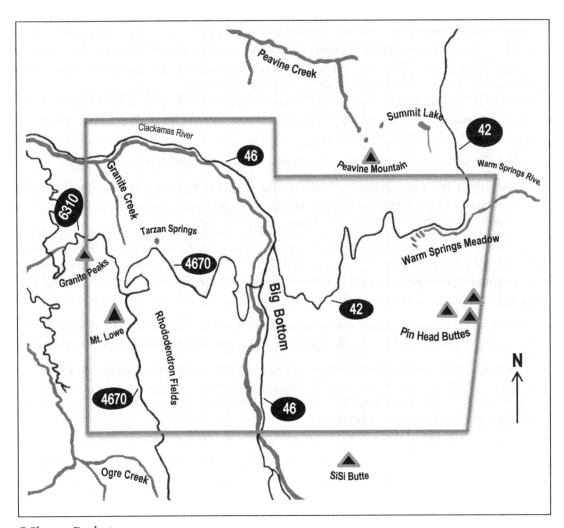

©Sharon Beelart 2015

Area 5 OBH Mile Markers

Miles from Estacada: from Detroit

28.4:	41.6	Collawash junction: Intersection of Roads 46 and 63
29.0:	41.0	Palisades of the Clackamas
29.8:	40.2	Big rock talus on north side of the road
31.5:	38.5	Austin Hot Spring, south side of the river
36.4:	33.6	High voltage power lines over Road 46
36.2:	32.8	Bridge and Road 4650 intersection
36.5:	33.5	Devils Ridge Road 4660
36.6:	33.4	A mile of old beaver ponds begin-end
39.5:	30.5	Junction with Road 42 to Mt. Hood
40.7:	29.3	Road 4670 to Mt. Lowe and Granite Peaks on left
45.5:	24.5	Upper (and last) Clackamas River Bridge
46.5:	23.5	Road 4690 to Olallie Lake
50.5:	19.5	Unmarked crest of Road 46
52.7:	17.3	Willamette National Forest sign; power lines; view turnout

District 1: The Big Bottom Stretch of Scenic Highway 46

Caution: Be especially careful driving the 11 miles south of the Collawash junction to the Road 42 intersection. Sometimes there is congestion at Austin Hot Springs; and, there are many flat, blind curves in this stretch of Road 46.

Control your speed and watch for on-coming traffic. But perhaps the greatest road hazards are deer and falling rocks.

District 1 of Area 5 covers Forest Service Road 46 from Mile 28.4 (41.6) to Mile 52.7 (17.3). These 34 ½ miles begin at the Collawash / Bagby Hot Springs intersection and end at the north boundary of the Willamette National Forest.

Along these miles the reader will experience some of the finest scenery in Oregon's high Cascades. And, in these pages the reader will learn this is Bigfoot's summer retreat, a land of plenty and solitude where the creatures can lead their lives almost as they did in times of old.

Less than a mile from the Collawash junction explorers pass high raw granite ramparts we call the *Palisades of the Clackamas*. Bigfooting explorers are now in the heart of the upper Clackamas River drainage. Now is a good time to think about the distant past of this wonderful place.

Imagine the last ice age when huge blankets of ice covered this land leaving only the tops of the highest mountains and ridges visible. At the end of the Ice Age raging torrents of melt water as high as the Palisades of the Clackamas roared through these narrows, leaving only barren stone.

The next major feature of District 1 is Austin Hot Springs on the south side of the river. Then, about seven miles after the Collawash intersection explorers enter the north end of Big Bottom, a fantastic huge bath tub shaped depression. Big Bottom was filled with a vast late Ice-Age lake as

evidenced by wave-made terraces on each side of the Bottom and on buttes in it.

When the Big Bottom ice dam near the Palisades, as well as similar ice dams near the mouth of Roaring River and the Collawash River melted, or more accurately, lifted, they drained the lakes behind them. These roaring melt-off waters and the boulders they carried were so massive and powerful they cut the great canyon known as the Clackamas gorge south of Estacada.

Austin Hot Springs. Photo by Joe Beelart.

In this age, during spring runoff, the Clackamas still grows wide in the Big Bottom flats as evidenced by erosion, sandbars, and bare rocks. In summer slightly elevated parts of this flood plain becomes a lush forest paradise filled with every sort of plant under high tree canopy including the exceedingly rare, carnivorous insect-eating plant *Darlingtonia californica*, or Cobra Lilly.

In Big Bottom, there are pure natural green cathedrals waiting for hikers to find them, to pause in them, to contemplate, to meditate where beauty and serenity abounds in nature's glory. These words are not overstatements, the majesty of Big Bottom is so impressive, so unique, that in 2009 it was turned into a part of the Clackamas National Wilderness.

District 1 geology #1: Palisades of the Clackamas: OBH Mile 29 (41 from Detroit)

Approx. GPS coordinates: 45 01 53.07N 122 02 52.51W, the approximate elevation at summit of the bare rock cliffs is 2000' which is 500' above river level.

District 1 geology #2: A Large Rock Talus: OBH Mile 29.8 (40.2 from Detroit)

The large round rock talus on the north side of the road is an example the tourist-explorer can see up close. Some talus are on top of ridges made of very dangerous plate rock. For example, see Ref. 70 describing the first Thomas sighting later in this chapter.

District 1 geology #3: Austin Hot Springs: OBH Mile 31.5 (38.5 from Detroit)

After the rock talus, travelers may notice a steam plume on the south side of the Clackamas River. This is Austin Hot Springs which surfaces at the north base of Burnt Granite (a mountain).

Two warnings: Austin Hot Springs is on private property and has no established bathing pools. The temperature of the spring varies. An unfortunate incident occurred in the fall of 2009 when two women and a child were severely burned over much of their bodies during a scalding water emission.

Do not try to park on the side of the road near the springs. If you want to see the hot springs, drive about one quarter mile east, park, and walk back. When parking, beware that like at Bagby Hot Springs, Austin often attracts unsavory characters with a liking to break into vehicles.

District 1: Monster 500 kilovolt power lines: OBH Mile 36.4 (33.6 from Detroit)

The electrical power lines running down the Clackamas River from the Oak Grove Fork power house to Estacada are "little" 115,000 volt lines. Further up the Clackamas hearty Bigfoot explorers will see two sets of monster Bonneville Power Administration 500,000 high voltage lines. The first crosses Road 46 in Big Bottom, the other at the Breitenbush River canyon breaks.

Power lines not only transfer electricity from Columbia River dams to users, they make raw highways through forests and mountains. In addition, power

Note the size of the winter slide tree trunk compared to my Tundra. Photo by Joe Beelart.

line cuts provide edges, miles and miles of edges. And as we all know, edges are important to animal survival as well as for watching animals.

Trimmed brush under power lines also provides forage fields for elk and deer. And, where there are elk and deer, there are large predators like cougars, and now possibly gray wolves that have migrated from eastern Oregon.

District 1: *Big Bottom*: **Forest Service Road 4651:** OBH Mile 36.2 (33.8 from Detroit)

After driving at modest speeds for over an hour and a half from Estacada, travelers arrive at OBH mile 36.2 (33.8 from Detroit), an intersection where there is only a turn to the south. This is where Road 4650 begins and climbs to Burnt Granite and Granite Peaks. Nowadays Road 4650 is bulldozed shut to all but foot and mountain bike traffic; but don't fret, views along the road are not particularly interesting.

Originally, Road 4650 was a horse trail used to supply fire lookouts, and for other forestry work. Later it was developed into a gravel log hauling road. Even later, when plans called for clear cutting the area south of Burnt Granite, 4650 was paved, but most of the planned timber sales were never made.

About 100 yards past the river bridge is the Road 4650 junction with Spur Road 4651. Spur 4651 is important in that is where your Big Bottom Clackamas Bigfootin' exploits began. But first, let's look at important Bigfoot history which happened on the western ridges above Big Bottom.

In 1967 and early 1968, on the west side of Area 5, Glen Thomas of Estacada had four sightings and a track find. Thomas' accounts occurred roughly between Mt. Lowe and Granite Peaks. We decided to begin reports from Area 5 with the Thomas sightings, because of their historic importance and the details recorded at the time by John Green.

About John Green on the 1967-1968 Glen Thomas Sightings

John Green of Harrison Hot Springs, British Columbia, is the historian emeritus of Bigfoot. His Bigfoot books culminated in *Sasquatch the Apes Among Us*, a giant, never paralleled work of over 175,000 words. *Sasquatch the Apes Among Us* was first published in 1978 and remains in print through Hancock House, a prime publisher of quality Bigfoot books.

Green is a newspaper man with more than three decades in the business. Paralleling his newspaper experience, he spent over 40 years conducting Sasquatch field research, including extensive on-site work at the Patterson-Gimlin Bluff Creek film location. Green accumulated and analyzed over 4,000 Bigfoot reports throughout Canada and the United States. Stories he selected for print are fact-filled, lean, and entertaining.

Mr. Green's various brief synopses and conclusions remain cornerstones of Sasquatch science and literature. His no-nonsense style set the standard for serious Bigfoot reporting today. So, I considered it a great honor when Mr. Green gave us permission to reprint his Clackamas and Collawash River reports.

After getting word of the Glen Thomas sighting in October 1967, John Green and René Dahinden traveled to Estacada to interview Thomas. John told me they timed an Estacada Friday evening surprise arrival which left no time for Thomas to make special preparations for them. The next morning, they went up mountain.

Both Green and Dahinden were duly impressed by Thomas' reports and the area in general. Next, Green reflects on the character of Glen Thomas.

John Green assesses the credibility of Glen Thomas

Begin John Green quote:

"Considering how rare it is for a person to see a sasquatch once, it always seems suspicious when someone reports that it has happened to them twice, although there is certainly nothing impossible about it. Unfortunately, from that point of view, four of the most informative of all sighting reports come from the same man. Nor does it help much that all those sightings took place within a period of a little more than a year. But the man had been spending every available hour since the first encounter trying to find the things again, and he lived where he could be in good country within minutes after leaving his home.

All his reports seemed entirely reasonable, and there was no indication that he was not a reliable person. He did not gain anything by telling the stories, in fact he did not tell them unless asked, and was most insistent that his name be kept secret for fear his neighbors would find out what he was doing. While the rest of us were wondering how he could possibly have seen so much, I expect he was wondering how we could have been fooling around for so long without seeing anything.

But, his most recent sighting was more than eight years ago now, and he has been hunting most of that time. It is my personal opinion that he is telling the truth. If he isn't, I don't know who is."

End quote from Green, John: *Sasquatch, the Apes Among Us*: second edition, 2006, Hancock House Publishers, Surrey, B.C. Canada: p.420–421.

Your authors' comments concerning the credibility of Glen Thomas:

Glen Thomas said this to Green about his first sighting, words that say a lot about what the experience meant to a long-time forest hand:

"At that time, I was a little bit nervous.... I'm not sure, now, about half of it seemed like it was a bad dream for a while. I just couldn't believe it was really happening. It just couldn't be, but it is."

In part, Green's opinion was validated by Millie Kiggins to me. She said Thomas took Green and Dahinden to the Kiggins' home to record Grover (father to Millie) and her reports of Sasquatch visits to the Kiggins property reported in Ref. 2. There Green learned about Thomas' friendship with Grover Kiggins and his visits to Grover soon after each of his sightings.

About the Thomas locations: While Thomas did not take Green to the location of all of his sightings, there are strong reasons to believe all of them happened on the western mountains and slopes above Big Bottom. There are three reasons the authors believe this. *First*, Thomas took John Green and René Dahinden to the talus site, so that location is certain.

Second, when Thomas told his talus story to Green, he mixed up the location with an area just to the southeast of Mt. Lowe. Lowe Creek, Mt. Lowe, and Jims Meadow are about two air miles from the Thomas site and are not likely to be misidentified by a logging road contractor.

Steve Kiley researched both the site and notes in Green's book. Kiley pointed out the rock talus site where Thomas led Green and Dahinden is a misidentification in Green's book. On inquiry, Green researched his notes and responded in writing that where Thomas led him and Dahinden, and where Thomas reported as the site location was correct.

Combining John and René's surprise arrival and what was probably a long day of talk, it is very reasonable that Thomas misspoke his locations. This thought led us to believe one of the Thomas sightings was near Mt. Lowe. Indeed, I later found a second talus with excavations south of Mt Lowe. That site is covered with rounded rocks.

Third, Green writes about Thomas ".... spending every available hour ...." continuing to search after his first sighting. This is a basic reaction characteristic of many people who witness a sasquatch. For a working family man like Glen Thomas, it is likely he returned to where he found gold, rather than prospecting a new area. In fact, Green notes on p.425 "The other sightings were all in the same general area ..." thus confirming the environs of Big Bottom in 1967 and 1968 was one of the best sasquatch sighting locales on record.

Thom Powell standing on the Thomas Site in 2014. Photo by Sharon Beelart.

Tony Healy (Australia) at the Thomas Site. Photo by Joe Beelart, July 2007.

Glen Thomas' first sighting is in Area 5, District 2 near Road 6310 in the Granite Peaks area. Green's report of Glen Thomas' October 1967 sighting follows. For the purposes of this book, Thomas' first sighting is designated as Sighting 22 (S22). Eating the ground squirrels is Bigfoot Related Incident 46 (I46).

A reminder; a *talus* is a large rock covered area bare of vegetation. The find of a similar site by Jim Henick and Thom Powell was reported in Area 3. Another similar site found by Steve Lindsey is reported in this section. From John Green, *Sasquatch the Apes Among Us,* Hancock House Publishers, Surrey, B.C. 2006, pages 420 to 424 and from John Green, *The Sasquatch File,* Cheam Publishing, Agassiz, B.C. 1973) "Ape Canyon to Estacada."

Wording is per John Green.
Begin quote:

"I have spent only one day out in the brush in Oregon as compared to months in California and British Columbia, but I rate that day as the most productive I have ever spent. The man who made it possible refuses to let his name be made public but he put his story on tape, as follows:

"I was supposed to be watching a catskinner as he was fire trailing, but it was awful cold, and I walked a mile or so down the trail, because he had no need of anyone at that time, and I thought I'd warm up and see the country. Up where he was, it was a cold east wind blowing; a little further down it was a west wind coming in. It was late fall, the last weekend in deer season I think, in 1967.

It was a mountain trail – they have several of them up there – footpaths, and for horses. The elevation was between four and five thousand feet. I came out lower down, into the fog, before I saw anything, and the fog was freezing on the trees because it was so cold, but the wind would blow, the fog would break, and fall off. That made it kind of noisy, it sounded like walking.

I came around a bend – well, first I noticed some rocks that were turned over. All the other rocks were wet, because of the fog, but these rocks were dry. Then I looked up, about forty or fifty feet, up on a ridge of rock, and I saw these animals there – looked like human or just about. Large male; the female wasn't so large; and a small baby – well not really small. It was moving with them. It was standing up, mostly.

The two older ones were squatting down and sort of bending, as they picked up rocks and smelled them. They were kind of careful. They moved on for a few minutes, and then finally the male found possibly what he was looking for and dug real fast down into the rocks, which were large boulders – not the round-type of rocks, but the flat, sharp kind.

I could not explain why these rocks were there; there hadn't been a slide or anything. They were on top of the ridge, so they wouldn't have come down from anywhere. They are loose, quite a few holes underneath them, and they are as if they had been broken up – definitely not the round river-type rock.

But, they (the animals) would pick them up, and after they smelled them, they would lay them down, on top of each other. They didn't just lay them back where they had picked them up; they stacked them up, in piles. And when the male found what he was looking for, he really made the rocks fly. The big rocks weighed 50, 60, or even possible 100 pounds; he just jerked them up with his hand. He didn't seem to take any precautions for his safety. Later on I looked, and there was some rock there that could have fallen on him, but he wasn't concerned.

He brought out what appeared to be a grass nest. Possibly some stored hay that small rodents had stored there. He dug through that, and brought out the rodents. It seems they ate them. The rodents appeared to be in hibernation, or asleep, or something. There were about 6 or 8 rodents. The small animal, I noticed, only got one, but the others got 2 or 3 apiece.

But about that time they became aware of my presence. And well, just became alert. I was alongside of this trail that follows the ridge. I didn't remember getting there, but I was squatting down beside a small tree when I became aware of where I was. As soon as they realized I was there, they suddenly began to move, real quiet, behind some low hanging limbs on a tree there. I didn't see them again after that.

I tried to follow their tracks in the direction I thought they would have to go, but I couldn't find any, although there was frost there. But the next day I found 2 tracks, 1 heel print, and the front part of the foot, the toes, but they were in a different direction – the direction from which I had come – and I never did get to connect up with exactly which direction they had gone or know anything about them.

The footprints, I would say, but there wasn't enough of the track to tell. They were possibly 5 inches wide, I don't know at the widest point. I don't think they could have been 6. I didn't know if it was one of the animals I had seen that made the footprints.

I saw the toe print as it came out of the old landing. I saw the heel print as it went in. The heel print gave me the impression that the heel protruded. The tracks were in dirt. It was just as if you had a level piece and scooped it out for about 2 feet deep, and it would cave in some. It (the animal) had stepped down into that and left a heel print, and as it stepped out on the other side you could see the toe print."

Pause.

"When I left the catskinner, he was on Lowe Creek, but I had walked to Jim's Meadow, possible a mile or more. I saw the footprints between where the catskinner was, and where I had seen the other animals.

After the animals disappeared I watched and looked for a few minutes and then decided I didn't want to go in that direction. So I just headed back. I didn't tell the catskinner about seeing them. I didn't tell anybody about it until (name redacted) asked me to ask among my crews, maybe some of them had seen them. That was the only time I had even mentioned it to any of the fellows out there, because I didn't want anyone to think I was a nut or something or other.

The only time I saw their faces was when they became alert. They gave me an impression of having a face a little like a cat, without the ears. I couldn't remember seeing the ears. It seemed like the nose was much flatter – it didn't stick out like a human's. The upper lip was very short, and seemed very thin. I couldn't remember that it had a chin, like a human has. So somehow or other, I felt that it was a face more like a cat than a human.

The male was darker than the female, a dirty brown, where the female was a buckskin or fawn colored animal. The male had much longer hair on shoulder, head, and neck, and hung in strings, like you see it on an Angora goat. He was much heavier in the shoulders than the female. From just above the hips, the male got larger; he had a very wide "small" of the back. From there on up, he just got bigger and bigger. They

had very rounded and stooped shoulders. The head was set lower on the shoulders than on a human. They don't seem to have the neck "stand up" as we do.

Most of the time they were not standing, but were squatting down and leaning forward to pick up the rocks. I didn't see them stand actually erect until they became alert that I was there. I didn't see them walk, as such. The only movement I saw was when they made a quick, short dash to get behind the limbs of the trees. I saw them move alright, but in a humped-up, stooped over position, just moving across the rocks. But they were upright when they made that quick dash at the end.

It seemed to me that the mother picked the baby up on her lap and ran holding the baby in front of her, possibly right below the breast, and her breasts hung real low, much lower than on a human.

I couldn't say how thick through the body these animals were, but they were very heavy set – particularly thick and heavy at the small of the back, and on up through the ribs. I think the male was over 6 feet tall, but I'm an awful poor judge of height and weight or anything. I didn't think the female was as tall as the male, in fact I think she came possibly up to his shoulder, but I saw them standing up so little, I didn't know, but they were much larger than a human, much bulkier.

The baby didn't come up to the mother's hips actually, I don't think, but I don't remember for sure. The first time I saw them standing up was as the male stepped out of the hole he dug with the grass, but it was only a very short while until they took off. I didn't see them after that.

Q: How did they eat?

"They ate by just taking it in their hand and eating it as one of us would if we were eating a banana. They ate it skin, feathers, and all just bit it in two, and as they would bite part of it well then just cram the other right on in. The little one though, he had a little more difficulty, because he didn't' have quite enough room for it all of it, where the older one did. It wasn't' like a human would hand the food to the baby, he had to get his – he was scratching through the grass that they had and got it himself, and the female did the same thing. They gave you the impression in that way of not taking care of the baby like people would. I've been wondering now if that group lived together as a family, and I hope to go back and look into it deeper.

Q: Did you form any impression of the proportions of, say, the legs in relation to the rest of the height? Would they be like a long-legged man, or short legged?

"I don't know; I couldn't say for sure; but the arms were such that when they squat down they have to bend forward to pick up anything – their arms are not long enough to reach. This one that was digging just seemed to go right on down. I didn't remember seeing him get up, but as he was down here, he was just digging and kept going on down, and ... well, at that time I couldn't see exactly where he was, because I was down, and they were up a little bit on the side of this rock, which kind of levels off some, and he went down, and so I couldn't see exactly what he was doing in there, but I did see when he came out. At that time I was a little bit nervous ... I'm not sure, now, about half of it seemed like it was a bad dream for a while. I just couldn't believe it was really happening. It just couldn't be, but it is.

Q: Did you notice the hands at all?

"I noticed that it had hands; I did not notice if it had thumbs. I couldn't tell from the way it worked; it didn't seem to use the thumb. And I didn't see any ears. I didn't see any knees projecting when it squatted.

They were in an awkward position because of the rocks, and they couldn't just squat down like we would on a floor. They would be on different levels; and off too far to be comfortable. That's as close as I can explain it.

When they went from place to place they would shift in position, according to the terrain. The male, well, actually both of them, seemed to be moving in a certain direction, possibly from tracing the small rodents. I thought possibly it was the scent left by the rodents coming up through the rock, because it was not a runway that they could have been picking, because they were just picking the rocks up anyplace, and as they picked them up, they'd turn it over and smell it, and then lay it on the stack. They left it very definitely in a pile. They would leave anywhere from three to fifteen or twenty in one pile, as they would reach back, and then, oh, six to eight feet farther, they would leave another pile—start laying them in another."

Green visits the site:

"With René (Dahinden) and my daughter Kathryn and son Jim, I went with this man last July to the spot where he had seen the three creatures. We found the piles of rocks to which he referred, not only at the spot he showed us, but on almost every other area of broken rock we found in two hours of scrambling around on the mountain. They were obviously piles manufactured by something or someone, the rock could not have rested that way naturally, and there were dozens of them.

The hole he saw the male sasquatch dig was about five feet deep and almost as steep sided as a well. No bear or anything else without hands could have lifted out the rocks. A man could undoubtedly figure out a way to do it if he had any reason to take the trouble, but in this case the story had only come out as the result of an inquiry from someone else who had seen footprints in the snow in January of this year, and there was no reason to expect that anyone would be coming to look over the site."

End of quote

Note: The persons who reported "footprints in the snow" to local television, to John Green; and ultimately, the British Broadcasting Company, were the Kiggins mentioned in Ref. 2. The witness to the sighting Green just detailed was Glen Thomas, a close friend of the Kiggins.

Four notes concerning the Thomas site:

- Important; the visit described by John Green was the trip mentioned by Millie Kiggins in her interview (Ref. 2). It also bears repeating that Glen Thomas and Grover Kiggins, Millie's father, were good friends. Thomas repeatedly visited the Kiggins' to talk about his sightings. Millie said the sightings upset Thomas, who was Native American. She said he sometimes questioned why the spirits allowed him to see the creatures and not some other person.

- Be aware there are other rock stacks in the general area of the Thomas site. However the only probable sasquatch "diggings" we've found is on a small rock scree about 100 yards southwest of the Thomas site.

- There is a probable second talus excavation site about four air miles south as mentioned by Thomas to Green in his interview. Not far south of Mt. Lowe Kiley and Beelart found a talus slope with excavations similar to the first Thomas site.

- In the spirit of sharing information, we wanted to list the GPS of the Thomas site in this book. However, a Forest Service official informed us of a nearby archeological site so we do not list it. However, we can say it is within a mile of Tarzan Springs.

Warning: If you happen upon a talus site like the Thomas site, we cannot emphasize enough the danger. People have smashed faces, broken wrists and ankles, and severely cut themselves falling on it. Even when the plate rocks are dry they are unstable and dangerous. When the talus is wet or icy the site is treacherous.

Ref. 71: Glen Thomas' Second Sighting

John Green: Glen Thomas' Second Sighting is listed as Sighting 23 (S23): Eating the leaves is labeled Bigfoot Related Incident 47 (I47). A reminder, Mr. Green does not capitalize the "s" in sasquatch. From Green, p.425:

"In the spring of 1968 he (Thomas) was looking for a place to take some sighting-in shots with a gun when he noticed at a distance of about 100 feet an animal eating leaves off a willow bush. He climbed up on the bank by the road to get a better look. The creature was a female, with breasts like a woman's, but in a lower position on the chest. He estimated it to be only five or six feet high, but it was very heavily built and covered with short, dark brown hair.

As he watched it strip leaves and shove them in its mouth he had the impression that its thumbs were not used. They seemed to be farther back on the hand than a human thumb. He had watched it only a few seconds before it noticed him and ran off into the trees. Although not many miles from the location of the first sighting, it was at much lower elevation."

Note: "... not many miles ..." is the key here. This sighting was probably in or just up from Big Bottom. There are flats there for long range shooting and many willows near water.

Ref. 72: Glen Thomas' Third Sighting

District 2: Glen Thomas' Third Sighting in November 1968 is designated Sighting 24 (S24) with Track Find 34 (TF34): Sleeping drawn up on stomachs is Bigfoot Related Incident 48 (I49): Cleaning and eating roots is Incident 49 (I49).

An inference is possible from Thomas' third sighting report. He mentions crossing a 3,500 foot high ridge. This means he probably dropped into the Collawash drainage (Area 4). From high up the only roads down into the Collawash from the Mt. Lowe – Granite Peaks ridgeline are via Road 6310 at Granite Peaks and Graham Pass via Road 6350 near Mt. Lowe.

Both roads lay between steep drop-offs which would account for the sasquatches walking on them for some distance. This reference, especially if the route was Graham Pass Road 6350 lends credibility to Steve Kiley's contention that part of Glen Thomas' finds were near Mt. Lowe and Jim Meadow.

From Green, p.425 – 426:

"For the next half year he hunted without success, but in November he hit the jackpot. Crossing a ridge at about 3,500 feet, he found two sets of tracks, both about 16 inches long, and followed them for several miles in the snow, going down a logging road. They were not always on the road but kept coming back to it.

Eventually they reached a level where the snow was petering out, and where we lost them in the woods. Next day he went back to where he had left off, and while casting about for more tracks he saw something dark on the snow across a small open area.

Using binoculars at a distance of less than 200 yards, he found himself looking at two sasquatches sleeping out in the open, with their backs to the sky and their knees and elbows drawn in under their bodies. He settled down for a long vigil, and they slept for about an hour, with very little movement, then one got up and then the other.

They went to a creek a few feet away and began pulling up and eating water plants. Both were obviously females, with more pendulous breasts than the ones he had seen before, and one appeared to have a swelling in the genital area and kept rubbing itself. It also gave an occasional loud call, which he described in a computer interview as 'like a scream in an echo chamber.'

He also saw one defecate in the creek. It stepped up on a wide, low stump that was in the water, 'bent forward about 45 degrees with its knees slightly bent and let fly.' It then wiped itself with one hand, and licked the hand briefly.

Ref. 73: Glen Thomas' Fourth Sighting

District 2: Glen Thomas' Fourth Sighting in December 1968 is Sighting 25 (S25): "… arms raised in threating way …" is designated as Bigfoot Related Incident 50 (I50).

From John Green, p.426:

"His final encounter took place only about a month later. He was following some elk tracks, walking on top of old, deep snow, when he happened to look back and saw right behind him, only about 10 feet away, a scruffy looking, dark brown sasquatch at least nine feet tall.

Ref. 74: Glen Thomas' 1969 Track Find

District 2: Glen Thomas' last sasquatch contact reported to Green was a track find near an unknown road in February 1969. This is labeled Track Find 35 (TF35). Purportedly eating grass is labeled Incident 51 (I51). From Green p.426:

After feeding for about half an hour, working their way up the creek from him, they lay down again in a new location for about an hour, then, both got up and crossed the road. The female with the swelling climbed a few feet up in a dead yew tree and wailed, then, both moved off into the timber above the road.

He estimated them to be only about six feet high, but very heavy. They were both dark brown, covered with shaggy, dirty hair. When they lay down they did not seek shelter, although there were trees nearby, and at one time there was snow falling. After they left, the observer went home. He said he was 'too spooked' to go over where they had been. Next day there was new snow."

It had both arms raised in what he took to be a threatening way, and he scrambled to try to get a revolver out from under his rain clothes. However, the animal quickly ran and ducked behind the roots of a blown-down tree, and since it was leaving anyway he did not shoot at it. Instead, he 'left the area running.'

His impressions of that individual are pretty spotty, but he realized afterwards that it had a mild smell, 'like an old outhouse,' and that it had a long upper lip that fluttered as it blew through its mouth. He also noticed that its hands were very large and long, but with the thumb 'not up where a human thumb is.'"

"(Thomas saw) … the tracks of two creatures, one with a 14-inch foot, the other 11-inch, that came out of the forest into a field, where they appeared to have been eating the lower stems of clumps of grass … What particularly interested him was that the two tracks were always near each other but never right together."

Ref. 75: Green on the Thomas Sightings

John Green brilliantly summarized the principle elements of Glen Thomas' sightings and track finds. Again, with Mr. Green's written permission to quote, from page 427 of *Sasquatch, the Apes Among Us*:

"Bearing in mind the hazards of basing too much on reports from a single source, there is a wealth of information in those (Thomas') observations. They picture creatures that do not have an effective opposable thumb, or if they do, don't use it much. There are three accounts of sasquatches actually eating something— rock rodents, willow leaves and water weeds—and circumstantial evidence that they eat grass stems.

The observation of the infant avoiding the male (in the first sighting) suggests that the trio was not a family group, and the tracks in the field suggest possibly a juvenile still hanging around its mother, but not welcome. The other pair was made up of two adult females, again suggesting that family groups are not the norm.

Female chimpanzees have to put up with large sexual swellings when in heat, but other apes do not, and there is no other report of a sasquatch in that condition. That, plus the calling, indicates reproductive arrangements unlike those of any other ape, but perhaps suitable for a species very thinly distributed. On that point, however, note that he describes a total of seven individuals, all different, and tracks that appear to belong to two more, all in an area of about 200 square miles.

Finally, one of them defecating into running water, at the same place where it was eating, might indicate a complete lack of concern about such bodily functions, or it might possibly be a set pattern of behavior. If so, that would certainly cut down the chances of collecting sasquatch droppings. It would also give the people who safeguard domestic watersheds from pollution something to think about."

The end of John Green quotes.

Ref. 76: Sasquatchian McCoy comments on the Thomas Sightings

By Leann McCoy:

"A great chapter, but I don't agree with all the conclusions John Green makes on the Thomas sightings. For example, because Thomas saw two females together Green thinks family groups are not the norm. Seeing two females together in no way means Sasquatch family groups are not the norm any more than seeing two human females together without the presence of a male means human family groups are not the norm.

Assumptions like that may have been based on the hundreds, even thousands, of interviews and investigations John Green

conducted prior to meeting Glen Thomas. However, they can't be made from Thomas' reports alone.

Also, Green makes no comment on signs that Thomas may have had experiences with the Sasquatch beyond simply seeing them. A careful read of Green's notes leaves me with a feeling something else may have happened to Thomas as his words show hallmarks of close encounters as reported by many other people, including accounts earlier in this book.

Thomas: "*... about half of it seemed like it was a bad dream for a while.*" Anytime a person reports a "dream-like quality," or other strange feeling it may not be due to shock. Something beyond the physical may have happened, something due to some other mental mechanism the Sasquatch people induce on humans.

Thomas: *"I don't remember getting there but I was squatting down beside a small tree when I became aware of where I was ..."* This statement by Thomas clearly indicates something else likely happened to him which he did not recall.

Thomas' experience is similar to other close encounter reports which indicate Sasquatch can hypnotize people, or freeze them in place, or perhaps even "freeze time." How the Sasquatch People do this is unknown and the reasons they may do it are varied. Three of the reasons are simple. They may do it to take a close look at a human, physically move a human as perhaps in Thomas' experience, or simply to get away.

Here is another comment which I've found true in my own research. People who are alone, and perhaps even on a subliminal level, seek out additional contacts generally have more contacts when they seek them. Green tends to confirm this through his assessment on the veracity of Glen Thomas.

Joe, I appreciate you letting me comment on John Green's reports of Glen Thomas' sightings. One thing I'd like to make clear is that I greatly respect John Green's long newspaper career, his decades of Sasquatch research, and his books. My comments here simply illustrate there may have been more going on with Glen Thomas than even Thomas knew."

Ref. 77: Henick and Powell find a Thomas type site

If we assume the Forest People live up there, as they do, we can also assume the first Thomas site is not unique. For that reason your Clackamas Sasquatchians have spent much time exploring talus for additional Thomas-like excavations. One of the finest examples was found in 2013 by Jim Henick and Thom Powell. Their story follows. For the purposes of this book the Henick-Powell find is designated Happening 17 (H17).

In the summer of 2013 Jim Henick and Thom Powell were prowling the ridges above Roaring River. There are several bare rock talus slopes on those ridges, as well as an extensive network of lava tubes, well-hidden, but known to advanced spelunkers. Bushwhacking across a ridge, on a remote talus Henick came upon a group of rock excavations very similar to those at the Thomas site. It is important to note the place is not enroute to any summit or near a hiking trail.

There are five clear excavations, one down about five feet to bedrock. Like the Thomas site the excavations seem to follow a pattern; and, as at the Thomas site, there is clear evidence of ground squirrel habitation. However, thinking this could be a sacred Native American vision site, Powell invited an archaeologist who specializes in northwest Native American culture to visit the excavations.

The archaeologist was experienced with over 20 years with a major Federal government agency. He pronounced the site not Native American, but offered no explanation of why it was made. He was also impressed at the size of some of the rocks that were removed from the holes.

In August 2013 Powell invited me to see the Roaring River site. Just getting "near" the place required traveling one of the worst forest roads I've ever driven. Thom had prepared a campsite that was simply magnificent. Standing in full view before us was Mt Hood in all its bare summer majesty. At night Timberline Lodge and Government Camp were wonderful beads of crystal light.

Camp was at the edge of a very steep slope which we proved by rolling a big rock that seemed to bust brush forever. (Don't do that at home; we shouldn't have, but it was too tempting.)

Thom Powell on the site he and Jim Henick found in 2013. Photo by Joe Beelart.

I found the talus moderately steep and dangerous, a better place for athletic Bigfooters like Jim and Thom. I was afraid of falling, but the temptation to see it was great. The excavations were all, and much more, than Thom had told me. There was no reason for the place to be Native American as it only faced the event of winter solstice and would then be covered by deep snow, a far trek from low altitudes.

However, as the slope faced the southeast, snow on it would melt early in the year providing Sasquatch an opportunity to catch hibernating ground squirrels. (See Ref. 70.) Weather aging and lichens on various excavated rocks seemed to indicate the excavations had been renewed or added to in recent years.

The next morning, I got up early and made some effort to approach the site from another direction with no success. Back at camp Thom had perked hot coffee and was prepping his really great pan breakfast using early potatoes from his garden. Four

Excavation at the Henick-Powell site, (5' walking staff.) Photo by Joe Beelart.

ears of boiled fresh garden corn were left over from the evening before so, hungry from my hike I ate one cold with fresh butter. Later we used the others as offerings.

When the pan was done ... potatoes, eggs, cheese, bacon, onions, mushrooms, and magic, Thom's son Jack and his friend went after it like the polite, ravenous teenagers they were. I must say, that breakfast and perked Folgers combined with the morning view of Mount Hood, was one of the finest and most memorable I will ever have: "Thank you Thom."

Ref. 78: Sasquatchian Lindsey finds an old Thomas type site

Happening 18 (H18) was on April 29, 2014 when Steve Lindsey and I drove up the hill to look around. As expected, we were blocked by snow about 1,000 vertical feet below Tarzan Springs, so we drove across Big Bottom and went up to the Big Rock Quarry.

On the east side, there was still snow up there that we plowed through in 4WD. On the west slope, afternoon sun had melted the snow and dried the road so we were fine. Lower on Forest Service Road 5731, a little south of the intersection with Road 5720, we stopped for a walk

Steve chose the east side of the road so I got the west, the big flat between Devils Ridge and the twin crests of Oak Grove Butte. One advantage of hiking this time of year is foliage on brush and annual trees are not out, so you can see well. I found a few deer tracks, but that was it; just a pleasant walk for me.

Steve had better luck. He led me to a little narrow scree about 150 feet long by 30 feet wide. The approximate center is at GPS 45 02 32.14N 121 53 47.53W at 3333′ which is an amazing number, given randomness in nature. There were rodent dens all through it and on the nearby rocky hillside.

And, there were four excavations. Three were bowl type about 10 feet across and one was a smaller, roughly two foot box type. Decaying small branches and rock weathering indicated the excavations were old, but for sure they were excavations.

Important: Lichen marks showed on the sun side of many rocks. Lichen does not grow in direct sun; it likes shade or dark. Those rocks, and there were many of them, were turned. Some were obviously stacked.

The bowl type excavations indicated these were not old Native American hunting blinds, too shallow, plus open all

Photo by Joe Beelart

around. They were not prospector test holes; this scree was all volcanic rock. While the area was logged, probably about 30 years ago, these were not bull dozer pits. Plus, there was one other telling sign. There was no human debris like expended cartridges, beer cans, plastic, cigarette wrappers, etc. lying around.

Our conclusion was Steve Lindsey found a Thomas type site where Bigfoot moved rocks to hunt ground squirrels. We are giving the GPS so other researchers can verify our claim. The find was a short distance from the road, maybe 150′ or so, but it is well hidden in summer by brush.

Also of note is that 100 yards or so north of the site is the beginning of the west access road to the top of Devils Ridge. In old times, this road was probably an Indian trail which also gave Sasquatch an easy access route to the top.

Warnings: (1) This scree has very unstable rocks. Be extremely careful walking on it. (2) The pot hole from hell is lower on Road 5730, about a quarter mile up from Timothy Lake Road 57.

District 1: Big Bottom, a Wilderness

Big Bottom is now a designated national wilderness, one of the five part Clackamas wilderness system. Each wilderness is separated from the others. They include Big Bottom, Clackamas Canyon, Memaloose Lake, SiSi Butte, and the South Fork of the Clackamas.

On maps, Big Bottom looks like a dog leg. On the ground, it looks like a huge bathtub with the drain downriver. It is a magnificent place to hike, a river bottom scoured by runoff each spring, rebounding into lush vegetation each summer and fall.

Huge water loving trees grow in the Bottom. Indeed, Oregon's biggest red cedar, a true monster, is only about an hour hike from Road 46. Everywhere there are big trees, some fallen by nature to regenerate this special part of the forest. In summer, the canopy makes Big Bottom a cool, inviting place to hike and explore. But as hikers soon learn, landmarks are few, paths indistinct, and getting lost easy.

Carry a compass. If you do become disoriented in Big Bottom, *do not panic*. Depending on your jump-off, just walk west to Road 4651 or to the river and follow it out. Be sure to pack plenty of drinking water. And, we advise using a staff or walking stick. Beware lying directly on soft detritus covering the ground. If you do, you'll soon figure out why.

Ref. 79: The Green Click

Big Bottom #1: The Green Click is Happening 19 (H19).

Road 4651 parallels the west side of Big Bottom and the Big Bottom Wilderness. Several stories came from game cameras set along Road 4651; this account combines summaries of several of them. These were trail cameras from the old days, not the economical super convenient weatherproof trail cams available today; which take half the fun from the art of using them.

But for now, let's skip the technical details of assembly and camouflaged set-up and get on to results. To provide an idea of the quality of photographs my archaic camera gets see page 101.

1999 Big Bottom Camera Traps

In Spring 1999 we set our game cameras in Big Bottom along Road 4651. At the time, the road was closed by a heavy steel logging road gate requiring hikes to set and service our gear. That was no problem as Road 4651 is a pleasant walk.

June 1999: I went up alone to set our infra-red actuated cameras in Big Bottom. The day was hot and sultry. I set one in a little basin at the base of Burnt Granite (a mountain). The attractants were simple, just a trapper's feather lure Steve made and raccoon trapping scent which smells sweet, like peppermint.

Then I walked at least another half mile south on 4651 to where the back and rib bones of an elk were bleaching in the sun. I dropped off the road toward the river on an old logging road now covered with vine maple. The glen I selected was surrounded with old growth and big downed trees. The place was very green,

green all over except for gray-tan fallen and broken wood.

My set up aimed at a big game trail. This game trail was well-used with no tracks. Surely, in my mind, it was another *Devils Trail!* I set fishing spinner blades here and there for lures, spread scent and managed to get a little bit on me. Swell, at least it wasn't "Big Stinky." That stuff smells ugly rotten and takes days to get off.

The first Road 4651 camera traps worked well except for no photos of Bigfoot. Most of the time when people find a camera set they either smash it or steal it, but fortunately, I've been lucky and haven't had one stolen. The most famous click we got was when someone came across one of our trail cams and gave us a moon shot and we ain't talkin' the space moon kind.

Another shot was more important. The infrared actuator was only supposed to work out to 60 feet. The *Green Click* image happened under old-growth tree canopy on a very still, breezeless day at slightly over 105 feet! To confirm, Steve and I later measured it with my long tape. I call it the *Green Click* because all the foliage was spring green and the sun was just right overhead to illuminate the greenness of the place.

I was proud of the *Green Click* and made several hard copies of it to send to various people, clearly explaining the distance and situation. At the time I was on one of the early Bigfoot Internet discussion groups and sent a hard copy to a member in Texas. They think big down there.

The gentleman was retired from a large company and seemed to have his feet on the ground. But, he went a bit zany over the *Green Click*. In the photo he saw a Bigfoot for sure. So, unknown to me, he took the photograph to his old office, scanned the *Green Click*, and posted it online. (At the time, scanning was a big deal.)

Pretty soon, I started getting emails, and even two telephone calls; one from a TV production company, wanting to use my Bigfoot photograph. I wondered, *what the hell is this all about?* After pointedly questioning a caller, I figured it out.

So, I called Texas on the telephone. "Where's the Bigfoot?" Before he answered, he started going on about the beast carrying a dead deer and a club, etc. I told him I just didn't see a Bigfoot, just me walking in to the camera trap.

I laughed, told him to blow up the image on his computer screen and he'd find me with my hiking stick angled toward the camera (the club) and my Duluth pack hanging from just one shoulder (the dead deer). So ended my "blob Squatch" photograph episode.

Unfortunately many, many people in the Sasquatchin' game don't take much care with what they think they see and as a result "blob Squatches" abound on the Internet. And, stuff on the Internet hangs around forever. Occasionally someone will still come across the *Green Click* with Tex's caption and post me about it.

Ref. 80: Kiley sees a Bigfoot

Big Bottom #2: Steve sees a Bigfoot in Sighting 26 (S26) along with Track Find 36 (TF36): The aggressive initial *ROAR* is Bigfoot Related Incident 52 (I52). The "whacks" on wood are labeled Incident 53 (I53). The moderate calls made and returned by the critters are Bigfoot related Incident 54 (I54).

Approx. site location, but very close is GPS 45 00 40.02 N121 55 11.05W ~ 2190'.

If following on Google Earth, watch the elevation rise along the tree line to 2190' and then begin falling. The high point is where Kiley's sighting happened.

Saturday June 19, 1999: It was a very nice day up the hill. First we checked out Road 42 that goes between Big Bottom and Mt. Hood. A few miles up, a big, bushy tailed coyote jumped out of the brush and jogged up the road in front of us, which was really fun to see. High on the ridge, snow turned us back just past the headwaters of Warm Springs River. Along the snow line beautiful arrowhead bear grass was blooming.

After kicking around Pinhead Buttes for an hour we went down to Big Bottom to wander and service the trail cameras. We parked at the closed gate on Road 4651 and hiked about a half mile to a Forest Service "keep'em out" road.

A "keep'em out" road means a place to explore so we crashed brush paralleling the torn-up road to a seasonal creek where we entered a strip of old growth about 200 feet deep. Behind it, a bowl of about 20 or more acres was filled with new growth 10 to 15 feet high. The Forest Service does that, leaving a band of old growth to hide the destruction logging leaves behind.

Steve led me along a game trail right beside the old growth. As we walked along we saw the big clear cut rising from the bowl up slope toward the northeast corner of Burnt Granite. We mention this, because the lay of the land proved important that day, and in three days to follow.

It was also here, in the old growth buffer tree line, we found another Devils Trail. Unfortunately, due to a later fire brush clearing operation, this Devils Trail is now obliterated. Note: By the end of 2013 we found seven Devils Trails spread throughout the Clackamas Ranger District and Breitenbush drainage.

Anyway, back to the story: I was following Steve by about 70 feet. He came to a small rise and from the brush just in front of him came a great, long rolling roar that rose in pitch and then died off. It lasted a long time, like a jet fighter taking off, not like an irritated bear.

Steve later described it as "enveloping." It hit me hard, like a rock concert speaker test; and I was way behind him. I ran up the trail. When I got to Steve, he was dumbfounded and obviously in a mild state of shock, I saw enough of that from my years in the Marine Corps to know. Steve stared into the new growth and pointed south.

He says he didn't say it, but he said, "It walked that way." Very interesting, that word "walked." I said some calming words, which I forget, and we both quieted down a bit. So that was it for the first part of Sighting 26.

Game Drive

We decided I should make a big circle to the south and see if something might come out. (In retrospect, I wonder about this plan ... monster in the trees, me in the trees ...) Steve was to stay on the mound with his little video camera. I borrowed his 44 magnum revolver, made sure it was loaded and then dove into the brush.

I went into the band of big trees where amazingly enough I found a reasonably well used deer trail that paralleled the Devils Trail. This was another pattern we found, deer and elk trails near a Devils Trail, but only crossing tracks on the Devils Trail, and even those tracks are very few.

Carefully, I made my way south into older regrowth and in the skungy trees, I turned west to parallel the torn up road. Finally, I got to a place where I couldn't penetrate the stuff, too many limbs. Important for our "drive," Steve later said I was making plenty of noise.

Note: Keep this area where I hiked into the regrowth in mind. It comes up again soon in another report when Cliff stands at the edge of it; and even later when an incident happened to me.

Anyway, several hundred yards into the trees, I turned back north (right) to complete my circle. The Forest Service had dozed a "keep'em out" road here too. It was strange; there were hardly any deer tracks even though tender, new browse was profuse. Maybe they had simply migrated to higher elevations for the summer.

After a while when I was taking a breather, I saw Steve maybe a hundred yards or a little more to my right. While I was standing and looking around, something started pounding on wood in the old growth where I began my circle! The whacks were loud, but not fast. "Whack ... whack ... whack."

The "whacks" were very clear to me. There were three whacks, no more; but they were very robust, very powerful wood-on-wood sounds. They weren't hurried at all. This worried me somewhat, so I cut off my planned hike and crashed brush over to Steve. We list the "whacks" as Incident 53.

Later, Steve told me something else that happened when I was in the trees which we labeled Bigfoot Related Incident 54. In an uncharacteristic, almost hesitant voice he shared something which obviously bothered him.

When I was circling in the regrowth, the creature called out again only not in a roar; it was in much quieter tone, and made sound breaks in what may have been in a primitive language. He said there were two replies – one from the slope to the south, and one from the northwest side of the bowl.

He said the first call was definitely a question and the return calls made him feel they were a *"Yes, I am here"* sort of response. He said there was no way the sounds were made by bears.

Steve also said, "Out of the corner of my eye, I saw a tall shadow go through that opening." He pointed to a door-way like space about 30 yards away.

He said, "I didn't see any form or color or hear any noise, but it darkened the space. Then, a few minutes later, a doe deer minced through the opening. She showed color."

It was after the deer passed by that Steve heard a long, loud, distant call from Big Bottom, the direction my wood knocks came from. It was briefly answered from the northwest side of the basin. His distinct impression was this was yet another *inquiry* call from a fourth creature; and most startling, was a response that came from yet another part of the basin.

In a quiet worried voice Steve said, "Just how many of those things are out there?"

He went on, "Then, about 10 minutes later, you went by the opening making plenty of noise. You were taller than the deer, but at least a foot or more shorter than the shadow. I could see your colors good."

Note: The above is a paraphrase, but it is very close to what Steve saw in 2012. Steve approved these notes for the book. We would also like to note that either the beings in the basin moved very fast and very quietly or there were at least five creatures in the general area.

So, the shadow was bipedal and about 7 to 8 feet tall and made no noise. This spooked us. Next, close together, this time with the 44 in Steve's holster, we explored the basin. In shallow dust, Steve easily found the track line from where it came out of the trees in front of him, turned, walked north along the old skid road and where the animal turned into the trees.

Unfortunately, the run of tracks, which we label Track Find 34, were too shallow to cast and the high sun didn't show much in photographs, mainly because we were so excited we didn't think about cutting branches to make shade. Oh well ...

After the Incident

Well, we were a little unnerved, but decided to look around some more. I went over to the dry runoff creek on the north side of the clearing and worked my way up slope. Steve went into the woods, crossed the road and scouted Big Bottom toward the Clackamas River. More than an hour later we met on the road. With extra adrenaline pumping, we both had made good distances, allowing for elevation, and were tired. We ate lunch and about 2 PM began our drive home; surprisingly, having little to say.

Ref. 81: Cliff Investigates: More Big Bottom excitement!

Big Bottom #3: Cliff investigates Steve's roar and finds himself stomped at, plus other sounds not right. The wind sounds and stomping Cliff heard, we label Bigfoot related Incident 55 (I55).

In concurrence with his detail-minded electrical career, and natural curiosity, Cliff Olson adopted a serious investigative interest in Steve's sighting and vocalization incidents. While Steve and I revisited the site, we did not do it as many times, or with the detailed vigor of Cliff.

Once, when he went up alone, again, Cliff reported as he walked up the "keep'em out" road, he began to hear wind blow. Hehe: Wind blowing in the forest; that's big news, right?

Cliff stopped and scanned the area. He didn't see anything, but the sound was unmistakable, wind blowing in the trees. And the sound kept on but Cliff did not feel wind, and when he looked at the tree tops they were not moving. "In fact, not a damn thing was moving."

Then, the wind noise slipped into a whistling wind, not a blowing wind. For some reason, Cliff began counting this sound down. The light whistling wind lasted for about 30 seconds, a long time.

Next Cliff heard heavy footfalls in the tress, but yet, he couldn't see any movement. The heavy footfalls got near, and louder. They became stomps! Cliff said later he thought, *OK, here he comes!*

But Cliff wasn't particularly worried. He was carrying his legal short barrel 12 gauge shotgun loaded with Sabot slugs, the same loads Alaskan fishing guides use to stop giant brown bears. He said he slipped off the safety, but kept his finger off the trigger.

Since he had a foreboding when preparing for the day, Cliff also belted on his 9mm Browning Hi-Power pistol, but he said he never even thought of pulling the precision weapon. He later said, "No need to just make it mad."

Then there was a silent standoff between Cliff and the invisible forest giant. Neither made a sound. Then tired, or bored, with the intrusive human, the unseen creature smashed through the thick trees away from Cliff. That was the end of the day for Cliff; he was ready to drive home.

By Google Earth, the place where Cliff was standing was about 100 yards south by southwest from where Steve had his sighting. After we went to the "wind and stomping" place with Cliff, we have collectively decided Cliff probably had the closest encounter with Sasquatch of any of us, anytime. The odd thing was even though he was very close and heard sounds very clearly; Cliff *did not* see so much as a shadow.

Approximate GPS of Cliff's wind and stomping event: 45 00 37.33N 121 55 08.75W ~ 2190'. Remember this spot.

The film makers go up

Blake Eckard and Alec Jennings were in Portland, again, to do more work on their Bigfoot documentary. Cliff told Blake about his wind and stomping encounter, and Steve's sighting. They wanted to go up, so a day was found when everyone could go along.

Later, we found it a bit shocking that on the day we took Blake and Alec to the site it was a day with lots of "action." If they had their doubts about Bigfoot being real, they didn't have them by the end of this adventure.

First we showed them the Devils Trail. Cliff remarked he couldn't remember anything like it, but of course back in his hunting days; he wasn't looking for Bigfoot trails. Cliff pointed out it was also clear of hanging vines, which were common right and left along it. Then, while Steve, Blake, Alec, and I walked the sighting area, Cliff wandered off to again investigate the area bordering the south side of the basin.

Then, to our great surprise, two very loud, long calls, not roaring calls, but yelling calls happened. One was from near Cliff in the trees and the other came out of Big Bottom to the east. The calls made, and returned, were not whistles and seemed to hold some sort of message. Alec and I hiked into Big Bottom, so we didn't hear the next exchange.

The sounds near Cliff changed. He heard what he thought was chest pounding but again, couldn't see anything. Steve said he heard what sounded like chest pounding coming from near Cliff. Blake heard it too. Later, to our great laughter, Blake said he envisioned a giant invisible gorilla pounding his chest in front of Cliff. Then something happened that Cliff, Steve, and Blake all agree on.

They heard loud wood knocks coming from Big Bottom. This was strange, since Alec and I did not hear them. Steve said the knocking happened four or five times. From their description, I thought the wood knocks were the same as I heard the day Steve had his sighting.

Then, almost in the same place as where it happened before, Cliff heard faint heavy footsteps recede away from him. From their vantage point, Steve and Blake again heard wood-on-wood knocks south of Cliff. Then all went silent for the rest of the afternoon.

Alec and I decided to climb back up and join the others. Steve and Blake were now with Cliff. When we got there, we older folk heartily encouraged the filmsters to gain fame and fortune by going in and filming the creature concerned.

Well, it doesn't take a Harvard professor to figure out the worst thing you can do is go into thick trees after a thoroughly irritated forest giant. So, they cooked up some excuse or another to stay in the clear with us, something about the lighting, or camera film jammed or something equally lame. These two guys were in really good shape and had the ability to run really, really fast if they needed to. What were they worried about?

In retrospect, Cliff thinks Blake was correct when Blake said the creature itself was making vocal wood knocks and was not pounding on a tree. Blake's observation also accounted for the tree knocks continuing as the shy beast walked away from Cliff. Cliff also thinks the creature's volume control was probably why Alec and I didn't hear them since we were "far" away.

Cliff agrees, saying they have huge lungs and can probably make a lot of different sounds, just like elk. He thinks they whistle too, but over the years, collectively, we've rarely heard whistling. He also thinks that maybe the creature made counting knocks; five of us; five knocks, and later, too many of us, so more knocks.

Anyway, Cliff simply asked, "How often can you find a stick on the ground that isn't rotten and big enough to pound on a tree?" Cliff is right; it is rare to find a big strong stick in the woods. But, on the other hand, maybe some of them carry well tested clubs ... speculation, speculation.

Ref. 82: Another Roar and Parting Trees

Big Bottom #4: Road 4651, again: Bigfoot related Incident 56 (I56): Another great roar in Big Bottom, then trees part as the creature stalks away up the hill.

June 30, 1999: The day before my birthday I decided to go up the hill to pull trail cams due to the upcoming Fourth of July weekend. I was happy to find they weren't stolen and had clicks. I thought about their locations and decided to take a chance and leave them. So, I changed batteries and film but I pulled our orange marking ribbons. Anyway, the bleached elk ribs were a good enough marker for the jump-off point to the cameras.

I was curious as to what was still wandering Big Bottom. I thought most animals had migrated to high ground by now, but maybe there was still a doe hanging around. As I hiked down 4651, I was semi-comatose, just ambling along, enjoying the day, trying to take a picture of my shadow walking when I heard, a deep "HNNNH," a sound like something big clearing its throat.

Damn bear, I thought. It was clear I'd just woke something up behind a big fallen tree on the high bank to my left. Then the "HNNNH," turned to a huge screaming roar! (Not a roaring scream.)

I recognized the roar. This was the same critter that surprised Steve a month earlier only a quarter mile away and this time, I got the dose of its volume. Before I could think, I had the 357 out, jumped into the shadows, and was in firing position.

No sun was in this boy's eyes. It was like I was back in the USMC. Strangely enough, I wasn't scared at all, but I felt my eyes scanning the woods like crazy. And I thought, just how long can that damn thing roar!!

Then it abruptly stopped with no trail off. The roar just stopped. Next I saw 3 inch plus trees parting at their tops as the beast walked up the slope of the hill into big timber. It was walking, whether on fours or twos, I couldn't tell, but, whatever it was, it was absolutely in no rush. It was simply moving away from me and was parting trees, like a bead curtain, trees a big man could only shake, at best. Whatever was walking up that hill was big and strong.

When I couldn't see the trees moving anymore, I scrambled up the steep four foot dirt bank and over the log. Something big had smashed the duff down behind the log in roughly a 10' x 6' rectangle and from the looks of it the bed had been in use for a while. One thing was certain, it wasn't a bear or elk's balled up circle. I didn't see hair, but that wasn't remarkable, animal hair in summer is short.

Then I started into the tree but quickly decided the hell with it ... too thick. Besides, something could surprise me in there and tear me up good; what do coroners call it ... "death by wild animal maul" or something.

I just marveled at the event, decided to leave, and walked north on the gravel road at speed, adrenaline was all through me. After maybe a hundred yards, I started to think again, and began wishing the filmsters were with me ... fame, fortune, and all that if they just followed Mr. Big up the hill.

A moment of daydreaming aside I slowed and began paying close attention to the forest around me. As I walked, listening to the gravel crunch, I thought, and then I knew ... I knew ... it was not a bear. The roar lasted too long. And, black bears are stumpy critters; even a big one only stands about four feet off the ground. There was no way a bear would separate trees like the creature that walked up the slope.

Oh well, no sighting, no camera clicks, and no courage to follow it in the thick. My mommy didn't raise no dummy, no Sir. Maybe just not too smart a one; after all I'm wasting time and dollars chasing nothing, aren't I?

After a while, I turned east into the big trees along the river and hiked down among them until I came upon an open glen. It was probably an acre, with good visibility. I walked over to a downed tree on the north side and sat down and thought about what had happened today and on the trip up with Steve when he got roared at, and what happened with Cliff when he went up on his own to check things out, and the day with Blake and Alec.

I ate a little lunch but my stomach was a bit upset from being startled. I thought about the weird feeling I had had when I set up the trail cam in the green glen. That day when I walked into the glen, I felt like something was intensely watching me. That was only about a half mile south of where I was sitting, maybe because of the turn I'd made, only a quarter mile.

Anyway, I hadn't even thought about it since I set the camera, but I remembered I had taken out my 357, without looking up and laid it in plain sight on a stump and very shortly afterwards, the watched feeling left me. I had forgotten completely about that.

Cascade Oregon-grape, *Mahonia nervosa*, grows to 20" with blue berries. Similar to *Mahonia aquifolium*, the symbol of Oregon, which grows 3' to 6'. Photo by Sharon Beelart.

Off to Tumble Creek

When I felt a little rested, I shouldered my Duluth pack and walked up the little slope to the gravel road and back to the truck. Then I drove down to Tumble Creek.

It's quite a few miles, at least 20 I'd say. I spent the rest of the day wandering around that neck of the woods.

While I walked, I thought about things that happened in Big Bottom. About all I came up with was I was glad I didn't follow that Bigfoot into the trees. I thought about slopes. Slopes are mainly transit and escape routes.

By the time I got to Jims Meadow, I decided I'd had enough of Big Bottom. Three rounds of bad things were enough. The next time things might not go so well. I decided to go up after the 4th of July, pull the cameras and explore another part of the forest for a while. We had talked about the headwaters of the Warm Springs River and that neck of the woods. That would do OK.

I was sure the others would go along with the plan if we worked it out together; after all, we had a mountain of forest to explore. A little tired, I hiked back to the truck and left. That's when I figured out I hadn't worn a hat and got a good sunburn.

Approx. GPS of where I was roared at and the following report about the furry, crazy little coyote pups: 45 00 38.99N 121 55 04.66W at ~2150'

Call blasting & coyote pups!

Big Bottom #5: Happening H2O (H2O) Flute music brings out coyote pups.

One day in the mid-2000s, as good Sasquatchians are given to do, Cliff and I decided to go up the hill to simply look around. I was driving, so Cliff packed a first-class lunch and he brought along the big boom box from his shop. The weekend before, he and his wife Patty-Sue went to a festival and amongst the performers was a group playing Andean flutes. Cliff liked their music and bought a CD which he thought might be just the tunes needed to attract Bigfoots.

We decided to drive Road 4651 ... after all, by now we had two sightings, vocalizations, the great tree parting, and Cliff's mighty strange wind and stomp incident with an invisible heavy breather. Given the locale, with Big Bottom on the east side of the road and the low flank of Burnt Granite (a mountain) on the west, who knew, we might attract a Bigfoot out in the open with Cliff's flute music. Not much chance, but no try, no chance, right?

Fortunately, the gate was open so our plan proceeded. Before we got on the spur road, I put a tarp in the back of my pickup as a cushion; Cliff set his boom box on it, touched the play button and turned it up loud. At one time, Cliff had a big shop; he bought a big boomer radio that played loud and clear so he could hear it at the far end of the shop. The music played loud and clear all right, it was so loud, I closed the sliding rear window in the truck.

We drove Road 4651 very slowly, windows open, drinking iced tea and gesturing since talking was a bit difficult, although, in an odd way, the Andean flute music was rather soothing and peaceful. When we got near the "keep'em out" road we began to hear small barks, yips, and cries on the west hillside; it sounded like a pack of happy puppies and their calls were immensely pleasing to the ear.

Then, shortly after we passed the "keep'em out" road, a pile of cute little gray coyote pups fell all over themselves as they rolled and zipped and sprang out of the brush onto the road. Were they happy! Obviously something in the flute music told them they were about to have coyote lunch.

But then, looking up at the massive short legged "animal" before them, an "animal" (my truck) with a huge face and making strange growling noises through a mouth that could instantly swallow them all, their ears perked and they silenced themselves. The too cute little guys stared for a second, and then all of them scrambled back into the forest as fast as the klutzy little honey-gray fur balls could go, falling over each other as they skedaddled.

It was such a pleasant, fun event we decided to include memories of it in this book. And while they probably wouldn't have any part of it, we both still think of how huggable those fat, little lively guys and girls were that day.

Well, that's the story of another day up the hill. Very occasionally we still call blast with Cliff's boomer, but not too often; doesn't seem much sense in it. First, what do Our Barefoot Friends like to hear? At what time of day? Does music make them throw back, or does it simply irritate them like teen music does to some adults?

Sometime afterwards I bought a small boom box on sale and tried broadcasting western, as in the western part of country & western music, on it a few times. I also bought a CD of flute music, but couldn't find the one Cliff owns. Anyway my boomer was too cheap. It sounded tinny so I gave it to Goodwill.

Organic Soup: A Bear Visits: Not Quite Lost.

Big Bottom #6: Wind Follows the Sun. Organic Soup. A Bear visits. Not Quite Lost: All labeled Happening 21 (H21).

It was a simple enough plan ... nothing could go wrong ... could it? Thom Powell, Jim Henick, and I were going to spend a night in Big Bottom to see what camping there was like. Plus with all that Steve and Cliff experienced west of the road, we figured we might run into one of the big fellows.

Except for the river bed and flood plain, Big Bottom is covered with trees and has a high forest canopy. Vegetation and brush is lush and thick excepting where spring runoff is strongest. In those channels there are shallow waterway cuts and duff, duff in many hues of chocolate, especially on high points and in clumps near tree roots.

In places the earth is moss covered, trees tall, and the wind is breathless. Here an explorer is provided a rare feeling of nature's spirituality. It was in one of these spots Thom proposed a night out, a night to become in touch with unspoiled land with no expansive views, little wind, and few stars which are all parts of camping high and open.

It was late August. Thom had scouted the site and thought it perfect since there was an open place for a fire. With the duff so dry, we decided on making an Indian's fire, not a white man's inferno, for even with a well-constructed fire ring and with the ground swept clear all around, a flame might escape, maybe through a rotten root, to start a wild fire. Before blankets, we were careful to rake the fire and douse it *and* surrounding ground with water until it was cool to the hand.

After setting up camp we exercised hard by exploring the Bottom in different directions at good pace. Part of our planning was for offerings, so we came up the hill with the goods. We set offerings of old in-shell salted peanuts on logs, hung big plastic bags of stale cereal from trees, laid apples and carrots no longer in their prime on fallen trees, and put out whatever else was old in our refrigerators; but no meat or meat products.

Later, Thom cleaned vegetables fresh from his Monet-like garden on my camp table, and in a big pot, boiled them into a wonderful spicy vegetable soup. Cooking the soup took a long time, maybe an hour and a half, maybe longer—no one was keeping track.

While we waited for organic soup, we sampled salami, olives, and cheese, and talked and laughed. We talked about places we discovered wandering the Bottom. Truly, this was one of the rare, glorious, perfect outings which happen now and again.

Time went quickly. Thom and Jim both had years of experience as kayaking and float trip guides, and as a result are camp chefs sans aprons and tall hats. Complemented with fresh baked garlic-butter bread Thom's soup was delicious. Full and warm, we became silent and had a quiet time around the fire.

Soon, it was pitch dark; the trees shaded us from the Zodiac glow but here and there a star, a heavenly jewel shone through the trees. Then it was time for bed rolls. Tired and contented, it was no problem to go to sleep.

It was also no problem to wake up about 2 AM when the bear came around. Scent follows the wind, and wind follows the sun, going down at night and up during the day. Since we were camped on the upper west bench of Big Bottom, the scent from Thom's soup swept down stream, undoubtedly attracting the bear.

Anyway, this bear was bold for an Oregon bear; it was noisy, stomping away on the duff and huffing, letting us know it was there. Not much to do; we shined lights, including my million power spot light toward it. Maybe we caught a glimpse of hairy bear butt dashing into the gloom, or maybe we saw just an illusion we wanted to see.

The next morning we all shared in making a first class camp breakfast. The reader can imagine what we ate, it really doesn't matter as long as the good camaraderie is there. Jim Henick had to leave, so with a full travel cup of coffee perked in my Cabela's pot, which for some reason, seems to make the best coffee in the world, Jim was off to civilization.

Not Quite Lost

Thom and I decided to follow Thom's track from the day before. He wanted to show me one thing or another, I forget what. Maybe it was the patch of the insect eating plants he found earlier, a veritable *Little Shop of Horrors*, Clackamas River Big Bottom style.

Now, let's be clear, it is impossible to really get lost in Big Bottom. First, you can follow the river out to the three bridges in this district. Where there's a bridge, there's a road, right? Or, a person who is disoriented can walk straight east or west and find one of the roads paralleling the river and the Bottom. After over an hour of exploring south from camp, that's what we decided to do. No! We were not lost!

Sasquatchians don't get lost. That's a rule, a gold standard. (Kiley says we just get turned round for an hour or two.) Anyway, we just didn't know where we were, that's all; we didn't recognize any landmarks under the canopy, after all, patches of skunk cabbage or hillocks covered with duff look rather the same, don't they? Well, after a while they do, that's sure. So, we decided to walk straight west, up to Road 4651. Simple enough except we didn't think of one thing.

At the time I was in reasonably good shape. So, we'd covered some ground since Thom, who is in great shape, was leading and I was just following along. So, we eventually found we had crossed and zig-zagged the Bottom, from river side to the west tree line for over a mile and ended up at Kansas Creek. No problem, just parallel

Kansas Creek up to Road 4651. So, reader, seriously, what's wrong with this picture?

Right, since the ground around the creek was well irrigated and fertile from soil washed down the mountain, we had a fierce tangle of brush to fight through. And, it was late August, so the brush was in fine condition which meant we couldn't see far in front of us.

We were in a miserable tangle, for the Cascades are a rain forest. That day, there, it was truly a hot, humid jungle; an intertwined mass of viney maples, little trees, and big leaf bushes scratching at our faces and catching our boots. To make it worse we were far enough downstream so the slope rose quite a bit. Climbing in our jungle, we both worked up first rate sweats. Finally, we saw daylight. The Road! We struggled through the last of the brush; it is always thickest next to a sunlit open edge, remember that.

Reader, you guessed it. We were hot and tired. And with all our experience and planning only a short hike, we didn't bring along a water bottle. Suddenly, in the mountain sun, we were both thirsty and we had a mile walk back to camp. What to do?

We don't drink mountain water unless it's coming out of a spring; you'll get beaver fever (giardia) and your liver might not like you forever. So, we walked back to the truck wondering about our "misjudgments."

Anyway, we had one fine hike and ample exercise before it was over. Even though we were thirsty, the sun felt good. Plus, remember the good part from a few words ago? We climbed uphill, so the walk back to Truck was downhill. Then we got to worrying that the bear might have come back to the scent of breakfast and it turned out he or she had.

But luckily Mr. or Mrs. Bear left the camp intact which was amazing since we had cooked a skillet of bacon. It only ate the cereal bags at camp, plus some of the other offerings, all of which were placed a distance from camp. Our Bear Friend seemed to take well to old peanut butter; where we ladled it on logs it was gone, licked clean. Fortunately our Bottom bear friend didn't rummage the cooler, and bite our cold, refreshing beverage cans like another bear did.

So the good Big Bottom camp ended. However your authors ask, what important note have we left out about this adventure? Please think a minute before scanning the next sentence. ... Before we departed camp Thom and I went to extremes to ensure our campfire was completely out.

Ref. 83: Steelhead & Bigfoot along the upper Clackamas

The following three accounts are Happenings 22, 23, and 24 (H22, H23, H24). While these accounts are probably better categorized as Bigfoot Related Incidents, we rank them as happenings because no secondary evidence of Bigfoot, such as footprints, or prior activity are associated with them. However, Bigfoot literature provides repeated precedents of all three happenings; i.e. rock throwing, fish stealing, and teeth clacking. Teeth clacking is also a well-established primate trait.

Summer steelhead fishing is probably the toughest fishing in the Northwest and Steve Lindsey, one of our Clackamas Sasquatchians, is good at it. There is no greater thrill than having a powerful, silver summer steelhead jump, shining in the clear air of a summer morn, and then have it race up river and down looking for a stump, a rock to wrap your line, or just toss the hook.

Steelhead are hard to hook (thus their name) and much harder to land. But wily Steve gets his share, and maybe more. One hint Steve shares on summer steelheading: The water is low and clear so the best time to fish is early morning when shadows are still on the water. Steve says camping is the best way to keep from having to get up at 3 AM for the drive up river.

Anyway, on our first Bigfooting trip to reconnoiter the upper Clackamas beyond Big Bottom, Steve pointed out three of his favorite summer steelhead holes. By the time we got to the snow line, I think he wanted to bite his tongue; but, I already knew about the holes but didn't tell him until he read the first draft of this report. And as we drove along, he told me about three strange happenings at those holes which he could not attribute to any usual animal. To me, as I heard him describe the events, I saw more brushstrokes in the detailed painting which shows us Bigfoots still live along the *Oregon Bigfoot Highway*.

Happening 22: A large rock is thrown at steelhead fisherman Steve Lindsey.

Steve remembers this event well, even though it happened in July of 1987 or 1988 at about 7:30 AM. The river runs close to Road 46 near the hole Steve was fishing. He was drifting eggs and sand shrimp (No scent for those really interested and this was before the lure only regulation.) The fish were persnickety as usual; Steve could see them in cool, deep pocket water holding their positions, rejecting his bait.

Then, one made the maddening soft bite that steelhead make; Steve saw him do it and he had one on! As the fish jumped and threw the hook; over his shoulder, Steve saw a "big" splash in the river. This bothered him as he knew it must have been a thrown rock. He scanned the road; no one there.

The cliff was far away from the river on the other side of the road so the rock wasn't a land fall. On the near side, there was no cliff, just a little table of bare spring runoff rocks. Something had to have thrown the rock.

Now keenly interested, Steve took a break from fishing. He quickly found it took a rock about the size of a bowling ball to make a splash like he'd seen. Then, there was nothing more to think about it. He went back to catching, err fishing, as smoked summer steelhead is about the best eating around.

Happening 23: Something steals two summer steelhead from Steve Lindsey.

This happened a little earlier in the season; June of 1992 to be exact. Steve's sure of the year because it happened a summer after a happy family event. Summer steelheads come in after spring Chinook salmon to eat spawned salmon eggs. While the Chinook protect their spawning beds which are called "redds," small clumps of eggs come loose in the current and float downstream for steelhead to gobble. At this time of year, summer steelhead are still ocean fresh and full of fight, but at 6 to 8 pounds they run a little smaller than winter steelhead.

Steve said he had good luck that morning, landing two steelhead about 18" long. To keep them cool, under thick shade, about five feet away from the water line he laid them on a flat rock. He was particularly careful of where he put his fish because a family of river otters lives along that reach of the Clackamas.

The morning before he'd watched the mother and father otters, and their three kits, fishing and playing. He said they were very much fun to watch, but knew if he wasn't careful they'd steal his fish.

However, he thought they may have moved up or down stream as he didn't see otters that morning.

Now in catch-and-release mode, Steve fought a third steelhead which moved him downstream a little ways out-of-sight of his truck and landed fish. After releasing the fish, Steve walked a short distance back toward his truck, only to find his two hard-earned steelhead had disappeared; and to be specific, cleanly disappeared. This bothered him considerably and he determined to figure out what animal took them.

First he ruled out humans. He'd camped out the night before, was on the river very early and had not heard or seen passing traffic. Next, he thought the friendly otters had taken advantage of him, but there was no evidence of the fish being dragged to the river, plus otters leave a wet trail from their fur when near the water.

The other possibility was birds, specifically an eagle. An eagle could possibly take one, but hardly could have flown off twice without Steve noticing. The fish were too big for osprey. In any event one reason he put the fish under heavy cover was so birds couldn't get to them. Finally, birds would have left scales as they set their claws.

The last options were skunks, coyotes, cougar, or a bear. A bear could have quickly wolfed down the fish, but would leave a mess and tracks as bears almost always do. Skunks, coyotes, and cougars might have pulled away one fish, but probably not two; plus they would have had to haul them across the road which would have left a scale trail. In the end, Steve just didn't know what could have silently approached, gilled, and lifted his prized steelhead without leaving a sign.

Happening 24: From heavy cover, something clacks its teeth at Lindsey.

This happened either before or after the 4th of July in 1995, the year before the 1996 floods closed the upper Clackamas for three years. Steve and friends were taking a three day weekend based at one of the established campgrounds upstream from the Ripplebrook Guard Station.

In that reach of the Clackamas, spring run-off leaves a long, bare rock bar along the river. Along the west side of the rock bar, the river has a deep pool where anadromous fish hold in the shade near the bank. It is important to note the rock bar also provides a fine view of what is happening along the river.

Well, before the fish woke up, Steve got up early one morning to serve them breakfast. A "mid-size" steelhead picked up his bait and then made quite a fight of it, running up and down the long-dark pool, jumping as he went; and, undoubtedly attracting the attention of any nearby forest denizen.

Steve decided the pool was too disturbed to keep fishing, so carrying his prize, he headed back to camp on a trail cut through riverside brush, which is very thick in places on the upper Clackamas. Not far up the trail he paused, thinking something was watching him. Then, the something, which he could not see because of the angle of the sun and the thick brush, clacked its teeth at him. "It was a very clear clacking sound; unmistakable."

Steve said he looked intently into the brush, but saw nothing. Then the presence clacked its teeth at him again, three times, just like the first time. Steve knew bears clacked, but this was probably not a bear, the sound was too high off the ground. The noise was too firm, too big for a squirrel to make, plus it was definitely clacking teeth, not chattering. After a short while, less than a minute, whatever it was clacked its teeth a third time, again three sets in a row. Still not seeing anything, Steve decided it best to move on, which he did.

Steve said he thought about the clacking a lot at the time, and occasionally since. Back then he just "put it off as one-of-those things." Then after he retired in 2011 he started reading Bigfoot books; he said he didn't read much before because his career required him to read technical manuals and computer stuff all day. In one book, he can't remember which; he read about Bigfoot clacking their teeth which connected him with the 1995 incident. He says he's fished the pool many times since, but the teeth clacking remains a one-of-a-kind happening.

District 2: Slopes, Ridges, & Mountains west of Big Bottom

Aside from the Clackamas River itself, the high places west of Big Bottom and Road 46 are the longest geographical features in the Clackamas drainage. It is literally the backbone of the upper Clackamas, and is shaped like the backbone of an elk with one half a rib cage. The ribs lie on the east side of the ridge and offer a moderate descent into the Bottom. On the west side, the side with no ribs, it drops off into the Collawash drainage with dramatically steep cliffs.

Road 4650, which in old times was a horse trail climbing up Burnt Granite, is on the far north end of the long dividing ridge. Burnt Granite is a long flat topped mountain with moderate slopes on the east side. The west slope of Burnt Granite is steep and covered with big rock talus.

Just southwest of Burnt Granite is a group of prominences called Granite Peaks. A little south of Granite Peaks is Saddle Springs. Going along the ridge, further south is a high bench covered with magnificent old-growth white fir trees which roughly end at Mt. Lowe. Mt. Lowe at 5334' is the high point along the Collawash River basin topping East Mountain at 5330' by an impressive 4 feet.

South of Mt. Lowe is Rhododendron Ridge. The far southern boundary of District 3 is roughly defined by the Sugar Pine Botanical Area on the west; and on the east by the intersection of Olallie Road 4690. The exit from the ridge system to the south is Road 6350. Road 6350 connects with Road 46 a tad more than a mile above the north border of Willamette National Forest. Yes, it took a lot of exploring, driving, and hiking to get this geography straight in my mind.

Primary access to the ridgeline system from the south is from Detroit via the aforementioned Road 6350. From the middle of Big Bottom, Road 4670 is the only route to the ridge. For our purposes, the beginning of Road 4670 at Road 46 in Big Bottom is the mile marker for discussions about this district. (*OBH* mile 40.7 (29.3)

Why so much time talking about roads on the west side of Big Bottom? The authors know of at least two instances where out-of-state people got lost in the area, even after receiving excellent instruction on which roads to use, and maps with marked directions. Both had to spend unplanned nights out.

Their main problem, which is ubiquitous, was that vandals often use signs for target practice or steal the road signs. To the uninitiated who are not prepared, unplanned nights can become very dangerous. Thus we encourage adventuring travelers to carry a current, good map and medical essentials when venturing off the main highway.

Significant GPS Points

Granite Peaks GPS: 44 58 47.40N 122 00 13.57W at 4991'

Burnt Granite GPS: 44 59 34.70N 121 57 31.35W at 4989'

Mt. Lowe GPS: 44 57 21.84N 121 58 22.48W at 5334'

Approx. GPS of Sugar Pine Botanical Area: 44 54 32.79N 121 57 49.05W ~4500'

GPS of intersection of Roads 46 and 4670: 44 57 59.39N 121 53 15.78W ~ 2325'

GPS of intersection of Roads 46 and 6350: 44 49 30.26N 121 53 13.85W ~3520'

GPS of Rd 46 & Olallie Road 4690: 44 53 28.23N 121 52 54.30W ~2770'

Rosy Pink Pacific Rhododendron, *Rhododendron macrophyllum*. Photo by Joe Beelart on Rhododendron Ridge.

Ref. 84: Finding the first Thomas Site

Granite Peaks #1: Our finding the Thomas site was simply through map research and luck. We designate the find as Happening 25 (H25). The big rock that was tossed out of the hole by something with immense strength we consider a Bigfoot Related Incident and therefore number it Incident 57 (I57).

Amazingly, no one we talked to at Western Bigfoot Society meetings knew where the site was located and no map known to us marked the site. Later we found out Henner Fahrenbach had been up there, but when we were asking, Henner wasn't around. Cliff only knew it was high above Big Bottom.

Like many people at the WBS, Cliff heard the story in Glen Thomas' own words from a tape recording made at Millie Kiggins house. From that, plus USGS topographical maps, and carefully reading John Green's book, we figured the all-important Thomas site was near Saddle Springs. So one summer Saturday, Steve and I decided to find it.

When out exploring, generally, it's best to park on the main road and walk the side roads. But, at the time, Cliff's knees were in rough shape from his years working at PGE, so he decided not to explore with Steve and me as he figured there might be a bit of hiking involved. Since, Cliff has had both knees replaced and is almost back to being the old mountain billy goat he was.

On discovery day, to our surprise, there wasn't much hiking to it, only about a mile. True, we'd gone on a good hike down low early in the day, so we were tired. At 90° the high altitude summer sun was unrelenting which tired us more. While it wasn't much of a hike, it was through high mountain scrub which shielded us from any breeze, and there was a fallen tree to jump here and there; or, more accurately, a fallen tree to crawl over or walk around.

My notes of Happening 28 are sparse. Maybe it was just the relief of finding the site. Maybe I was tired when I wrote them that night. So, here are the basics from my field notebook:

"Parked at what was probably an old log dump as remnants of a plywood field shack is nearby. Hiked to the Thomas site through some very picturesque regrowth. Site is a big talus. Only one deep hole.

Flat rocks, not round. Very unstable. Dangerous. Piled rocks looked recent although some look the same as in Green's photos. Some piles were fresh ... still showed dirt and lichens from where they were overturned.

Nearby southeast cliff very steep, high. Did the creatures walk up from the northeast? (Road 4650) Need to explore there.

Lots of tree root holes in the area. Didn't find any evidence of bedding, although Steve found some fresh digging. No bear tracks. No trash. Someone cleaning it up?

Very tired. Afraid of slipping on the jumbled rocks. These flat, plate kind rocked when we walked, not round rock like most talus. Nothing to grab; slip and you break something, probably a wrist or cut hell out of self.

Went walking past the talus out toward the point of the mountain. Too far to go all the way. Found some more talus hidden in the trees. Much bigger than the Thomas site. Too tired after morning hike down low to really do much good looking around. Safety is important. We should have come here first."

Bad Road Warning

Side roads up high are often not suitable for use by rental cars. I have received two angry telephone calls from tourists who were directed into the area by a Portland area Bigfoot enthusiast. They called me because the aforementioned Bigfoot enthusiast also mistakenly told them I ran Joe's Towing Service.

Anyway, neither found the site, even when told in detail where it supposedly was. One tourist drove a stick through his rental car radiator. Another knocked out his rental car oil pan draining the engine oil. Both had a difficult time getting back to Estacada. Total expenses in each incident were many thousands of dollars.

Once, for a person I trusted, I marked the Thomas site on her forest map and drew a detailed route to it. She never found the site and because road signs are normally vandalized or stolen, she got lost and had to spend a night "somewhere." The next day, almost out of gas, she met a forest worker who led her to the Detroit road. These stories go on and on.

Blake Eckard at road slump. Photo by Joe Beelart.

Three Thomas Site Notes

(1) Amazingly, the Thomas site is kept clean by something or someone, or just not used much by man, even in hunting season. We, in our collective memory, do not remember finding cans, cigarette wrappers, bottle lids, or other common trash on or near the site and we've been going up there yearly for over a decade.

(2) As noted earlier, but it bears repeating, one year a large boulder fell into the hole, perhaps because of a mild earthquake or through slippage caused by melting ice. The rock easily weighed 250 pounds. Since the edges of the hole didn't seem disturbed, we figured the rock just slid in; that it was probably not tipped in by vandals.

The next year the rock was not only out of the hole, it was laying several feet away as if it was lifted and tossed by an extremely powerful, long armed beast. It was not pulled from the hole by humans as there are no scraped or chipped rocks inside the hole. As of 2013 this large boulder was still located northwest of the hole. Since this unusual event was presumably done by Bigfoot we assign it Incident number 57 (I57).

(3) In 2013 I led Cliff Barackman of *Finding Bigfoot* fame to the site. We arrived late in the afternoon after first pitching a most pleasant camp several miles away at the Tarzan Springs gravel pit. For the first time, in low afternoon shadows, it was suddenly apparent to me there was a systematic pattern in the various excavations which strongly collaborate Glen Thomas' observations.

I also showed Cliff Barackman a similar excavation on a small rock scree about 100 yards west of the Thomas site. We Sasquatchians have watched this secondary site for years with no convincing evidence that the excavations have been reused, although some rocks seem to move indicating "sniffing."

Cougar #5: A pre-dawn Encounter

Granite Peaks #2: Road 6310: Cougar #5 (C5): A very close pre-dawn cougar encounter by Beelart

GPS: 44 58 12.73W 121 58 36.71N at ~4945'

This brief account of a close-up cougar sighting (C5) may interest readers. It was the week before Labor Day weekend 2006, probably *the* holiday weekend for Bigfooters to avoid wandering the mountains. I decided to go up high to see far, both into the heavens and Central Oregon. The best place for this is a small turnout on Road 6310 on the ridge way up the hill above Tarzan Springs.

There are two things about that camp. One, don't get drunk and fall over the side. And two, since it is next to the berm it has really fantastic predawn lighting.

I've camped here alone several times, but only once with a companion, who was to put it bluntly, not taken with the place as he sometimes walks in his sleep. So, that night, to solve that problem, we set his shoes away from his bedroll so he'd have to walk on gravel, which hopefully would wake him up before he walked off the 700 foot cliff as checked on Google Earth.

The camp was at 4,945 feet. West behind camp, almost exactly 100 yards away, and only about 135 feet higher, was the crest of the ridgeline at 5,180 feet. In a way, way up there, I felt a little like a mountaineer. Well, wind likes ridgelines, and it sure wasn't dead that night so I only

Years ago after taking Rick Noll to the Thomas site, he strongly advised me to document both a photographic and GPS survey of the site and then periodically review the survey. Unwisely we never have done it. In this regard, qualified, funded candidates may apply for information.

stayed up until about 10 PM listening to the wind roar through the virgin white fir forest on the narrow ridge crest.

By about 3:30 AM, I was pretty well rested and mostly awake, peacefully watching stars fade as the silver sheen slowly plated the eastern sky. I had an excellent view as I sat up in my bedroll in the bed of my truck, only four feet from the edge of the berm which keeps people from launching vehicles off the cliff.

Then, suddenly on the berm at the foot of my truck bed, in the silence of the dawn and backed by the sky's silver sheen, I spied the motionless profile of a giant cougar.

This thing was huge; its shadow filled my vision; I knew I was about to be cougar Spam in a pickup can. I mean, after this beast turned me into breakfast he'd barely have to lick up afterwards as I was only wearing my shorts!

Rats, what to do? I watched its shadowy tail slowly swing from side to side against the silver sheen. The cougar was watching me, I was watching it.

Really, what should I do? I was all for very coolly calculating my move, of which I didn't know what; but for some reason I was not scared or panicked. Time slowed. It seemed like things were taking a long time to pan out. And even with five years of college, I hadn't a thought ...

"Should I make a move for my 357 magnum? I'm right handed. It was on my left side with the holster still snapped.

Should I jump up and wave my arms; or just scream?"

What I did, because of the cold, high altitude predawn air, was lightly cough. Well, that was quite enough for my gigantic feline intruder. It leapt into the air, and momentarily profiled itself suspended against the sky! No! After it jumped, I didn't wet my underwear; I was too scared. Was it coming for me?

In mid-air, the beast was as colossal as an Ice Age saber tooth tiger and for a millisecond it was looking right at me! Thank God, instead of jumping on me (thus you could not read these words), it made an "about face," charged a few feet north on the berm, crossed the road like a gravel spewing rocket, and smashed through low brush south along the ridgeline. Then, the forest became extremely quiet.

Well, after that, I was definitely awake; so I had nothing much else to do but roll out and in the light of dawn, pull on my jeans, shake critters out of my boots before lacing them up, light the propane stove to perk coffee, watch the sun rise in all its glory over Central Oregon, and when there was enough light, listen to a colony of ground squirrels begin their day just to the south of my truck on the lower east side of the berm.

Then, I knew what I'd done. As a human intruder, I scared a mountain lion from his breakfast. After I heard the squirrels squeaking and squalling in ground squirrel speak I knew. And in a small way, I was sorry. On one hand a squirrel was saved. On the other there was a hungry cougar out there and it was my fault.

Afterwards I thought of Thomas reporting Bigfoots eating golden mantle ground squirrels, which probably were the variety in this den. Honest ... I turned to the virgin white firs behind me intently looking for a Bigfoot; a Bigfoot waiting in line at a mountain McDonald's for its McGroundSquirrel breakfast. But I saw none, although one may have been hiding in the magnificent white firs, hiding from the morning sun which was now illuminating the forest like a floodlight from the eastern heavens.

Ref. 85: How Tarzan Springs got its name

Tarzan Springs #1: Sighting 27 (S27): Surveyors Jake 23 and Jake 24 (J23 & J24)

Directions to Tarzan Springs: from Road 46 at mile 40.7 (29.3) turn west onto Road 4670. Driving carefully, go uphill for about 7 miles. OBH Tarzan Springs is on the north side of the road. In spring, it is a little beautiful pond. In fall it is generally dry, but very lush with grass. The buttressing rock talus and a gravel barrow pit on the east side will tell the traveler, he has arrived.

OBH Tarzan Springs GPS: 44 58 41.91N 121 57 34.87W at 4208'

Real Tarzan Springs GPS: 44 59 05.08N 121 57 05.72W at 4187'

Important note: The seasonal lake I call Tarzan Springs is to make it easy for adventurers to find.

The exact location of the geographically correct Tarzan Springs is about half a mile northeast behind the ridge. In about 2010 the road was dozed closed but for the exact minded, it is an easy quarter mile walk.

In early 2001 at a Western Bigfoot Society meeting I listened to a rather weird discussion about how Tarzan Springs got its name. Unconvinced by the opinions offered, I decided to check it out. First I sent a letter to the Mt. Hood National Forest headquarters in Sandy, Oregon. They informed me that they didn't have the information.

On their recommendation I sent another query to Forest Service headquarters in Washington, D.C. Months went by. Again, I received a letter saying they didn't have the information; that I should ask the U.S. Geological Survey.

So, I did a web search, found an address for the USGS and sent them a letter: "How did Tarzan Springs get its name?" More months went by until it became 2002. Then one day, a person at the USGS in Colorado left a message on my telephone asking me to give her a call, which I did.

The "Tarzan Springs" close to the road. Photo by Joe Beelart.

After I identified myself and purpose, she laughed and said words to this effect: "Let me tell you, you've made quite a stir around here." Amused at her response to what I thought was a very simple request, I asked, "How so?"

She replied it was a little difficult to explain, that she worked in a bureaucracy where various levels of approvals must be given to documents submitted to the public. My request about the Tarzan Springs name happened to fall into one of those categories. She said they were most interested in whether I worked for a news agency, or some other widely distributed media. I told her no, unless our book becomes a best seller, and explained my situation. My reply both relieved and amused her.

Then she said words to this effect: "Well, after we began looking into your request, we got just as curious as you. It took quite a bit of digging to find the answer. However, we are not going to give you a response in writing; I'll just tell you the story."

In 1922 and 1923, surveyors were sent through the south Clackamas area to make plans for roads, locate fire lookout towers, do basic timber surveys, and other functions preparatory to changing vast stands of magnificent virgin timber into dimensional lumber. She said in a record book describing the Mt. Lowe quadrant, they found a note saying the surveyor's encountered an "old prospector who was living with a group of apes."

At the time Edgar Rice Burroughs' book *Tarzan of the Apes* was hugely popular in the United States. So, the surveyors named the nearby springs, "Tarzan Springs." For our purposes, we shall term the surveyors as Jake 23 and Jake 24. Their sighting, although reported via a secondary source, we label Sighting 27 (S27).

Notes on Bigfoot activity near Tarzan Springs:

- When looking at Tarzan Springs on Google Earth or a similar program, the wooded slope to the left of the springs is where Steve Kiley found tracks early in the summer of 2003.

- Neiss and Beelart heard wonderful drumming at Tarzan Springs in the night from the high ridge to the SW of Tarzan Springs. (See Ref. 86.)

- The gravel pit where the Bigfoot drawing was made and the critter came into camp (see Ref. 87) is 1/2 air mile from OBH Tarzan Springs on a heading of 214° at GPS 44 57 58.92N 121 58 14.58W at 4262'.

- The High Rock Quarry is one-half air mile away on a heading of 173° at GPS 44 58 13.51N 121 57 30.00W at 4444'.

Ref. 86: Drumming above Tarzan Springs

Tarzan Springs #2: Bigfoot related Incident 58 (I58): Neiss and Beelart: Road 4670

Every year I try to camp out somewhere special near my birthday. In 2000, it turned out I managed exactly the night of July 1st. The plan was simple. I asked Todd Neiss, a well-respected Bigfoot researcher, along. Todd had heard my stories about the High Rock Quarry, but hadn't seen it, so we were going to spend the night there, experiencing whatever might happen.

Every winter really big trees break off the steep slope on the ridge above Tarzan Springs. Like huge unguided dud missiles, at highly acute angles, they slam into the road below. Huge white firs blocked the road. So, with our progress halted, we decided to stay in the somewhat secluded gravel pit at Tarzan Springs.

After a supper of grilled steak and green salad, accompanied by a good bottle of cabernet, we sat around the fire talking very little. Then, to our surprise, about midnight, from the ridge above us came a series of three very deep, hollow, melodious wood-on-wood knocks. Each set was spread over about 5 minutes, or about 15 minutes total.

This happening, this incident was magical; it was a combination of the absolutely unexpected and wonderful; it was hauntingly beautiful and eloquently appropriate. We talked quietly. The drumming from the ridge was most probably not made by humans. Just beyond us the road was blocked and Rd. 6310 up from the Collawash and Rd. 6350 from Detroit were still closed by snow. We concluded the drumming was made by one of Our Barefoot Friends.

In patient anticipation, we waited for more. About 1:30 AM, we heard quiet noises at the south end of the gravel pit. I clicked on the spotlight only to find a bunched up herd of five or six curious does looking at us, ears up! They stood like superb statues, dazed, so I clicked the light off. Then we heard them quietly drift into the forest.

About 2 AM we walked the road without a flashlight. The night was amazingly clear. While I have often walked under only Zodiac glow at high altitudes, our walk that night was exceptional. The mountain air currents were so stable we saw Olallie Lake Resort's night light 18 air miles away. A new moon's very thin, faint crescent rose on the southeast horizon, not luminous enough to affect the tremendous star shows in Sagittarius and Scorpius. But sadly, we heard no more of the wondrous drumming.

On Clacking Sticks and Tree Knockers

While the drumming was a mystical event, in some small degree we often use the same technique, only with carefully tuned clacking sticks. Basically, clacking sticks are about 18" long, well-dried pieces of small wood. On quiet nights, and days; sitting away from the noise of a fire, gently clacking the sticks together attracts nearby Sasquatch, at least in our minds; plus they make naturally restful music. Very occasionally something strange has happened after using them.

Tree knocks are also sometimes used by Bigfooters on the assumption that if Bigfoot whacks on trees, they will respond to the same. We occasionally "knock," but it is easy to overdo this. Some people use wood (not metal) baseball bats, but they don't carry the spirit of a natural, well cured piece of wood. Many people new to the mountains are surprised that fallen limbs don't make good knockers; they are mostly brittle or rotten.

Ref. 87: "You should be more observant."

Lowe Springs: Sighting 28 (S28): Bigfoot related Incident 59 (I59) has four facets; a night walker in camp, thermal imager finds, tracks, and a urine line. Joe's two companions are Jakes 25 and 26 (J25 & J26).

Late July 2005: The situation; a Bigfooting friend of mine wanted to explore the upper Clackamas and bring along a young friend of his. Planning the trip during winter, I easily convinced him exploring the Tarzan Springs area was a good first-time choice.

My friend is a tenured Ph.D. in a highly technical and statistically oriented field of science. He works and teaches at a university highly regarded in his specialty. This was his second camping trip up the hill with me. For convenience, let's call this Ph.D. scientist Jake 25. Jake 25 has a long interest in Bigfoot, but vigorously avoids public association with the subject.

Jake 25's companion, Jake 26, was close to obtaining his Ph.D. degree in a biological science from another prestigious university. He has since succeeded and is into his career.

Since they were coming from Salem, Oregon, I told my friend where to meet me in the mountains since I planned on camping for two days before they arrived. My friend said he was starting to get uneasy and felt mighty relieved when they came upon my pickup. I wandered out of the woods about 30 minutes later and we commenced to ramble around the rest of the day.

The Location

About 3 PM I encouraged setting up camp in the *High Rock Quarry*, but they wanted to be a little lower, in a more sheltered place, so we settled on the Road 4670 maintenance gravel pit partly because it is backed by a steep cliff which shelters it from wind. The gravel pit is about one mile southwest of Tarzan Springs. At the pit, the road makes a dog leg letting us see a lot of ground.

Immediately south is an area that was logged some 20 years ago. The regrowth there is easy to bushwhack making for interesting hiking up to Jims Meadow. To the east, directly across the road is about 15 acres that was logged maybe ten years ago. Beyond the ten-year regrowth, the forest was logged maybe 30 years ago and is filled with 30 to 40 foot trees.

The pit is about 100 yards north of the spring that makes Lowe Creek. Along the east side of the road, Lowe Creek flows past the site and on a moderate slope, continues down mountain just to the left of the 30 year regrowth. On our side, the spring side, below the cliff is a patch of old growth fir, but at that altitude, the trees aren't huge, just big and wonderful. It's a place one of my tree-hugger friends loves to wander; and yes, he does...

Sasquatch fans—take a deep breath at that thought. Yes, this friend, a Clackamas Sasquatchian tried and true, is a real tree hugger. He hugs trees, or as much as his arms will let him and he softly says lovely words to them, but to be honest, I don't know what he says, because when he starts hugging, I back off. Who knows? It might be contagious. Anyway ...

At Camp

While I set up camp with my tables, chairs, etc. Jakes 25 & 26 busied themselves making a good fire ring and gathering a big pile of downed branches. Between their branches and my firewood, we had the makings of a fine fire.

Settling in for the night, I parked my truck alongside a game trail next to the old growth. It's important to note my engine end pointed cliff side. They parked their little RV next to the camp setup. As normal in good weather, I quickly spread my bed roll in the open truck bed and was ready to relax; I'd done some serious walking the last two days.

While my friend and I occupied ourselves catching up, Ph.D. candidate Jake 26 took his notebook and walked around observing and partaking liberally of designer beer; after all he was on vacation. For some reason, Jake 26 became very interested in the ten year regrowth across the road from our camp.

He silently walked up to camp, rummaged through their RV for a pair of binoculars, took one of my director's chairs, always a favorite with visiting campers, and walked to the gravel berm separating the pit from the road. After trying a couple of spots, he situated himself to look into the trees, especially the edge bordering the taller 30 year regrowth and Lowe Creek.

Occasionally J26 scribbled furiously in his notebook. Once in a while he walked back to camp for another beer from the cooler. But, he always returned to intently look into the timber.

J26 watched and watched and made notes until the intensity of his goings-on were remarkable to J25 and me. But after a while we paid little attention to J26. He was a biologist in training, so taking field notes was part of his business. And, we had decided to wander the old growth and check out the springs.

Back at camp, Jake 25 showed me the electronic toys he packed for this year's trip. One of them was a high quality thermal imager he'd checked out from the university science laboratory. After he carefully showed me how to operate the thermal imager, I prepared the fire, but didn't light it.

Using the propane stove, I soon had supper ready. Whatever kept Jake 26's interest apparently disappeared when the dinner bell rang. He was ready to eat and drink. We all were.

After a pleasant day, food and drink tastes especially good at altitude. We talked, but J26 stayed very quiet. He was thinking about something.

Cool evening air set in just after sunset. The fire was ready, so I lit it. Then, I took a short nap so I could spend most of the night awake. After a couple of hours I woke up. It was really dark. We couldn't see stars to the north because of the cliff. In the east, they burst from the night sky.

I always try to get people to go for a night walk. If campmates won't go, I do. This time, primed by my old companion, my new friend was ready. It was easy going on the gravel road. We had no moon. No matter, at that altitude the Zodiac glow is enough to walk a gravel road. We walked well past Tarzan Springs and then back. There is little more comforting than the sound of boot soles slightly crunching gravel. When we stopped, there was no sound. None.

We walked by the 30 year timber twice in the dark, once going, once coming back. Each time J26 lingered, staring into the gloom. We did not use flashlights, but talked quietly, so it is possible we attracted the attention of a creature in the trees. By the next morning, for several reasons, we thought this highly probable.

This wasn't the first, and I doubt the last time I've been trailed or watched by one of Our Barefoot Friends while walking a long ways on forest roads in the night. But I don't worry about the Forest People. My only real concern is stepping in a pot hole and twisting an ankle, or perhaps a night run-in with a cougar; a very scary thought indeed.

Anyway, it took us well over an hour to make the walk. How do I know since I didn't put on my watch? The fire still had embers, but was about out. Since there was no wind, and because the fire was widely surrounded by gravel, we shoved the big wood aside and let the coals burn when we left. We sat and talked. Jake 25 said he'd been on night hikes using flashlights where people have seen fifteen Bigfoots.

With my experience, in the USMC and up the hill, I said I thought we'd seen lots of trees and shrubs gently moving on mountain wind currents. It was late, maybe 12:30 PM, but for some reason instead of staying up and watching the night, suddenly I was ready for my bedroll. It was almost like something was putting me to sleep, like I was a little kid.

My companions were tired too, partly from the drive up to meet me, and partly because of the effort it took to set up our camp. So off we went; me to the back of my pickup and they into their little RV.

A Walk Through

Time: About 1:30 AM. I generally have a solar powered watch I keep at my side, along with a bottle of water, a Maglite brand flashlight, my .357, a roll of toilet paper in a clean coffee can, and a couple Handi-Wipes. Anyway, when I checked the time I heard one of my companions taking a big pee in the gravel near the camp setup.

In fact, I thought it was the biggest, longest pee I could imagine, but I was tired. Out of politeness, I didn't rise up to look and decided to wait until morning to suggest going to the tree line for that. Then I dozed, but didn't go to sleep.

Well, damn if I didn't hear footsteps cross the gravel to below my truck. "Oh well," I thought, "one of them is just looking at the stars."

Then the footsteps started up the animal trail next to the tree line and, next to my pickup. Now, I became attentive, very attentive and wide awake. For some reason, I figured it was for my betterment to not move a muscle.

The footfalls were definitely much longer, and more purposeful than those a night walking Ph.D. or Ph.D. candidate would make. The footsteps stopped by the side of my pickup bed. I was looking up at the stars, trying to force myself not to move. *It* was looking down at me, breathing. I was looking straight up, hardly breathing.

Whatever it was took deep, long breaths. I knew it was looking at me. I knew this was a really good chance for me to be torn into raw McJoey tenders, forest style. Something that tall could reach in and pick me up like a doll and slam me into a tree; an equaling discomforting thought. Now, I was positive my night watcher was not Jake 25 or Jake 26; much too tall to be one of them. Within moments I didn't give a hoot what it was so long as it would go away.

Then an odd thought came through my mind. I knew what it was but one thing was missing. It didn't smell bad, which is their reputation. I wondered if I was dreaming, but no, I wasn't. It was real and it didn't smell. That made my mind flash … can they turn smell on and off? But there were more important immediate considerations at hand.

I felt for my .357; small comfort. Should I rise up and shine my flashlight on *It*? It didn't take long for me to figure that probably wasn't a good idea. I regressed to some of my military training and tried to keep my eyes as shut as possible, yet wide open … nothing. The beast had the dark of the tall old growth behind it; the SOB knew how to use terrain to keep concealed.

Well, after a while it walked up the trail. The footfalls were long. Soon I couldn't hear them. I carefully rolled out of my bedroll, slipped on my moccasins, and made my way up to the camp table. Jake 25 had put the thermal imager on the table under a towel in case one of us wanted to use it in the night.

I looked at the little RV; all dark and silent. I felt for the thermal imager under a towel on the table. There. I felt for the switch … it clicked on. It was working! The imager lightly hummed as it warmed up. A little diode told me it was ready to use. The first thing I noticed was the heat signature of the engine and brake pads on my truck.

I swung the thermal imager to the forest. "There! An image! Something tall and thin!" We'd tried the imager earlier in the night to check for false positives. This was not a rock. Maybe it was a heat blooming tree stump; but, not likely, since J26 had specifically scanned for one earlier.

A quick scan of the pit showed me a heat line running from just beside the ice chests down the quarry slope, to an end about 20 feet away. Only later with a spotlight did we see the "drill hole" the beast made when it urinated beside the ice chests.

I have to get them up!

What the hell is it with people that they won't wake up in the night when something's going on? I've always noticed it. I shook and shook the side of their little RV. I beat on the windows; finally, a groggy answer.

Poot! Up went their door and out they came, boxers, tee shirts, bare legs, bare feet and all. I know they were barefooted because of the #$%& they both said when their bare feet hit cold gravel.

I quietly commanded, "Shut Up!" They obeyed. "Here."

They looked through the night scope. "Hmm."

"You want to go in there?"

"No."

"Hey man, its dark."

I thought, even a Ph.D. has common sense.

"You two go in there, OK? I'll watch the road to see if it comes out there," but I was really thinking, not me in them trees, no siree, not me.

Jake 25, "Should we use the spotlight?"

We quickly, and very quietly decided the million power light would only yield a quick glimpse, if that, given the number of trees and bushes. By now, the "stick" figure in the thermal imager was aware of us and moved away to the northeast. Soon, the image was gone.

Jake 25 and Jake 26 then appropriated the thermal imager and began a study of the area. From the foot heat signatures we saw where the creature walked out of the low regrowth, crossed the road, stepped over the low gravel berm separating the pit from the road, and strode up to the ice chests where it mightily relieved itself. In the berm, we rough measured three footprints in the gravel; whatever it was took really long strides (about 60″ heel to heel).

Then, using shorter steps, it strolled below my pickup. A little heat sink told us where it stopped for a minute and then decided to walk up alongside me. It was simply amazing to see individual steps and the variances in them as shown on the imager. Where the beast stopped to look me over as I was "sleeping" in the back of the truck there was a big heat sink from multiple foot shifts.

Then, the forest person walked about 60 feet up the trail and veered right into the old growth along the creek. That is where we saw the tall thermal image from camp. J25 said why they didn't want to go into the forest with the imager, "If that thing gets damaged, I've got a really big bill to pay." So, we walked down to the road scanning the trees with no luck. The creature had vanished.

By now, it was about 3:30 AM and the silver sheen of very early light was edging across the eastern sky. We all went back to our bedrolls and by all accounts slept well. I got up about 7 and started the coffee in my first-class, wonderful, magnificent Cabela's percolator; have I ever mentioned how highly I regard my Cabela's coffee pot?

Morning

Since it was the last morning for me up the hill, I got out the fry pan and cooked up all the bacon, opened canned peaches, and some other stuff. But, I didn't cook eggs. I don't fry eggs up the hill, even in fresh hot, spackling bacon grease; I bring hard boiled eggs in the Dahinden tradition, but that's

another story for next time. My campmates seemed to respond to the scent of frying bacon. They were soon up and at the coffee pot.

We marveled at the drill hole in the gravel where the creature relieved itself. We roughly measured how far down the slope the urine traveled under the gravel. We walked the creature's route. I laughed at my scare. If I'd jumped up, shined my flashlight on the beast, it probably would have simply walked off, maybe.

In the forest duff, there were plenty of 16 to 17 inch imprints, but nothing to cast. I told them a few years before, in the early summer, Steve Kiley found an old but distinct line of tracks about 17 inches long at nearby Tarzan Springs. Could it be the same creature?

Just after we packed up camp, which didn't take long, Jake 26, our Ph.D. candidate, walked over to my pickup with his notebook. He said he wasn't going to give me something but after the "excitement" of last night, and what we'd found this morning, he decided he would.

He carefully separated a page. "I drew this yesterday afternoon."

It was a detailed sketch of a Sasquatch standing beside a tree. He pointed to the far edge of the regrowth area, next to the bigger trees. He said, "It was watching us from over there."

Then Jake 26 gently chided me, "You should be more observant."

I asked him why he didn't call us over for a look. He said he wasn't sure why, maybe it was because if the creature felt it was attracting attention it would go away. Besides, he said he only got glimpses of it, the creature was very shy.

"Why didn't you photograph it?"

His reply was succinct, "Because I didn't want my career to end before it started." From his quiet, firm tone, it was clear Jake 26 thought about taking photographs.

"Has Jake 25 seen this sketch?"

"No. It's just for you and me. Now it's yours."

I was perplexed by Jake 26's secrecy, but he seemed comfortable with it, so that was that. Whether he later told Jake 25 about his sighting I don't know.

After I led my two scholars down into Big Bottom and handed them off to Thom Powell, I drove back up the hill to walk the area that J26 watched. In the thick forest duff, I saw large indistinct foot-like imprints made by something heavy.

For the record, we label Jake 26's sighting as Sighting 28 (S28). The night walker and thermal images are recorded as Bigfoot related Incident 59 (I59).

Perseid Meteors, Perseid Cougar #6

First encounter with HRQ Cougar #6 (C6). Mt. Lowe #1: Night in the High Rock Quarry (HRQ): The Perseid meteor shower.

Background information: The Perseid meteor shower that occurs in the second week of August is one of the major meteor showers of the year. Every year the Perseids fly in the northeast sky on the night of August 12th or 13th depending on Leap Years. They are not great light poles roaring through the sky like the Leonids in cold, early winter, but they are fun to watch with 60 per hour not uncommon at bombardment zenith.

Earlier in the summer I was driving on the Granite Peaks Road when I glassed a big open rock quarry with my binoculars. On another trip I drove to the quarry, which is at about 5,000 feet, a good elevation and found it had an exceptional view to the southeast which is necessary for a full night of Perseid watching. An added bonus was that the surrounding area was prime country for the Forest People, so I decided to use the High Rock Quarry to watch Perseids that August.

After a day of Bigfooting, I set up camp in the quarry. The sky was clear until just after dark when clouds rolled in from the Pacific. I saw four good shooters through cloud breaks, but then the night sky went dark. That was it for the Perseids that year. That's nature for you, can't contest it, and so might as well enjoy it. I felt a big storm brewing. I kept the fire going and hunkered under my rain poncho as I sat close to it.

Northwest corner of Area 5 looking Southeast into Area 6.
Photo by Sharon Beelart

Soon after I sat down I began hearing cat-like calls from the southeast side of the quarry. The calls were intermittent, and got louder, coming for sure from an annoyed animal. When the critter circled the southwest side of the quarry toward the road I tried to record the calls with my little recorder's external microphone. Too much wind noise to get anything.

Next, I threw enough wood on the fire to get the light umbrella to jump to the edge of the quarry. This seemed to irritate the critter even more. It cried out in a much different tone than before, more of a growling snarl than a call. Since it was going to rain I didn't set up the cot, but with a beast scouting me, I wasn't about to sleep out anyway. That's what truck cabs are for.

I tried to stay awake while the persistent creature kept at it. Now, it was wailing in long sets, and then going silent. Then it started crying; but it didn't scream. This thing had a bunch of sounds in its repertoire and seemed to be using them all as it circled the big quarry *twice* more; I was

The High Rock Quarry Cougar, again

Mt. Lowe #2: Cougar #6 (C6) again.

One weekend I decided I needed to get out of town for a reality check, so in late August 1999 I went up the hill to the *High Rock Quarry* again. I wanted to walk the ridges north and south of it, I wanted to explore. And, while we don't want the reader to become bored with High Rock Quarry stories, there are a couple of things to learn from this outing.

Here's the long and short of that trip up the hill. While I brought along some wood I stopped and chopped four knots off the big white fir beside the road. Woodcutters left the knots, the best parts. High elevation woods always burn beautifully, so I'd made a real find. With

certain it was getting a good look at me, probably deciding if it wanted to attack! About 1 AM, I finally got into the truck, leaned the seat back, got out my pillow, spread the bag over me, left the window down so I could hear and went to sleep.

When I woke in the morning, it had rained. There wasn't going to be any hiking today, too wet. As I drove down the mountain to Big Bottom the rain stopped. From this I learned a major nature lesson, something I hadn't noticed before. I'd spent the night near the ridgeline crest. High ridgelines make their own weather. Down in the Clackamas River basin there was no rain or mist, just overcast with darker cloud shadows near the ridges.

While I didn't know it at the time, I later found the cat making the calls was a mountain lion, not common bobcat. I label this animal as Cougar 6 (C6). The reader will meet C6 again. Cougar 6 is very protective of its territory, which includes the High Rock Quarry and probably Tarzan Springs.

lots of wood for a white man's fire I set up a fine camp, even though it was really just the same as always. Then, slowly, a beautiful evening descended onto the mountains. In the southeast, a quarter waxing moon rose. It was about a perfect camp, a perfect evening.

The evening was perfect until Cougar 6 started making its damn cat calls again. I scent-marked around my cot and kept the fire going. Once again the calls weren't regular and again, the cat circled the quarry. Again it changed the calls from small wails to growling snarls to other vocalizations, but fortunately, no screams.

This was interesting. I stayed up. The cat was obviously becoming more annoyed with me and was circling closer. One call came from just inside the south tree line only about 100 feet away. About 2 AM I fired two 357 magnum warning rounds into

High Rock Quarry, 1999. Photo by Joe Beelart.

the rocks. Fire really comes out of that thing in the dark! What a blast!

The calls stopped. Now I was uneasy. Where was the critter? I stayed up till about 3:30 AM; I know because the stars were dissolving into early morning light. The hard knots still burned in the fire circle. Finally, I had to sleep; as usual in good weather I slept on the cot with no tent or tarp over me.

When I woke up I found strange scat just past the urine scent line I made around my cot. When I got back I confirmed with Steve that the scat was cougar because it looked like a sausage with a circle indented in it every inch or two. My immediate thoughts: dangerous, lucky. Steve also thought a cougar might have a den in the area and was upset by me. The rocky hill side would sure be a good place for a den. But, on the other hand he thought I might have misidentified the scat and that my cat was really a big "bob" (bobcat).

It really was a cougar

The first ramification of that night out was a "huge" discussion among Cliff, Steve, and me about whether I encountered a bobcat or cougar. The upshot of it was—and folks, this is almost impossible to believe— Cliff, Steve and I decided to drive up to the rock quarry the next Saturday to look at the scat. If the scat had ring marks about an inch apart from being squeezed out it was cougar; no rings meant it was a bobcat.

So on Saturday, we piled into Truck and drove 2½ hours up to the High Rock Quarry. Yes, it took all of 2½ hours, if not a little more. We looked at the scat, now dried in the sun. Sure enough, there were ring marks on it. Cougar for sure, plus Steve said it was too big for a bobcat. We went down to the low point in the quarry, the place that holds water after big rains. In the mud, we found a line of mid-sized cougar tracks.

Steve and Cliff then both opined that a female cougar probably has a den somewhere around the quarry, probably where dynamite blasting left an opening in the rock. Since this was the time of year mama cougar was raising her cubs I opined that it was probably unwise to search for the den.

Cliff said that I shouldn't worry about mama cougar; I'd be fine if I crawled around for a look. After genuinely thinking about it, I proved I'm not quite as stupid as I look; I declined. Cliff and Steve laughed. They weren't about to climb rocks for a look either.

Anyway, the total trip took us about seven hours since we stopped at the Carver Café for lunch where we had a good laugh. We had used up $60 in gas to accomplish what? A five minute look at an eight inch long piece of dried out cougar turd ... So, that's it for the *HRQ*, but we still have lots of stories from there, including what may have been a set of wolf tracks.

Commentary: Not so Good ole' Boys

Unfortunately, the high rock quarry also seems to attract nasty people.

First, bumping into bad boys in the mountains is more common than a flat-lander might think. In former years, the North Fork part of Area 1 was notorious for meth labs. Always, it seems the lower Memaloose in Area 1 is littered with drug paraphernalia. We've found car stripping ops in Area 1, up Indian Henry in Area 2, the same in Collawash Area 4, and a long-suffering, formerly very nice Subaru in Area 5.

In Area 3 we found an old marijuana plantation complete with irrigation piping and volunteer plants still hanging on. One morning a friend of mine woke up to the crack of semi-automatic rifle fire and lots and lots of bullets whizzing over his head smacking into the trees around his camp ... it was just joking around by some local rednecks ... he hoped. Anyway, after what "seemed like an eternity," they quit firing.

Trail head parking areas are notorious for theft and vandalism. Bagby was especially bad until prevention measures were taken circa 2010. You will know you are in an extremely bad place when broken auto glass covers the ground.

Some criminal activities up the hill are almost comical. Once I came back to camp to find my ice chest rummaged by some wicked soul. Whoever it was took all the beer and went through the sandwich box, picking out his favorites, which were roast beef and salami, leaving the Velveeta cheese sandwiches.

Well, this time the joke was on him. Velveeta sandwiches are my favorites. Plus, I had corn chips and an emergency tin of Spam so I was set for another day. Anyway, I was lucky, most of the time they just steal the whole ice chest.

Other thefts are more serious. A common one is siphoning valuable gas leaving adventurers stranded. Occasionally you might encounter drunken poachers out of beer, blocking the road with newspaper taped over their license plates, demanding your beer. Or the worst might be just plain mean, psychotic, or drug crazed men looking to make trouble.

Take our word for it. Sooner or later, you will meet all of the above, and more. Our advice is to be aware of your surroundings and have an exit route in mind. Remember, in the mountains, you are on your own. Help, if you can call for it, is hours away.

District 3: The High Buttes east of Big Bottom

District 3 of Area 5 is a mountainous sector shaped like a huge rumpled square. The north boundary follows the line made by the curvy Road 42. The east boundary is the straight border of Warm Springs Indian Reservation. The south boundary is roughly the line midway between the south bases of Pinhead Buttes and the north base of SiSi Butte. The west boundary is Road 46.

Along the southern border of District 3 and Olallie Butte is a big, low, no-man's land, an almost flat basin containing few creeks. This land grows little more than dense jack pine trees, many of them now dead and decaying from an invasion of bark beetles. One of the creeks in the basin is "Slow Creek" indicating the flat boring, drooping branch, decaying nature of this forest waste land.

While there is a wealth of habitat in District 3 for Our Barefoot Friends to comfortably live, we didn't get a sighting report from Area 5's District 3. This is probably for two reasons: (1) Not many people hike this often beautiful area outside hunting season, and (2) While there is

ample water in much of the District, there are no practical fishing grounds.

But, the Bigfoot lives up there, at least during part of the year. A reservation Native American told the authors the Reservation's west boundary – the east boundary of District 3 – is a migration route for Sasquatch. And the reader will soon find secondary evidence of Sasquatch is abundant in the District through independent reports and our own nights camping up there, many times in full view of majestic Mt. Jefferson.

Ref. 88: Lumber Jack saves Bigfoot

District 3: In the vicinity of SiSi Butte: Happening 26 (H26): Road 4680-1

Readers will undoubtedly remember Lumber Jack, the Estacada lumber baron profiled in Area 1. Well, Lumber Jack didn't exactly save Bigfoot; he saved Big Bottom from becoming a tourist Mecca which would drive our Clackamas River Bigfoots from their lofty homes. So, in a way he *did* save our Clackamas Bigfoots.

Happening 26 transpired because Lumber Jack had sharp-eyed attorneys who read every clause in a timber sale contract, when they wanted to do so, whereas, at least this one time, Forest Service attorneys did not. Now, reader, please transport yourself to the area between Pinhead Buttes, Lemiti Butte, and Olallie Butte and think about the brown-gray waste land of Slow Creek and worthless dead jack pine trees.

What do you see? Mountains? No. A low altitude basin? Yes. Think about winter. Think about a tourist highway direct from Portland to Central Oregon. Starting to get the picture?

The idea of a low altitude passage to Central Oregon was not lost on post-World War II Oregon planners who envisioned tourism as a major Oregon "industry,"

which it has become. By the 1950s financial visionaries also saw Central Oregon as a profitable paradise, which it also later became.

Indeed, by the early 70s, Sunriver, the first major Central Oregon destination resort, was built and proved an immediate success. Mt. Bachelor Ski Resort opened and swiftly attracted world-wide attention for its quality powder snow and slopes. Black Butte resort followed, and then, by the 2000s, many more.

But before all that came about, a good highway was needed from Portland to Bend. From the central Willamette Valley, Highway 20, which is continually under improvement, gave people access to Central Oregon. But, Oregon's major population center and international airport was in the Portland metropolitan complex.

Portland needed a first-rate route to Central Oregon. Highway 26 through Government Camp existed, but needed costly on-going improvements and maintenance to carry heavy weekend traffic.

Plus, Government Camp lies at about 4,000 feet on the flank of an 11,249 foot high mountain. State highway maintenance workers, the Highway Patrol, and travelers have to contend with major winter weather in the vicinity of Government Camp.

Planners quickly found a solution to the Mt. Hood problems: Build a new road through Big Bottom to Central Oregon. There were many advantages to such a road. First, the route's crest was about 3,000 feet, 1,000 feet lower than Government Camp. Also the Clackamas basin crest is narrow and slopes are moderate meaning few sharp curves and easier snow plowing. Perhaps most importantly, being away from Mt. Hood meant no mountain effect and therefore much less extreme mid-winter weather.

The planned road gradient was much more advantageous to road building as it first followed the Clackamas River, rose through beautiful Forest Service land and continued on through the remote southern part of the Warm Springs Indian Reservation. This meant the Big Bottom route would be easy and cheap to construct. It would be favorable for commercial traffic, as it would provide a much more direct, fuel efficient route to and from central Oregon and for truckers, many less miles requiring tire chains.

So, the plans were made: Improve Hwy 224 to Estacada and up the hill to Ripplebrook Ranger Station. Road improvements past Ripplebrook to Road 46 would be easy, mainly by constructing sweeping curves. The planned route would only require building two bridges between Big Bottom and the Reservation line. Due to terrain, Road 46 was to remain two lanes with a passing lane. However, from 46 past SiSi Butte the plan called for an eventual four-lane interstate style highway ending at a major intersection near Redmond, Oregon.

The Cascade hot springs were attractions in themselves. Speculators anticipated turning Austin Hot Springs and Bagby Hot Springs into major summer tourist destinations, so improvements on the Bagby road and a bridge to Austin Hot Springs were planned. The main road and development plans were perfect, except for one unexpected complication, Lumber Jack.

No #$%& white campers allowed

Lumber Jack, his cohorts and the Forest Service, wanted no part of the plan:

- First, the plan wrestled control of land from the Forest Service to Oregon government, thereby igniting a governmental turf war. And you know how bureaucrats are about turf!

- Second, sleepy Estacada would no longer be sleepy as many thousands of vehicles roared through town each weekend scattering kids and dogs left and right. Even worse, planners called out *bicycle lanes*. Rumors spread the road would be just like tourist roads in Europe, and "you know those people."

- Third, tourist vehicles impede log trucks on a tight schedule, and the greatest portion of the upper Clackamas still wasn't logged. Imagine log trucks and Forest Service vehicles stuck behind fifteen #$%& campers and bicycles. WOW!

- Fourth, and perhaps worst of all, the plan allowed for a small village in the area north of SiSi Butte for a gas station, restaurant, maintenance yard, emergency vehicles, and a rest stop – a Clackamas River Government Camp. This alone established a precedent of civilian incursion into National Forest lands which might have serious repercussions throughout the United States.

- Fifth, rumor also has it that there were nefarious developers planning a land exchange with the Forest Service to turn the "Clackamas River Government Camp" into a destination summer and winter resort, a snowmobile and cross-country skier paradise.

Well, Lumber Jack and the timber tycoons of Idanha and the upper Santiam valley didn't exactly think in national terms, they just didn't want tourists clogging up their logging roads. And they sure as hell didn't want a development in the middle of "their" forest. Allegedly a deal was struck among the lumbermen. Lumber Jack was to do what he did and, for his troubles, timber sales fell his way to make up for dollar shortfalls he suffered.

But who knows if this rumor is true since all that is ancient, undocumented business history. And, since almost all real business history occurs behind closed walnut boardroom doors, or perhaps in this case, in the back corner of the Safari Club's bar under the never seeing eyes and frozen lips of the club's wildlife menagerie, it too is also undocumented. Whatever happened, from the lumberman perspective, it was very successful.

What Lumber Jack did was buy a key square mile timber sale which was the first clear cut needed to start building the new highway. Timber cutting was supposed to begin the next summer, first by clearing the right-of-way, and then the boundaries of the sale.

However, cagey Lumber Jack knew the terms of sale let him hold the timber for up to ten (10) years before he had to log it; so, that's what he did. Lumber Jack paid for the sale and left the timber standing. Why the time clause was not changed for that sale was never determined. I can imagine a faceless Forest Service bureaucrat saying, "Just a mistake; it will never happen again."

No amount of cajoling got Lumber Jack to log the sale. "Hey, right here in the fine print of your contract it says I've got 10 years to cut." Again, as rumor has it, the Forest Service was less than pressing in getting him to fire up the chain saws and get on with that logging show.

Waiting 9 or 10 years for logging the key timber sale, plus years more to finish logging right-of-way, and build the highway and bridges, set completion of the Clackamas road to Central Oregon far into the future. Also, environmental lawsuits were just starting to raise their venomous heads toward developers and planners. Delay might last long.

Effectively, the Clackamas highway plan died. The result? At considerable expense, the road over Mt. Hood through Government Camp was improved. Today, as the primary route from Portland to Bend, it is maintained at great expense.

Anyhow, how did Lumber Jack's obstruction of the new Central Oregon road save the Bigfoots?

Without a major road through the area or a rest stop to gas up, human activity in the Clackamas drainage region is limited mostly to loggers, hunters, and a few hearty outdoorsmen and women, with only the occasional intrepid but naïve tourist trying to get lost. Without the human pressure, animals thrive in their native habitat, as do our Bigfoot Friends.

South Pinhead Butte **Adventure #1**: A most excellent track find no. 37 (TF37) is made by me and Jake 28 "near" Road 4230 while friend Jake 27 watched the truck.

In late July 2007 I took two older long-time friends on a very long day trip to show them Big Bottom. My friends are labeled Jakes 27 & 28.

Surprisingly, neither J27 nor J28, then age 70 and 67, and both avid outdoorsmen, had been high in the Clackamas. After showing them Big Bottom from Granite Peaks they wanted to drive across the Bottom to SiSi Butte, to get a look at the Forest Service tower. I told them the road to the tower was closed with a heavy gate, but we could get a nice view from Pinhead Buttes, so we drove up there.

Jake 28 and I decided to hike up the butte to see what we could see at the top, which is a marvelous jumble of giant volcanic rock surrounded by trees. The timber on the south side of the Butte is all magnificent white firs, except for the brush barrier of about 30 yards that exists on the sunny edge of most stands of timber. That day it was really beautiful under the canopy. The sun was edging toward the west, illuminating trees in superbly filtered light.

On the way to the top I stopped cold by the spring line. There were five very well defined Sasquatch tracks in the damp soil, perfect tracks for casting. Out loud, I cursed myself for not bringing casting material.

Jake 28, who is a life-long, somewhat grizzled outdoorsman, had no interest in what I was doing and made some remark about me talking to myself. So, not wanting to have him consign me to the loony bin crowd, I pointed up and we continued our hike.

On the way back down, excusing myself, I stopped at the track line again. Jake 28 wandered off, occupying himself with the verdant nature of the hillside. I found the tracks were about 17 inches long, perfectly imprinted with dermal ridges showing; they were fresh, but because of shadows, my little digital camera took no good photographs.

Anyway, by now, J28 had taken an interest in my observations and the rough measurements I made by breaking a branch to the length of the tracks. He looked and looked, finally saying:

"I don't know who's walking around barefoot up here, but whoever it is sure has great big feet."

Then, he realized what he'd said and shut up. During the drive back to West Linn Jake 28 only mentioned the tracks in jest to J27. He's since taken a passing interest in the Bigfoot phenomena; I've heard him wittily entertain friends with overdone details of his great track find and the monster that made them.

End note: I had to work the next two days. By then a really big rainstorm came through. I figured the tracks were ruined, plus it had to be a day trip as my schedule didn't allow for a night out, so I never cast them. Three weeks later when I went back up, a few of the outlines remained.

Ref. 90: A Bigfoot Playground

South Pinhead Butte **Adventure #2**: In late July 2008 I find a Sasquatch Playground which is designated Bigfoot Related Incident 60 (I60).

Hoping that the habits of Sasquatch are seasonal, after finding the tracks on South Pinhead in 2007, I spent a few nights up there in late July and early August 2008. I really had a good time walking the high plateau, cresting the buttes, and exploring the reservation line, always looking for something other than a game trail.

I didn't have any luck with tracks, but on the other hand, the only wet ground in the area is on mid-slope seep lines, by creeks, and the little high swamp to the northeast of South Pinhead Butte. Beyond that the next wet place I know of is Trapper Springs Meadow a couple of crow miles north.

My camp there in early August was only for one night, and I was alone. It was absolutely wonderful, although I put on one too many blankets in my truck bedroll and got pretty hot by morning. Why I didn't just throw one off still amazes me.

In the evening, I lit two wax fire logs since I didn't want to tend a fire. Wax logs are just right for a little fire, and if not burnt by blanket time they are easy to extinguish. These burnt out because I stayed up until about 2:30 AM; thus sleeping in and getting sun hot.

Another thing I do on almost every camping trip is to light one or both of my propane lanterns. If fire danger is high, or I just don't want a fire, the umbrella of light from a lantern sitting on the ground is comforting. Plus, in my mind, if one of the hairy fellows is watching, it resembles a campfire.

If I light more than one lantern I take the old one some distance from my camp as a signal someone is in the area. That is what I did that night; I carried it about a quarter mile down the road to the west and parked it against a sand slope. Sand slopes really reflect light and I try to keep an eye out for them as a place to set a lantern.

In the morning I packed up and decided to go for a walk up the butte before leaving. This time I angled to the northwest, being careful to keep my bearings, although with enough walking and a compass there is always a road. In this instance the long road was to the west. As I was looking around I came upon the strangest thing alongside a fallen tree. The tree was one of the big ones, so it made a natural wall.

On the west side was a bare spot. Bare as in clear of forest duff, fir needles, limbs, etc. The only thing on this bare spot was a little coincidental debris like blown in twigs, a small limb and the like. The bare spot was a square of about 15x15 feet. There was no human debris in the surrounding area. Since the spot was on a moderate slope, it was certainly not cleared as a tent site. It was smooth, as if it was swept by a forest broom made from a fir branch full of needles. Indeed, along the edges were rows of swept needles.

I must say I marveled at the place and sat contemplating it a long time, for truly, this was a rare, unusual find. As sun filtered in from the west I determined the bare spot was made to be used in the afternoon for it was a warm, shadow dappled, breeze-free space. I took a photograph or two. But what I was seeing was simply a mystery to me until much later when I saw a woman in a park spread a blanket for her baby to play on. Then it hit me. I had found a Sasquatch playground!

Yes, I have returned to the site several times. It has been maintained. Oddly enough, there are no marks or tracks on the playground. It is always swept clean and clear after use. Why haven't I set trail cams there or watched it with my spotting scope?

Well, for the first reason, I think it extremely rude to interfere with a mother raising her young, no matter the species. The second reason is the Bigfoots will know you are there and not use their playground when humans are about. This was partially confirmed when I returned two weeks later in late August.

Sasquatch playground. Photo by Joe Beelart.

Ref. 91: Night Walker

South Pinhead Butte **Adventure #3**: Bigfoot related Incident 611 (I61) is a bold night visitor.

Late August 2008: Perplexed by the bare spot on South Pinhead Butte two weeks later I drove back up to look at it again. While I still had no idea what I was looking at, I was certain it was not made by humans, bears, deer, elk, or a cougar. Nonetheless, I decided not to bother it and patrolled wide of it, except to pass north of it and look down at it with my binoculars.

I found a game trail I'd overlooked before. This well used trail was not a *Devils Trail*. It was a spring-fall migration trail for elk and deer going to and leaving the high country. Depending on the season, it led west-to-east, or east-to-west, virtually over the top of Pinhead Butte to within 100 yards of the summit. I followed the trail east and patrolled the reservation line being respectful to not enter it, even though I was sure the nearest human was miles away. I didn't see any animals.

On this trip, as on many, I didn't see a person or hear a vehicle after I left Big Bottom Road 46. That's a day and a half

alone, 15 miles from Road 46. Also I knew where the reservation line was because the clear cut is on the Forest Service side.

The night was superb and warm. There was no need for a fire and the moon was waxing about one-third, so I didn't light my lantern. About midnight I went to blankets as usual in the bed of Truck. I stayed awake, but it was for no good reason because moonlight washed out the great southern star constellations.

There must have been a reason I stayed awake. Maybe it was to watch a beautiful moon rise over Mt. Jefferson and then slowly illuminate the Collawash Mountain, after which the silver orb illumed *The Horns of the Devil*. Maybe those were the reasons I stayed awake, but then again, the mountains are so full of wonder, sometimes it is difficult to sleep while taking in the majesty of it all.

At about 2 AM by the light on my Casio G-Shock watch, I knew I was not alone. A branch broke not far from my truck, which was pointed north. The bed where I was sleeping was open to the south. The branch breaking was southeast in the open regrowth and I think the break surprised the animal just as much as it did me because for a very long time there was silence, from out there and from me.

Remaining quiet wasn't difficult. I was in bed, heck, I could even move a little under my dark blanket to relieve stiff joints and muscles. Rather suddenly, it dawned on me this was my second chance to be torn into raw McJoey tenders forest style. All I had to do was jump up, fire my million candle power light at the noise maker and wait for the inevitable. So, I decided there was nothing better to do than stay silent. I sure as hell wasn't going to shoot my 357 into the night because a stick broke.

After what seemed like a long time, and for once, I didn't check my watch for this intrusion was all too interesting to miss, I stayed awake and alert. Then the creature took another step, and then another, and then it stopped.

Now, with three distinct steps to its credit, I was sure an intelligent bipedal creature was watching my truck. Another species of animal would have just wandered off. Plus, what I heard was *step, step*; not *step, step, step, step* as made by a four legged heavy bear or a curious deer mincing its way to safety.

I was sure the creature saw me as the truck bed was illuminated by moonlight. What to do? This was assuredly new territory for me, even after the Tarzan Springs gravel pit thermal imager incident. I decided to modify what some people do when introduced to a new dog, only different.

When meeting a dog, often times holding hands open and below their muzzle calms them. So what I did in a gesture of peace was to rise up, lean against the front of my truck bed, hold the palms of my hands up, fingers spread in the direction of the noise, white side out. I was sure the moon illuminated my hands and they were seen by the night walker.

Incident 61 was soon over. The Bigfoot was standing, I figured, about 30 feet south of my pickup. I was trying desperately to sight it but among 8 to 10 foot trees, a tall figure was difficult to define in moonlight; in moonlight, trees and Bigfoots look about the same.

After what seemed like a minute or three, but no more, the Bigfoot or whatever was out there, strode away to the west. The creature made no attempt at silence. It was going "crunch, crunch, crunch" on fallen limbs. Whatever interest it had in me was over; it was time to go on with Sasquatch night work. Incidentally, *strode* is the right word, and for sure, whatever strode in the moonlight that night was certainly bipedal.

I never felt threatened during the incident, I felt no messages. What happened, happened. I went back to sleep and woke refreshed at about 6 AM. When I searched the area for tracks I found none because of the thick layer of forest debris. It was then I also resolved to not go back to the "playground" for a while. Let the Bigfoots live in peace; once you've found one of their special places, don't disturb it.

I did return in 2010; the playground was still there. In 2011 the road was ripped up and I didn't want to leave my truck with my instrument pack and most of a tank of gas alone on Road 4230, so I've never gone back.

Finding a Bear Den

South Pinhead Butte **Adventure #4**: Finding a bear den is Happening 27 (H27).

Bears, although rarely seen, are common along the *Oregon Bigfoot Highway*. In 2012 the Oregon Department of Fish and Game estimated as many as 30,000 black bears live in Oregon. Interpolation by me, which was double checked by a professional wildlife biologist, indicates an average of about 450 black bears live in the Clackamas and Breitenbush drainages.

Bears are very rarely seen, even by forest professionals. One reason is they are low to the ground. A really big 400 pound boar will stand only about three (3) feet at the back. Another is they don't go out in the open much. What is there to eat in an open area like a meadow? Which leads to a third thought: if they are so many, why aren't they often seen crossing roads? A few are, but few is the key word. What about campsites? Sure, bears investigate campsites, but due to hunting pressure generally avoid Oregon camps.

The best thing to do is not encourage black bear and human interaction by leaving food scraps out after a campout, or to entice them in with other than normal cooking scents. As I've noted, I don't leave offerings within 100 yards of camp, and then only rarely, and generally around a quarry. Bears do come around and they make noise, after all, bears have four feet to crush fallen twigs, although with 200 to 400 pounds distributed over four paws, impacts can be close to silent.

Anyway, by accident one day I found a bear den on South Pinhead Butte. Structurally, the den really isn't a big deal. It's just a hole clawed into the ground under the south side of a big fallen tree. The den is near the south edge of a virgin timber tree line which means it probably warms early in the spring. For three summers I visited the den. The sides were always smooth indicating a bear repeatedly hibernated in it, "polishing" the sides.

Two more bear notes: Certainly, witnesses have seen bears standing on their hind legs and confused them with Bigfoot. Bear double strike paw imprints are easily confused with Sasquatch prints by those new to field research.

One key is the heel. If the heel is narrow and the imprint tapers wide to the

Entrance to bear den. Photo by Joe Beelart.

ball of the foot, almost like a pyramid triangle, you have found a bear track, even if claw marks don't show. Don't be disappointed if you find a bear track instead of a Bigfoot track. Bear tracks are fun; and finding one means an adventurer is paying attention to spoor.

Ref. 92: The West Pinhead Butte Camp

Four Finds, Events, or Happenings

West Pinhead Butte **Event #1**: Track Find 38 (TF38**).**

After finding that the road into South Pinhead Butte was torn up, I needed to find a new place to camp for the night. One of my key requirements was a view; the second was a good place to park my truck, and third was a place for a fire ring.

Knowing the area fairly well, I decided to drive a few miles north and maybe find a campsite on West Pinhead Butte. I found a good one, and while it was right alongside the road, since the site was shielded from traffic by a two foot diameter fallen tree, I figured it was safe enough.

Actually as it turned out I didn't need to worry much about night traffic. I camped there a total of five nights (seven days) during 2010 and 2011. Only one pickup drove by when I was near camp and that happened one afternoon when I was napping to get ready to stay up that night.

The real value of the roadside campsite I settled on was a tremendous view of Mt. Jefferson, a view even better than from South Pinhead Butte where the mountain is partially hidden by Olallie Butte. I also knew it was probably the best site around because it had the only substantial fire ring along the whole road. So, I adopted it and this campsite became the base for the several notes I made about things around West Pinhead Butte.

One reason I know West Pinhead is not frequented by people is there are still large amounts of firewood left from logging, probably from the late 90s. The first night I was there I took advantage of firewood from a slash pile across the road, plus limb knots knocked down during the previous winter, to make a little bonfire. It was a really good

fire, but not a huge fire. I know it reflected for miles because the back of the campsite was sandy bare earth left from bulldozers.

My first night there the moon was big and supreme, so star watching was nil. The night was most comfortable thanks to a fire; turkey sausage cooked well over coals and eaten trapper style; radishes, celery, a bowl of peaches; and a glass of cabernet. Sometime, not too late I rolled into my blankets in the bed of Truck.

Not much happened all night. I'd marked my territory around Truck, but then, if a cougar comes around, I'd never know it anyway. In the soft light of dawn I awoke, very happy to be alive, to see the sun glowing on Mt. Jefferson's snow fields, defining the mountain's every crag from the glorious orb's constant movement in the northeastern sky.

When I walked around the fallen log to my camp table to fire up the propane stove and perk coffee I discovered I'd had a visitor during my very first night at this camp. In the soft soil around the fire ring there were shallow imprints, human-like barefoot imprints. Even stranger were spear-like holes made in the soil alongside every other track. The night walker was using a walking stick, a walking stick with a very strong point.

It only took about a 100 yard walk north of camp to find where the night walker dropped off the butte and walked down the road to the fire ring and camp table. Then, it walked back out to the road and stopped alongside my truck. It may have spent a little time watching me sleep before it walked southeast down the road another 100 or so yards and veered off into the woods. I searched, circling in the forest, but couldn't find more imprints, although I found a couple of holes that may have been made by its walking stick.

This nightwalker's tracks are listed as Track Find 38 (TF38). After coffee and breakfast another thorough circle of the hillside above my camp revealed the following: The critter sat on the butte above my bon fire, making a butt imprint in the duff. I suspect it sat or stood there for some time watching my camp, probably when I was still up.

After I hit the sack and camp was clear the creature walked north on the side of the butte, dropped down to the road where I found its tracks and continued to inspect things. Due to the nature of soil on the butte, there were few complete tracks, but many toe impressions. There was absolutely no evidence of claw marks.

I long puzzled about the creature's walking stick, and then settled on

Photographing Uranus

West Pinhead Butte **Event #2**: Road 4230: Photographing Uranus is Happening 28 (H28).

When I went up for my second camp on West Pinhead the moon was barely new, just a sliver low in the southeast sky and Uranus was rising. My purpose that night was to photograph Uranus, a wonderfully aqua blue planet I'd never seen other than through a telescope.

After settling in at camp, I circled around the butte, both high and low to look

A Very Special Rock Present

West Pinhead Butte **Event #3**: A rock present is Bigfoot Related Incident 62 (I62).

On the weekend after Labor Day I decided to go up the hill for the third night at my "new" West Pinhead campsite.

something most campers know. If you season the end of a hardwood stick in a fire, you can temper a very hard point. Obvious uses for a hard point are as a penetrating instrument to kill, maybe probe a bee's nest, or for a longer lasting walking stick.

When I got home, I couldn't find another Bigfooter to go back up the hill with me the next weekend. Cliff was still recovering from his hip surgery; Steve had orders to fill, etc. Since I told everyone else that the camp was small, alongside a road, on a dry slope, dry as in no water, and they might not see much of anything Bigfoot wise, no one wanted to go. When I was making the invites I purposely didn't mention the view of Mt. Jefferson. If someone wanted to come, that would be their big bonus.

for spoor (scat, tracks, or other evidence of an animal). I found none. Comfortable I was reasonably alone I relaxed and thought of my goal, photographing Uranus.

Late that night, after many tries, I finally did it. I captured a photograph of Uranus with my digital camera at only 3X optical, its maximum. In fact, thanks to stable night air, I captured several good images of the beautiful planet. In my little world, this was a substantial accomplishment. The photograph displayed here is Happening 31.

Sharon was gone and I didn't have anything else to do. Since I wanted no responsibilities camp wise, I didn't invite anyone along, although I probably should have because I did some serious cross-country hiking on the untracked north and northeast side of the butte.

Basically I spread a lot of scent, not to mention I built a nice fire and charred up another turkey sausage. I set out offerings alongside the road, never within 100 yards of camp, and some over three miles away.

In the night, I woke and became uneasy. While I stayed awake for a long time, I heard nothing. In the morning I sensed my barefoot friend again when I saw vague imprints in the soil, easily distinguished because they were made in heavy night dew. I also found a playful gesture on the part of him or her.

What I thought was really important about that night was once again one of the beasts came in to watch me sleep. How do I know that? Next to my left rear tire, just under where I was sleeping in the bed of Truck, was a stone placed tight against the tire. Finding this stone I label as Bigfoot Related Incident 62.

I know it wasn't there because as usual, I carefully cleared the area around Truck during the day for three reasons: One, to get sharp rocks away from my tires, two to leave a clear path for any heavy footed night walkers; and three, clear the ground in case I wanted to get in the cab in the dark.

This stone was not moved by my tires as there was no disturbance on the roadbed within many feet of the truck. I think the stone was set there in appreciation of the offerings – pastry tarts, apples, and other fruit I'd left on Pinhead Buttes the day before, and all during the summer, or maybe, it was just a signal to let me know I wasn't alone.

Jim Falls in the Fire

West Pinhead Butte **Event #4**: Another example of sudden accidents: Jim falls into the fire. This is Happening 29 (H29)

This is a very simple tale to illustrate how suddenly serious accidents can happen while exploring the *Oregon Bigfoot Highway*. After my first September 2011 trip up the hill, I informed Thom Powell I was going up the hill the next weekend.

Thom, always a gentleman sport, and very intellectually acute, jumped at my unsaid suggestion that he come along. Since I was planning a two night outing I asked him if he thought he might keep busy on a high, dry camp for two nights and roughly three days. Thom allowed he might, so the deal was done.

On the appointed day, up the hill we went. Thom heartily approved the site saying he'd never seen a more magnificent vista of Mt. Jefferson. Amazingly enough he turned on his cell phone and from somewhere got a connection.

Thom called our friend, Jim Henick and told him to stop work and come up to the camp; that the view alone was worth the trip. Unfortunately, Henick, who is seemingly easily led astray by Powell, said he'd drive up the next day from southern Washington bringing along Ben, his new apprentice.

Jim was his same wiry self and Ben proved a cheerful man in his early-30s who hadn't camped much, other than a few youthful experiences. The apprentice wanted to know if we could have a big fire. "Sure."

Used to using his hands, he speedily and enthusiastically hauled a pile of firewood into camp, something we all appreciated. The rest of the day was spent exploring. In the evening we enjoyed Ben's fire since normally, the fire is named after the person who did the most work to make it.

For some reason, about 10 PM I excused myself way early and rolled into the blankets in the bed of my truck. My companions remained around the fire, quietly talking, remarking on the moonlit view, laughing, and having a good time. They weren't drinking much at all, no boisterous behavior. It was easy for me to go to sleep.

I slept well, especially during my two hours of deep sleep. Then Jim shouted something! I woke up quick and clicked on my trusty Maglite, which is always in the truck bed beside me. Jim shouted something more and then Thom and the apprentice began yelling "put it out!"

Oh God, what's happening? One thing I knew from my years in the USMC, when excitement starts, don't jump into the fray until things start settling out. Holding back for only a few seconds is generally a good idea. Become oriented to what's going on.

What went on was Jim stubbed his toe on a rock and fell into the fire, not only lighting his shirt on fire, but smashing his upper arm into the fire ring rocks. At this point I must make it clear, Jim's fall was not because of drinking too much; in the dark, he simply stubbed his toe on a rock while picking firewood from the pile.

After things settled down I asked Jim if I needed to drive him to an emergency room. After what seemed like a long time which was actually short, Jim spoke from the umbrella of fire light.

"No, we don't have to go to the hospital."

"Sure?"

"Yes."

Later, Jim went to the doctor and ended up wearing a flexible shoulder brace for a couple of months. So, for the heck of it, let's call Jim's accident Happening 32, and respectfully, please let it be a lesson to the reader.

One of the benefits of being the camp designated driver is going to bed early. The bad part, if you think it bad, is being alone to watch the morning rise and listening to your campmates snore. In this case I was very happy I was sober and fully capable of driving in case I was needed.

Also, most of the time in camp, I pour left-over morning coffee from my genuine Cabela's coffee pot into my Thermos. That way, if I do need to drive at night I have some coffee to stimulate me a little. Fortunately, over the years, I've only had to haul a man to an emergency room once and myself thrice with one of those times being when a bush wacked me in the eye and embedded a wood fragment in it.

Caution: the authors encourage one person in every camp to be a designated driver.

Ref. 93: Bigfoot Photographed

West Pinhead Butte: Bigfoot photographed is Happening 30 (H30) as reported by Jake 29: Misery road is Happening 31 (H31).

The west boundary of the Warm Springs Indian Reservation north of Pinhead Buttes is a rich area for Sasquatch research. Both authors have seen a pin map of Bigfoot sightings and incidents on the reservation made by a reservation resident, and they are many. Both authors have also heard a tribal representative speak about Sasquatch living on the Warm Springs Reservation and their place in Indian society.

At one time I had a connection to a non-Native American who worked as a classified US government employee on the reservation. Let us call him Jake 29. Jake 29 said a Shoshone elder took offense at young people talking disrespectfully about man-like creatures in their history. So, the elder went to the south part of the Reservation between the Metolius River and Olallie basin and took three clear photographs of a tall, dark, hair-covered, naked man-like being standing in a small clearing.

When the elder showed the photos to the disrespectful youths he also allowed J29 to see the photographs. We designated that event as Happening 30 since J29 directly related it to me. The elder's sighting is not given a sighting number since it happened beyond the east boundary of Area 5 of the *OBH*.

Jake 29 said the elder then either put the photos away or burnt the photos, he wasn't sure which. My understanding is, and I may be wrong, that in their culture, seeing a Sasquatch is ... it's hard to translate ... but the phrase is something like "bad luck."

I remained in contact with Jake 29 after he was transferred from his position at the reservation. After I gently jabbed him a couple more times, J29 firmly told me he would not tell me the elder's name, that he had to respect the wishes of the elder to keep the photographs secret. He repeated he did not know if the photographs were destroyed.

Nonetheless, seeds were sown, so Beelart and Olson made several ventures to the Reservation's southwest boundary. With one exception we did not step on to the Reservation. The exception was to allow Olson two steps in to pose for a photograph at a remote reservation boundary sign. It was quite amazing to find a small sign that wasn't shot up or stolen, but in this case, "remote" means remote.

The reason we did not trespass, and continue to not trespass, is simply due to respect for our Native American citizens. Respect is the key, because, in the far reaches of the reservation there are rarely humans around to see a trespass or Tribal Police available to enforce such laws. That is wild country down there, still almost, but not quite frontier.

Misery Road

This is a "heads up" account to warn you to not only be careful what you do in the woods, but to think ahead. In this case, a couple hundred yards of hiking would have spared me a lot of misery and a near death experience.

Happening 31 (H31). I was driving a really, really bad road. Do not try to drive Pinhead Buttes Spur Road 120 for any reason unless you have a 4x4 pickup with big tires and a chainsaw.

One day I decided to leave West Pinhead Butte via Spur Road 120. It took me about three hours to go one and a half miles. Along the way I almost had a heart attack from having to manually saw, chop, and remove a tree that fell across the road. Due to the sunken grade of the road I could not turn around and one section was too steep to back up, even in 4-wheel drive with rocks piled in the bed.

After Road 120 the two miles to Road 42 went relatively quickly. Too tired to walk to Warm Springs meadow, I explored the springs that are the headwaters of the Warm Springs River. Again I was amazed at how water, lots of water, percolates out of the ground up high.

The sun was just right, so I watched little trout dart about. At that altitude, it was mid-summer so Oregon grape, salmonberries, and other berries were still hanging on here and there. It was really beautiful and restful after the ordeal on the sunken road. Then, ever curious, I walked up a partly washed out side road and found the *New Rock Quarry*.

Tony Healy (from Australia). Photo by Joe Beelart.

A Splendid Stage!

District 3: Finding the New Rock Quarry (NRQ) is Happening 32 (H32).

GPS of the New Rock Quarry (NRQ):

44 59 14.48N 121 47 14.09W ~3875'

At first sight, I knew this quarry was fabulous! It is a much better place to attract our Barefoot Friends than the *High Rock Quarry*, or the *Big Rock Quarry*; both of which have proven very productive. This quarry is absolutely wonderful! So wonderful, its discovery we designate as Happening 35 (H35). So what makes the *New Rock Quarry (NRQ)* special in our Bigfoot research?

Basically the quarry is laid out like a theatre. At the south end is the "balcony" which is backed by virgin timber. The land south of the balcony is fairly level, making access easy from miles around. The balcony railing is made of large boulders set there by the Forest Service to keep people from proving Darwin's Theory. The middle of the quarry is theatre seating and on the north end of the quarry is a slightly raised stage.

The *New Rock Quarry* (NRQ) is faultless as a place to attract our Barefoot Friends. Shielded by boulders and trees, big hairy beasts can watch actors (Bigfooters) from their orchestra boxes, as if they were at a grand opera. Stage illumination is perfect.

The only drawback to the New Rock Quarry is sun, baking sun. Unless the day is cool, the stage is not for a matinee. The day I discovered it, after the ordeal on Spur Road 120, it was hot, very hot. But then, I was also tired, very tired.

Opinion: With the protection offered by the Indian Reservation, the upper Warm Springs River area must be loaded with Bigfoots. And as always, there is so much else to see around the *New Rock Quarry,* so much to study. Yes, my last Clackamas field day of 2011, even given the horrible road trip, was a spectacular success! Bravo Nature! Bravo Big Bottom!

Note: A smaller stage is found directly across Road 42 where well-hidden up in the trees is a talus used as a small rock quarry long ago. This quarry has more shade than the New Rock Quarry and provides excellent "look down" opportunities from trees on the slope above.

In June 2014 I showed this quarry and the strange circles in it to Steve Lindsey. He promptly labeled it the *Indian Ceremony Quarry* because of old, relatively flat, manually cleared areas in the talus which showed no signs of mechanized manipulation.

This site is a talus so in old times it was open to the sky; a good place for summer or autumn Native American ceremonies and celebration of harvest; huckleberries still abound in the area, but I'm not saying where. The circles were certainly not made with bulldozers and the rocks around them show signs of long weathering. There is absolutely no evidence the circles were used by white men for any purpose.

For anyone with Google Earth, we encourage a look at this site to see the ceremony rings. The west ring is small, only about 12' by 15'. The center circle is about 30' in diameter. The east circle is shaped more like an egg because of underlying rock and is about 30' by 25'. GPS: 44 59 26.90N 121 47 24.45W at 3829'.

From the far northeast edge of the talus an old trail goes toward the Reservation line. However, we suspect these circles were in use far earlier than when the Reservation was established in 1855 in a ten acres for one acre "land exchange" with the Federal government.

I have never driven into this quarry and talus site. For some strange reason, from my first exploration, I had a feeling it was better to walk uphill for a quarter mile to where the talus begins. It is a feeling I still have. The grade is moderate. Beautiful virgin timber borders the road. For some reason I feel I am walking on what was an ancient trail.

Note: I am placing confidence in the integrity of Bigfoot researchers by giving the specifics of this location. Please do not move any rocks and please do not litter if you visit the site. Someone is keeping it clean for a purpose.

This ends reports from Area 5.

Palisades of the Clackamas on Hwy 46. Photo by Sharon Beelart.

A stretch of the historic Oregon Skyline Road near the headwaters of the Warm Springs River. Photo by Sharon Beelart.

Area 6: the Southern Region

Area 6, the southern part of the *Oregon Bigfoot Highway*, is a region of untamed mystery. It is a place where binoculars are the traveler's friend, whether glassing magnificent Mt. Jefferson, the old fire lookout tower on SiSi Butte, (pronounced "sigh sigh) the Breitenbush River gorge, or edges of chiseled canyons everywhere. All along it, wild places, and the wild creatures in them, parallel this stretch of the *Oregon Bigfoot Highway*.

What are the boundaries of this largely unfettered semi-wilderness? The center southwest point is easy to find. That is at the small town of Detroit and Detroit Lake. Most of the southeast border is the lower flank of Mt. Jefferson. The southwest line of the Warm Springs Indian Reservation is the east border of Area 6. The western boundary is roughly the west end of *Bull of the Woods* and *Opal Creek* wilderness.

SiSi & Lemiti Buttes

Functionally the northeast boundary is the desolate low plateau which lies between SiSi Butte and Lemiti Butte. This is a basin crowded with beetle-infested jack pine that loggers will not stoop to saw.

There are few animals in it and only one sorry, slow, bug infested creek. But, this plateau is a natural route from Portland to Central Oregon and at the west end of it is where Lumber Jack bought his infamous no-road timber sale.

Unlike the waste land basin, the area south of Olallie Butte and north of the Mt. Jefferson Wilderness is covered by numerous lakes. In the distant past, this region was probably either a big post-ice age lake, or a huge swamp. It is a verdant land with worthy trees that remains good habitat for all kinds of animals.

The north central point of the boundary is before the Olallie Lake turn-off

on Road 46 (Mile 46.5/23.5). From there, the north boundary runs west just above Ogre Creek to the western line of the Opal Creek Wilderness. For fit Bigfooting adventurers, hiking the northwest boundary of Area 6 may generate important results.

SiSi Butte forest fire lookout tower in the fire smoke of 2012. Photo by Sharon Beelart.

Camping in Area 6

Area 6 is rough and wild. Few people frequent the interior of Area 6, except near Olallie Lake where there are eight established campgrounds and a summer lodge. As a result, few reliable, non-Internet Bigfoot reports come from the area.

There is only one campground on the west side of Road 46 which is at Round Lake. But, to put things in perspective, there are *zero* established campgrounds in Area 5 which is the largest area along the *Oregon Bigfoot Highway*. Surprisingly, Area 5 also generated the largest number of reports and incidents for this book.

The Southern Ridge Crest

The crest at *OBH* mile marker 50.5 (19.5) is where explorers can stop to see the steep "V" of the Breitenbush River canyon falling away to the southwest. The Breitenbush canyon is a severe steeply sloped fissure, more gorge like than the Clackamas River canyon south of Estacada. Like the Clackamas River gorge, the Breitenbush gorge was carved at the end of the Ice Age by huge, speeding floods carrying boulders which worked like nature's router to make the "V" before you and beyond.

Bigfoot in the Breitenbush

While the Breitenbush canyon is narrow, steep, and rocky about every 4 or 5 miles along Road 46 logging roads penetrate the mountains. Still, the steep terrain immediately surrounding Road 46 does not seem particularly hospitable for regular habitation by the Bigfoot creatures, so they are seen less in this area, and reports are few.

The southwest part of Area 6 is the remnant of a great glacial basin that runs to the mountain crags surrounding *Bull of the Woods* wilderness, and the Opal Creek Wilderness further west. This sink is certainly not as big as Big Bottom, but still, it is easy in one's mind to see the ice that filled it and later create great floods to roar out of the basin and carve the Breitenbush canyon.

We can also deduce how rugged *Bull of the Woods* country is, as the southern Bonneville Power Administration 500 kilovolt power line from the Columbia River dams turns here to avoid the *Bull of the Woods*. The power lines then follow the Breitenbush River to near Detroit where the line again veers west to the population centers of the mid-Willamette Valley.

Power lines, like water, tend to follow the path of least resistance. It should also be noted that the power lines were constructed decades prior to the establishment of Bull of the Woods Wilderness. Since the power line route is the "easy" route, it is also probably the path of Sasquatch, especially through the Olallie Butte region.

Even after substantial attempts to gather accounts for Area 6 of this book, the authors found only five "genuine" items and one drawing for Area 6 even though there are undoubtedly many more hidden away in people's minds. Also, please keep in mind we did not use web based reports for *OBH*. Only one written report contained a sighting, an event with "meat" in it.

However, the five items were very close to the 1:4 ratio of Bigfoot sighting reports to non-sighting incidents reported in Areas 1 thru 5. That is about one sighting report to four reports of incidents such as track finds.

Finally, our sole hoax story comes from Area 6. It was really not much of a surprise since a tornado of hoaxes and fantasies swirl around the subject of Bigfoot. And, I perhaps guaranteed myself a hoax story but, I was hoping for something more sophisticated.

Also, in the spirit of Bigfootolgy, Area 6 offers the only "Blob-Squatch" photo in this book. When the photograph was submitted to the authors for possible inclusion, the photographer, a man of good character and with a responsible job, did it in good faith believing he had photographed a Bigfoot at night.

At first glance, the night time "Blob-Squatch" photo certainly did resemble a tall, massive animal, which was indeed the truth of it. We hope readers will smile while enjoying this story.

Breitenbush canyon, looking south from Road 46. Photo by Sharon Beelart.

Area 6 OBH Mile Markers

Miles from Estacada: from Detroit

52.7:	17.3	Willamette National Forest sign
53.5:	16.5	*15 MPH* curves
55.7:	14.3	Power line crossing
58.5:	11.5	Road 4685 intersection
58.9:	11.1	Intersection with Road 4688; power lines
60.5:	9.5	Breitenbush Hot Springs Road 4693
65.0:	5.0	West side: this forest was thinned in Nov. 2009
66.3:	3.7	Breitenbush River Bridge; power lines
69.0:	1.0	Upper arm of Detroit Lake
70.0:	0.0	Detroit: intersection of Rd 46 and Hwy 22

The end, or the beginning, of the *Oregon Bigfoot Highway*

From the left: Olallie Butte, Mt. Jefferson, and Lemiti Butte (forward, lower butte). Photo by Joe Beelart.

Map of Area 6

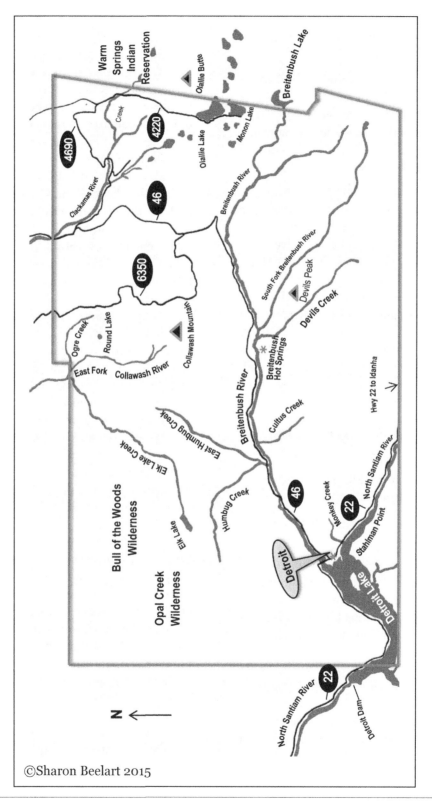

©Sharon Beelart 2015

The time of this long, convoluted tale of a night with all kinds of strange doings was late August 2007.

Location: Lemiti Butte on Road 4220: Being trailed and stomped at, at night, is Bigfoot Related Incident 63 (I63): Track Find 39 (TF39) was made in the morning, in and around camp. Bigfoot braiding a horse mane is Happening 33 (H33). The horse person is Jake 31 (J31).

Little People is Jake 30 (J30). *Little People* got his moniker because on the morning of the first day of this adventure, he drove to my house to meet David Mann and me. While I finished packing the truck, Jake 30 cornered my wife in the kitchen and talked to her about *"Little People"*. She knew most of, and genuinely liked my Bigfooting friends, but to her great astonishment, this was a pine tar curve ball. I had no time to talk to her before the three of us headed up the hill, but when we returned she looked askance at David and me and referring to J30 as *Little People* and it stuck.

Lemiti Creek camp GPS: 44 54 05.04N 121 47 43.39W at 4210'

Horse camp GPS: 44 54 19.49N 121 47 19.75W at 4224'

I only go up the hill with people whose company I enjoy, or think I will enjoy. In this case, David Mann, who was one of my favorite camping chums brought along his friend, who was a long time Bigfooter, on this "adventure."

Mostly campout companions, other than the Sasquatchian bunch, are quietly vetted before trips to find their interests and level of experience. Reasons for not inviting people for field research varies, but mainly it has to do with physical conditioning, lack of camping experience,

unreasonable expectations, propensity to "see things," etc. Sometimes field research techniques don't match well.

This was one of those times, but it all turned out OK. Jake 30 is a pleasant, intelligent, intense, experienced, and unique in our circle in that he advocates the existence of Little People over Bigfoot. He may be right; numerous Native American legends speak to Little People.

Little People make certain, and perhaps even better sense as an ecological fit to the land. Anyway, Jake 30 said he had many encounters with Little People. He said, showing Mann and I how he attracts Little People would add a useful facet to our research.

My plan was simple enough, but was foiled at the onset. I wanted to go to Pinhead Buttes to spend the night so we drove there. David rode with me in my truck and J30 drove his big SUV. After chain sawing a large fir which fell across the road, we finally arrived at my favorite campsite.

When Jake 30 found out there wasn't water nearby, he chastised me for not telling him. He likes to camp near water. Apparently, the best places for Little People are near water, which is also the best place to find raccoons.

Very honestly, that does not mean I think J30 mistakes raccoons for Little People, but new researchers might. Anyway, due to the expansive view of Olallie Butte directly in front of us, he knew there was water down there because he'd heard that the Olallie Lake area harbored a number of Little People. As it turned out, J30's idea was a good one.

So we drove down mountain, across the flats on the east side of SiSi (sigh, sigh) Butte and came upon Lemiti Creek. I already knew it was Lemiti Creek but my companions were finally convinced of it when we came upon a little Forest Service sign reading "Lemiti Creek" mercifully ending that discussion.

According to J30 this was a good place. And David and I agreed it was nice, almost idyllic. There was a grass filled glen alongside the creek and on the southwest side of the creek a small hill offered both a late afternoon sun screen and perhaps, a wind break.

Unfortunately, this was also the point in our campout where I learned *Little People* forbade campfires. His reasoning was in part that while a small fire is small to us, it might be frightening to the Little People and keep them away.

While I don't build a campfire every night I'm out, I was planning on one that evening to roast hot dogs and sit around if we stayed up late. As a result, I had loaded up a pile of wood. "Oh well, I like my dogs cold too and the wood will keep."

After we unloaded the trucks David helped J30 set up his sound broadcasting system which I'd heard much about. I would have helped, but they had done it together before. I was surprised at how quickly the set-up was done, considering J30 brought along all the speakers, wiring, battery boxes, and gear adequate to power a small rock concert.

Jake 30's reasoning for such a system was that in addition to entertaining most of a township, it projected into Little People's underground homes better than a more modest system. However, I must say, I wondered what all that acoustical power did to their little ear drums.

Shortly after dark, *Little People* fired up his sound system, which was to be sure, very powerful, and broadcast, to my horror, circa '80s love songs at full volume. It truly was amazing. Given Jake 30's age, those songs may have attracted girls to him back then, but I had sincere doubts those songs would bring in any starry eyed Sasquatches.

Since we couldn't talk, I went for a walk away from camp and still heard the broadcasting. That's when I decided it was time for my night walk, only a little early. *Just how long can those batteries last, anyway?*

So, I walked back to camp and rested a while listening to elevator music gone bad. After a while I let my intentions be known, pulled on my Duluth pack, picked up my walking stick and took off up the old asphalt haul road. The moon was about a half, so I didn't need a light, which is normal.

Trailing & Stomping

After about a quarter mile I came to an intersection where a gravel logging road headed east, so I turned up it. I walked for about another 20 minutes according to my hardy Casio G-Shock watch, when I came to a strange juxtaposition of big trees on the south side of the road.

Sometime in the past a strong wind blew the trees together. One of them was big and sans bark, a veritable *Bigfoot Beacon*, as I call big buck-naked, sun-bleached trees. It was time for a break, so I unbuckled a pouch on my pack and enjoyed a drink of

water. It was then I heard the crunch of footsteps near the tepee of trees.

Deer? No. The steps were too heavy. Bear? No. Not enough brush crushing. Then it dawned on me and I snapped out of my journey into black oblivion, a place where I often go on night walks; those were bipedal footsteps and ... in a race of imagination ... I "saw" the beast taking those steps to watch me, to follow me.

I was still without a light, and didn't click one on all night, so all the critter in the woods saw was a dark, short, bulky form standing on the road. Was I friend or foe? Was I something interesting to investigate, or not? But, out on the road I was thinking just now might be an opportune time to head back to camp before I became the *carte du jour* in a Sasquatch fine dining establishment, or cave.

What happened next we label Bigfoot related Incident 63. It was a mile back to camp, or maybe a little more. Roughly a decade earlier, that part of the forest was attacked by an invasive beetle species which killed most of the trees in the basin. As a result of the trees slowly decaying, there is a lot, *as in a lot* of limb debris on the ground. Normally, nature would have taken care of this problem with a big wild fire, but one hadn't happened yet.

What all those fallen limbs meant was, as I walked along the road in the dark of night, I could hear my forest companion walking in the trees to my left, paralleling me. When I stopped, it took a step or two and then stopped. When I started, it started; when I suddenly stopped, it took an extra step or two and stopped. Really, it became kind of a game.

When I arrived at the asphalt road intersection of Road 4220, in my mind, the game got serious. Then, whether it meant to or not, the beast in the woods east of the road made a display *by stomping* forest duff and fallen limbs, some of which didn't sound too small from the way they cracked.

What is that all about? Am I nearing someplace it doesn't want me to go? Is the land behind the beast its territory and the stomping a sign of a fence line?

Conversely, in retrospect, it may have meant me absolutely no harm and was transmitting to me, for my own good, "Don't go that way!" Maybe earlier it heard *Little People's* music from Lemiti Creek rupturing the forest quiet.

Anyway, the creature paralleled me back to our idyllic, fireless, now silent camp on Lemiti Creek; gloriously silent because the batteries gave out. When I walked in, my companions were sitting in my director's chairs which always get used because they are the most comfortable.

I fiercely whispered, "Shusssh," then pointed with my walking stick at the woods on the far side of the road. The creature therein again performed a *stomping display* which, to some degree, caught my companions' attention since whatever was doing that stomping sure as hell wasn't a Little Person out there in the night shadows.

It was now about 1 AM. I decided it was time for a nightcap, so after again "shushing" my companions, I poured myself a stiff one to help me settle down a little. Then, I tilted one of my director's chairs to indicate to the occupant, "off" and sat down. I was tired. I'd walked in the dark, without a light, for almost two hours.

Sitting quietly and shushing my friends was a good thing. In part, it let us listen to the quiet burble of the creek and the creature as it crossed the road, splashed through the creek, and climbed the hillside southwest of our camp. When things got quiet on the hillside, then things got way quiet on our side and stayed that way. From that hillside, we knew the critter was looking at us, which was a bit unnerving.

The quiet was somewhat disturbing, so disturbing in fact, that after I finished my nightcap, I thought of taking out my 357 and placing it beside my bedroll in the back of my pickup; but thought better of it since two people were in camp with me. The next morning, we found where the creature sat watching us; it was less than 120 linear feet from our chairs.

Little People went to bed inside his SUV. In the morning, I saw Mann had pitched his wonderful little bivouac tent with a mesh top in the center of the meadow in the glen beside the creek. We all also saw the grass around his tent was smashed down, like he was being circled by Sioux warriors in a plains battle.

It was obvious the creature was curious about Mann, and because it could see through his tent's mesh top, it watched him sleep from several angles. While there were many partial prints, all about 17 inches long, because of the grass mat none were good enough to cast. Also, since Lemiti Creek is a spring fed creek with grass shores there were no castable tracks along it. We label the tracks along the creek and around the tent Track Find 39 (TF39).

Braiding a horse's mane

In the morning, *Little People* said the Little People came out very late that night. He said they came from the hillside and pranced and celebrated on the old log in our campground. When they came, their cheerful little voices woke him and he got out of his SUV to watch them dance and sing and be happy. He also said he heard nothing from our heavy footed friend during their visit.

Unfortunately, while visions of the Little People are pleasantly stowed in our minds, we don't have a category for them, so thoughts of their appearance are a happy memory, not a number.

Also, while we were drinking coffee, my companions chided me for being gone so long on my own and not telling them where I was going (*How did I even know?*). Then both of them made mildly disparaging remarks about my claim of walking a mile one way in the dark.

So, #$%&, I decided to show them. We drove to the crunched trees of which I actually drew a drawing before we left, and to their unwashed knowledge of happenings in the dark, found the tree crunch was slightly over a mile from camp.

Satisfied, *Little People* departed for Portland. My buddy Mann and I decided to

drive up the logging road. In short order we encountered a horse camp. One horse was on a tag line stretched between two trees, the other horses were in trailers. We asked to pass through, which was granted even though it was a Forest Service road open to all, and came upon a pothole lake and a tree fallen across the road.

So, we turned around and again stopped at the horse camp. Mann noticed the horse tied to the tag line had intricate braids in its mane. He motioned to me that Bigfoot braid horses manes, and said he'd also seen weaving in llama hair in Tennessee.

People came out of their trailer so we started to chat. I inquired about the intricate braids in the horse's mane saying something to the effect, "You probably have a lot of time to do that sort of thing up here."

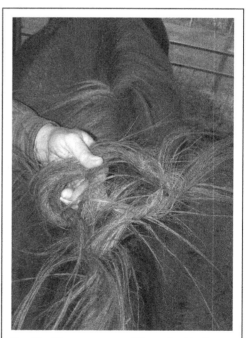

Braided horse mane. Photo by Beth Heikkinen.

The woman promptly answered, we refer to her as Jake 31. J31 said in a worried tone words to this effect, "No, someone has been doing that in the night starting the second night we camped here."

Then, one of the men standing near J31 interrupted saying that "we don't know what to make of the braiding." He also said he was a little surprised we noticed it.

"Are you horse people." "No." Then the woman (J31) promptly chimed in saying they were not sleeping well, and were hearing quiet noises in the night. But, the horses didn't whinny or seem spooked.

She pointed to the horse on the tag line saying the ground wasn't pawed up like it would be if the horse was upset. Then the second man broke his silence, anxious to say that at first they thought it was someone in their camp pulling a practical joke, but everyone had absolved themselves from the strange doings.

Jake 31 was positive the braids were not made by wind, partly because there had been little wind, they didn't ride fast, and because the braiding was intricate and repetitive. The woman said she was glad they were leaving that day. One of the men nodded in firm agreement.

We consider the horse mane braiding at the pothole lake an unusual event and important enough to label it Happening 33 (H33). Since there was no direct connection to Bigfoot it was not assigned an Incident number.

Notes: Bigfoot creatures playing with horses and braiding or plaiting horse's manes is occasionally mentioned in the literature. Russian researcher Dmitri Bayanov, *In the Footsteps of the Russian Snowman* (Crypto-Logos, Moscow 1996) is especially expansive on the subject of plaited horse manes as he devoted ten pages to the subject. We wholeheartedly agree with Mr. Bayanov that habituating Bigfoot through prolonged horse camps, or remote homesteads might provide very useful research results.

Washington Bigfoot researcher Beth Heikkinen has long investigated the braiding phenomena and has graciously provided photographs to the authors of examples of braided horse manes made in other parts of the northwest. Beth is adamant that her photographs do not show wind braids.

Map notes: The location and number of the side road that I walked, and where the horse camp was located are good examples of mistakes in maps. My 1983 contractor–fire fighter grade map labels the road as Spur 015, my official Forest Service 1993 map labels it as Spur 4207, which is no big deal, unless one person is referencing an old map and someone else a newer edition.

My 2003 detailed, official Forest Service map does not list a spur number. However, it maps the side road south of Lemiti Creek, when in fact the side road definitely intersects with 4220 about one quarter of a mile north of Lemiti Creek. The side road and pothole lake are easily seen on Google Earth. The end result of this little treatise is to caution researchers to double check in the field what they see on maps.

Ref. 95: The 1953 Round Lake Sighting

Round Lake is in the north-central part of Area 6. In August 1953, Bigfoot watches young men in camp and fishing.

This is Sighting 29 (S29): The witnesses were Jake 32 (J32), Jake 33 (J33), and Jake 34 (J34). The bad odor is Bigfoot Related Incident 64 (I64).

Round Lake GPS: 44 52 32.10N 121 58 13.98W at 3597'

In 1953, the closest road to Round Lake was Hwy 22, which was about 25 miles south at Detroit. Detroit was also the southern hiking and pack horse trail head into the upper Breitenbush and Collawash Rivers. On a side note, Detroit was "new" in 1953 because in 1952 the original 1890s village was relocated as the Detroit Dam reservoir rapidly filled.

The nearest northern trail head to Round Lake was at the confluence of the Collawash River and the Clackamas River. This trail head was also about 25 miles north of the lake. Road 6370 now passes Round Lake and there is a nice campground there.

Late August 1953 was a time when the Collawash River was still wild in the way the Indians knew it. Only foot and horse trails existed, trails that were the predecessors of Forest Service Roads 63 and 70; roads which later destroyed most of the ancient trails.

The Sighting

It was on the main Collawash River trail that three hardy young men, one 16 and two at 18 years, carrying all of their gear plus a raft, walked 25 miles from the Collawash and Clackamas River junction to Round Lake to fish. These are Jakes 32, 33, and 34.

Only one of the three young men is alive today, but after almost six decades, he remembers the Sasquatch encounter well. However, during his talks with me, Jake 32 is still somewhat reticent to claim a Bigfoot sighting although his two companions repeatedly told without equivocation their sighting of a big hairy naked man-like being at Round Lake.

The deceased gentlemen are Jake 33 and Jake 34. Through some circuitous Bigfoot telegraph Jake 32 found out we were writing a book on the Clackamas so he sent me an email saying he had an old experience that might interest us. It did.

In late April 2012, Jake 32 granted me a telephone interview, a follow-up interview, and then I sent him this report for his approval. J32 is retired from a professionally licensed field requiring four or more years of university study. Surprisingly, although he is succinct in words, his memory of events which happened 59 years previous was incredibly precise.

Our three youthful, highly energetic adventurers hiked to the lake, quite literally fishing for their supper. The second day on the lake one of the 18 year olds, Jake 33 remained in camp while Jake 32 and Jake 34 went trolling in the raft. But, while still on the beach, all three noticed an obvious "new stump" standing in shadow near their camp on the lake shore.

They didn't think much about the "stump," only that it seemed out of place and was roughly 7 feet tall. Keep in mind Round Lake only covers about 4 acres, so something nearby is nearby. At least twice in the interview, Jake 32 said the "stump" was "close" to camp, at the very most, 100 yards away, and always, keeping in the shadows.

After Jake 32 and his raft mate paddled around about an hour, Jake 33, the young man at camp, began waving and calling out for them to "come back, come back!" So they rowed back to find the shore side teen thoroughly scared.

Apparently, the "stump" walked from where it was near the beach, into the forest, and then to the brush surrounding their camp. In the brush it expressed its displeasure at their presence by banging on trees, throwing rocks and limbs, and making growling-roaring vocalizations. The vocalizations were so loud even before J33 began waving and calling, the two youths in the raft heard the roars and started paddling for shore to see what was up.

While the acts by the invisible intruder disturbed the young man at camp, some minutes later he really got scared. Less than 50 feet away a huge man-creature suddenly appeared from the forest and presented itself to him in an "aggressive" arms raised posture. An undetermined amount of time went by with the youth frozen in place wondering what would happen next. Then, when the man-creature saw the raft approaching, it silently retreated into the virgin timber.

The Jake at camp was not to be consoled. He had seen an upset, very large, very naked "man–animal" (words used by J32) that was close enough to allow him to smell a bad odor. He was adamant about the odor; it was really foul. Jake 32 said it was still present when J32 and 34 explored the brush. We designate this odor as Bigfoot related Incident 64.

For Jake 33 it was a mostly sleepless night. Jake 32 said he slept well and remembers nothing happened in the night unlike Jake 33 who was convinced the "man-animal" returned to the brush close to camp and raised a commotion. Jake 32 still thinks Jake 33 was just having nightmares about his day time visit by the monster.

By morning, Jake 33 convinced his companions to hike out of the Collawash, which was good, because the Forest Service was after them. It was prime forest fire season and smoke from their fire was seen by one or more of the fire-watch towers in the area, probably the one in what is now Bull-of-the-Woods Wilderness or on SiSi Butte.

Anyway, for one reason or another, the Forest Service knew the identity of the teens at Round Lake and they wanted them out, pronto! Wild fires in roadless, rugged country were basically uncontrollable and destroyed valuable timber.

So, that was pretty much the end of the story. Officials were waiting when the youths walked out of the Collawash onto Road 46. Later Jake 32 wrote a report for the Forest Service in Estacada which is still on file. In J32's report to the USFS, he barely mentioned the "man–animal" which he regarded as a harmless noise making hermit.

J32 said, even after all these years, he still remembers the official's comments about the reference to a wildman. He recalls they said words to the effect: "They're out there but they don't bother anyone. They're probably crazy hermits."

As best as J32 can remember, the officials weren't much interested in the wild man, but they were very interested in the trout species the three caught in the lake. Jake 36's report recorded bull trout, or Dolly Varden, along with rainbows, but no eastern brook trout. Bull trout is a fish now on the endangered species list, but not back then because "endangered" was not part of the conservation lexicon.

Researchers searching Forest Service archives at Estacada should not look for the word Bigfoot in J32's report. The term "Bigfoot" did not exist in 1953, and would not for five more years until Jerry Crew's 1958 find was reported in a northwest California newspaper. Unfortunately, Jake 32 cannot remember the exact name of the report

Cougar #7: A cougar trails Kiley

Cougar #7 (C7) follows Kiley near Olallie Butte.

It was the last day of late elk season in 2006. Light snow covered the ground and visibility was very good. It was cold. Steve Kiley was out elking the east side of Area 6 with his reliable old 30-06. Steve had followed elk tracks over and around a partially open area proven in the past to hold late season elk. While the area remains confidential, it may become apparent to those who study the habits of large, hoofed, ungulate mammals, and who study topographical maps.

Basically, the story was simple. It was late in the day. Somehow, the big herd bull Steve was following got wind or sight of him. Perhaps the bull was warned by his harem. In any event, the hunting day was done when the elk crashed away through the forest to parts unknown.

Following them further was dangerous. Steve was high up the hill above camp; a winter storm was approaching. He needed to get back before dark. So, to make it easier, he hiked cross-country to an old logging road that intersected with another road he could use to hike down to camp.

After about a quarter mile of hiking down the road, Steve had a feeling he was being watched. He turned. Silhouetted against the sky on the road above him was a cougar, standing, watching. As Steve continued down the old skid road, he stopped from time to time. Each time he turned the cougar was there, following him at about 150 yards, being careful to not give Steve a rifle shot.

When Steve got down to the bottom, he once again turned to look at the cougar. Fortunately, this time it was nowhere to be seen. That was the end of the event. He said maybe it followed him further staying out of sight in the trees. He never felt threatened, he just thought the cougar was curious about him or because Steve might lead it to a gut pile.

Ref. 96: Four Hunter Stories

#1: Jake 35 (J35) makes Track Find 40 (TF40) near Breitenbush Lake: **#2:** North of Olallie Butte a forest giant shakes Jake 35's truck producing Bigfoot related Incident 65 (I65). **#3:** Jake 35 describes a deadly silent forest in the same area which is Happening 34 (H34). **#4:** On the north central slopes of Mt. Jefferson hunter Jake 36 (J36) reports a second deathly silent canyon which is designated Happening 35 (H35).

The authors note all four of these episodes happened along the proposed Sasquatch eastern migratory path described in Appendix IV. We also note the forest is often very silent while at other times it is *very, very silent*. Happenings H34 and H35 are examples of *very, very silent* as reported by responsible, highly experienced outdoorsmen.

#1: A track find at nine

Breitenbush Lake GPS: 44 46 10.20N 121 46 38.98W at 5510'

In yet another weird turn of events, Jake 35 somehow, through the wood knocking telegraph, heard this book was being written. So, he got in touch with me and asked if I would like some stories. After talking to Jake 35 a few times, and checking out his qualifications, I was more than willing to include three of his hunting tales.

However, Jake 35 wanted two things; he wanted to write his stories and he wished to remain anonymous. J35 is an avid outdoorsman who lives south of Portland, Oregon. He emphasizes respecting the Reservation boundary line.

Jake 35 on Track Find 40 (TF40). Begin quote:

"The only time I saw tracks was when I was nine years old. The year was 1973 and I was with my aunt and uncle and we were on a camping trip between Breitenbush Lake and Olallie Lake. There's a ton of small lakes in the area and I can't tell you which one it was because I was nine and wasn't paying attention to where we were. We had made a stop to make a sandwich. While my aunt was making sandwiches I wandered away to take care of hydrating a plant or two.

While I was waiting, I wandered around and found a small lake about a hundred yards off the road from where we were parked. I added to the lake water table and was walking around doing what kids do when I stumbled onto a set of huge footprints. Just seeing them scared the crap out of me! At that age I could only imagine what made them. The tracks walked into the lake about fifteen feet then came back out and then continued around the lake into the woods.

My uncle, aunt, and I back tracked the prints up to the road and found that they came off the side hill across the road and down to the lake. They didn't seem to be faked. They had deeper depressions in the heel and ball of the foot and distinct toes. We left and ate our sandwiches elsewhere.

During that trip I thought about those tracks every night when I was lying in my sleeping bag in the tent. The thought of them in the night gave me the jitters. Later, in the fall of the year I phoned John Green about my tracks and John Green put the story in one of his books." End quote.

#2: Bigfoot shook my truck

Jake 35 on Bigfoot Related Incident 65 (I65). Begin quote:

"During the 1993 archery season I was in an area east of the Clackamas drainage along the southwest border of the Warm Springs Indian Reservation. My buddy worked second shift and was going to drive up and meet me after work. That would have put him up there about 1:30AM.

I (J35) got up to our spot about 6:00 PM and it was drizzling rain. I got camp set up and since I had about an hour to an hour and a half of daylight left I thought I'd go out and elk call a little. I found some fresh sign and rut activity and proceeded to throw out some cow calls and a few bugles using a diaphragm call. I didn't have an archery elk tag that year because I drew a rifle tag so I could hunt with the old man during rifle season.

Wouldn't you know it, here comes Mr. Big, Mr. REALLY Big ... This bull was a whopper and I could do nothing more than appreciate his majestic beauty. He would have scored well over 300 and gave me a nice 20 yard broadside shot.

That's great, but no archery tag. Naturally I got all excited, but it was dark and time to head back to camp and get a small fire going. I didn't spend any time getting firewood and used a little wet stuff that was around camp.

I heated up a can of the old standby Dinty Moore stew and sat next to my pitiful wet campfire that barely burned and listened to the Blazers (Portland's basketball team) play whomever they were playing that night. The game must have been out of town because I remember it ended at about 8:30 PM and I decided because it was still drizzling and I had such a lousy fire I called it a night. So, I climbed into the back of my Toyota, closed the canopy and crawled into my sleeping bag.

I snuggled in and relaxed, thinking about the next morning's hunt and how I hoped I could call that bull back in for my buddy when I thought I heard something. This was within five minutes of going to bed. I told myself it was my imagination and closed my eyes when my truck moved. Something was pushing it! I couldn't hear anything else after that but my heartbeat.

Here I was, 65 miles from Estacada with nobody within probably 20 miles of me so I know somebody wasn't playing tricks on me. It was pitch black out and I couldn't see a thing because there was no moon and something is being pretty forward with me. Off and on for about the next three hours whatever it was hung around camp messing with stuff though it never got into a cooler or anything else food related. That made me think it wasn't a bear.

But, was it a bear? I don't know? I finally manned up and got mad and fired a round from my .357 out of my canopy window into the ground and it left, but then came back for a while then left for good. My buddy showed up a little after 1:00 AM. When I told him what happened he laughed at me. He doesn't believe in anything other than what is proven. His logic said bear, not something else. Anyway, whatever it was shook my truck with me in the back of it. Bear? Maybe? Maybe I think not." End quote.

Note: Jake 39 made a point to twice say to me that he found no claw marks on his truck after it was shaken. Bears cannot retract their claws.

#3: **Dead Silent Canyon no. 1**

Jake 35 on Happening 34. Begin quote:

"The next year I (Jake 35) was up in the same place during bow season. I parked at that same camp spot and took off on a morning hunt. The bulls up there are hard to get (Aren't they all?), so I started bugling. It usually takes about 20-30 minutes of constant bugling to get them going. I finally got a bull bugling then more joined in. I was probably a mile and a half to two miles from my truck and had elk all around me!

I had a little three point bull come within 40 yards of me, but didn't shoot him. His little three points were a perfect little crown to cradle a baseball bat. He wandered away and I continued calling. Bulls were bugling, cows were mewing, and the sun was shining. It was a great morning. Then it was like something turned off the elk switch.

My wind was good, I'm always aware of that, so the elk did not catch my scent. Then, the woods just went dead silent. It was about nine in the morning and I figured it was time to start hiking back to the truck which was close to two miles away. As I was walking I felt like I was being watched and I felt real uneasy. I was getting that hair on the back of my neck standing up feeling and moved a little faster.

I was traveling through some pretty heavy patches of brush and Rhodies at times and my mind went back to the story when I was nine. I thought to myself that today is the day that I'm going to see something I don't really want to see. I got back to the truck and never saw anything, but I know something was there. I'd never had that feeling before that day or since. Maybe it was a cougar? Maybe it wasn't? I will never know, but it was something." End quote.

Bunchberry dogwood, *Cornus Canadensis*. Low trailing evergreen shrublet, 8"tall. White blooms in summer, bright red berries in September. Photos by Sharon Beelart

#4: The Breitenbush silent canyon

Near the Mt. Jefferson Wilderness, hunter Jake 36 (J36) reports a deadly silent canyon which we record as Happening 35 (H35).

Breitenbush Hot Springs GPS: 44 46 52.67N 121 58 31.65W at 2254'

Devils Peak GPS: 44 45 33.58N 121 56 22.67W at 4507'

The Breitenbush Hot Springs and Road 46 intersection is about 9 miles from Detroit and about 60 miles from Estacada. To ground reference this Silent Canyon report, see Willamette National Forest Roads 4685, 2231, and Spur 870.

Bigfoot tales spring out of the most unexpected places. This is an example. One day when I was visiting a factory, a long time pump mechanic told me this story while I ate lunch with the men. We call this man Jake 36 (J36). Jake 36 is a no-nonsense, salt-of-the-earth sort of fellow who works hard and plays harder. He hunts deer and elk, but not small game and birds.

How J36 found out I was interested in Bigfoot is unknown. I've never asked, and he's never said, but after that lunch he's brought up the subject at opportune times. Anyway, like many Bigfoot stories his tale is short, simple, and without a sighting or incident involved. The reason he even mentioned it to me is vague.

Essentially he said he and a friend, or two, have hunted deer almost every year for a long time in the mountains east of Breitenbush Hot Springs near the Mt. Jefferson Wilderness. (Hunting is prohibited in the Wilderness). He said in October 2006 something happened to change their hunt and, J36 said 2006 wasn't the first year something like it happened.

They set up camp on Friday, and on Saturday entered their favorite canyon before dawn. All morning long they hunted but saw no fresh tracks or spoor. They heard no birds. The canyon was deathly silent. In previous years this same thing sporadically happened. They knew hunting in the silent canyon was futile, so they moved camp.

The next time I saw him, I brought along a topographical map of the area. I spread it, pointing to the general area of Devils Peak and Devils Creek, the major creek which meets the Breitenbush River near the Hot Springs. He said I was in the right vicinity.

Except for our later general conversations about Bigfoot he didn't bring up his hunting territory again except to tell me the next year they dragged two good bucks out of the canyon. I've always felt Jake 36 has more to say about the silent canyon happenings but isn't ready to talk.

Note to the attentive reader: Devils Peak near Breitenbush Hot Springs is not one of *The Horns of the Devil*. It's also interesting that Devils Peak, Devils Creek, and Monkey Creek are all in the southern part of Area 6. Finally, Devils Mountain is near Mt. Hood.

Ref. 97: Breitenbush River: A fly fisher sees Bigfoot

Willamette National Forest Road 46: In Sighting 30 (S30) Jake 37 (J37), a fly fisherman watches Bigfoot.

Approx. sighting GPS: 44 45 55.89N 122 06 29.62W at 1715'

Henner Fahrenbach, Ph.D. told this report to us. It is important to the authors because we both have known Dr. Fahrenbach for many years and know he has a keen, clear, questioning approach to the phenomena.

Note: While Dr. Fahrenbach told us about this sighting, he originally investigated it for the Bigfoot Field Research Organization. See www.bfro.net for BFRO Class A Report #11818.

The general location of the sighting was about four miles up the Breitenbush River southwest of Humbug Campground near where Road 46 bridges the river. Dr. Fahrenbach said the witness was fly fishing

when he heard the loud snap of a breaking branch across the river. Soon, at no more than 75 feet away, he had a sighting which lasted perhaps fifteen seconds until the beast disappeared into the trees. Nonetheless, the sighting was impressionable as the witness told Henner the creature was big, had a barrel chest, and no neck.

What impresses the authors about this report is that Henner talked to the witness in June 2005 only two years after the sighting. At that time the witness stated, "I believe it was in June 2003 ...." He continued, "As best as I can remember, it was between 12 noon and 4:00 pm ..." Clearly, the witness is unsure of the time. And, he even seems unsure of the month.

From that the authors concluded two things. One: It is an indication that to some people, a Sasquatch sighting is so inherently unexciting, or such an everyday event, they forget common details. Or, two: Perhaps the creature affects the mind of the witness so details become bleary or are forgotten.

It is up to the reader to read the detailed BFRO report and consider the impression the sighting made on the subject. While he definitively mentioned the time frame, Dr. Fahrenbach offered no opinion or comment on our ideas.

This is designated Sighting 30 (S30) and the witness is designated Jake 37.

Ref. 98: Bigfoot Advertising

Advertising for Bigfoot stories has its pluses and minuses. In 2008 I decided to write this book. In 2010, in an attempt to find more accounts along the Breitenbush River and near Detroit, I designed a simple store window advertisement reading in bold, big type: *Bigfoot Experiences Wanted by Author*. Then during one long day, I drove to Detroit and down the Santiam River highway stapling my notice to Forest Service notice boards, in Post Offices, and other opportune spots.

I told my story in small shops, especially convenience stores, where,

Readers may also note Cultus Creek flows into the Breitenbush about one-half mile from the sighting. Cultus is one of several Native American terms for evil forest beings, or a place inhabited by them.

In contrast to the cool approach of J37 to his sighting, in the Detroit Lake sighting report, three accounts hence, the witness had a very animated reaction to his sighting. Now ... let's have a little Bigfootery fun.

generally after a laugh, or smirk, they let me tape a notice to a window with masking tape I had brought along especially for the purpose. Twenty notices lasted me until Mill City on the road to Salem. I also mailed copies to Breitenbush Hot Springs Resort and Olallie Lake Lodge to post on their bulletin boards.

At Mill City I bought a copy of the local weekly paper. It was just right, so for $40 I ran a small advertisement twice. This was the most productive promotion I did as it resulted in discovering the important Jacoby Track Find described in upcoming Ref. 99.

Smokin' up a good one

Olallie Lake: Happening 36 (H36) is the story Jake 38 (J38) and friends concocted.

Olallie Lake GPS: 44 48 26.44N 121 47 18.15W at 4946′

First, on Good Calls

After my advertising I was pretty sure I'd field a tall tale or two, but was pleasantly surprised by the quality and sincerity of the few calls I received. While only one respondent supplied material suitable for the book, they were all interesting and I thanked each with genuine enthusiasm.

For example, one of the most unusual responses was from a local Federal employee who said she gave my request for information to one of her sisters. She said years ago her sister had a close-up, extremely frightening encounter near Idanha, which is two miles south of Detroit.

According to my caller, her sister was hanging clothes out to dry when a Bigfoot walked out of the forest, watching her. This of course scared her. They watched each other and then the sister got a terrible foreboding the beast was going to kidnap her. She ran to the house. Unfortunately I never heard from the sister.

The call that had to happen

Finally I got the call I dreaded in an amusing way. It was just when I thought it would come, at about 8 at night. It was from a young man who worked at one of the resorts. I'll call him Jake 38. I closed my eyes and was sure I smelled the smoke of a popular, illegal bud product wafting through the telephone line, and from his intermittent laughing, I suspected he smoked the product profusely while he was thinking about making the call.

No one would ever make up a Bigfoot story, would they? Well, we admit there are a few stories out there which are Bigfoot urban legends and this was one of them. It was an adaptation of the hunter having to hole up in a cave with a Bigfoot during a three day blizzard.

Compared to some versions of this story, what this kid thought up was fairly bland. But, I was convinced he thought it an original idea, so, I enthusiastically led him on. And he went on, with sporadic stops to recharge, or destroy brain cells as one could look at it.

However, I soon suspected the story's inspiration wasn't entirely his because at one point where he thought it especially humorous he stopped to "heehee." In the background I heard muted laughter and encouraging commentary which suggested to me perhaps some other folks and maybe even beer was mixed in with the water piping.

I decided to play along because it was harmless fun. As we went along, I made gusto for what he was saying. I asked relevant questions and repeated details which he eagerly, but hazily developed after several "umm's." Anyway, due to my exceptional memory, I found no reason to take notes.

By the time the young man hung up, I feel I convinced him I truly believed his account, and would feature it, which I have, labeling it Happening 36. I smile just thinking of those hosers sitting around a campfire, tokin' it up, slinging down beers, and contributing to the literature.

Brief aside: Another common Bigfoot story is when five Bigfoots (why never three or four is beyond me) surround a man sleeping under his pickup canopy. The Bigfoots terrorize him in various ways. To escape, he always squeezes through the cab's slider window, sounds the horn and drives away.

Bigfoot, Blob-Squatch, or ... ??

Happening 37 (H37) is a game camera photograph submitted by Keith Patterson, a career pilot in his early 40's. Keith's photograph was clicked about 200 miles south of the southern boundary of the *OBH*, but we liked it.

At worst, we figured the photo would make an excellent example of a "blob-squatch," a type of photograph ever so common in our pursuit. And since it was the best "blob-squatch" we received we chose to run it. Yes, people submitted photographs insisting they were excellent shots of Bigfoot when in fact they were limb shadows, stumps in shadow, etc.

Keith's photograph came our way via an electron Bigfoot advertising roller coaster. Cliff told his son about our book. His son is an outdoorsman who works in the telecommunications business. He told people about the project. They told people.

Somehow word of the *OBH* got down to Medford where a man said, "I've got a photo of a Bigfoot, it's not a very good one, but I think it's real."

What we initially and correctly saw in the high resolution submittal were two massive legs, hair, one fairly well defined foot, and what looks like an exhaust of lung air making a big steam cloud, Bigfoot breath if you will, since the photo was taken in cold weather. As we contemplated the photo, we ventured that Squatch breath may smell as sweet as roses, or not; anyway, on with the analysis.

The Basics

The photograph was taken about 25 miles SSE of Ashland, Oregon near Pinehurst State Airport (GPS 42 06 36.78N 122 22 58.04W at 3611') on October 18, 2012 at 20:21 hours or 8:21 PM with a Tasco 5 MP color trail cam with IR illuminator

(flash). After sensing a subject, the camera was set on 5 second repeats.

Trail cam photo by Keith Patterson.

The camera was placed about 5 ½ feet up a tree next to a heavily used deer trail at the end of an old logging road passable only by dirt bike or on foot. There are Mule deer in the area, but no elk. A herd of wild horses roams there. The bait was Deer Cocaine which is a mix of minerals and maple syrup which brings in all kinds of animals.

On the day preceding the photograph the trail cam took several photos of wild horses, probably attracted to the Deer Cocaine. Then there was nothing until a click of a tree only, as if the camera was twisted in position. Next was the subject photo. Finally there was a photo showing nothing but black.

Large Human-Like Tracks

There were large human-like tracks in the dirt in front, and near the camera. These tracks were what initially caused Patterson to think he might have photographed a Bigfoot, especially since they clearly showed separated, splayed toes. (Since it was out of our area, Patterson's track find is not included in this book's track find totals.)

After several enhancements of the photograph in Photoshop, I submitted a copy to a science analyst for examination. It was his opinion that the creature is a wild stallion throwing its head. Due to night time low shutter camera speed, when the stallion tossed its head, the image gave the impression of steam. Shifting its legs gave the impression of massive legs and a foot.

The impression of steam is real; it is the stallion's mane flowing.

That settled, our only comment is that Bigfoot is known to like and associate with horses. (Crazy thought — *Bigfoot atop a wild stallion galloping through the forest!* Told you it was a crazy thought). As a reminder, Bigfoot and horse association was reported in Ref. 94, and our citation of Russian researcher Dmitri Bayanov.

Ref. 99: Beaver Pond Track Find

Two miles west of Detroit Lake Track Find 41 (TF41) was filmed with an early video camera: Bigfoot related Incident 66 (I66) is a partially eaten beaver. People involved include Jakes 39, 40, 41 and 42.

My newspaper advertisement led to one of the most significant secondary reports in this book. A man from Salem called me with a beaver pond report. He said in late July 1994, his future son-in-law found a series of what he took to be Bigfoot tracks in a beaver pond on state land near his grandfather's property. Since the site is also near the Santiam River, we call this the Santiam track line or Track Find 41.

The location is about two miles west of Detroit Lake and three miles south of Bull of the Woods Wilderness. GPS coordinates are: 44 45 02.12N 122 21 20.49W at 1265'. The beaver pond was about 70x150 feet.

A large rural power line runs over the site. Giant 500 KV Bonneville Power Administration power lines are an easy 150 yard walk from the pond. These are continuations of the same power lines described earlier near the Mt. Hood & Willamette National Forest border.

If you are able to look at the site on Google Earth, notice the beaver pond has dried up and is now a small meadow. Further, the pond site is next to the Santiam River which is probably both a territorial

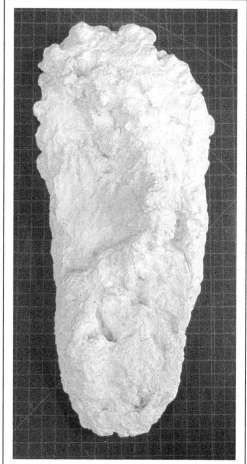

Mold of track find. Photo by Cliff Barackman.

boundary and a salmon fishing site for Sasquatch.

A few days after the find four family members returned to the pond. We therefore label them Jakes 39 thru 42. Using plaster-of-Paris they cast a single track.

The father-in-law also filmed the site with his low resolution digital video camera which was quite modern at the time. Video of the track line showed the creature walked out of the forest, crossed the pond's muddy perimeter and then walked about 15 feet into the pond.

From the day the tracks were found to when the casting party arrived on site, something happened to the pond's dam such that the pond had drained about 4 inches. So, the film unmistakably shows where the Sasquatch stood in the pond, turned, and then in a banana shaped pattern walked out of the pond leaving several well defined tracks both in the pond and on its banks.

The video, which was sent to me, clearly shows the feet remain parallel, both in the bank mud and in the shallow water. While water and sun had somewhat deteriorated the tracks, they were still clear and impressive at about 17 inches long and over 6 inches wide.

The stride averaged about 3½ feet or about 42 inches. Four (4) toe marks were well defined. A fifth (the small toe) was somewhat distorted due to the foot sliding in mud.

The father-in-law also filmed a partially devoured beaver found near the pond. It has long been speculated that Bigfoot damages beaver dams and kills the beaver when it comes to make repairs. Then Bigfoot eats the beaver. Indeed, beaver tails were considered a delicacy by early trappers so why not by People of the Woods. The father-in-law was emphatic that there were no trap marks on the beaver. The low

resolution video tends to confirm his contention.

The pelt was attached and partially pulled off, not torn. Selected parts of the beaver were eaten, as if they were tasty morsels, but the carcass was not mauled as by a hungry coyote. In fact, the men were a little surprised a predator or hawk had not fed on the beaver carcass.

In 2010, Sasquatch track expert Cliff Barackman visited the father-in-law at his Salem home and verified the Santiam track story. After examining the original casting, Cliff's opinion is that it shows the mechanical reaction of a two part foot. He also received permission to make a mold of the original casting.

End Notes

The father said he'd never given much credibility to the idea of Sasquatch, but the tracks made him "kind of a believer." He said the sight of their size made "the hair on the back of my neck stand up". The grandfather, an old logger, "pooh-poohed" the idea of Bigfoot. However, after the track find, grandfather took to carrying a shotgun when he visited his property near the beaver pond.

We also note the Santiam track find validates Kiley's dictum on the importance of beaver ponds to forest flora and fauna. Researchers should always make attempts to circle beaver ponds, being careful of beaver tunnel dens and in-ground hornet nests.

Finally, this track find also indicates what we have repeatedly stated in this book. Power line cuts are forest highways. Watch them for crepuscular animals, animals active at dusk and dawn; watch the edges. At night when the weather is right, enjoy their displays of static electricity and search their edges with night vision. Who knows, maybe a nearby unclassified hominid is also enjoying the static electric show.

Comparing the Santiam track with the London, Oregon tracks

Background: In February 2012 a long track line was found in wet mud in the Cottage Grove Reservoir near London, Oregon. About three days after it was discovered Thom Powell and I drove 2 ½ hours to examine the track line. Later, comparing my photographs of the London tracks with the Santiam tracks, we were amazed, in fact startled, to see some photographs of the London tracks showed almost the exact same two-part foot suction pattern as the Santiam track.

The Clackamas Lake Ranger Station Historic District located on Road 42, SE of Timothy Lake, was established in 1905 by first ranger, Joe Graham. In the 1930s the Civilian Conservation Corps built the eleven buildings still existing today. In summer, volunteers conduct interpretative tours. The original ranger residence is available for rent. GPS 45 05 55.05N 121 45 03.52W at 3360'. Photo by Sharon Beelart.

Ref. 100: The Detroit Lake Sighting

This is the last sighting we report along the *OBH*.

The location was near Hoover campground at Detroit Lake adjacent to Willamette National Forest Road 10. Jake 43 (J43) was the terrified witness; his sighting is designated as Sighting 31 (S31).

Jakes 44, 45 and 46 (J44, J45, J46) talked to Jake 43 immediately after his sighting. Todd Neiss investigated the sighting on-site within 24 hours.

The Bigfoot's display of aggression becomes Bigfoot related Incident 67 (I67). Tracks found by Todd Neiss at the lake and up the hill are Track Finds 42 (TF42) and 43 (TF43): Incident 68 (I68) is collecting unclassified hominid scat: Night roars from above the lake are Bigfoot related Incident 69 (I69).

GPS of Hoover campground: 44 42 50.83N 122 07 26.35W at 1589'

Approx. GPS of the sighting: 44 42 57.05N 122 07 46.14W at 1580'

What follows are notes from my logbook on July 22nd and 23rd, 1999 expanded by Todd Neiss: During early evening on July 21st I got a call from Todd Neiss. He wanted to investigate an incident that occurred the day before at Detroit Lake and asked me to come along. We planned a quick trip in my truck so we had room to pack gear.

Detroit Lake is about 50 miles straight east of Salem, Oregon or about 100 miles south by southeast of Portland. It is a major boating, hiking and camping destination. Bull of the Woods Wilderness is north of Detroit Lake and the low northwest slopes of Mt. Jefferson are the eastern banks of the lake.

We drove to Hoover campground, which is on the south side of the lake at the base of Stahlman Point (a peak). Timber land rises up slope behind the campground. The little town of Detroit lies about a half mile across an arm of water. At the Hoover campground is a narrow, wooded, flat area bordering the lake.

While Neiss had conducted several field investigations, this was my first so I mainly listened. Careful to not use leading questions, Todd interviewed two alleged witnesses. It turned out they had not seen the Bigfoot. However they had talked to the witness at the campground immediately after his sighting.

According to Jake 44, at dusk on July 20th, a fisherman who we will call Jake 43 (J43) was walking along the lake back to the campground. At a spot about a third of a mile west of the campground something growled deeply at him. The witness turned toward the wooded slope (south). About 15 feet away, a huge Sasquatch rose from deep, lush ferns and stood with its arms raised. Then the giant roared mightily at Jake 43. We designate these displays of aggression as Bigfoot Related Incident 67 (I67).

The witness dropped his gear and ran, fast. Jakes 44 and 45 said when he passed by their campsite, the witness was running absolutely as fast as he could run, that it was like watching a man running in a movie comedy scene, only this was obviously serious stuff. Upon his return, the witness quickly told them his story, immediately packed his gear and departed. We label this incident as Sighting 31 (S31).

Jakes 44 and 45 stated they clearly heard the roar from the campground. They were closest to the roar and it scared them very much, so after the witness departed, they also packed up and left.

Then, in some convoluted Bigfoot tree knock telegraph way, that night Jake 44 was referred to Todd. Then Todd called me. The next day, J44 and J45 drove from Portland back to the campground, a distance of about 100 miles simply to talk with Todd about the sighting. Near the sighting Todd found a bedding site in two foot tall ferns of about 8 foot by 4 foot. Apparently the walking fisherman startled the beast awake. Todd also found some fresh, wormy scat and took a big sample of the scat. Later he said it was analyzed and reported as coming from "unknown primate origin." We designate this important scat find as Bigfoot related Incident 68 (I68). The tracks around the bedding site and going up the hill we label Track Find 42 (TF42). We decided to spend the night at the campground; we stayed up late and made a small fire next to the tent. I decided to sleep outside. About 3 AM, sets of long screaming roars from high on Stahlman Point woke me. By the time I woke Todd, which took some doing, the roaring was over.

Background note: Many people fall into such a deep sleep for the first few hours that they are very difficult to wake. This was the case when I tried to wake Todd. This trance like state is also something to also be aware of when camping alone. Beware what is around, or can approach you, before nodding off.

The next morning, above the lake on a dirt embankment along a new logging road Neiss found tracks with a long stride. There were clearly two Bigfoots, one large and one smaller, each making distinct footprints. The tracks were about 150 yards up hill from the lake side sighting. We note these tracks as Track Find 43 (TF43)

.

Stahlman Point, one mile southwest of Detroit. Sighting was near the beach on the far side of the water in the center of the photograph. Photo by Sharon Beelart.

While TF43 were clear tracks in soft ditch dirt, we did not have casting material with us. This was truly a loss as the tracks were well defined and many showed dermal ridges. Unfortunately, due to distance and work, we couldn't return to cast them.

More Details

Another camper we interviewed said it was comical watching the witness run through camp with his arms flailing at full speed. This fellow was a Good Samaritan we will call Jake 46 (J46). Jake 46 said he and J43 had camped next to each other and shared coffee for several days.

J46 said J43, the witness, was a stable fellow using up a week of vacation. Anyway, J46 jumped in his truck and drove after Jake 43 who was still running like mad, but was tiring and slowing down. J46 signaled him to stop.

Jake 46 said he drove the witness back to camp and gave him a couple of beers to calm him down. Then exhausted, shaky Jake 43 packed up and left, saying he'd had enough vacationing. J46 said J43 wouldn't return to the site to retrieve his fishing rod and he didn't want to wait for J46 to do it for him.

What witness J43 told Good Samaritan J46 about the Bigfoot matched what the witness told Jakes 44 and 45 who were camped on the other side of Jake 43. When Neiss interviewed them, Jakes 44 and 45 were still shaken from the events of the previous day, but Jake 44 calmed down after talking to Todd and volunteered to walk with him to the site. Jake 45 wanted to remain at the campground.

Willamette National Forest Road 10 borders the south shore of Detroit Lake. During our field investigation of the site we quickly found a newly installed logging road gate on the south side of Road 10. The road was covered with big jagged crushed rock used on logging roads. This type of crushed rock is so sharp loggers are happy to get only 15,000 miles out of a set of tires. By the time civilians get on logging roads, this rock is generally crushed down by heavy log trucks.

Anyway, the fresh jagged rock was too sharp for the beasts to walk on. This resulted in Track Find 43. From where Todd found the two sets of tracks, the ground rises very steeply from 1570' at lake level to the peak of Stahlman Point at 3045'.

Due to time constraints, we didn't explore back roads around Stahlman Point. But, after finding the tracks we walked logging roads until we were tired. We did not find another track line. That was the end of our field investigation.

I'd like to note there are benches in the mountains southwest of Stahlman Point which may be good to research. Hikers have driving access via Willamette Forest Road 1003 and its spur roads. Google Earth is your friend when planning trips into this area.

Even more notes: The three sets of roars I heard from high on Stahlman Point were very loud. In the morning, I talked to two other campers who were also awakened by them. The roars were deep, and as one of the other campers said, lasted a "long" time each. They were modulated indicating something with huge lung capacity made them.

One can only speculate on the reason for the roars. One conclusion is certain; due to their length and modulation, they were not bear roars or cougar screams. After talking to the other campers who heard the roars, I decided to label them as Bigfoot related Incident 69 (I69).

Stahlman Point, one mile east of Detroit. Sighting was near the beach on the far side of the water in the center of the photograph. Photo by Sharon Beelart.

This ends reports from Area 6

.

Photo by Sharon Beelart.

Warms Springs Meadow after spring melt, near Road 42. Photo by Joe Beelart.

Commentary on Areas 1 through 6

From the number of longstanding reports made by a wide variety of responsible people, the authors surmise that prior to logging operations, a sizeable number of Sasquatch populated the upper Clackamas drainage. From relatively recent reports, the authors also theorize a self-sustaining remnant population of Sasquatch continues to live along the Clackamas and Breitenbush Rivers from Estacada to Detroit. We finally conclude through good field techniques, a persistent researcher may see a Sasquatch.

How do they live?

Some things are obvious from reports in this book. They appear to live without the benefit of clothes, fire, or building permanent shelters. They seem to be omnivorous with an emphasis toward vegetation in their diet, supplemented by fish, especially salmon, and finally deer and elk meat as opportunities allow, or possibly got through coordinated group hunts.

In the Clackamas and Breitenbush drainages they seem to live in social structures of dispersed hunter-gatherer groups somewhat like those found near the Arctic Circle; South Pacific islands, Amazon jungle, or parts of Africa. Perhaps the majority of their life is spent looking for food while simultaneously avoiding human contact.

Undoubtedly, parental duties are very important to them. Tending the young, teaching life basics, "guarding the flock," and lessons on how to avoid humans are probably primary concerns. Finally they almost certainly engage in ritualized reproductive ceremonies which are unknown, indubitably unique; but present in all animal groups, and which may represent the culmination of their life pleasures.

One of the most important aspects of their lives is avoiding humans. This is a highly specialized and practiced skill common among all animals in the forest, except for birds which simply fly away.

Seemingly, Sasquatch's primary attitude and reaction toward humans is avoidance and unhurried flight. By unhurried flight, we do not mean running in panic. Reports in this book indicate Sasquatch prefers leaving the presence of humans by simply walking away, sometimes in apparent indifference or disgust. We have no reports of a Sasquatch running in a panic as do some animals in the forest.

In rare situations, under particular circumstances, they seem to develop trust in certain human beings. Generally this happens near repeatedly used camp sites or human homes bordering the forest. This type of activity is generally termed "habituation."

Where do they live?

Steve Kiley helped answer this question using his huge assembly of USGS topographical maps on his study wall. As we pinned sighting reports and track finds both from this book, and other sources, patterns became apparent.

Sasquatch lives at high elevations in summer and near the snow line in winter. The winter snow line in the upper Clackamas fluctuates around 1,500 feet or roughly the elevation of Ripplebrook Guard Station. We surmise that in winter part of the Clackamas summer population travels south of the Willamette Valley then west to the Oregon Coastal Range to feed on anadromous fish runs, and to escape being crowded at lower Clackamas elevations.

Unless they are traveling or foraging for food, our Sasquatch probably live in trees, secluded glens, under rock overhangs, caves or lava tubes, or perhaps, old mine entrances. Generally they live near mountain meadows and water sources such as streams and beaver ponds.

From our area reports and our population estimate in Appendix III, we think that they have well-defined territories. Where small groups or individuals live, almost undoubtedly there are easy-to-use natural escape routes with each route exiting a given point in substantially different directions.

Surprisingly, given the immensity of the forest, after extensive field work and study of topographical maps, the number of places where Bigfoot might have ground based safe abodes seems small, perhaps only a handful in each area. However for now, our list of such places must remain confidential. If they use trees at least part of the time for rest, their domicile opportunity list grows very large.

Where do I go to see a Bigfoot or find tracks?

Where do I go to see a Bigfoot or find tracks in the upper Clackamas and Breitenbush drainages?

The answer to this excellent question comes in three parts. The simplest is where to go in winter. Stay around the snow line. The Ripplebrook area and lower is generally open most of the year.

Snow comes and goes at lower elevations in the Collawash basin. Indian Henry is also sometimes good in winter, but beware of black ice on the roads. It's best to park and hike into the meadows. Go carefully, slowly, and silently and you may see a herd of elk. Attention: Do not confuse elk track melt-outs with Bigfoot tracks.

Big Bottom is generally snow bound from December through March, if not sooner, or longer. The high elevations sometimes take until the first week of July to open. I know this because my birthday is July 1st and I like to make the first high camp of the year about then.

The Breitenbush canyon is generally snow bound from December until March, again, with surrounding high country not opening to June. Check with Olallie Lake Resort to see when they open, or stay there for an exploration base. It's a nice place; as is Breitenbush Hot Springs Resort.

One of the least explored, but productive track find places is in Area 1 on and near massive Goat Mountain and the west access road to Skookum Lake. Goat Mountain is easily seen from the gorge viewpoint south of Estacada.

Look to the southwest for a long-massive mountain with antenna towers at its center. Steve Lindsey specializes in this area and says he quit casting tracks there because at certain times of the year there were too many; he says it got boring.

How does a person see a Bigfoot?

With luck and persistence, or chance; those are the only ways. Persistence has little probability of success. But alternatively, without persistence, failure is virtually guaranteed. Lack of persistence is the primary cause of neophyte Bigfoot "researchers" dropping out, generally after one or two summers of trying.

Another problem with persistence is it costs money, a lot of money. We figure a day up the hill costs at least $50 with most of the expense for gas money. Nights up the hill cost more; I plan on $100 per night.

Expenses can rapidly build, especially for those folks who insist on attempting to see the critters with help from technology, and those who rush from one technology to another. After using trail cameras, recorders, etc. we think the top way to look for Our Barefoot Friends is just old-fashioned careful observation. Be sure to spend a little time each day glassing trees.

The best way to pursue the search is to budget time and money comfortably within your means. The next critical part, as mentioned, is to carefully plan outings. Enjoy the forest in peaceful, quiet pursuits.

Hike, photograph, fish, watch the night sky, study weather; learn to identify trees, plants, and flowers; maybe have someone teach you mushrooming. Set out offerings in great anticipation, but don't be disappointed. In short, enjoy the forest, the mountains, in all the ways nature intended. Then, with a little luck, you will see what you wish to see.

What techniques do you recommend to see a Sasquatch?

For practical observing purposes, Sasquatch is a *crepuscular* animal, meaning they are active at dawn or dusk; which in turn means those are the best times for people to see them. Of course they wander the night, but people without powerful technology are limited in what they can see in the dark.

It is best to keep your techniques simple. (1) A must is a set of good binoculars or a spotting scope with a tripod. (2) Watch edges. (3) Be happy and conversational. (4) Don't play loud music. (5) Innovate.

Try playing a guitar or a traditional Indian drum like Thom Powell, or native flutes like Leann McCoy and David Mann.

If you must sound blast, we recommend melodic tunes like Andean flute music or mellow tunes from female vocalists like *Jewel*; or groups like *Sons of the Pioneers*.

We recommend setting up camp in an open area where the Sasquatch can look down upon you from a hidden place. Quarries or meadows with nearby ridgelines are perfect. Sleep in open air.

The next step after finding a comfortable place like this is to arrange an on-going camp. Be sure to set out offerings on a consistent basis far enough away to not attract bears and coyotes. And, don't leave food stuffs out in plastic bags; pesky, cheery chipmunks will chew through them.

Why are they so hard to see?

First, there are few of them; second, the forest is big; and third, the forest is full of big trees. When I decided to research the Clackamas River Ranger District I asked myself, "where could I hide a company of Marines (about 170 people), for two weeks (no fires allowed) and not be detected? After studying topo maps the answer came in short order; the upper Roaring River basin. As reported, the upper Roaring River basin is difficult to access, and is a veritable northwest jungle making it difficult to see animals of any kind.

Now consider the cougar, bear, elk, and deer enigma. The Clackamas Ranger District combined with the Breitenbush drainage covers more than 1,000 square miles. There are at least 20 cougar, about

400 bear, several hundred elk, lots of coyotes, and more than 1,000 deer in the area. The average person in a day trip, hiking for hours, rarely sees more than one or two deer.

Thus the enigma: If there are that many animals to see, why are so few seen?

Transfer that thought to Sasquatch, a creature with more reasoning ability than any of those mentioned, or perhaps even more than humans, and you can see your observational problems.

The Tree Option

The tree option is one factor we have barely mentioned. Perhaps trees hold a common sense clue as to where some Sasquatch, especially smaller ones, live in their off-the-ground hours. Was there a really unique reason "Monkey Creek" was named "Monkey Creek?" Then think of the observational problems just discussed and multiply it by a factor of ten. That is the problem of observing trees.

What human spends much time looking into trees? Most humans when they walk, unless they have military or special training, tend to look at the ground for footing.

Reader, ask yourself: "When was the last time I looked carefully into a huge tree

to see what was up there? How long did I spend looking into the trees during my last trip? How much time have I looked into trees this year or for that matter, for years?"

Perhaps it is time to start tree looking logs by hours spent and areas observed. Will the Hewkin-Sullivan guideline of one significant Bigfoot event for each 200 hours of boots on the ground apply to tree observations? Who knows; it might be more productive, or less. If you decide to watch trees find some big, old-growth. They have big limbs and often undergrowth is open offering easier observing. Keep a detailed log.

Characters: Ant Man, Moss Man & the Hurk Meister

While researching for this book, the authors met characters and eccentrics, some seemingly larger than life. But unfortunately, there is no space to tell about everyone we met. The three characters I call *Ant Man, Moss Man, and the Hurk Meister* are examples of the eccentric.

High in the mountains in late summer 2009 at Summit Lake Cliff and I met *Ant Man* where he was simultaneously running out of potable water and deep into researching carpenter ants for his Ph.D. dissertation. He was from the flat land of east Texas and after a week in the mountains was a bit awed, both by the

scenery, the expanse of forest, and huge ant colonies living in rotting wood.

He was wonderfully happy about all the ants he'd found but he was down to his last quart of water. "Do you have extra so I don't have to drive down?" "Of course." We asked him about Our Barefoot Friends. He was startled. Then, after a pause, he said words not uncommonly heard by Bigfoot researchers. "You will never believe what happened two nights ago." "Oh, we might."

Moss Man was a little different. He held a Ph.D. and was a biology professor at a major eastern university. Referred to me by a colleague, *Moss Man* called me saying he was coming to Portland for a conference.

He wondered if I would take him into the mountains during the usual discovery day off. "Sure, I'll take you up the hill; we'll meet at 6 AM." That hour usually sorts out the casually interested, but not *Moss Man*. "I'll be waiting."

Moss Man was a really fun person. We had a great time getting a start up the mountain when suddenly he shouted, "Stop here!" So I stopped, wondering "Was this gentleman like *The Hurk Meister*, a fellow I took up who got car sick going around two curves?" Without exaggeration, *The Hurk Meister* made me stop over 20 times in one day, but refused to go down mountain. He was from a big city far from Sasquatch land and he was not about to let a little nausea ruin his Bigfootin' day in the high Cascades.

Anyway, *Moss Man* scrambled out of Truck and scurried over to a small waterfall where he proceeded to get out a monocular, looked intently at the green, and finally scrapped a specimen into a glass vial which he put in his leather case. With a huge smile he marched back to the truck, obviously proud of his trophy ... moss.

And so it went. As we drove along he showed genuine interest in my stories about Bigfoot and mountain history, but he was more interested in stopping to collect specimens of his botanical specialty, moss and lichens. Finally, I told him, "If you really want to go high and get back at a reasonable hour, we've got to get up mountain." So, I got him as far up the mountain as I could reasonably get him while he used every minute allowed to scrape moss. By the end of the day, *Moss Man* was a very happy camper, even though he was staying in one of Portland's finer hotels.

This ends commentary on Areas 1 through 6

High valley (ancient lake bed) with Peavine Mountain in background. Photo by Joe Beelart.

"Keep'em out" road. Photo by Joe Beelart.

Area 52: Bizarre Happenings

The following accounts *are not* for faint-of-heart or closed-minded readers. All three of these seemingly unearthly reports come from the Upper Clackamas.

One of our Sasquatchians championed Area 52. The original draft contained twelve such Area 52 reports made by nine different people. From those twelve reports, we have chosen three representative accounts.

The first report is a fantastic UFO and Bigfoot sighting, the second is a most curious story about huckleberries and *Little People*, and the third is a night of bizarre contact with Sasquatch beings. All were told by people seemingly in control of their faculties.

Why are these accounts included when they are so different from the physical encounters related in Areas 1 thru 6? Many people think Bigfoots are connected to UFOs. (See *The Psychic Sasquatch* by Kewaunee Lapseritis.) While some of these feelings come from anecdotal sighting reports, others may have arisen from the *Star Wars* movie series.

As one reader said after being told we were going to delete this section from the draft, "*They've* made billions of dollars from Bigfoots on space ships. It's what the public wants, so keep it." So we did. Here you go, hang on tight.

In early June 2012 a person, Jake X1, learned of this book and asked to meet with me. I found him a well-educated part Native American with impressive credentials from a long professional career in an intensively detail-oriented field. After looking over the outline and hearing the gist of my flesh and blood stories; and the nature of Sasquatch as I thought of it, the man paused, looking at me.

Then he said I was welcome to three stories which immediately came to mind, but I was to know they were very extraordinary. He began with a phrase I'd heard before in conversation with Native Americans; and, read in their histories. He said:

"These things really happened."

We repeat because we feel this is important; the meaning of "really happened" does not translate well from Native American languages to English. As the reader will soon find, "really happened" is not a warranty of truth; *truth is assumed*. Rather, the phrase is a kind of exclamation point.

The stories he told were short and without elaboration. This was the first. His second and third stories are not included here.

Ref. 101: UFO with Bigfoot Crew

Note to readers: this story is akin to a dream derived from a motion picture. After some discussion, we finally decided to include it for its entertainment value, the veracity of the teller, the consistency of him repeating the story, and his relative sobriety which we tested during a high Cascades campout.

Jake X1's first Bigfoot encounter was not in the Clackamas drainage. However,

after that experience, JX1 often went alone to Fish Creek to search for Bigfoot because he was told by the Native American in the Introduction it was a good area to encounter supernatural phenomena.

Fish Creek, which is in Area 1, is close to Portland where Jake X1, a well-educated professional person, holds a respected position. Its relatively close proximity to his home made day trips possible.

While he told the story willingly, it was with some reluctance he allowed us to use it, even without his name.

The time was late August in the early 1990s. Fish Creek road was open and angling was allowed back then, so Jake X1's excuse to his wife was to go for challenging late summer dry fly fishing. His real reason was to try for another encounter with Bigfoot. In this he succeeded, although in a most unusual way.

As JX1 walked into the open area near the Wash Creek confluence with Fish Creek, which is about five and a half miles upstream from Hwy 224, he was absolutely astounded to see a flying saucer parked in a clearing. He said the saucer had probably just landed because he had heard a "whooshing, humming" sound minutes earlier, plus the space ship was still buttoned up (that's aviation slang for no open hatches).

The sight scared JX1, but also mesmerized him. He couldn't make himself go away, partly because of his legal logic and investigative training. On the other hand he said he felt nothing was keeping him at the site and he said he never felt he was in harm's way. He said it was a very unusual sensation, something he'd never felt in his life (at the time he was in his mid-40s). So he moved into dark shadow and settled in to watch, for as he said, "You just don't see something like that every day."

He said the craft was out of the movies, silver with windows, round like two soup plates mated together with a circular cockpit on the top that had a row of windows around it. The ship had angled tripod legs with saucer shaped pads on the ground. Somewhat familiar with engineering, Jake X1 said the legs seemed too small to support the structure, so he suspected they were made out of an exotic metal.

The base of the craft stood about 10 feet off the ground and was perhaps 30 feet high at its apex. His immediate impression was that it was designed to land in moderately rough terrain and was an exploratory craft from a much larger mother ship. He saw shadows moving in the cockpit.

Then the damnedest thing happened. A staircase lowered and a Bigfoot climbed down it carrying a bag, like a big, strong doctor's bag. The creature looked about, didn't see Jake X1, or anything else which seemed to disturb him, for it was a "him." Then the Bigfoot proceeded to an access hatch and opened it. The creature took components from the mounts in the craft and replaced them with parts from the bag. It then made communication with whomever, or whatever was in the craft.

Things were apparently declared OK because the Bigfoot loaded the old parts into the bag and climbed back into the spacecraft. The ramp closed, a humming noise began, and then with a gentle "whooshing" noise, the flying saucer rose, turned and climbed out to the southeast past Fish Creek Mountain and Whale Head, disappearing into the afternoon sky.

Jake X1 described the Bigfoot as about 7 feet tall, not particularly massive, and covered in moderately long "mahogany" colored hair which showed tinges of red in sunlight. He said the genitals were not large. He said the hands had an opposable thumb. The face was mostly covered with hair. The ears and nose were small in proportion to the rest of the size of the beast.

It had rectangular lips which were not especially full. He didn't get a look at the teeth. The eyes were a dark color, but he didn't know whether they were black or brown. He said the creature moved with grace and strength.

He guessed the feet at about 16 inches because that was the approximate length of the impressions they left in the forest duff. He said the saucer's pads didn't penetrate the ground; they only made impressions. There were no burn or radiation marks he could see, although when he approached the landing site, he felt warmth.

He estimated the whole event lasted somewhat in excess of 15 minutes, so he had time to study things. But, he was so startled, he didn't know what to concentrate on, and, he was intent on staying perfectly still and in the shadows. JX1 said he sorely wished he had a camera, any camera with him, but he had accidentally left his in the car. He repeated he was not scared or did not feel threatened at any time during the sighting.

Jake X1 forcefully and repeatedly stated his sighting did not reflect subliminal association with any motion picture, still photograph, or television series. He said he forced himself to observe as objectively as he possibly could, given the shock of the situation. JX1 also repeatedly said he did not see any writings or symbols on the craft.

On the spot, he decided to never return to Fish Creek. "Too many weird things go on up there." He has only told the story to a few carefully selected people as he didn't want such a story attached to his name, yet it was such a disconcerting event he says he sometimes needs to share it to get it off his mind.

Ref. 102: An Old Berry Picker & Little People

A Sasquatchian told of an unusual encounter which warrants Happening status. The incident happened in Area 5 high under the crown of Mt. Lowe or, about three air miles south of Granite Peaks.

There is a great huckleberry field in the area but, for obvious reasons, we keep it a secret. When the year is right, this particular huckleberry field is heavy with fruit, rich, juicy, full-bodied, turn your lips and teeth blue, huckleberries. When winter is harsh, or there's a late freeze, sometimes there are few berries in the patch, which is an old timber sale where for some reason regrowth hasn't taken hold or rhododendrons haven't weeded up the place.

It is the author's opinion that huckleberries south of Estacada are the best, perhaps not the plumpest, but the best. Why this is, we don't know. Perhaps it's because they get less rain and more sun than those in the north Mt. Hood National Forest, or the Washington Cascades, and therefore flavors intensify.

Whatever the reason, I go to the field every year I can, always with great expectations for either a day of basket filling or, if the berries are sparse, just for eating. Generally I see a deer or three munching up, becoming fat and sleek for winter. One year I rounded a shrub and came face to face with a really big buck in late velvet. He simply looked at me in disdain, took a couple of more bites and walked away – amazing!

Some years ago, I took the Sasquatchian who told this story to the field. Now, he seems to try for those berries before I can get to them. There are ways to test the limits of friendship; being an early huckleberry picker at a field made known to you is one. But, he's polite enough to ask me along so I know when he's beating me up the hill.

Anyway, one afternoon, our Sasquatchian climbed up from the field with a loaded bucket, happy and ready to go home. The harvest was good and he was quite satisfied with his pickings. As he slowly drove north hoping to spot a bear or a deer he rounded a corner and came upon an old Native American woman walking.

She was dressed in the old way, the way seen in museums. She wore a triangular shaped hat woven from reeds, or something like reeds, that shaded her well. She wore well-padded moccasins. The cloth of her clothes was unusual, rustic, unfamiliar, and hand sewn. She was carrying a wonderfully woven basket filled to the rim with huckleberries.

Our Sasquatchian drove by her, stopped by the side of the road, got out of his SUV and approached her. She stopped, gently piercing him with dark, dark eyes. He asked her if she would like a lift to where her people were parked.

In soft well-spoken English she responded. "No, I do not need a 'lift.'"

He said the way she said "lift" made him think the word was new to her. Our Sasquatchian complemented her on her berries. She had picked them nicely, mostly free of leaves and unripe ones. That made her happy. She smiled.

Then, she said something which surprised him. Her words were very close to these, "This year I got them before the little people." She looked down toward the field and said, "If you watch carefully and quietly in the evening, you might see them come out from the forest to gather their fraction of the harvest."

Then, she said goodbye and cradling her basket in her arms, began slowly walking to where, our Sasquatchian did not know. He slowly drove away careful to not toss a stone, or kick dust on her with his tires.

As he drove down slope, careful to not tip his baskets filled with prized cargo, he thought about how she pronounced her words and why she used "fraction." He thought about her dress. He wondered where her people were. He did not see any people or even a car until about ten miles later on Road 46 in Big Bottom.

Late in the harvest he spent a night at the field, but saw no little people. Then, hesitantly, our Sasquatchian shared two other things about his encounter, which he said seemed to be imprinted on his mind. He said she talked with no accent. And, it took him a long time to realize the old woman's lips did not move when she talked.

Ref. 103: Squatch Noir

I thank Sasquatchian Kirk Sigurdson for suggesting this nifty title. Onward: As demonstrated in courtrooms across the country, there are often differences in how events are recalled, especially stressful, unusual events. So, it was no surprise to me that Blake Eckard remembers *Squatch Noir* somewhat differently than I did, even though both of us made long notes shortly after that camp.

Background: As funds and time have permitted, Missouri filmmaker Blake Eckard has worked over a decade on his much anticipated Bigfoot documentary. Blake has camped for many nights along *The Oregon Bigfoot Highway* with me, his friend, Alec Jennings, also from Missouri, Cliff Olson, and other Bigfooters. With few exceptions, at each camp we take a night walk without using flashlights.

After reviewing the draft of this book, on June 21, 2013 Blake wrote me a long email containing his notes about the night of September 30th and October 1st 2008. To me, which version is more accurate is of little to no importance. If Blake says this is what happened, this is what happened.

The following is a quote with only paragraph breaks inserted here and there, plus a few minor word changes. For professional considerations, Blake's friend's name is changed to Jake X2.

As Filmmaker Blake Eckard Remembers It

Begin quote:

"I drove my pick-up to Boise, Idaho to attend the Idaho International Film Festival, where (my movie) *SINNER COME HOME* was playing. The lead in the film, Jake X2, met me there. After the festival the two of us drove on to Portland, where we both have friends. I particularly wanted to get some camping in and planned to go up into the Cascades for 2 nights.

Jake X2, being the real city slicker he is; was eager to say he'd actually camped out in the wilderness, and so off we went. My long-time Bigfooting pal, Joe Beelart, came out for the first night with us, suggesting a place I'd never been, which sits in high Cascade country and has a rather interesting name: Devil's Ridge.

It turned out to be the strangest night of my life, with a lot happening over a period of several hours. There was no visual sighting, but *something* was around us for most of the night. Here's what happened as best as I can break it down from memory (still very vivid) and notes I wrote immediately after.

We drove up into the hills, JX2 in Joe's truck, me following. We stopped a few times to take in views and listen to Joe's notes on significant places we were passing. About mid-day we pulled into the rock quarry.

It's a big, interesting place that's been blown up for rock to a good 40-50 feet below the road. To the north is an amazing view of Mt. Hood. From the right places, Mt. Jefferson can also be seen quite well to the South.

We spent the afternoon in the pit, drinking some beers, talking, setting up camp, etc. Jake X2, who is a ball of energy and was beginning to annoy Joe and myself, was ordered to take a long hike. He did just that, totally oblivious to being told to "take a hike." As he left, headed down the lower road, I saw him put in earphones. Typical of him.

As nightfall came things were absolutely still and silent. No wind, no nothing; truly an eerie strange silence in hindsight, although at the time none of us mentioned it.

After nightfall Joe decided we needed to go for a night walk up the gravel road.

The walk was quick, I don't think we even went all the way to the top before turning around, but we took our time. As we re-entered the gravel pit about halfway to our fire was a black patch on the ground. Having been out in the dark for a good 30 minutes, the dark spot showed on the dusty gravel like a beacon.

Approaching, we quickly realized it was a puddle...a puddle none of us remembered seeing on our way out, and I frankly don't know how we could have missed it. We all got down next to it, and Joe put his finger in it and sniffed. *"That's urine."*

Jake X2 and I each got down and smelled the dark dust: I remember thinking it smelled just like dirt. The puddle was quite large, maybe 36"x30" that even seemed to show a "trailing off" pattern – just the sort of thing one would expect to see in a urine pattern left from a man standing and taking a leak.

What we decided to do was spread out in the big pit and each take a leak ourselves; to see if anything happened, I guess. At this point I distinctly remember feeling like I was being observed. I recall looking all around when my friend, way off to my left and out of sight, started calling my name.

I didn't answer, but the damn city boy kept saying my name, so I finally calmly said *"yeah,"* and he came wandering over to my voice. *"That shit's got me spooked, man. That's the first time I've been spooked since we got up here."* I just kept listening to the air. Nerves or something else, don't know, but I had the weirdest feeling I couldn't shake.

About an hour later (might've been longer) we'd moved back to the fire. I was sitting in a lawn chair, just looking into the flames. Joe and JX2 were off to my right, rummaging around in a cooler and laughing when I heard what can only be described as "talking" from above us, on the upper road, I'd guess from memory 75 yards away.

Chatter & a Jelly Jar

The sound lasted, at most, two seconds. It came and went, just as if someone was speaking in a normal room tone. But I immediately recognized the "talking" as something I couldn't understand. Brief as it was, it gave me the impression of Asian-sounding chatter.

Neither my friend nor Joe who were talking, heard it. I made a noise of surprise and was pointing – knew right where it had come from. When Joe asked me what it sounded like I told him *"Japanese gibberish,"* to which he responded *"That's them. They're here."* My friend (JX2) looked like he was going to (poop in) his pants.

Deciding to put out some "offerings" we took stock of what we had: Apples, hot dog buns, and a jar of jelly, courtesy of the Idaho Film Fest. We moved out, putting things at various places within the huge gravel pit, eventually getting far beyond the visual of camp. Nearly to the rock wall, directly opposite of our fire, we came to a large, flat rock, perhaps 3'x5' in circumference, and maybe three feet high. I put down our last "offering" – our jar of jelly.

As I set it down, I put a quarter turn on the lid, then backed off. We all stood there listening for the longest time when there came an audible vibration sound. I think it actually made me slightly jump, as the atmosphere was DEAD STILL. We all looked down at the rock and jar of jelly, when suddenly, the lid to the jelly jar popped right off the jar...the sound we had heard was the lid un-screwing.

As we all stood there the lid, lying on its back, next to the jar, suddenly started quivering. Then it STOPPED. No more than a few seconds later it started to drag to the right, away from the jar. It moved, perhaps 5 inches and stopped. Silence. Then it began to tremble *again.* The trembling stopped, then it moved another 5-6 inches, and stopped.

At this point I distinctly remember saying (asking) *"What the #$%& is doing that?"* to which Joe responded *"There are Sasquatch in those trees..."* pointing to the quarry rim above us.

After a long time of silence my city friend (Jake X2) suddenly said aloud, *"I want to walk into those trees."* It totally unnerved me. He sounded spaced out and zombie-like. Joe says we had to physically restrain him from climbing up the slope. I do not remember this at all, and strongly disagree.

From the time the lid came off the jar we never left the spot in front of the flat rock before departing back for camp. The trees in question, and the slope below them, were a good bit of distance away. At this point my legs began to tremble uncontrollably. I almost couldn't stand – I even grabbed Joe's hand and had him touch my knee.

Joe asked, *"What do you think?"* to which I responded, *"I think we need to move."* He responded, without hesitation, *"Then we need to move."* After no less than two steps, I felt much better, like (I was) walking out of a sauna.

After this, we found it difficult to find our camp because we couldn't spot the fire. Imagine that! In a huge, flat gravel pit! Finally, we saw the white of my pick-up. Once back, we realized why we hadn't seen a flame; our fire was nothing but embers.

Checking the time, *we were all shocked* to see it was almost 1:30 A.M. We'd previously noted the time at 11:00 before we left camp to put things out. All of us estimated we'd been gone perhaps 30-40 minutes, max. I remember feeling like I was in a *Twilight Zone* episode.

Joe goes into the dark

Soon after Joe came over to JX2 and me, he handed us a high-powered spot light. "Take this, but don't turn it on. I'm going to make a big sweep out there. Talk normally. Don't whisper. Just act like you're standing here minding your own business."

Then he took off (*into the dark with no flashlight*), leaving JX2 totally baffled. I would have been, too, had I not camped with Joe before and known him for doing things like this.

Quite a bit of time went by and JX2 had grown very nervous, thinking Joe might have fallen down and knocked himself out. He started calling his name, and I might have, too. Then Jake X2 turned on the spot light and started waving it all around.

From way, way out there came Joe's voice: *"Shut off that goddamn light!"* The light went out, and sometime later Joe came ambling into view. He poured himself a Scotch and sat down.

"They're all over out there."

"What do you mean?"

"I could feel the vibrations of feet running on the earth. I even laid down and put my head to the ground. I think they're out there having a good time, playing with us."

Joe had hoped to see one of the things cross between him and campfire light, but never did. We were talking when I suddenly became aware that JX2 wasn't with us. Neither Joe nor I had noticed him leave; he just wasn't with us anymore.

Pretty quickly, Joe found him asleep in his sleeping bag, in the back of Joe's pick-up; something I found completely at odds with JX2 and his amped up personality. Then, Joe turned in, leaving me beside the fire.

I think I had another beer before calling it a night -- being up alone, after all that had happened, I wasn't feeling exactly at ease. Up to this time, I had always thrown out my sleeping bag in the back in the bed of my truck and slept under the stars. Not this time. I climbed into the cab, locked the doors and remember thinking I would see something look in the window before I went to sleep. That didn't happen, and eventually I drifted off.

Watching Jake X2 "sleep"

What I didn't know for some time was what apparently happened to Jake X2 only 30 feet away. Deep into the night, in back of Joe's pick-up, face-down and asleep, JX2 awoke as the passenger side of the truck suddenly lurched down; as if something of tremendous weight had leaned down over the passenger wheel well. Immediately, my friend found himself petrified with fear.

Lying face-down, he couldn't see anything, but heard heavy breathing *right there*. Deliberate, heavy breathing you would picture coming from a gaping, open mouth. After what he said felt like hours, JX2, utterly exhausted from fright, fell back to sleep or, as he suggested, passed out. He told me all of this, for the first time, two months later at the St. Louis International Film Festival, where we were again showing *SINNER COME HOME*.

He had never told me any of this before, and for years later downplayed all events of this night. I once said to him, *"Something put weight down on the truck and woke*

you up. You told me that." All he would say in response was, *"Had to be Joe moving."*

Update: Joe says he slept that night on the ground, as he has every night he's spent in this particular rock pit, on soft gravel. Since JX2 went to bed before us, he was only under the assumption that Joe slept in the cab.

Even still, it's worth mentioning that had Joe been in the cab, he doesn't have the size to shake a full-sized pick-up in the way my friend describes, especially within the confines of the cab.

For the first time in front of anyone, my friend more or less agreed all of this happened on the set of *GHOSTS OF EMPIRE PRAIRIE* when, one evening after filming, I told (two names redacted) the story. The four of us were sitting outside drinking beers after shooting all day, with (name redacted) leading a conversation about ghosts. This naturally segued into me and Bigfoot. After I told this story, as I have written it here, JX2 said something like:

"It's one of those things a guy doesn't want to believe, because agreeing it happened means it happened."

Oddly enough, it's how I feel, too."

End quote.

It's important to note that Blake's version, and mine, when coldly compared, agree on most major action points and on seven basic issues:

- Sasquatch using speech,

- Sasquatch causing inanimate objects to move,

- Sasquatch controlling our minds, at least partially.

- Sasquatch causing us to make physical actions,

- Sasquatch probably inducing sleep in Jake X2,

- Sasquatch inducing memory loss, possible time loss, or change in memory, and perhaps most important,

- Sasquatch activity in trees.

This ends reports from Area 52.

Reader, this ends *The Oregon Bigfoot Highway.* The authors hope you have enjoyed this journey. If you drive the highway, enjoy the sights, but if you don't see a Bigfoot, don't be disappointed. They are rare, but they are there. Sometime during your drive a Sasquatch will probably watch you pass by.

Thank you. Be careful.

Appendices

The first appendix profiles the Clackamas Sasquatchians. These are the people who provided much of the material for this book.

The next five appendixes summarize information from this book. Due to the scarcity of solid information on Sasquatch, these appendixes are brief, to the point, and based on data collected from this book and maps of the upper Clackamas and Breitenbush drainages.

The next two appendixes are warnings and disclaimers, in other words, the fine print, only here in regular print so you can easily read it. Literally, your well-being may depend on what is in Appendix VII and VIII so please spend a minute with each. The title of Appendix IX speaks for its self.

Sasquatchians around a smoky camp fire in Big Bottom on November 17, 1999, during a four night research expedition. From the left: a Jake friend, Jim Henick in wool hat, Steve Kiley, Woody Woodworth, Cliff Olson, Bill Harper, and Thom Powell. Note the Cabela's coffee pot next to the fire. Photo by Joe Beelart.

I: The Clackamas Sasquatchians

As noted in the Introduction, the Sasquatchians are fourteen loosely associated people; not a formal club or society. Our common interest is researching Sasquatch in the Clackamas and Breitenbush River drainages. In addition each has his\her own personal outdoor interests. Those pursuits include camping, hiking, kayaking, hunting, exploring, prospecting, star gazing, mushroom collecting, photography, etc.

There are no criteria to become a Clackamas Sasquatchian other than to possess keen observational techniques, campfire storytelling skills, and a penchant to occasionally go to breakfast during winter to tell ... err, relate experiences. Plus they must have camped at least five nights up the Clackamas, or spent in excess of 200 hours of boots-on-the-ground in day trips up there, and exhibit sufficient knowledge of the area to be informally approved for inclusion by other Sasquatchians.

Sasquatchian experiences, or knowledge of history, resulted in many contributions to this book. However, for reasons noted in Appendix IX, most of their accounts are not attributed by name. In alphabetical order, we are:

Joe Beelart

West Linn, Oregon

B: 1947. Until he was 16, Joe was raised on a farm /ranch in the north Nebraska sand hills where the outdoors was recreation. There was no TV! In 1962 the family moved to a ranch in the Oregon Coast Range foothills. In 1970, Joe married Sharon, his long-suffering wife.

Joe became interested in the phenomena in 1993. After exploring a handful of books he decided to study the creatures in the Coastal Range and the upper Clackamas River. In 2000 he expanded his areas of interest to the Wind River system in southern Washington. Joe has camped at unimproved sites for as many as 23 nights in one year.

Henry J Franzoni III

Deer Island, Oregon

B: 1956. Henry Franzoni is the intellectual, the guru, the futurist of your Clackamas Sasquatchians. He is a musician with over 18 albums to his credit, a major body of work in itself. In real life Henry is a computer scientist, a practical fisheries biologist, a statistician, and a historian. Raised in northern New Jersey, Henry's first encounters with wild lands were the New Jersey Pine Barrens.

Henry became interested in Sasquatch when he was engaged as computer consultant to a large Bigfoot research project. Using Sasquatch as the vehicle, Franzoni was the pioneer in programming Internet discussion groups. He developed early websites for a series of Bigfoot notables and has contributed to numerous books and articles about Bigfoot. He has appeared in six movies about Sasquatch and has spoken in many venues on the subject. He lives with his wife Pam, and their cats, on a homestead in the Oregon Coastal Range.

Jim Henick

Washougal, Washington

The man who literally fell into Bigfooting

B: 1953. Jim Henick, the athlete of Sasquatchians, was raised near Portland. While he had an interest in sports, he didn't fish or hunt, but in his late teens he took up rock climbing and spelunking (cave exploration). With his interest in the outdoors heightened, Jim next went kayaking. This is how he met Thom Powell and together they instructed many beginners.

One of Jim's favorite campfire stories is about hiking all over Saddle Mountain which is about 17 miles south by southeast of Astoria, Oregon. Saddle Mountain at 3287 feet, GPS coordinates: 45 58 08.31N 123 41 07.58W is the high point of the north Oregon Coastal Range.

He and a friend had walked through little dog hair firs, and then an extraordinary old growth forest on a trail that they found rather odd. It was used and open, but there were no elk or deer tracks. (In our Cascades, we call this type of trail *A Devil's Trail*.) He especially remembers the path going between two huge fir trees. They followed the trail to a jumble of blown down timber left by a powerful Pacific storm. Jim was walking on the huge fallen trees when it happened.

Jim slipped and fell. For a moment, he was scared. Falling in the forest is dangerous doings. The ground often has exposed rocks to break bones and broken branches to spear bodies. But to his great surprise he didn't hit hard. Instead, he crashed through the roof of a cavern like structure and hit bottom on a soft floor lined with small limbs and moss.

Jim said he quickly took stock of his situation. The "room" was large, with a roof line taller than his 5' 8." It was obviously "something's" home and he was not only intruding, he had ruined the roof which was made of interwoven branches. Jim figured he was in deep trouble and the only way out was up. Jim said he "leaped" out of the cavern with magical strength he didn't know he had. Then he and his friend bolted from the area.

Later, combining his experience in the Coastal Range with his inherent drive toward energetic hiking adventures, he got to know the upper Clackamas well. Partly because of its beauty and solitude, Jim became very interested in the Roaring River basin which is now a designated wilderness. Over the years he has spent at least twelve nights in the Roaring River basin alone, which is an arduous hike.

Steve Kiley

West Linn, Oregon

B: 1953: Steve Kiley is our mountain man. Steve was raised in an outdoor-loving family near Chicago. During his youth he spent summers in northern Wisconsin canoeing, camping, and fishing; becoming proficient in all manner of outdoor skills. Carefully studying the ways of animals in the wild he became an expert tracker and hunter.

In 1999 he met Beelart and Powell and became interested in the Sasquatch phenomena. After spending many days and nights in the Washington and North Oregon Cascade Mountains his conclusion to date is:

"They are up there, but how do you prove it?"

Steve Lindsey

Portland, Oregon

B: 1952. For over 30 years Steven N. Lindsey has been going up the Clackamas to hunt and fish. He says he's camped approximately 300 nights above Estacada, mostly during the times when fishing was good, and also during deer and elk seasons.

In the mid-70s during a hike near Elk Meadows on the northeast slope of Mt. Hood he found his first tracks: "Unmistakable, knew immediately what I'd found." Steve first cast tracks in the Clackamas near Skookum Lake in 1987, the first of several good casts he took from that area. In May 2014 he found a Thomas-style site on Devils Ridge.

David Mann

In 2015 he is on a remote Philippine Island

B: 1937. David Mann is possibly the most strident protector of the environment among the Clackamas Sasquatchians. This is not to say he is an environmentalist, rather, as a professional engineer, he devoted most of his career to keeping water clean and so, he simply respects the environment.

Through decades of outdoor life he has also developed deep feelings about nature and man's place in it, and Bigfoot's place there too. Mann loves trees and sees them as one of nature's finest, most majestic creations. David is adamantly convinced Bigfoot is a type of human. Occasionally in the book, Sasquatch is referred to as *Forest People*. This is in deference to a request by David Mann.

Leann McCoy

Beaverton, Oregon

B: 1959: Leann has worked in engineering for over 25 years. As a youth, she said the McCoy family enjoyed peaceful contact with the Sasquatch at a cabin they built at the headwaters of an Oregon coastal river. Leann first met the Sasquatch at age 3 ½ and feels blessed to have had the unique opportunity to see, experience, and interact with the *Sasquatch People* throughout her life. McCoy says:

"My hope would be that people seek peaceful contact without hidden agendas of entrapment, aggression, or fear and come to appreciate the uniqueness of these amazing entities.

Talk to them if you feel they are around and treat them as friends. Seek contact with a clan that is OK with contact. Food gifts should never touch the ground (place them on a rock, stump, or up in a tree) and tell them it is a gift for them. Control your thoughts as they are highly telepathic. Give them boundaries so that both you and they feel comfortable.

They have a most surprising sense of humor so make it fun for them. Emit positive energy around you. Go alone, but if others are with you stop talking amongst yourselves and talk to *THEM*. Be patient, it can often take years ... if they decide to allow contact."

Besides seeking peaceful contact in all seasons with the Sasquatch, Leann's interests include Native American studies, ancient archeology, and geology. Her favorite areas include the Oregon coast range, south-central Washington, and the Clackamas River drainage which she said, "Is a most exciting place!"

Todd Neiss

Dockside, Portland, Oregon

Todd Neiss five days after he returned from his tour in Iraq.

B: 1961: Todd M. Neiss was born and raised in the Pacific Northwest in a family that thrived on outdoor activity. Hunting and fishing were simply a way of life for him. Todd's penchant for spotting wildlife, and his duties as a career soldier ultimately brought him to see three Sasquatch during army maneuvers.

Due to his thoughtful approach, and integrity, Neiss has become one of the more respected and widely known Bigfoot researchers. Due to his camera presence and well said presentations, Neiss is sought after by the media and has made appearances in nearly 20 documentaries, plus many other venues. But perhaps one of his most significant accomplishments was establishing **BeachFoot**, a highly anticipated, annual, invitation only gathering strictly for researchers.

Cliff Olson

Oregon City, Oregon

B: 1932, Astoria, Oregon: Cliff came from a northwest Oregon coast family where everyone, including aunts and uncles fished and hunted bountiful northwest Oregon, in part propelled by the Great Depression. When he was old enough, Cliff logged for four years in the Seaside area and at a remote Diamond Lake logging camp in Central Oregon. When the Korean War began Cliff joined the Navy, became an electrician, and sailed the north Pacific supply route.

After the war, Cliff joined Portland General Electric and worked at the Clackamas Oak Grove Power project for thirteen (13) years. During those years he lived with his family in the heart of the Clackamas at PGE's Three Lynx housing project. For the remainder of his thirty-nine (39) years of service with PGE, Cliff lived in rural Estacada and worked as a Power Dispatcher at the company's Portland headquarters.

While Cliff was an experienced outdoorsman, when he saw his first Bigfoot track on Oak Grove Butte in 1957 he was taken aback, but given the scarce amount of literature available on the subject, there was little to learn about it. In the early 1990s he discovered and became active in Ray Crowe's Western Bigfoot Society. Within three months he met veteran Bigfooter Peter Byrne who was running his Hood River research project. In following years, Cliff investigated and reported on three major sightings for the Byrne project.

In 1997 Cliff met experienced Sierra Nevada Bigfoot Researcher Ron Morehead at the WBS Carson Bigfoot Daze. They have remained friends since. At the 1998 Bigfoot Daze he met Joe Beelart and by early 1999 Cliff, acting as chief guide, was sharing the upper Clackamas drainage with Joe. Shortly thereafter Thom Powell and Steve Kiley "joined up" and the informal group of Clackamas Sasquatchians began.

Thom Powell

Oregon City, Oregon

B: 1956: Thom Powell was raised in Ohio where he engaged in numerous outdoor pursuits and athletic activities. He graduated the University of Ohio with a Bachelor of Science degree which eventually led him to a science teaching career. For some years in summer, Thom guided rafting expeditions deep into Idaho's Salmon River.

Thom has a long interest in Bigfoot. He was a key person in the Skookum Expedition where he was the first to find the imprint which he helped cast. In 2003 he wrote *The Locals*, a seminal book on the phenomena. In 2011 he wrote a fictional bigfoot novel based primarily on historical events titled *Shady Neighbors*. Currently he is working on a book of scientific incongruities, including obvious problems with the Sasquatch phenomena. Due to his combination of knowledge and humor, Thom is always in demand as a speaker. He has spoken in many venues on Sasquatch including conferences as far away as Ohio and Oklahoma.

Jeff Rone

West Linn, Oregon

B: 1963. Jeff Rone loves outdoor activities like bicycling, skiing, and camping, however, Jeff is not a hunter or fisherman. With virtually no interest in Bigfoot research, over the years he gradually worked his way up the Clackamas basin on his motorcycle "searching for roads I've never been on."

Then, as described in Area 4, the events at Bagby Hot Springs and Camp Broken Arrow happened to him. Since Broken Arrow, Jeff has taken an active role in field research in the upper Clackamas drainage with his most recent expedition being a July 2014 adventurous, productive three-night outing between Oak Grove Butte and Devils Ridge.

Jeff's good nature and field expertise regularly attract people from afar to go on his expeditions. Frequent campmates include Jim *Elk* DeMain of Idaho; Sue Funkhouser of Central Oregon, and Thom Cantrall, the author, from eastern Washington.

Kirk Sigurdson

Portland, Oregon

B: 1966: Kirk Sigurdson was raised near Salem, Oregon on property that bordered forest. His parents were avid outdoors people who did "tons" of camping. "We camped and hiked everywhere," said Kirk, "especially around the base of Mt. Jefferson."

Then, an odd thing happened. Kirk began to feel compelled to hike the upper Clackamas; he was "pulled" to the area. From about 1995 to 2005 and mainly alone, he camped in the drainage"...at least 50 times" developing a particular interest in the Goat Mountain area. In 2005 Sigurdson connected with Powell and Beelart who introduced him to Devils Ridge and other parts of the Clackamas. He has since proved invaluable with his knowledge of Area 6.

Diane Stocking

Portland, Oregon

Diane was raised in south Florida near the great Black Swamp and the Everglades. In the early 70's the many "Skunk Ape" (Sasquatch) reports generated in South Florida, "grabbed" Diane's attention and subsequently, became her life's passion. She founded Stocking Hominid Research, Inc. in 2007. Since moving to Oregon she has taken a particular interest in the Collawash River drainage and because of it, is now well known throughout the northwest Bigfoot community. Also, for years, Diane has been a key to the success of Todd Neiss' **BeachFoot**.

Woody Woodworth

Wood Village, Oregon

Woody has an understanding of the ways of wild animals. The authors think the stories about how he gained this understanding, plus his particularly unique introduction into Bigfooting will interest readers.

B: 1943: Woody Woodworth is the trim, tall Iron Man of the Clackamas Sasquatchians. He grew up in Washougal, Washington and was very active in sports; to this day, he exercises hard. His father was not a hunter, but was an ardent steelhead fisherman (steelhead are the prized sea run rockets of Northwest rivers). So, as a youth, in addition to sports, Woody "fished" all the time.

He and his father "did lots" of hiking and camping near Mt. St. Helens (before the eruption blew off the mountain's beautiful white dome). As camping and fishing spots Woody's father also favored

Trout Lake, and Mosquito Lake, before it was flooded by Spirit Lake Reservoir. Later, after college, Woody played semi-pro football.

Woody's father, the true outdoorsman he was, never talked about Bigfoot, he put little faith in the legend. Then, decades later, after a fishing trip near Davis Lake in central Oregon in which everyone had their own tent, he told Woody, "I heard your Bigfoot screaming in the night." As an experienced woodsman, he knew the sound could be made by nothing else. Surprisingly, the incident happened during the night after the Woodworth's saw and heard Army personnel practice explosives training, much like what happened in Todd Neiss' sighting.

In 1989 Woody took up archery. This led him to bow hunting in the early 1990s, specifically traditional bow hunting which means he hunts with bows made in the style used by Native Americans. Also, in the mid-1990s Woody was introduced to Ray Crowe of the Western Bigfoot Society, and then to Peter Byrne who was managing a Hood River based Sasquatch research project. After getting to know Peter, Woody conducted several field investigations for him along the west side of the Clackamas with one being a habituation situation in which the subject said the Bigfoot made "peacock" calls in the hills above his place.

Nowadays, Woody is an accomplished traditional archery hunter. This means his hunts require the skills of Native Americans. He has had multiple successes with elk, bear, and deer. Also, Woody has nearly harvested the elusive, swift, Oregon desert antelope. In addition to knowing how to observe and approach wild animals; he knows their ways and, he has a close appreciation of nature. He has to. *A long shot* for traditional bow hunters is about 40 feet (not yards). Yet, with his thousands of hours afield, Woody has not seen a Bigfoot.

Woody's first real exposure to Bigfoot came in about 1970 when he attended an airing of the Patterson-Gimlin film at Benson High School in NE Portland. Someone, maybe Roger Patterson, narrated the film, but exactly who it was Woody's forgotten. Woodworth's interest in the phenomena began in earnest during the late summer of 1976 in what is known in Northwest Bigfoot circles as the Dixie Mountain incidents.

The Beast of Dixie Mountain

From an interview with Woody Woodworth on January 8, 2013.

Dixie Mountain is in the Oregon Coast Mountain Range about 20 miles northwest of Portland city center and southwest of Scappoose. During the summer of 1976 two or more sightings of large, hairy, naked "men" crossing roads were reported to authorities and local newspapers. Many more sighting reports circulated among the locals. More particularly intense was a series of incidents which happened at one of Woody's coworker's Dixie Mountain homestead. Since the basics of the story are important in many ways, but do not involve the Clackamas drainage, the authors report it here.

At the time, the Dixie Mountain area was still Coast Range timber land with only a handful of homesteads up high and a few farms down low along river bottoms. A coworker reported horrible "screams" that drove his dogs under his cabin and got his geese to cackling like mad. A neighbor had a sturdy rabbit hutch that was ripped apart and his rabbits went missing.

The screams continued for over a week. Then one day Woody's coworker came in very troubled. The night before, the beast was screaming close to his cabin. Well, for Woody, there couldn't be a better mid-week diversion than a half case of beer and a trip to the homestead for a night of monster fun. Only, it turned out not so fun.

Woody said when the screams started about midnight, they were very impressive. The calls were not coyote as Woody secretly suspected and as they went on, Woody was deeply impressed. The calls lasted as long as 40 seconds (Woody recorded them, but has lost the tape.) They began with a guttural growl and grew into a final long, high pitched scream.

Whatever was making them was probably a mile away at first, and worked its way through the timber to less than a quarter mile from the cabin. The monster had huge lungs. Finally, the monster was close, screaming from a ravine below the cabin.

The man had six dogs. As usual, when the calls came near, the dogs retreated under the cabin and stayed there. The calls, which came at cycles of about 20 minutes, lasted a long time, the homesteader said usually about two hours.

There was nothing else for Woody to do but go back to the homestead the next night. At midnight the calls began again. This night the homesteader said, "If you want to see it, go down by the mailbox (about a hundred yards away down at the road). It walks down there." One of the man's six dogs was an "ankle biter;" the rest were watch dog types. He told Woody, "When the beast is calling .... my little guy is the only one that will go down there with me." He also said his little guy was a brave soul who once ran off a cougar attacking one of their young calves.

He elaborated; "the last time I went down there, my little guy (dog) went with us. When we got down to the mail box, it ran down into the ravine where the calls are coming from. Then he came racing back, squeezed between my wife's legs and would not move unless she moved."

He also described the huge bipedal beast which they saw in full moon light. From the ravine, the calls became closer. They were penetrating. Woody decided to not go down to the mailbox alone.

According to the homesteader, the calling incidents ended one night about a week later when the calls started, as usual, about midnight. That night, from across the valley, another beast answered. In the distance, the screams came closer and closer together; then the calls were heard no more. Sightings ceased. The locals surmised the calls were a mating signal; answered.

Fog and Orb

The most disturbing occurrence of all the Dixie Mountain incidents to Woody was his final night on the mountain. He took a female companion who was looking for adventure up the hill late one night to drink beer, socialize, and smoke cigarettes (long ago he quit smoking). Anyway, the moon was up, the stars were out and they were parked above a farmer's stump patch and below a wooded ridge.

Not long after they stopped, a low fog enveloped the stump patch, which was quite large as it was intended to become a cow pasture. About 1:30 or 2 his companion asked, "What's that." "That" was a white globe with a bright white halo shining in the fog, only about 100 feet off the ground.

Woody studied the situation. He quickly decided the "globe" was a solid orb. And, he decided there was no way the light was a human wandering in the dark and the fog. It was steady and not bobbing. There was no habitation in the area. It was not a barn light. Because of hills behind it on the far horizon, the orb was not a star, planet, or fog covered moon.

Then the orb slowly began approaching Woody's car. His car was a Dodge Charger hard top with a 440

Magnum engine, one of the most powerful production engines ever made. They rolled down all the windows. There was a strange scent in the air, Woody thought maybe it was lavender, but then they decided, "No." After about two cigarettes and one beer, "What do you think it is?" "I don't know."

The orb, the halo, and the fog came nearer, and as the orb neared, silent and becoming larger and larger, and the fog became more foggy, through their open windows, ".... all of a sudden from the timber slope above came crashing," the crashing of a bipedal animal running toward the car. It was obvious the light, the orb had zeroed in on the car and now a monster was charging down the hill in attack mode.

Woody said, "That's when I fired up the 440 and floored the Charger."

So, on that gravel logging road in the Oregon Coast Range late that night the car badged "Charger" justly earned its name.

Even though the orb incident remains a mystery, the seed was planted in Woody that there may be a connection between the stories of UFOs and the Sasquatch. He has never seen anything like it since. But, the mating call screams made more sense to him. If Bigfoot gestation is about the same as humans, mating in mid-to-late summer means birthing in spring. That leaves the summer for baby Bigfoots to grow and prepare for winter.

This ends the Clackamas Sasquatchian Appendix.

II: Bigfoot Characteristics

This list of characteristics is from the stories in this book. It is representative and does not include all characteristics mentioned in the text.

Behaviors	Ref. No. in this book	Area & Report
Aggression		
Aggression toward humans		
Aggression #1: not seen	8	Stones a car
Aggression #2: close encounter	9	Backs out fly fisherman and children
Aggression #3: not seen	17	Throws limb at campers
Aggression #4: close encounter	21	"Gorilla" backs out prospector
Aggression #5: not seen	41	Possible stomping at Cliff
Aggression #6: not seen	51	Throws stone at intruders
Aggression #7: close encounter	73	Raised arms in "threatening way"
Aggression #8: close encounter	80	Great roar in Kiley sighting
Aggression #9: not seen	82	Second great roar in Big Bottom
Aggression #10: not seen	83	Throws rock at fisherman
Aggression #11: not seen	83	Clacks teeth at fisherman
Aggression #12: not seen	94	Stomping at Lemiti Creek
Aggression #13: close encounter	95	Raised arms in Round Lake sighting
Aggression #14: close encounter	100	Raised arms in Detroit Lake sighting
Concern with Human Activity		
Befriends old prospector	85	How Tarzan Springs got its name
Watches human activity daytime #1	10	Sits on snow-covered bulldozer seat
Watches human activity daytime #2	87	"Be more observant:" Lowe Springs
Watches human activity daytime #3	95	Round Lake 1953; youthful campers

Curiosity & Humor

General

Likes Horses

Screams & Wails for Sex

Nightly screams until returned	---	Dixie Mtn. Beast. See Woodworth bio.
Wails; loud: swollen genitals	72	Thomas' third sighting

When first seen

Remains motionless, squats or balls	---	Several instances
Departs area immediately #1	3	Leave Blank's vegetable garden
Departs area immediately #2; night	16	At tire change; strides upslope
Departs area immediately #3	42	Two cross road in night
Departs area immediately #4; night	58	Collawash sighting; strides upslope
Departs area immediately #5	82	Roar, then parts trees leaving
Departs area immediately #6	97	Breitenbush River sighting
Departs area immediately #7	100	The Detroit Lake sighting

End of Behaviors

Diet

Beaver	99	Beaver pond find; site video filmed
Elk food, processed	41	Ripplebrook sighting follow up
Fish	Inferred	See "Fishes"
Grass, purportedly	74	Thomas' Feb. 1969 track find
Human food stuffs	3	Blank's vegetable garden sighting
Human food stuffs	7	Sweetcorn field; tracks; roaring
Human food stuffs; seems to want	42 & 58	Two tossed stews
Leaves, willow	71	Thomas' second sighting
Minerals from rocks	19	Licked rocks
Rodents, small	70	Thomas' first sighting
Roots	66	Kiley finds cleaned root & tracks
Skunk cabbage #1	33	Kiley find #1: cabbage root bitten

Note: Care was taken not to list feedings by deer, bear, coyote, birds, raccoon, mice, etc.

Physical Characteristics

Arms longer than human	58	Collawash moonlight sighting
Body odor: Good, natural perfume	4	Jake the Recluse
Body odor strong: Produced at will?	12	South Fork incident
Body odor: None	55	Cabin Creek camp
Body odor nauseating, acrid	57	Green report on Collawash
Body odor like outhouse	73	Thomas' fourth sighting
Body odor: May be able to turn off	87	"Be more observant" account
Body odor "foul"	95	Round Lake sighting
Breasts lower than human female	72	Thomas' third sighting
Breaths deeply	42, 57, 87 & 102	Close to very close encounters
Ears small	9, 55 & 70	Backs out fly fisherman, plus
Eyes: large and bloodshot	3	Both sightings at the Blank farm
Eyes: blue color	4	Jake the Recluse
Eyes: black or dark	9	Backs out fly fisherman
Face complexion black or dark	55	Cabin Creek sighting
Face similar to a human	55, 57 &58	Collawash moonlight sighting, plus
Face similar to cats	70	Thomas' first sighting
Foot length: 9 inches to 17 inches	Various	Track finds at many locations
Foot: "padded like a dog's"	40	Ripplebrook sighting
Foot: two parts probable	12, 43, 44, 99	Beaver pond track cast
Gorilla, looks like	21	Backs out prospector
Genital area; female; swelling	72	Thomas' third sighting
Genitals, male, not large	9	Backed out fly fisherman
Hair: arm hair long	40	Ripplebrook sighting
Hair: color reddish	40	Ripplebrook sighting
Hair: color dark brown, short; no. 1	71	Thomas' second sighting
Hair: color dark brown, short; no. 2	72	Thomas' third sighting
Hair: color dark brown, short; no. 3	73	Thomas' fourth sighting
Hands: large	9	Backed out fly fisherman
Head : Top crest or peak	40	Ripplebrook sighting
Head: Top round, not pointed	58	Collawash moonlight sighting
Intestinal parasites unique no. 1	26	"Mother of All Turds"

Intestinal parasites unique no. 2	100	Detroit Lake sighting
Neck: None	97	Breitenbush sighting
Neck: Short	70	Thomas' first sighting
Shoulders: Wide, body tapers	58 & 70	Collawash night & Thomas' first
Teeth: white, large, square	9	Backs out fly fisherman
Temperature: Feels cold to touch	17	Leans against tent
Temperature: Feels warm to touch	61	Leans against tent #2
Thumb: In non-human location #1	71	Thomas' second sighting
Thumb: In non-human location #2	73	Thomas' fourth sighting
Waist & legs large	13 & 72	In fire smoke & Thomas' third
Walks: Feet parallel unlike human	2	Two instances in the Kiggins reports
Walks: Feet parallel unlike human	28	Whale Head track find
Walks: Feet parallel unlike human	53	Track line photo at Devils Ridge
Walks: Feet parallel unlike human	99	Beaver pond track film
Walks "humped-up, stooped over"	70	Thomas' first sighting
Walks up steep slopes with ease	16 & 58	Fish Creek & Collawash sightings
Walks using knuckles	6	Culvert sighting

Rocks

Rocks: Excavates for food #1	70	Thomas site
Rocks: Excavates for food #2	70 notes	Talus south of Mt. Lowe
Rocks: Excavates for food #3	84	Scree near Thomas site
Rocks: Excavates for food #4	77	Jim & Thom Roaring River talus site
Rocks: Excavates for food #5	78	Lindsey talus site
Rocks: Possibly plays with	24 & 50	Circle of small rocks & pyramid
Rocks: Stacks	19 & 70	Licked rocks & Thomas' first sighting

Shelters

Builds primitive structures	3	Bud Blank finds "lean-to"
Builds primitive structures	32	Todd Neiss finds "shelter"
Lives in caves or old mines	15	Law Enforcement Officer report

Sound Making

Chattering	A52: 103	Squatch Noir: night on Devils Ridge
Drumming; melodious	86	Above Tarzan Springs
Loud, long roars not bear #1; day	12	South Fork incident
Loud, long roars not bear #2; night	26	Silver Tip incident
Loud, long roars not bear #3; day	80	Kiley sighting
Loud, long roars not bear #4; day	81	Parting of trees
Loud, long roars not bear #5; day	100	Detroit Lake sighting
Loud, long roars not bear #6; night	100	Detroit Lake sighting
Whistles in the night	17	Bigfoot leans against tent
Wind sound: makes in the day	41	Cliff's unseen aggressor
Wood knocks	81 & 82	Big Bottom sighting

Telepathic Ability Possible

Felt "being watched"	---	In several references
Induces sleep in humans	55 & 103	Cabin Creek & *Squatch Noir*
Makes "invisible wall"	20	Forest Service biologist
Summoned to the Collawash	60	Bagby & Broken Arrow
Summoned to the copse of trees	103	Squatch Noir
Told to leave area	63, 64, 65	Collawash blow downs
Unseen but causes human anxiety	17	Fish Creek campers
Unseen but causes human anxiety	18	Fish Creek watchman
Unseen but causes human anxiety	42	Ripplebrook habituation by FSE

Territorial Identification

Territorial Identification	Maps	Surmised from ridges and rivers.
Possible Territorial Identification	11	North Fork scotch broom twist-off
Possible Territorial Identification	50	Kiley finds tree breaks
Possible Territorial Identification	43	Filmmaker's Ripplebrook track find
Possible Territorial Identification	48	1957 on Oak Grove Butte

Tools

Tools, use of	12	South Fork fish clubs photograph

Trails & Travels

Devils Trails: Trails easy to walk on. Not used by other animals	41, 42, 51, 63, 66 & 79	Six found in four areas
Possible migration routes	App. IV	Warm Springs elder & map study
Travels on ridgelines	No ref. no.	Native American elder & Kiley map
Travels along streambeds #1; day	6	The Culvert Sighting
Travels along streambeds #2; day	41	Ripplebrook investigation
Travels along streambeds #3; day	72	Thomas' third sighting
Travels along streambeds #1; night	57	Green's Collawash report
Travels along streambeds #2; night	58	2nd Collawash night sighting

Trees, use of

Jumps off steep slope; lands in trees	56	"French visitor's first time luck:"
Possibly lives in trees	A52: 103	Squatch Noir
Uses for camouflage	90	Baby play area
Uses for concealment	87	Lowe Creek camp
Uses to make shelters	3 & 32	Bud Blank; and Todd Neiss

Types described

Big and aggressive	4	Jake the Recluse
Big (large)	Several ref.	See "Behavior"
Smaller, friendlier	4	Jake the Recluse
Little People	15, 94, A52: 102	Memaloose, Lemiti Butte, Mt. Lowe
Possibly two Cascade species	46	Photo of Yeti like tracks

Winter Range

Lives at about 1,500 feet in winter	Maps	Kiley wall map & sighting maps

III: Bigfoot Population Estimate

How many Bigfoot are there along The Oregon Bigfoot Highway? Without scientific proof how did the authors make an estimate? Mainly we guessed based on the Areas and reports in this book. While we have no way of knowing, we hope these estimates include the number of individuals required to maintain an on-going population.

Area 1:

North Fork & Squaw Mountain	2
Memaloose and South Fork	2
Fish Creek	0

Area 2:

Roaring River & Mt. Mitchell plateau (Indian Henry is the Area 2 wintering ground)	2

Area3:

Oak Grove Butte & Devils Ridge	2
Peavine Mountain & Summit Lake	2
High Rock plateau	2
Timothy Lake district	5

Area 4:

The Collawash drainage	2

Area 5:

Pinhead Buttes to Lemiti Butte	2
Mt. Lowe	2

Area 6:

Olallie Lake area	2
Bull of the Wood Wilderness	2

Roving:

Mature males	2

Others

Such as immature & and pass through Bigfoots	2

Total summer population:	31

Due to topography and experience in the area, we consider the Fish Creek drainage a transit or temporary feeding zone without a sustained population of Sasquatch.

In summer, the Timothy Lake district is very large and hospitable. Cliff Olson has closely studied it and feels there are a relatively high number of individuals in that area, some of which may be transients. Please see the Migratory Route map.

If Sasquatch spends most days in trees, and the few caves that are along *The OBH*, we think our population estimates make even more sense.

After our estimate was made, we were surprised to see our population density is close to the number of individuals vs. square miles mentioned in the 1967 Thomas sightings (Ref. 70-73). In Ref. 75 (1978) Green writes Thomas saw "...seven individuals, all different, and tracks that appear to belong to two more (Ref. 74), all in an area of about 200 square miles." Extrapolating, the area of the Clackamas Ranger District is about 800 square miles. 7/200 vs. x/800 = 28 individuals. Our population estimates factor only sightings, *not* track finds.

Clackamas meadows at the intersection of Road 57 and Road 42. Photo by Sharon Beelart.

IV: Bigfoot Byways or Migration Routes in the Clackamas

Native Americans and long-time Bigfoot researchers believe Bigfoot travels along mountain ridges. There are several reasons for this belief with perhaps the most important being a relatively straight line is the shortest distance between two points.

The second is that river bottoms tend to be clogged with trees and brush making swift transit difficult. While dense river bottom cover also means concealment, it conversely means limited vision of activities in an area. Both points lead to a major third reason for using high ground for a byway, or throughway; high ground generally has more open ground and better visibility.

The *Oregon Bigfoot Highway* is amongst three ridgeline Bigfoot byways. The attached map shows each byway. Each natural migration route runs almost directly north and south with a southerly terminus on the east and west slopes of Mt. Jefferson.

South of Mt. Jefferson the Bigfoot byways converge and then proceed on a primary southern route past Mt. Washington, the Three Sisters, and Crater Lake into southern Oregon's Siskiyou Mountains and the Sierra Nevada Mountains in California.

One side route to the Oregon Coast Range begins southwest of Mt. Jefferson and follows the McKenzie River to south of Eugene where it turns west to the Coast.

The second route to the Oregon Coast follows the Clackamas northwest to the Tualatin River and then follows the Tualatin west.

To the north, the Bigfoot byways pass on both the lower west and east slopes of Mount Hood. One famous Bigfoot explorer-researcher feels their primary route is on the east slope, crossing at about the level of Mt. Hood Meadows Ski Resort and ending on the south side of the Columbia River roughly across from Washington's White Salmon River. The west route is through Lolo Pass and ends at the south side of the Columbia River across from Washington's Wind River drainage; a place with many Bigfoot sightings and where the Skookum Cast was taken.

That the creatures used these routes is beyond doubt; on an old pioneer map, Todd Neiss found a place named *Ape Crossing* on the Sandy River close to the south terminus of Lolo Pass near Brightwood (a village). *Ape Crossing* is almost directly north of McIntyre Ridge which is a high north-to-south ridge rising from the Sandy River valley and extending to the Clackamas River Ranger District east of High Rock.

Map of Bigfoot Migration Routes

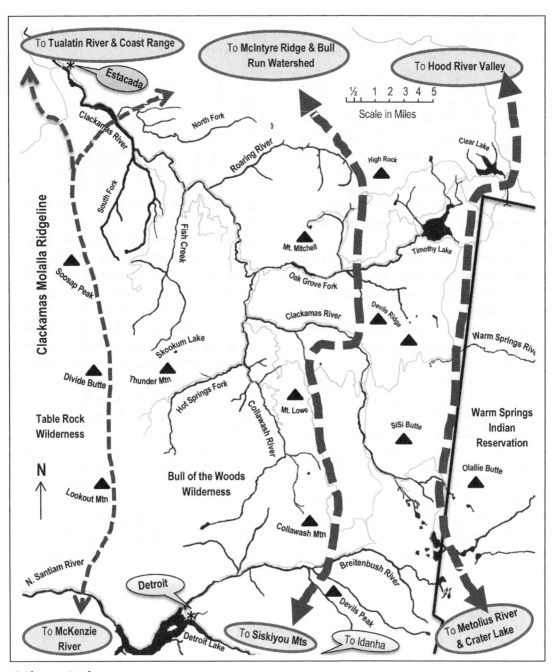

©Sharon Beelart 2015

Bonneville Power Administration lines in Area 6. Photo by Joe Beelart.

V: Meadows along the Oregon Bigfoot Highway

We include this list because meadows are perhaps more important than quarries as research bases. Names are transcribed per official USFS maps. It is common practice to omit the apostrophe on some topographical names, so Toms is spelled correctly per official maps. Sometimes the "s" is omitted, as in Bob Meadow and Jim Meadow.

The general location within an Area is noted by approximate location then Area: i.e. Austin Meadow is in the SW part of Area 2. GPS coordinates are approximate; elevations are rounded to the nearest 100 feet. Be aware that in spring some meadows are seasonal swamps, or submerged lake shores.

Field work indicates some map search engine locations are near, but not at the actual meadow location. Cornpatch and Cachebox Meadows are good examples. Also, there are numerous unnamed meadows along the Oregon Bigfoot Highway. A Google Earth scan near Olallie Meadow shows several easy-to-see unnamed meadows.

Locations are listed for two unnamed low elevation meadows in SW Area 2 near Ripplebrook Guard Station. These meadows are excellent for winter wildlife viewing but beware of winter driving conditions, especially black ice on shady roadways.

Austin Meadow: SW A2: GPS 45 03 24.84N 122 03 15.96W ~1500'

Black Wolf Meadow: N A3: GPS 45 08 52.12N 121 52 12.29W ~4100'

Bob Meadow: E A5: GPS 44 56 36.43N 121 58 47.95W ~3900'

Cache Meadow: NW A3: GPS 45 08 01.49 N 121 59 42.40W ~4400'

Cachebox Meadow: N A6: GPS 44 50 20.87N 121 57 04.95W ~4500'

Clackamas Lake Meadow: E A5: GPS 45 05 53.05N 121 44 43.97W ~3300'

Cornpatch Meadow: E A6: GPS 44 49 43.71N 121 48 05.89W ~4600'

Cottonwood Meadow: SW A3: W A3: 45 06 27.51N 121 57 41.17W ~4000'

Eds Meadow: W A5: 44 53 31.32N 121 55 18.23W ~3800'

Fawn Meadow: N A6: GPS 44 55 24.49N 121 58 12.87W ~4100'

Jim Meadow: W A5: GPS 44 56 45.85N 121 57 33.53WW ~4300'

Little Crater Lake Meadow: E A5: GPS 45 08 57.11N 121 44 53.68W ~3200'

Olallie Meadow: E A6: GPS 44 51 34.87N 121 46 16.26W ~4500'

Rhododendron Meadow: SW A5: GPS 44 55 17.59N 121 57 13.33W ~4200'

Round Meadow: N A6: GPS 44 51 27.80N 121 57 03.14W ~4900'

Squaw Meadows: E A1: GPS 45 13 22.07N 22 01 21.47W ~3500'

Toms Meadow: NE A4: GPS 44 57 48.28N 122 02 17.25W ~2000'

Trapper Springs Meadow: E A5: GPS 44 58 31.87N 121 47 27.79W ~3800'

Twin Meadows: N A6: GPS 44 51 32.55N 121 56 44.77W ~4900'

Wards Meadow: SW A2: GPS 45 04 13.67N 122 03 31.52W ~1400'

Warm Springs Meadow: E A5: GPS 44 59 12.09 N 121 46 54.88W ~3700'

Unnamed Meadow 1: SW A2: GPS 45 03 26.10N 122 03 31.52W ~1700'
Unnamed Meadow 2: SW A2: GPS 45 03 34.55N 122 04 50.75W ~1900'
Unnamed Meadow 3: N A3: GPS 45 10 46.44N 121 52 23.55 W ~3400'
Unnamed Meadow 4: E A5: GPS 44 56 54.75N 121 59 58.15W ~3200'

The importance of meadows to a field researcher cannot be overstated. They are (1) gathering places for animals, either in summer or winter, (2) they generally lie along the theorized *Bigfoot Highways*, and (3) they are excellent places for observation, especially watching edges.

Example: as reported in Area 3, in September 2003 Cliff Olson found an 82 imprint track way at a small lake near Cottonwood Meadows. Note elevations in reports, especially at lower elevations. They tend to support the theory of Sasquatch wintering below 2000'.

High up Indian Henry: An old beaver pond that has become a meadow.
Background: Whale Head in storm clouds. Photo by Joe Beelart.

VI: Pies for the Mountain Guys

The authors do not know the true and genuine reason for making offerings to the Sasquatch. One thing we do know is that before leaving the forest, setting out a gift of food or a small, shiny, non-dangerous object as an offering feels good, a little like leaving a small gift for a host after a visit.

Never set an offering on the ground. Place it on something like a fallen tree, a stump, a big rock, or a pile of dirt. It is generally best to not place an offering until ravens and crows fly to their roosts for the night. It is their job to scavenge the forest and they are both good at their job, and quick about it.

A Good Way & Gifts in Return

In our opinion, this is one of the best ways to make offerings. Take the offering, whatever it might be, and put it in a single generous piece of aluminum foil or wax paper. Fold the covering over the offering on an elevated place, securing the flap with a rock or some other natural weight. The covering serves three purposes: It shields the offering; it is reflective in night light, and is somewhat rain resistant. A final note concerning offerings; occasionally they leave a small gift of appreciation at an offering site.

Use of Words & Steve Kiley's Words

Some of us use words when we place an offering; the words do not have to be spoken aloud. We are quite sure when a person is connected with the Sasquatch, they can hear our thoughts. We are careful to not make appeals for the Sasquatch to do something in return. Rather, the words are thanking them for arousing our awareness of the beautiful world around us.

For decades, Steve Kiley has extensively studied and interacted with Native Americans. To some degree these words reflect Steve's respect and understanding of Native American history and teachings concerning interaction with nature and the creatures in it, including the Sasquatch.

"People of the Woods: We acknowledge and honor you with this humble offering. Please accept this offering in the spirit it is given. We have much to learn from you. Please direct us if you see fit."

Preparing offerings at dusk. Sharon's apple cobbler and a cookie. Photo by Joe Beelart.

VII: Common Sense & Courtesy - Forest Style

- Carefully obey all FIRE WARNINGS!

- Please, DO NOT LITTER! If you take it in, take it out.

- Watch out for Log Trucks!

- Bury your turds and tissue.

Pets: If you bring a pet, bring a leash. Dogs get especially excited in the woods, what with all the strange, beguiling scents washing over them. So, they tend to run off. Dogs are often difficult or impossible to find because they cover ground rapidly and your voice won't carry far, especially through timber. Rest assured, lost dogs will most likely be killed and eaten by either a pack of coyotes or a cougar. So, if you value Spot, keep him, her, or it on a leash.

What the authors carry:

While it's not practical for the casual driver or tourist, the authors almost always carry the following into the forest:

- A bucket, shovel, and axe (required in the old days)

- Hiking staffs

- Toilet paper

- Hand cleanser and hand wipes

- Gloves

- First-aid kit

- A signal whistle ("I am lost whistle"), compass, multi-tool, spare batteries, etc.

- An emergency box containing heavy duty jumper cables, a tow strap, flares, heavy gloves, safety glasses, and other handy stuff like duct tape.

What your Sasquatchians do:

- Each trip up the hill, we pick up and haul out trash, however little. This shows respect to the forest, and our Barefoot Friends like it. To this end, carry a plastic bag and cheap latex gloves

And One More Time: Mountain roads are curvy and generally without a shoulder, but, are not difficult to drive as long as drivers rigorously heed safe driving practices.

VIII: Book Reader Warnings

Your authors have encountered people and situations in the forest which cause us to mention the following points. This is not an all-inclusive list. Use common sense. For instance, do not go on weekend trips in October during deer rifle season, or when a winter storm is predicted. (Check with Oregon Dept. of Fish & Wildlife for season dates.)

Travelers of *The Oregon Bigfoot Highway* should agree with the following:

- Never leave Estacada or Detroit, Oregon without at least 3/4 of a tank of gas.

- Check for proper tire inflation including your spare tire.

- If planning to drive side roads, ensure the vehicle has adequate clearance.

- Always have supplies of medicine, bottled water, and emergency food rations.

- Bring a basic map, or a detailed map if venturing up side roads.

- A working flashlight and other basic equipment.

- Warm clothes, and in season, a blanket for each passenger.

- Obtain a valid visitor parking pass where required.

Travelers of the *Oregon Bigfoot Highway* should acknowledge that:

- I will drive carefully, with vigilance, within all speed limits; or slower when dictated by conditions. I will slow to the signed speeds on curves: 15 MPH means 15 MPH.

- I will let my passengers do the looking. When it is time for me to look at something I will pull to the side of the road at a safe and appropriate place, even if it means walking for some distance to get to the vantage point.

- There is very limited cellular reception along the Oregon Bigfoot Highway.

- Side roads are little used. If I get in trouble, I'm probably going to have to get out of it on my own or walk miles for help that will be very slow arriving.

- Dangers such as ice, rock falls, landslides, fallen trees, tree branches, grade slumps, potholes, and other obstructions are common along the highway.

- Hot springs, any body of water, and marshes are dangerous places.

- I will not enter an abandoned mine. Dangers lurk within.

IX: Truth & Privacy

The accounts in this book are based primarily on your authors' and your Sasquatchians' personal interviews with carefully screened individuals and a few very select newspaper and book accounts which we could authenticate. We did not include Internet based reports, however believable they may be, for obvious reasons. To the best of the authors' knowledge, each account in this book is true.

Writing a book on the Bigfoot phenomena presented many tricky problems for the authors. One major dilemma was getting stories from people who would not tell their story if their name was used. This was normally the case with United States Forest Service employees and other professionals, such as lawyers. So, this is how we solved this problem.

We used alpha-numeric identifications for people who did not want their name used, such as *FSE* for Forest Service Employee followed by the sequential number as they appear in the text. We use Jake, a moniker originally suggested by Ray Crowe of the Western Bigfoot Society, as a generic reference to people as events are described and when:

- The person, or people, involved are not available to interview (i.e. dead, have dementia, were seriously ill, etc.), and their basic story comes from a family member or other reliable source such as a law officer, making it suitable for inclusion,

- Events are long in the past and dim in memory (which is so noted), or

- A Sasquatchian told the story but could not contact the subject person, or

- The story teller did not want the family name connected to Bigfoot.

People's names are used in the book under three circumstances: (1) when the person specifically asked us to use their name; (2), where a person experiencing an event approved the text in writing and also gave specific permission to use their name; or (3) when the story was reported from print or broadcast media and we made a proper citation.

Index

INDEX by Reference Number							
Area	Ref. No.	Location & Report	Sources (a)	Sighting S1-S31	Tracks TF1-TF43	Bigfoot Related Incident I1 - I69	Happenings & Cougars H1-H37; C1-C7
		(a) Sources: SQ = Sasquatchians; LEO=Law Enforcement Officer; FSE=Forest Service Employee; Jake=Name withheld.					
Area 1		Estacada, North Fork, South Fork, Memaloose & Fish Creek					
A1		District 1: Estacada					
A1	1	Estacada 1: Lumber Jack and the Safari Club	Local history				
A1	2	Estacada 2: Millie Kiggins	Millie & Clackamas	1 & 2	1, 2 & 3	1 & 2	
A1	3	Estacada 3: Blank family	County News	3 & 4	4	3 & 4	
A1	4	Estacada 4: Jake the Recluse	SQ: Woody				
A1	5	Estacada 5: Through a glass clearly	M. Kiggins	5	5		
A1	6	Estacada 6: The Culvert Sighting	SQ: Cliff	6			
A1	7	Hwy 224 #1: The Corn Field	Jake 1		6	5	
A1	8	Hwy 224 #2: Stoning a '59 Chevy	Jake 2			6	
A1		District 2					
A1	9	North Fork 1: Bigfoot backs out fisherman	Jake 3	7			
A1	10	North Fork 2: Bigfoot sits on bulldozer in snow	Jake 4, 5 & 6		7	7	
A1	11	North Fork 3: Scotch broom twist-off	SQ: Steve & Joe			8	
A1	12	South Fork: Tracks, roars, scent	SQ: Steve & Joe		8	9 & 10	
A1	13	Memaloose 1: Running naked in fire smoke	LEO 1	8			H1
A1	14	Memaloose 2: BD crew see "fly fishermen"	FSE 1	9			
A1	15	Memaloose 3: LEO circles on map	LEO 1 again				H2

INDEX by Reference Number

Area	Ref. No.	Location & Report	Sources (a)	Sighting S1-S31	Tracks TF1-TF43	Bigfoot Related Incident I1-I69	Happenings & Cougars H1-H37; C1-C7
A1		**District 3**					
A1	16	Fish Creek 1: Bigfoot watches a tire change	FSE 1	10			
A1	17	Fish Creek 2: Bigfoot leans against a tent in night	Jake 7 & 8			11	
A1	18	Fish Creek 3: Watchman's nightmare	Jake 9			12	
A1	19	Fish Creek 4: Hike, rock marker, licked rocks	SQ: Steve & Joe			13	
A1		Fish Creek 5: Cougar stalks woman	Jake 10 & FSE 2				C1
A1	20	Fish Creek 6: Biologist hits a "wall"	FSE 2 again			14	
Area 2		**Roaring River, Three Lynx, Indian Henry, & Ripplebrook**					
A2		**District 1**					
A2	21	Roaring River 1: Hiker backed out by "gorilla"	J11 & Neiss	11			
A2	22	Roaring River 2: The Great Roosters Exp.	Jake 12		9	15	
A2	23	Under Mt. Mitchell 1: Steve's first track cast	SQ: Steve & Joe		10		
A2	24	Under Mt. Mitchell 2: A curious circle of stones	SQ: Cliff & Joe				H3
A2	25	Under Mt. Mitchell 3: The Mother of All Turds	SQs			16	
A2	26	Under Mt. Mitchell 4: Night roars & Cougar	SQ: Woody			17	C2
A2	27	East of Three Lynx: "A tall dark man"	Jake 13	12			

INDEX by Reference Number

Area	Ref. No.	Location & Report	Sources (a)	Sighting S1-S31	Tracks TF1-TF43	Bigfoot Related Incident I1 - I69	Happenings & Cougars H1-H37; C1-C7
A2		**District 2**					
A2	28	Whale Head 1: Hundreds of tracks in snow	SQ: Cliff & Joe		11		
A2	29	Whale Head 2: Blank clicks, covers opened	Jake 14 & SQ: Joe			18	
A2	30	Whale Head 3: Olson's Saddle	SQ: Cliff				H4
A2	31	Indian Henry 1: Crowe finds trackline	Ray Crowe		12		
A2	32	Indian Henry 2: Neiss Finds structure	SQ: Todd Neiss			19	
A2	33	Indian Henry 3: Tracks & bit skunk cabbage	SQ: Steve Kiley		13	20	
A2	34	Indian Henry 4: Bigfoot watches man sleep	Jake 14 again	13			
A2	35	Indian Henry 5: BF waits to cross road	SQ: Cliff & Joe		14		
A2	36	Indian Henry 6: Bit skunk cabbage #2	SQ: Steve & Joe		15	21	
A2	37	Indian Henry 7: High lake sighting	SQ: Cliff	14			
A2		**District 3**					
A2	38	Ripplebrook 1: Three year slide repair	Local history				H5
A2		Ripplebrook 2: Five Elk Pond	SQ: Cliff & Joe				H6
A2	39	Ripplebrook 3: "Bigfoot Logbook"	FSE 3				H7
A2	40	Ripplebrook 4: The Ripplebrook Sighting	FSE 4	15	16		
A2	41	Ripplebrook 5: Sighting report is investigated	FSE 4 & 5		17		
A2	42	Ripplebrook 6: Two more sightings	FSE 4 & 6	16 & 17		22, 23, 24 & 25	
A2	43	Commentary: Sasquatch Territories					
A2		Territorial signal #1: Film makers' track find	Jake 16 & 2 Filmers		18	26	

INDEX by Reference Number

Area	Ref. No.	Location & Report	Sources (a)	Sighting	Tracks	Bigfoot Related Incident	Happenings & Cougars
				S1-S31	TF1-TF43	I1 - I69	H1-H37; C1-C7
Area 3		**The Oak Grove Fork, High Rock, Devils Butte, & Timothy Lake**					
A3		**District 1**					
A3	44	Atop Mt. Mitchell: Cliff finds 82 tracks	SQs & J14, again				
A3	45	Hideaway Lake: A Night Watcher	Jake 16		19	27	
A3	46	High Rock Road 1: Tracks in snow	J13 & J17		20		
A3	47	High Rock Road 2: FSE points to "good place"	FSE 7			28	
A3		North of Timothy Lake: "The Snow Sweeper"	SQ: Joe				C3
A3		**District 2**					
A3	48	Oak Grove Butte 1: 1957: Cliff finds territorial track	SQ: Cliff		21		
A3	49	Oak Grove Butte 2: Log landing night stalker	SQ: Cliff			29	
A3		**District 3**					
A3		Devils Ridge 1: A beautiful happening	SQ: Steve & Joe				H8
A3		Devils Ridge 2: The Devils Wind	SQ: Joe				H9
A3	51	Devils Ridge 3: The Night Watcher	Filmsters & SQ. Joe		22	30	
A3	52	Devils Ridge 4: Devil on the Rim	Jake 18	18		31	
A3	53	Devils Ridge 5: Offering Incident	Joe & Sharon		23		
A3	54	Devils Ridge 6: Intrepid explorers and bears	Jakes 19, 20 & 21				H10

INDEX by Reference Number

Area	Ref. No.	Location & Report	Sources (a)	Sighting S1-S31	Tracks TF1-TF43	Bigfoot Related Incident I1 - I69	Happenings & Cougars H1-H37; C1-C7
A3		**District 4**					
A3	55	Peavine Mtn: Bigfoot watches Mann sleep	Sq: Mann & Joe	19	24	32	
A3		Timothy Lake area: the Green Cathedral & Solstice	SQs & FSE 8				H11
Area 4		**The Collawash River**					
A4		**Tromping the Collawash**					
A4	56	Under Granite Peaks: French visitor luck	Jean Roche & SQ		25	33	
A4	57	John Green: a Moonlight Sighting	John Green	20			
A4	58	Another Moonlight Sighting	Jake 22	21			
A4		A cougar stalks Joe; warning shot fired	SQ: Joe				C4
A4	59	What's in a name? Ogre Creek	Jake 23			34	
A4	60	Summoned to Bagby Hot Springs	SQ: Rone		26 & 27		H12
A4	61	Camp Broken Arrow Expedition	SQ: Rone & Assoc.		28	35 thru 42	
A4		**Tom's Meadow**					
A4	62	Toms Meadow 1: Cliff finds tracks on slope	SQ: Cliff & Joe		29		
A4	63	Toms Meadow 2: Track line in duff	SQ: Steve & Joe		30		H13
A4	64	Toms Meadow 3: Spooked again	SQ: Steve & Joe			43	
A4	65	Toms Meadow 4: "Leave here now!"	SQ: Steve & Joe			44	
A4	66	Toms Meadow 5: Cleaned, dropped Roots	SQ: Steve		31	45	
A4	67	Toms Meadow 6: Aggressive baiting	Sasquatchians		32		H14

INDEX by Reference Number

Area	Ref. No.	Location & Report	Sources (a)	Sighting S1-S31	Tracks TF1-TF43	Bigfoot Related Incident I1 - I69	Happenings & Cougars H1-H37; C1-C7
A4	68	Toms Meadow 7: Private Bigfoot Reserve	FSE 9				H15
A4	69	Toms Meadow 8: Bigfoot Watch Towers	SQ: Joe & Thom		33		H16
Area 5		**Big Bottom & the Mountains Around**					
A5	70	Thomas' first sighting: Three on a rock talus	John Green	22		46	
A5	71	Thomas' second sighting: Eating leaves	John Green	23		47	
A5	72	Thomas' third sighting: Watches two females	John Green	24	34	48 & 49	
A5	73	Thomas' fourth sighting: A "scruffy" old male	John Green	25		50	
A5	74	Thomas' February 1969 track find	John Green		35	51	
A5	75	Green's analysis of the Thomas sightings	John Green				
A5	76	McCoy comments on the Thomas sightings	SQ: L. McCoy				
A5	77	Henick & Powell find Thomas style site	SQ: Jim & Thom				H17
A5	78	Lindsey finds a Thomas style site	SQ: S. Lindsey				H18
A5		**District 1: Big Bottom**					
A5	79	Big Bottom 1: The Green Click	SQ: Joe				H19
A5	80	Big Bottom 2: The Kiley Sighting	SQ: Steve	26	36	52, 53, 54	
A5	81	Big Bottom 3: Cliff Investigates	SQ: Cliff			55	
A5	82	Big Bottom 4: A great roar & parting trees	SQ: Joe			56	
A5		Big Bottom 5: Call blasting & coyote pups!	SQ: Cliff & Joe				H20
A5		Big Bottom 6: Organic soup; a bear; lost	Sasquatchians				H21

INDEX by Reference Number

Area	Ref. No.	Location & Report	Sources (a)	Sighting S1-S31	Tracks TF1-TF43	Bigfoot Related Incident I1 - I69	Happenings & Cougars H1-H37; C1-C7
A5	83	Steelheading along the high Clackamas River	SQ: S. Lindsey				H22, 23 &
A5		**District 2: Mt. Lowe Ridgeline**					
A5	84	Granite Peaks 1: Finding the first Thomas site	SQ: Steve & Joe			57	H25
A5		Granite Peaks 2: Cougar before dawn	SQ: Joe				C5
A5	85	Tarzan Springs 1: How it got its name	Jakes 23 & 24	27			
A5	86	Tarzan Springs 2: Salad & drumming	SQ: Joe & Neiss			58	
A5	87	Lowe Springs: Be more observant	J25, J26, SQ: Joe	28		59	
A5		Mt. Lowe 1: Perseid Meteors; Perseid cougar	SQ: Joe				C6
A5		Mt. Lowe 2: It really was a cougar!	Sasquatchians				C6, again
A5		**District 3: Pinhead Buttes**					
A5	88	Lumber Jack saves Bigfoot	Lumber Jack				H26
A5	89	South Pinhead Butte 1: Four little adventures	J27, J28, SQ: Joe		37		
A5	90	South Pinhead Butte 2: A Bigfoot playground	SQ: Joe			60	
A5	91	South Pinhead Butte 3: Night walker	SQ: Joe			61	
A5		South Pinhead Butte 4: Finding a bear den	SQ: Joe				
A5	92	West Pinhead Butte 1: Four events.	Sasquatchians		38	62	H28 & H29
A5	93	West Pinhead Butte 2: BF photo & a bad road	Jake 29 & SQ: Joe				H30 & H31
A5		Warm Springs River: The new rock quarry	SQ: Joe				H32

INDEX by Reference Number

Area	Ref. No.	Location & Report	Sources (a)	Sighting S1-S31	Tracks TF1-TF43	Bigfoot Related Incident I1-I69	Happenings & Cougars H1-H37; C1-C7
Area 6		**The Southern Area: Olallie Basin, Breitenbush, and Detroit Lake**					
A6	94	Lemiti Butte Night Camp	Jake 30 & 31				H33
A6	95	Round Lake: A 1953 sighting	J32, 33 & 34	29	39	63	
A6	96	Near Ollalie Lake: Cougar follow Kiley	SQ: Steve			64	C7
A6		Crest line: Four Hunter Stories	J35 & J36		40	65	H34 & H35
A6	97	Breitenbush River: Fly fisher sights Bigfoot	Jake 37	30			
A6	98	Bigfoot Advertising: Smokin' up a good one	Jake 38				H36
A6		Wild stallion blob squatch	Patterson				H37
A6	99	Near Detroit Lake dam: Beaver predation	J39, 40, 41, 42		41	66	
A6	100	Detroit Lake: Sighting, tracks, roars, scat	Jakes 43-46 and SQs	31	42 & 43	67, 68, 69	
Area 52		**Bizarre Happenings**					
A52	101	UFO with Bigfoot Crew	Area 52 reports are not included in the Sighting, Track Find, Bigfoot Related Incident, & Happenings totals.				
A52	102	An Old Berry Picker & Little People					
A52	103	Squatch Noir					

INDEX

Map Index

Bibliography

References used in this book

Ham, Ray. *Encounters with Bigfoot Remembered*, The Clackamas Country News, Vol. 72 No. 24, July 25, 1979 (Ref. 2 and 3.)

Green, John. *Sasquatch the Apes Among Us*. Surry, BC: Hancock House, 1978 & 2006. (Ref. 57 and 70–75.) Mr. Green was quoted with his written permission.

Sasquatchian experiences or interviews (See Appendix I and IX.)

For further reading: Periodicals

Ray Crowe (editor). *The Track Record* (1991-2006). Available on CD from the North America Bigfoot Search, Los Gatos, California: **www.nabigfootsearch.com**. In every issue, Crowe warned his readers to "keep your skepticals on." The NABS CD contains about 135 accounts and mentions from the upper Clackamas drainage.

Daniel Perez (editor). *The Bigfoot Times*. Published continuously since January 1998, this highly-respected monthly mail newsletter covers all aspects of man-like beings and persons involved in the phenomena. USA subscriptions in 2015 are $17.50 per year, $21 international, from 10926 Milano Ave. Norwalk, CA. 90650-1638.

For further reading: Books

The following explore similarities between Sasquatch and unclassified hominids on other continents.

Bayanov, Dmitri. *In the Footsteps of the Russian Snowman*. Moscow: Crypto-Logos Publishers 1996.

Debenat, Jean-Paul, Ph.D. *The Asian Wildman*. Surrey, BC: Hancock House 2015.

Healy, Tony and Cropper, Paul. *The Yowie, in Search of Australia's Bigfoot*. San Antonio: Anomalist Books, 2006.

Other Titles by John Green:

On the Track of the Sasquatch. Agassiz, BC: Cheam, 1968.

Year of the Sasquatch. Agassiz, BC: Cheam, 1970.

The Sasquatch File. Agassiz, BC: Cheam, 1973.

On the Track of the Sasquatch: Encounters with Bigfoot from California to Canada (2 volumes). Harrison Hot Springs, BC: Cheam, 1980.

Photo by Joe Beelart

Study of Bird and Animal Sounds

Since misidentified night bird calls, especially those of the barred owl, are often attributed to Sasquatch we encourage researchers to study bird, and animal sounds.

First go to the Oregon Department of Fish & Wildlife site, *www.dfw.state.or.us/wildlife/living_with/* and select your animal, or try "Whooo_Am_ I" for fun facts about the 14 species of owls in Oregon.

In many cases, the site will then direct you to the Cornell University Department of Ornithology Macaulay Library of natural history recordings, *www.macaulaylibrary.org*, which is recognized world-wide as the best source of natural history recording available.

Black Wolf Meadow in late September. Photo by
Joe Beelart.

Notes

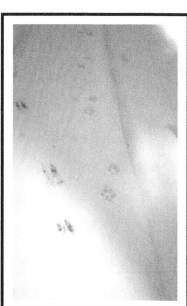

Large buck and coyote tracks in fresh snow over our tire tracks on Mt. Mitchell plateau, Nov. 2004. By Joe Beelart.